ꞌBlacklisting of trades unionists and workspace activists is one of the great scandals of the modern workplace. The story set out in this book provides a stark warning to all workers who want to organize for decent pay and conditions. Those who have campaigned on this issue deserve the support of everyone who believes in justice.ꞌ
Matt Wrack General Secretary, Fire Brigades Union

ꞌI recommend people read this book. Just by picking up this book, just by reading it, you challenge what I believe to be a state and corporate spying culture that is out of control.ꞌ
Mark Thomas Comedian

ꞌThis powerful book shows that blacklisting is more than about union members in one industry but is a human rights scandal which affects us all. We wait to see whether new procurement guidance in Scotland will force the guilty to own up, apologize and pay up. But we couldn't have got this far without the diligence of those ordinary men and women in the Blacklist Support Group who refused to give up. Their determination and campaigning is an example to us all.ꞌ
Neil Findlay MSP for the Lothians

ꞌThis book is a powerful and necessary exposé of a dark episode in British industrial relations – the blacklisting of construction workers for trade-union activities or for raising health-and-safety concerns in the industry. In exposing this scandal, the book points to the role of large corporations, the state and the security services in the surveillance of a wide range of activists. Above all, the book is a testimony to the bravery and integrity of construction workers in standing up to unbelievably hostile employers.ꞌ
Professor Sian Moore Co-director, Centre of Employment Studies Research, University of Greenwich

ꞌDave Smith has been at the forefront of the campaign to expose the loathsome and illegal practice of blacklisting of employees for trade union and political activities for many years. This book should be required reading for anyone interested in how big business covertly subverts democracy and trade-union rights. Please read it, discuss it and pass it on.ꞌ
Tommy Sheridan Former member of the Scottish Parliament and co-convenor of Solidarity

BLACKLISTED

About the authors

Dave Smith is a former construction worker from east London. He was blacklisted for his union activities after he complained about unpaid wages and raised concerns about safety issues such as asbestos. He is the secretary of the Blacklist Support Group, the campaign body that represents blacklisted workers and has given evidence to the parliamentary Select Committee investigation into blacklisting. Dave has a test case awaiting hearing at the European Court of Human Rights and was one of the claimants in the High Court group litigation on blacklisting. It was evidence at his Employment Tribunal that exposed the police link to blacklisting.

Phil Chamberlain has 20 years' experience as a journalist. He has written for a number of national newspaper and magazines, primarily on social policy issues. He is currently Associate Head of Department for Broadcast and Journalism at the University of the West of England where he specializes in investigative journalism. It was his article for the *Guardian* in 2008 on blacklisting which led to the exposure of the blacklist. No other journalist has followed the story as closely nor spoken to as many of the people involved.

Acknowledgements

This book has been very much a team effort. It could not have been written without the huge support of literally hundreds of people who are too numerous to mention. You know who you are: thank you. Dave and Phil would especially like to acknowledge the support from our families and close friends, whom we have sometimes neglected during the writing of this book.

BLACKLISTED

THE SECRET WAR
BETWEEN BIG BUSINESS
AND UNION ACTIVISTS

THE FULL STORY

Dave Smith and Phil
Chamberlain

Blacklisted:
The secret war between big business and union activists

This fully revised second edition published in 2016 by
New Internationalist Publications Ltd
The Old Music Hall
106-108 Cowley Road
Oxford OX4 1JE, UK
newint.org

First published in 2015
Reprinted 2016

Design: Juha Sorsa

Printed by T J International Limited, Cornwall, UK
who hold environmental accreditation ISO 14001.

MIX
Paper from
responsible sources
FSC   FSC® C013056
www.fsc.org

British Library Cataloguing-in-Publication Data
A catalogue record for this book is available from the British Library.
Library of Congress Cataloging-in-Publication Data.
A catalog record for this book is available from the Library of Congress.

ISBN 978-1-78026-341-0
(ISBN ebook 978-1-78026-342-7)

Contents

Introduction to the updated and expanded new edition

The book you are reading was never intended to be merely a reference publication gathering dust on a library shelf. It was always viewed by the authors, publishers and Blacklist Support Group (BSG) as an integral strand of the justice campaign for blacklisted workers. The first members of the public to see *Blacklisted* were those very workers at the BSG AGM in Glasgow on 7 March 2015. The rapidly unfolding story since the book was first published demanded this completely updated new edition.

Five days after the Glasgow event, it was standing room only when the swanky official book launch was held in the UK Parliament at Westminster. The authors were joined by Gail Cartmail from Unite and blacklisted activist Helen Steel. Chairing the event was John McDonnell MP, who six months later was to be elevated to the position of Shadow Chancellor of the Exchequer by his long-time political ally Jeremy Corbyn. There were speeches from Matt Wrack, the leader of the Fire Brigades Union, and from Dan Collins, a young electrician sacked from the Crossrail project after raising health-and-safety concerns. One person who wanted to be there but could not, fearing he would be arrested for breach of the Official Secrets Act, was former undercover police officer Peter Francis. Instead he sent a written statement giving further details of the scope of state surveillance of trade unions and political activists that was read out by John McDonnell. This was to cause political shockwaves which are still reverberating. The judge-led inquiry into undercover policing set up by the then Home Secretary Theresa May could shine yet more light on deliberately hidden anti-democratic practices stretching back decades. This updated version of *Blacklisted* brings together for the first time much of the material which has been extracted on the activities of the 'political police', as well as new revelations about the lengths to which big corporations will go to protect their profits.

Following the launch, *Blacklisted* did a tour of which many rock bands with a new album would have been proud – from inside the Sullum Voe gas terminal on Shetland during a walk-out over safety issues in near-hurricane conditions, to the summer sun of Glastonbury Festival and almost every independent bookshop in between. *Blacklisted* was shortlisted for the Bread and Roses Award for Radical Publishing and was warmly received at the historic Durham Miners Gala. The TUC passed its first-ever motion on blacklisting and undercover policing after a packed fringe event. The UK, Scottish and Irish parliaments have all debated the issue. Virtually every union conference had events, as did countless universities, Trades Councils, regional and branch committees, with many unions bulk-ordering copies of *Blacklisted* to distribute amongst activists. Photographs of construction workers reading the book on building sites flooded social media. Sometimes thousands listened, while at other times it was dozens in the back room of a pub. But the tour didn't stop at the UK border, with the story being told at the Irish Congress of Trade Unions in Dublin and the Maritime Union of Australia in Brisbane. Since *Blacklisted* was published, there have been two major developments above all others: in the High Court and the undercover police inquiry. Hold on to your hats, because it's been a busy 18 months, and you're about to read the inside story.

This edition, as with the original, has a quotation from Steinbeck's *In Dubious Battle* at the opening to Chapter 1: 'Out of all this struggle a good thing is going to grow. That makes it worthwhile.' The political developments outlined above, and explored in more detail in the pages which follow, are obvious examples of this hope realized. But there are other, unlooked for, good things which are worth highlighting. The blacklisting scandal has, for example, seen a flowering of artistic responses. Blacklisted former electrician turned graphic artist Jim Turner (not his real name) became the *BSG Artist in Residence*, producing 'Art-Hats' (made from safety hard hats), photo-collages and giant graphics that have been viewed by literally millions of people. Visitors who attended Banksy's iconic Dismaland at Weston-super-Mare could see works by *Art Against Blacklisting*, which also appeared at an exhibition at the University of the West of England in Bristol and during a guerrilla exhibition against BP at the British Museum.[1] The group's subvertising adorned building sites, *Strike!* magazine, the London Underground and the 2016 Glastonbury Festival.

Jim commented:

> ❝Tony Benn once said, "no matter what your skills are – writer, artist, driver, organizer or orator – use those skills to their best effect and bring about the changes needed for a just society". So *Art Against Blacklisting* was formed to help keep the flame of justice burning. It has opened doors unimaginable six years ago, such as invitations to take an active part in enabling art initiatives and direct actions by supportive campaign groups and some of the world's best-known artists. Turning the negative of blacklisting into a positive has been a personal journey of rediscovered talents and interests that I can truly say has been life changing... and bloody enjoyable!❞[2]

The veteran video activist collective *Reel News* has produced a string of agitprop films recording the fight against blacklisting that have played everywhere from inside the Scottish Parliament and the Victoria & Albert Museum via union conferences to the hedonistic Shangri-La corner of Glastonbury.[3] A new major documentary *Blacklisted* by the producer Tom Wood from Reel News was released to coincide with the launch of the updated edition of this book.

Artist and filmmaker Lucy Parker spent a year researching the blacklist story to produce an installation seen in London and Edinburgh.[4] The stories of the blacklist and associated spying have also been fruitful for dramatists. Mark Thomas's award-winning play *Cuckooed* toured the UK after premiering at the Edinburgh Festival and dealt with the impact of betrayal by a fellow activist in the Campaign Against Arms Trade.[5] The specific story of women drawn into relationships by undercover police officers was dramatized a number of times in 2016. The well-received *Any Means Necessary*,[6] written by Kefi Chadwick in collaboration with women activists, opened at the Nottingham Playhouse while, with some serious star wattage if a more problematic storyline,[7] the BBC showed the dramatic serial *Undercover*.[8] Forthcoming from the team which produced *McLibel* and *Age of Stupid* is another TV drama, this time based on Bob Lambert, the most notorious of the undercover officers.[9] Longer films are also in the works from Anna Burton's Neon Tetra Films and a documentary, *Spied Upon*, by Jason Kirkpatrick, which also considers the international aspects of the undercover police story.[10]

Musicians have also got in on the act. Early on, folk singer Chris Tymkow wrote a song called *Blacklist*. Then, in June 2016, the world-renowned singer-songwriter Sean Taylor released the BSG campaign single *Blacklist Number 1*,[11] which was produced by Gerry Divver, mastered by the legendary record producer Mark Hallman, and for a few days topped the Amazon Blues download chart. The chorus is already being sung on protests, picket lines and in conference bars, and it looks set to become a standard for the trade-union movement worldwide. The music video was inevitably produced by Shaun Dey from Reel News and mixes protest footage with terrible dad-dancing by blacklisted workers.[12]

As the authors toured the country speaking about the book, a familiar theme was that the story was not about victims. That word does not feature in the index – and deliberately so. This surge in creativity is one sign as to why. Far from gloomily accepting blacklisting, the story has been one of fighting back on many fronts, from conference platforms to theatre stages, from demonstrating on the street to protesting through the written word, in film or online. On Twitter the hashtag #spycops is now the tag-de-jour for journalists, activists, lawyers and politicians to share the latest information. There are now more members of the Blacklist Support Group Facebook page than there were names in The Consulting Association files.

They wanted blacklisting to be their dirty little secret. They failed. It became a story repeated and investigated and dramatized and painted and chanted. This is the story of that victory.

Dave Smith and **Phil Chamberlain**
September 2016

1 historyofbp.org/hard-hat/ 2 Interview with the authors. 3 nin.tl/BLreelnews
4 nin.tl/LucyParker 5 Guardian, 4 Aug 2014, nin.tl/Cuckooed 6 nin.tl/AnyMeansplay
7 nin.tl/Undercoverreality 8 BBC, nin.tl/Undercoverblurb 9 undercovers.tv
10 spiedupon.com 11 nin.tl/SeanTaylorsong 12 nin.tl/SeanTaylorvideo

Foreword
to the first edition
by John McDonnell MP

Two hundred years ago working people toiling in the fields and in the small workshops and emerging factories of the early industrial revolution discovered a secret. It was the secret of solidarity. The secret that individually they were weak and powerless in the face of exploitative employers and yet if they combined together they had a collective strength to secure better wages and working conditions.

Workers went on to celebrate this discovery by sewing the slogans of solidarity on their trade-union banners, still displayed with pride today. 'Unity is Strength', 'United We Stand, Divided We Fall'. In its more modern form the slogan of defiance, 'The Workers United Will Never Be Defeated', first chanted on the streets of Latin American cities, echoes the same principle of a belief in solidarity.

Employers, too, understood the threat that workers' solidarity presented to the unrestrained power they had over their wage labourers. That's why they devised a variety of means to break the organizational form the workers developed to exercise their power of solidarity, the early trade unions.

The mechanisms that have been used by employers over the last two centuries to undermine the collective strength of workers in their trade unions have ranged from physical intimidation and individual victimization to the use of the law and even the lockout.

Physical intimidation against trade unionists by employers or the state on behalf of employers has been a consistent feature of industrial relations in this country, with stark examples ranging from Winston Churchill letting loose the troops to fire on the miners at Tonypandy in 1910 to the horse-mounted police baton charges against the miners at Orgreave 70 years later.

The victimization of individuals to break the trade-union movement has never ceased, whether it has been the transportation of the Tolpuddle Martyrs in 1834 or the collusion by politicians, the security forces and the judiciary to imprison the Shrewsbury pickets in the 1970s.

Throughout modern history employers have also resorted to legislation to stifle the growth of trade unions and undermine their effectiveness. In the early 19th century it was the Combination Acts attempting to prevent the birth of trade unionism, while in the 1980s it was the anti-trade union laws of Margaret Thatcher, introduced to undermine trade unions' ability to take solidarity action to protect and promote the interests of their members.

While trade unionists have always had in their armoury the ultimate weapon of solidarity, the strike, employers have also repeatedly demonstrated that they too can take their own form of strike action, the lockout. Throughout the 19th and early 20th century when the movement of labour was inhibited by the limited transport available, local employers frequently put their competition temporarily aside and combined in order to break the unions by locking their workers out until economic necessity forced them to accede to employers' terms. In the recent Grangemouth oil-refinery dispute in Scotland we have seen the ultimate modern equivalent of the lockout, when the owner was willing to close the whole plant down in order to force the trade unions to accept job and pay cuts.

A further tactic used by the employer, usually covertly, has been the blacklist. It has been a simple but extremely effective weapon used by employers to attack trade unions. The blacklist works by employers identifying an individual trade unionist and then working together to prevent that individual gaining employment at any of their operations.

This is aimed to have three direct effects.

First, there is no doubt it aims to break that individual so that he or she is forced to choose between earning a living at their trade and feeding their family or relinquishing being an active trade unionist and therefore no longer an individual threat to the employer's power over their workforce.

Second, it aims to quarantine the individual so that, by denying them access to the workplace, they have no ability to represent, influence, persuade or mobilize others to stand up for their rights at work.

Third, it undoubtedly aims to send out a message to anyone else who may be tempted to join a union and play their role in representing others, that they too could be sent packing by the employer and find themselves in the dole queue as a result.

The constant problem for trade unionists is that, although they may believe that a blacklist exists, it usually operates in secret and is hard, if not at times impossible, to prove.

When a Labour government was elected in 1997, party policy committed it to outlawing the operation of blacklists and in some of its first employment legislation the government introduced the basis upon which this appalling practice could be made illegal. Unfortunately it failed to prioritize the enactment of the detailed secondary legislation that would have given effect to this primary legislation.

There was no sense of priority because government ministers were not convinced that blacklisting was still in operation. It was looked upon by New Labour ministers under Tony Blair as an anachronism, long extinct in a modern economy. In addition, Blair was constantly anxious to avoid anything that could be seen to be supporting trade unions and that might have upset the CBI or the Institute of Directors. Even the TUC and many trade unions put the issue on the backburner, citing lack of evidence.

In Parliament and with ministers, I regularly asked when the blacklisting regulations were to be published, to be met with a disdainful air, as if the question were an irrelevance.

When the raid by the Information Commissioner began to expose the role of The Consulting Association in the operation of a large-scale modern blacklist, I convened a meeting in Parliament of trade unionists who had suspected that they had been blacklisted and the Blacklist Support Group was formed.

At these meetings I listened to so many heartrending stories of individuals and their families who had been forced into unemployment and poverty simply because the blacklisted worker could not follow their trade or gain employment at all. Many families could not cope with the strain and fell apart. The pressure broke the health and shortened the lives of many of those that were blacklisted.

Thanks to the tireless work of the Blacklist Support Group

members and a number of their supporters, the blacklist story is now being told and redress is being sought. The operation of a blacklist is now accepted in those circles in the Labour and tradeunion movement that were in the past sceptical or dismissive. Indeed, we now know that some may even have been implicated in the operation of the blacklist.

There is still a long way to go to secure justice for the blacklisted workers and to bring to book those blacklisting companies and their directors who scarred the lives of so many workers and their families. Nevertheless a start has been made and this book will make a major contribution to securing the righting of an appalling wrong.

Preface
to the first edition
by Mark Thomas

It is 20 November 2014 and I'm walking through Nottingham city centre, past the hip tattoo parlours and vintage clothes shops, when a researcher from BBC Radio 4's *Today* programme phones. He's following up on a press release issued by the National Union of Journalists, which is backing legal proceedings against the Metropolitan Police Service for putting journalists under surveillance. The researcher is eager for me, as one of those NUJ members being spied on by the police, to appear on Radio 4 the following morning and, as is the way with researchers, he questions me about the story, so he can later brief the interviewer, Justin Webb.

'So do you think this has a wider significance?' he asks.

'Well,' I reply, 'I think our story is a small part of a much larger picture that shows police and corporate spying is out of control.'

'Goodness, that is a pretty controversial statement to make!' he blurts out, suddenly sounding like Bertie Wooster.

This moment stands out to me: it is the moment a journalist on the *Today* programme, the nation's agenda-setting news programme, showed how wilfully ignorant the well informed can be. This is, after all, a man who works in the news and must be aware of the accumulating stories regarding spying: the Snowden revelations; the women deceived into having relationships with undercover cops; the Stephen Lawrence family campaign being spied upon; the Ricky Reel family being spied upon; court cases collapsing amidst undisclosed evidence; dead children's names being used as cover names for the police; the construction blacklist and thousands denied work illegally. He must know all of this, yet to suggest this litany of wrongdoing shows either a collapse in oversight or an example of conscious overreach is a 'controversial view'.

I suppose Oxbridge types don't see spying as a threat to liberty and privacy; they see it as a career option if the BBC doesn't pan out for them.

The tiny, really tiny, part of the picture of spying that my story inhabits – alongside the myriad other stories – raises the questions of prevalence and accountability. How widespread is spying? Who has democratic oversight and control?

To the best of my knowledge I appear on three spying databases: one run at the behest of Britain's biggest arms manufacturer, BAE Systems; one run by the police; and one run by The Consulting Association, the construction industry blacklist. I have been spied upon by people who befriended me for BAE Systems, who worked with me, entered my home and know my family. The police have decided I am a 'domestic extremist' and therefore put me under surveillance; they note when I speak at political rallies, when I do fundraising benefit gigs and when certain documentaries I have worked on appear on TV. I have even had information passed to the police from the management at the Open University.

On a personal level the issue of whether spying is out of control is answered with these facts. I am a performer and writer. A comic. I have no criminal record. I helped the police put illegal arms dealers in jail. Yet it is acceptable for someone in a managerial role in the liberal establishment of the Open University to send information to the police about my appearance at their facility to give a lecture.

As I say, mine is a really, really tiny part of the picture, but for me that is quite a WTF moment.

The story of BAE Systems spying on activists broke in late 2003 when the *Sunday Times* ran a story that Campaign Against Arms Trade (CAAT) was being infiltrated. An ex-employee of the company's security service sold internal documents to the Murdoch paper showing reports on anti-arms trade activists garnered from moles planted inside the NGO. One of the spies named later by CAAT was Martin Hogbin, a friend of mine and many other activists.

There was a common reaction of disbelief amongst those outside of the anti-arms trade community. Although few people would use the word 'liar', there was a faint whiff of discomfort in the air, as if we were conspiracy theorists or fantasists over-inflating our own sense of importance and radicalism, somewhere between David Icke or Rick from *The Young Ones*. Indeed, some of my friends reacted by saying, 'Well, you'd be disappointed if you weren't spied upon.' As if I was actively seeking the attention as a way of validating my activism, a modern-day René Descartes, 'I am spied upon therefore I am.'

When friends doubt the accuracy or significance of being spied on, you tend to over-emphasize the facts. Forgive me, but it is worth being clear on them.

BAE Systems admitted in court they spied on CAAT in 2007. The company was caught in receipt of internal CAAT documents, was taken to court, where they named Paul Mercer and Evelyn Le Chene as the people they employed to do the spying for them (Martin Hogbin was sending information to Le Chene's company). The company has signed a legal undertaking not to spy on CAAT or its members in the future.

This is not a conspiracy theory; it is a conspiracy.

Back in 2003, when I heard a close friend had in fact been spying for an arms company, I felt embarrassed and humiliated; I wanted the story to go away. That is no longer the case. When I found the police were putting myself and others under surveillance, our first reaction was to ask if there was a chance of getting the police into court. There is. Currently six of us, including a *Times* journalist, are bringing a court action against the Met Police, after we demanded our files from the police using the Data Protection Act.

Incidentally, the case being heard before us concerns a man in his eighties, a veteran, with no criminal record, who happens to paint at protests. He is regarded as a 'domestic extremist' and the police keep him under surveillance too.

There is one thing I have found out for certain in these years of being spied upon and appearing on secret databases and it is this: spies and blacklisters operate in the dark, which is why they hate the spotlight of publicity upon them.

They hate being named and appearing in court.

They hate people appearing on the *Today* programme to talk about them.

They hate Parliament asking questions about them.

They hate people finding out about them.

Which is why I recommend people read this book. Just by picking up this book, just by reading it, you challenge what I believe to be a state and corporate spying culture that is out of control. Controversial, I know.

Introduction

by *Dave Smith* & Phil Chamberlain

On 23 February 1998, an explosion left a crater 22 metres wide and 7 metres deep in the playing fields of George Green School, on the Isle of Dogs in east London. Luckily it happened at five in the morning when the school was empty. If the explosion had occurred during school playtime, it would have been a major disaster. It was caused by compressed air in a tunnel extending the Docklands Light Railway under the Thames to Greenwich. The incident later resulted in the third-biggest fine ever handed down by a British Court for breach of health-and-safety legislation.

When I arrived for the start of my shift that morning, lumps of earth the size of a small car were stuck five storeys up on the outside of a block of flats 100 metres away from the school. I contacted my union and, at a packed meeting in the site canteen a few days later, I was elected as a safety rep for the building union, UCATT. From that day on, major construction companies started taking a keen interest in my activities − unfortunately, for all the wrong reasons. In the next three years I was repeatedly refused work or dismissed from building sites and found myself virtually unemployable, even though this was the middle of a building boom when the industry was crying out for skilled workers. By 2001, I could barely pay my mortgage and was forced to leave the industry I had worked in since I left school. For the next seven years, I hardly gave construction another thought, unless it was to discuss work with family members.

Fast forward to 8am on 6 March 2009 and the lead story on Radio 4's Today *programme was about a shady outfit called The Consulting Association. I listened while driving into north London and made a point of visiting the corner shop to buy the* Guardian *before going into work. I didn't realize it at the time but the front-page article I read that morning was written by Phil Chamberlain. Later, I watched as the Association's role in blacklisting was the lead item on the BBC 9 o'clock news. If I am honest, my overriding thought, and that of other builders I spoke to that day, was: 'Blacklisting in the* building industry? How on earth is this the lead news item? Everyone has known this was going on for decades.'

And that really is the point of this book. It is an attempt to expose the dirty secret behind all those construction hoardings and scaffolding you walk past every day – to name and shame the people who orchestrated the blacklisting of thousands and to expose the system which made it an integral part of doing business on building sites.

We wanted to hear from all those involved. So you will read interviews with people who were at the heart of this scandal: the bookkeepers and spies, the human-resources managers and security officials. We didn't gather gossip in secret; we wanted to know their motivations and practices. Many of them saw their work as part of a battle – hence the subtitle of this book.

Everyone who was involved with industrial relations in the building industry knew that blacklisting was rampant. It was an open secret. It was the price paid by anyone prepared to stand up for the rights of their fellow workers, to have the temerity to ask for decent facilities or even for wages to be paid on time. Managers used to boast about putting union people on the blacklist and making sure they'd never work again. Union conferences debated blacklisting year after year and some of the older guys told stories about how they had suffered years of unemployment or had been forced to leave the industry altogether to pay the bills. We all knew about blacklisting but only because we were right in the middle of it. But if you weren't part of it, the building game was another world.

When I was in my twenties, I listened to the old boys talking about the blacklist and violence against activists. I viewed it as a kind of oral history: how bad it was back in the day. There was a building boom going on and although I couldn't get a job for any of the big companies, I was working in supervisory positions via employment agencies or smaller subcontractors. Some of the outfits I worked for didn't even have a proper office; the subcontractor operated out of the back of his Merc. How on earth could he possibly know that, two years before, I had been a safety rep while working 100 miles away, for a completely different firm? Initially, I was sceptical.

But slowly it became more and more apparent that I was one of those on the blacklist. I didn't know the mechanism, but the effect was obvious. I was a trade-union activist in the building industry. And, as an elected union safety rep, I attended TUC training courses and I was able to apply for membership of the Institute of Occupational Safety and Health. As part of the membership application I had to provide a list of all the places I had worked where I had been a safety rep, my length of service and reason for leaving. Completing the form brought it home to me. I hadn't been sacked just once but rather every single time that I had raised safety issues on a building site. And the times out of work were getting longer than the times in work.

The mid-1990s saw the start of an unprecedented building boom with wages rising sharply as the shortage of skilled labour kicked in. I was a qualified engineer with over a decade of experience and had even started working in junior management roles. It was at this time that I also became more active in the union and started raising concerns about asbestos and overflowing toilets on building sites. The loadsamoney effect only lasted a few years with me. In 1998 I was driving a big 4x4. By 2000, I couldn't get a job as an engineer anywhere, and even employment agencies stopped phoning me. When, in desperation, I rang to ask why, one agency honestly told me that I came up as 'code 99' on their computer system, which meant that they had been told never to offer me work ever again. My tax returns that year show that I earned around £12,000 and I was now driving a battered old £300 Fiesta van with questionable paperwork – in the middle of a building boom!

When everyone else is taking their kids to Disney World in Florida, unemployment is not nice. For the only time in my life, I went to the doctors asking for sleeping pills. After another year, it was so obvious I was being blacklisted that I left the industry altogether. The trade unions helped me out again and I was lucky enough to get a job working as a TUC tutor, teaching shop stewards on the very courses I had attended a few years earlier. Teaching adults in Further Education doesn't pay what engineers were earning in a building boom but it covered the mortgage.

If the intention of the blacklist was to drive the activists out of the industry, then it worked. I left, and dozens of other union people I knew did the same or took lower-paid jobs in the public sector. My kids missed some school trips, we defaulted on our mortgage *payments a few times and, as a grown man, I had to borrow money from my parents. But others suffered much more than my family. Other blacklisted workers lost their homes completely, split up from their partners or had serious health issues. Some committed suicide.*

When I finally received a copy of my blacklist file in 2009, it was 36 pages long. The transnational building firms who set up and ran The Consulting Association had had me under surveillance from 1992 until 2006. My file contains my name, address, national insurance numbers, photographs, phone numbers and car registration. Copies of my safety rep's credentials appear on three separate pages. Leaflets I had handed out about asbestos were added to my file and speeches I made at UCATT and TUC conferences were recorded verbatim. My file contained information about my brother and my wife, as well as recording nearly every job I worked on for over a decade.

In mid-2009, I got a message about a meeting in the Houses of Parliament being hosted by John McDonnell MP. For the blacklisted workers who sat around the table that night, these firms had taken the food off our kids' tables: for us, this was personal. We knew that if there was going to be a successful campaign, then we would have to run it ourselves. It was the first time I had met many of the people who were to become good friends and comrades. But we were brought up in the building industry: we were all used to hard work and getting our hands dirty. Rather reluctantly, I agreed to take on the role of secretary temporarily. That was six years ago. It has been my honour to have met and worked alongside some of the most honest and hard-working people in our movement. Some of them suffered from the impact of blacklisting and some of them have fought in our campaign for justice.

And that is the other reason for this book: to tell their story. To give a voice to those blacklisted workers and their families who are often absent in the debates in parliament and the discussions among well-paid lawyers. We have interviewed over 100 blacklisted workers and their families, with more being quoted from TV, YouTube footage or from books.

During the writing of this book we have been given well-meaning and some not so well-meaning warnings. We had letters from lawyers representing parties who would rather we did not write about them. One time we were told to 'be careful' because we were 'poking very powerful people with a big stick and they won't like it'. Another time we were told that we were either 'very brave or very stupid – there is a lot of money and a lot of very dangerous people involved in all this'. We're not particularly brave. But, as one of the protagonists in the story is described, we're like a dog with a bone and we've been loath to let go.

During the seven years it has taken to be published, company directors, QCs, trade-union general secretaries, MPs, MEPs, US Senators, party leaders and the prime minister have all had their say. Legal cases are at the High Court and the European Court of Human Rights. The proven involvement of the police and security services has made blacklisting an accepted part of the political debate. This book is not an historical artefact. Most of the people we name as implicated have prospered rather than been punished. Many still hold senior positions and some have even been promoted. The ideology that encouraged the secret smearing and spying is still widely held by the powers-that-be.

One of the most difficult sections to write was the criticism of the trade unions. Both the authors are proud to be trade unionists. It is clear that without diligent research and campaigning by trade unions the full picture of blacklisting would never have emerged. Yet corporations have compromised the ideals of some and we do not shirk from looking at where these compromises have taken place and why. There are lessons here for anyone interested in industrial relations in the 21st century.

And, talking of compromises, writing a book was ours. The number of words is limited and the biggest battle was over what to leave out. In resisting the best intentions of lawyers to stifle debate, we gathered considerable amounts of documentary evidence, most of which we have not been able to find space for.

Virtually all of this information was already in the public domain, having been used as evidence in open court, quoted in parliament or newspaper articles – it just needed someone to collate it all. People have generously handed over documents they had held on to since the 1960s because they wanted to have their stories told, while others have shared information on their own blacklist files.

We could not have written the book without the generosity and support of literally hundreds of people too numerous to mention. You know who you are and we thank you all.

The constraints of writing a book mean that we will not have satisfied everyone. We apologize if certain aspects of the story are only briefly touched upon and that Court Orders have restricted the publication of some of the information we have gathered. This merely adds weight to our call for a fully independent public inquiry. If a freelance investigative journalist and an ex-construction worker with only partial access to the documentary evidence can uncover this amount of sordid detail, how much more would a public inquiry discover?

It was important to give everyone the opportunity to have their say and we feel we have produced a fair piece of investigative journalism. But journalism should not simply record events but, in the tradition of Upton Sinclair or Paul Foot, should strive to influence the agenda.

There is a genuine public interest in exposing the full story of corporate and state spying upon individuals involved in perfectly legal, democratic union activities. We hope this book will contribute to the ongoing debate: we've come a long distance but there is some way still to go.

March 2015

‘Out of all this struggle a good thing is going to grow. That makes it worthwhile.’

John Steinbeck, *In Dubious Battle*

1
A foot in the door

One Monday morning in February 2009, four investigators from the Information Commissioner's Office (ICO) knocked on a door in an alley off a street in Droitwich, West Midlands. It was opened by 66-year-old Ian Kerr. Looking straight at him was David Clancy, head of investigations at the ICO. Clancy had a warrant but he didn't want the door shutting on him, so the former Greater Manchester police officer inserted his boot and announced they were coming in. Clancy had spent eight months hunting for this address. It had begun with a newspaper article. The final piece of the jigsaw had been a fax number pinpointing a mysterious group called The Consulting Association. It was an organization that didn't appear on any official records and had no nameplate above its anonymous green door. Clancy didn't know what to expect on the other side.

The shabby two-room office had furniture dating from the 1970s and 1980s, an electric typewriter on one of the desks, a computer and a sophisticated photocopying machine. Almost immediately the investigators found a ring binder in a tatty plastic cover. Inside were pages of names, addresses and national insurance numbers. Next they found a card index with additional information typed onto each card. Clancy recognized the set-up: it was identical to how a police local intelligence filing system works. It was organized alphabetically and each card related to a name in the folder. In all there were 3,213 names. Eventually the repercussions from this raid would be felt in the boardrooms of transnational corporations, the highest courts in Europe and in parliaments around the world. A 30-year covert operation involving the country's top construction firms, with the co-operation of the security services, had just come to an end. The scene was more John Le Carré than James Bond. Kerr told Clancy: 'You realize you have destroyed, or you appear to be about to destroy, a very effective network in the industry.'[1] Having spent months tracking the organization down, Clancy's feeling was very different. 'It was like Christmas,' he recalled.[2]

For 16 years, The Consulting Association compiled a secret database containing files on thousands of construction workers. The files had their names, addresses and National Insurance numbers, comments by managers, newspaper clippings, vehicle registrations; a number of files even contained information about their spouses. The organization acted as a covert vetting service funded by the construction industry to monitor people applying for work on building sites. More than 40 of the biggest names in the business – including Tarmac, Carillion, Balfour Beatty, Skanska, Kier, Costain, Laing O'Rourke, BAM Nuttal, Trafalgar House and Sir Robert McAlpine – each nominated a few senior people in their human resources department or industrial relations section to act as contacts with The Consulting Association. When recruitment took place, these people would fax the names of those applying for work over to Ian Kerr at The Consulting Association (TCA) who would check his files. If the name matched they would report a hit back to the 'main contact' from the company. Invariably this would result in the job applicant being refused employment or, if already on site, dismissed.

The idea was simple; the effect was devastating. The building worker had no idea that their details were being checked in this way and no way of seeing if the information held was accurate. Once you had a file, it was added to over the years and you would never know – you would just be repeatedly turned down for work. Blacklisting was a secret tool used by companies to keep out people they didn't like. Those with files were often union members who had raised health-and-safety concerns or complained about conditions. Thousands of names were checked every month. There had always been rumours about blacklisting but now the files provided evidence for all to see.

Over the course of this book we'll reveal exactly what was on those files held by this covert organization. We'll also show who helped to keep Kerr operating. And we'll demonstrate that it wasn't just building workers this hidden organization monitored. The spying operation might have been set up by building firms but the security services and even some trade unions are implicated too. It is a drama whose origins date back to the years after the First World War and whose principal players range from Manchester electricians to company directors and police spies. It is a story about how far companies will go to boost their profits and the lengths to which workers will go to protect their rights. And it starts with a newspaper landing on David Clancy's desk in Cheshire.

The investigation begins

Back in 2008, investigative journalist Phil Chamberlain pitched an article to the *Guardian* suggesting looking at the issue of blacklisting. The construction industry seemed the obvious place to start researching this story and it wasn't hard to find examples. An approach to UCATT – the Union of Construction, Allied Trades and Technicians – led to contact with a number of workers who claimed to have suffered from blacklisting. At the suggestion

Phil Chamberlain

of UCATT, Chamberlain spoke to, among others, Steve Acheson, Colin Trousdale and John Winstanley. Winstanley, a joiner from Liverpool, spoke about the crushing effect of being refused work during the 1960s. Acheson and Trousdale had more recent experiences establishing a pattern of activism, jobs offered and suddenly withdrawn. Trousdale told Chamberlain:

> ❛I've had to change my address so that I didn't have a Manchester postcode because people saw the job application and thought I was one of the bolshie ones. All I did was speak up for some lads. People I know who have been blacklisted have suffered ill health as a result. They're under stress by virtue of the fact that they cannot get a job.❜[3]

The insidious nature of the practice meant that a pattern of behaviour might be established but evidence beyond the anecdotal was hard to find, though not impossible. The official position remained that blacklisting did not happen. Chamberlain spoke to the Construction Confederation, the industry trade body, about the existence of blacklisting. A spokesperson was quoted saying: 'We're not aware of it existing. If unions have evidence of malpractice by an employer, they need to share it. Blacklisting is not the practice of a good employer.'[4]

Chamberlain went looking for that evidence and his search led him to the Manchester Royal Infirmary (MRI) building project. This was a huge undertaking, close to the city centre and worth millions to the contractors involved. Behind the scaffolding a low-intensity conflict was being waged by contractors to keep control of who got to work there, targeting union representatives in particular. Acheson's solicitor passed to Chamberlain the judgment from an employment tribunal from 2007, which revealed what happened when some of the electricians carried out their lawful union activities.

Three electricians, Tony Jones, Graham Bowker and Steve Acheson, were working for a small electrical firm from Norwich called Logic Control at the £750-million Bovis project. The MRI was to be one of the largest new-build hospitals in Europe, employing thousands of workers over six years. Balfour Kilpatrick was the main electrical contractor, employing around 200 electricians. Logic Control had a separate contract running computer data cables and signals employing around 20. Tony Jones started first, in October 2005, followed by Graham Bowker in November 2005 and finally Steve Acheson in January 2006. It soon became apparent that not everyone was happy to have them there. Acheson recalled:

> I got summoned to the canteen by Kevin McGowan, my friend. He said: "Steve, I've got to have a chat with you. Balfours have been onto Logic saying you've got to get rid of this Acheson, he's a trouble causer".[5]

Bowker said that warnings came from several quarters:

> There was pressure being put from Balfour's to Logic to have us removed. The site manager for Logic said: "These guys are gunning for you." Even the site convenor, Lawrence Hunt from UCATT, said: "These people don't like you, do they?"[6]

The three electricians were sacked but applied to an employment tribunal, arguing they had been unfairly dismissed from working on the MRI project after they had raised health-and-safety concerns with their sub-contractor, Logic Control. The tribunal agreed, saying the trio had been: 'Unfairly selected for redundancy because of trade-union membership and activities'.[7] These were not complaints about tea breaks; they were fundamental concerns about safety raised by three people who between them had more than 70 years' experience. The result of raising the complaints was that all three got what was known in the trade as 'the tap on the shoulder'.

Bowker, like the others, had long suspected he was on a blacklist.

> ❝ We knew without knowing that there was something totally wrong. I applied for one very big project in Wales through the agency. I was told the job's now filled, and there's no vacancies. And, following my conversation, 300 more electricians went on that site. So that shocked me. Plus the amount of times I've been thrown off site, it's unbelievable. Or I've been given a job over the phone, an hour later it's gone. My phone doesn't ring at all now, never.❞

The electrician from Oldham was subsequently to find out that the file kept on him by The Consulting Association contained entries from Crown House Engineering, Carillion and Tarmac: all companies with which he'd found it difficult to find work.

The effect on Bowker was not just about lost wages – as with many others, his health and family also suffered. He said:

> ❝ I've had tinnitus, alopecia, got rheumatoid arthritis; they say a lot of this stuff could be stress induced. This is what the doctors have said. It's had a bearing on the family because I've totally changed character from being happy-go-lucky to dead snappy. It's frustration, I think. A lot of it because from working all your life to not being able to work at all, the slightest thing you get agitated. It's affected the wife. It's an old saying, like: "when money stops coming through the door, love goes out the window". Well, that's a true fact. I used to take three holidays a year, prior to 2000, and I probably get one a year now. Some years I've had none. My wife's supporting me now. I get no benefits because my wife works more than 16 hours a week. It's not fair on my wife having to support me: that's my role in life. The kids – when they had their weddings I couldn't

finance them. Two of my daughters got married while I was having all my problems and I feel guilty where I could give very little towards the weddings.[9]

Some workers found the debilitating experience of constantly being offered and then refused jobs too much. Mick Anderson, from Kerry in Ireland, who had more than 25 years' experience after leaving school, applied for 250 jobs and took courses to keep his skills up to date. He was out of work for 16 months. In 2006 he and his family moved to the Irish Republic because of his struggle to get work. He later found he had a blacklist file. Also with a blacklist file was Darren O'Grady, from north London, who in 1990 moved to America with his family to try to secure work.

Stewart Emms from Hull was on the blacklist from when he was an activist in the 1980s but managed to escape the worst effects when he was elected as an official of UCATT. He remembers what happened when he finished working at the union: he was repeatedly turned down for employment.

> I got bits and bobs now and then but when the building society threatened to take our house away, we knew we had to get out to survive. Bulgaria was cheap, so we moved here in January 2005. We were living in a house with an outside toilet and shower.[8]

Denise Emms, his wife and fellow activist, remembers the impact it had on her husband.

> Just dreadful: his legs were cut off. The worst time of our lives – out of work for two years, we thought we would lose the house at one point. He did part-time work scrapping around doing some little joinery jobs and they took it off his dole money. We're just managing now on our pensions.[9]

Electrician Jake McCloud was blacklisted after being involved in a dispute while working for the electrical contractor Matthew Hall on the Mossmorran oil refinery in Scotland in 1982. He said:

> It affected me very badly, because I didn't work after that for at least three years. I maybe got a wee week here or a wee week there but I didn't get anything concrete and I have

to be honest and say it was the end of my marriage. It was very difficult and I understand looking back now, how your missus and your two young kids looked at things. A guy, three doors down from you, he's got all the jobs in the world and you can't get one. And she says, "How come you can't get on that job?"

I tried to explain and it was alright for a wee while but when it goes on and on, one Christmas after another Christmas, it becomes very tiring and you begin to argue in the house. You want a pint but you've no money for a pint but you go for a pint anyway. All that sort of thing took place. I was only an ordinary bear but at the end of the day I fully appreciated that my missus couldn't take any more.❜[10]

Steve Barley, a blacklisted electrician from Cardiff, remembers the inability to find a job as a blight stretching back decades – one which devastated some families.

❛I was in the apprentice section of EETPU [the Electrical, Electronic, Telecommunications and Plumbing Union] in 1970 and the first real warning I had about the blacklist was in 1973 after the national builders' strike. Cardiff branch at that time was run by a man called Billy Williams, who was chairman, and two other strong trade-union activists, Pip Jones and Alan Marsh. There were fights on different sites to get these guys jobs. Other people working already on those sites were threatened with being blacked for trying to get those men back into employment. Over the years I've tried to get Billy a start at St Fergus in the north of Scotland and again at BP in Barry in 1979 but it was the same situation. They actually got a start at St Fergus for a company called Control and Applications from Swansea. They were on the site for a couple of hours and were actually frogmarched off by the police – that was in 1976. Billy Williams committed suicide in the 1980s.❜[11]

Steve Barley's friend was not the only blacklisted worker to take his own life.

Back in Manchester, after being dismissed from the MRI building site, Bowker, Jones and Acheson protested for more than a year outside. Jones said: 'Our principle was the main reason. We always suspected there was a blacklist but by Manchester Royal Infirmary we knew it existed.'[12]

According to the employment tribunal, Logic Control found itself under pressure from Balfour Kilpatrick to let the three go. As part of the evidence, the tribunal heard from a former human relations manager, Alan Wainwright, that blacklisting of union members took place. The tribunal did not find Wainwright's evidence pertinent but his submission placed on record a lot of inside detail, hitherto unheard of, about how blacklisting operated. Wainwright put in the public domain evidence that companies sent lists of new job applicants to an organization and, if a name appeared on their files, the company would refuse that person work. The Wainwright evidence added to the wealth of detail submitted by the electricians about why they had been singled out. The tribunal ruled that there was no evidence that Logic Control had used the blacklist but its written judgment records:

> ❛Disgraceful though it be, the Tribunal concludes that a blacklist exists in relation to certain workers in the industry in which the claimants work and that the claimants are all on that blacklist.❜[13]

The Manchester hearing gave authority to a suspicion many construction workers had but, as with thousands of other tribunal decisions made each year, its judgment was not reported. The industry's dirty secret was hidden in plain view.

Some of the detail on what happened at MRI can be gleaned thanks to the raid by David Clancy and the ICO. The seized files were now in the possession of the government's data-protection watchdog and workers who suspected they were on the secret blacklist could apply to be sent a copy of their own file. In 2009, two years after he was sacked from the MRI project, Tony Jones gained access to his file. The Manchester electrician said:

> ❛My family is riddled with debt and suffering. We had to do without food and clothing at times, no holidays. We were unable to ever apply for a mortgage and never knew why. We do now.❜

Acheson, Trousdale and Winstanley would also get their hands on their own blacklisting files. Winstanley, from Liverpool, found his file had been opened in 1975 by an organization called the Economic League and ended in 2002. It has details on his heart bypass surgery. One entry describes him as an 'old-style communist'.

Enter the commissioners

The *Guardian* article was published on 28 June 2008 and Chamberlain moved on to the next job. A few days later he got a call from David Clancy at the Information Commissioner's Office. The ICO is an independent authority set up by the government 'to uphold information rights in the public interest, promoting openness by public bodies and data privacy for individuals'.[14] It has the power to investigate data breaches and take to court those found to be breaking the law. At the time Clancy was part of a small group of investigators, all with police, military or Customs and Excise background. There was a sign on their office door saying: 'Abandon hope all ye who enter here'. The Monday after the *Guardian* article was published, a member of the ICO staff dropped a copy on Clancy's desk as something his team might be interested in looking at. Clancy spoke with Chamberlain and took details of the evidence he had collated. He then went to see Steve Acheson. The electrician recalled:

> ❝The day he turned up I had just received a letter turning me down for work. I told him he couldn't have come at a better time. To be honest I didn't think he would find much. I told him this but he said: "Once I get my teeth into something, I don't let go".❞

Clancy then spoke to Alan Wainwright, now working in the music business and unable to get a job in human resources or construction. Wainwright had started as an electrician, then ran a recruitment agency before getting a job with Tarmac. In 1997, while National Labour Manager at Crown House, a division of Tarmac (later to be rebranded as Carillion) he had been introduced to Ian Kerr at the company's Wolverhampton headquarters. Wainwright claims that the meeting was set up by HR manager Kevin Gorman, under instruction from the Group Personnel Director, Frank

Duggan.[15] It transpired that Kerr was employed to carry out checks on staff to identify undesirable employees. Wainwright met Kerr twice and was told that many construction companies supplied him with information. Wainwright worked for Crown House, Drake & Scull and Haden Young and told Clancy he found the same system operating with Kerr at all three companies. And all three were subsequently found to have subscribed to The Consulting Association.

After raising concerns about fraud, but disillusioned with the company's response, which denied the allegations, Wainwright left Haden Young in 2006. Before he did so, he wrote to its head office in 2005, saying: 'The company operates a blacklisting procedure for new recruits and hired temporary agency workers to check for any previous history of union militancy, troublemaking.'[16] He launched and lost an employment tribunal and became convinced that he too had been blacklisted. Wainwright's suspicions were later proved to be correct and his blacklist file includes the evidence he gave to the Logic employment tribunal. He started a blog and posted the names of electricians supposedly blacklisted after working on the Jubilee Line Extension, which had been the scene of industrial unrest. But no-one seemed interested in his story.

Unknown to Clancy, Wainwright's detailed evidence had actually been given to the government a whole 12 months earlier. The Department for Trade and Industry (DTI) had been contacted by Wainwright. Documents released to the authors under the Freedom of Information Act show that Wainwright met civil servant Bernard Carter from the DTI on 12 January 2007 at The Queens Hotel in Chester. The official note says:

> Mr Wainwright explained that the lists of people to be refused employment were kept by third parties. In 1997, whilst working at Carillion, he [Wainwright] had met the person involved, Mr Iain [sic] Kerr. Mr Kerr was self-employed, but Mr Wainwright did not know his business's name or its location. For a few months, he [Wainwright] was the main contact point between his part of Carillion and Mr Kerr, though that function was transferred after a few months to a senior person at Carillion's head office.

The memo records that Wainwright passed to the civil servants a list of names of Balfour Kilpatrick workers on three projects from the late 1990s and a set of internal memos within Haden Young 'asking for a check to be carried out on individuals who had been identified by agencies for work as electricians and plumbers'.

A clue as to what the DTI did with Wainwright's evidence can be gleaned from correspondence in 2009 obtained by the authors between his MP, David Hanson, and Pat McFadden, then the minister for employment relations. It discusses why the evidence was not acted upon. Dated 27 April 2009 – so more than a month after the ICO raid – McFadden reassured Hanson that Wainwright's evidence 'was considered carefully with the Department' and indeed 'was valuable and indicated that a vetting procedure of some kind had been operated'. However, and there is an almost audible sigh of *Yes Minister*'s Sir Humphrey proportions, the letter then says that there were 'important gaps' in Wainwright's knowledge, including the criteria used in the vetting process.

❝ The Department possesses no investigatory powers to uncover fresh evidence in such situations and, in consequence, the Department could not take the matter forward at that time.❞

It seemed that naming companies and individuals, as well as providing case studies, was not enough to warrant further action. Wainwright's subsequent experience mirrors that of many whistleblowers and, indeed, of the blacklisted construction workers – lack of income, stress and demoralization. 'It affects your relationship with your children, who are the most important thing in my life,' said Wainwright.[17]

However, it wasn't just the DTI that had been passed evidence of blacklisting. In 2007, Tony Jones, one of the claimants in the Logic Control tribunal, went to see his MP, Graham Brady, about the blacklisting he had suffered. It was the second time Jones had seen his MP about the issue. The first time had been around five years previously but, as Jones admitted, his evidence had then been limited. This time he had something more substantial. He had the tribunal's findings and Wainwright's statement. Subsequently the MP wrote to Harriet Harman, then minister of state in the Department for Constitutional Affairs, passing on the evidence and asking what response he could give to his constituent. Once again, Pat McFadden responded. Once again, the minister sympathized with the difficulties Jones had encountered. This time McFadden noted that the electrician had made use of an employment tribunal and so suggested the system of protection for workers was appropriate.

While one government department had not felt able to make use of the leads provided by the Logic Control case, Clancy saw that there were several firms worthy of further investigation. Following information from Wainwright, the ICO investigators turned their attention towards Haden Young. Using powers contained in the Data Protection Act, Clancy applied to the Crown Court for a warrant to effect an immediate search as he believed that giving a warning would mean evidence being spirited away. This power had never been used before in a case of this kind but a judge granted the search warrant and in September 2008 Haden Young's offices were raided.

The warrant documentation specifically mentions the Wainwright evidence as being *prima facie* evidence of blacklisting. Since this legal action was breaking new ground for the ICO, it would not have included this information unless it was absolutely sure. Yet it remains substantially the same as that given to the government a year previously. In that time tens of thousands of names would have been checked against the blacklist by subscriber companies.

On entering Haden Young's offices in Watford, the investigators quickly secured the fax number 01923 295109, which was the hub of the operation. They now needed to know where that led. After threatening British Telecom with a court order, the phone company disclosed to the ICO the name and address of Kerr and The Consulting Association. Now it was back to Manchester Crown Court for another search warrant and the Droitwich raid was on.

Alarm bells

At this point Kerr knew nothing about the impending knock at his door, yet all the signs were there. One of the tasks he pursued assiduously was checking the radical press. He provided a clippings service for subscriber companies – described as 'very useful' by one former TCA chair. Mary Kerr recalled that her husband would spend a lot of his time reading the newspapers and magazines that TCA subscribed to. 'He had a tremendous knowledge of current affairs. Everyone wanted him on their pub quiz team,' she said.[18]

When Kerr read Chamberlain's initial *Guardian* article, alarm bells rang, prompting him to take the precaution of temporarily removing all the documentation from TCA's offices. The construction companies' own media-monitoring services flagged up a concern but this did not lead to a decision to abort the operation. This is understandable since the blacklisting operation was compartmentalized within each company on a need-to-know basis. When Chamberlain contacted one firm, Skanska, after the raid for a comment there was genuine disbelief in the press office that it could be involved. It felt inimical to an organization with a headquarters in Sweden, a strong corporatist structure and so many public-sector contracts. It subsequently turned out, though, that Skanska was one of the largest users of The Consulting Association.

What is harder to fathom is why Kerr remained in the dark after the raid on Haden Young in September 2008. At any time a discreet phone call could have been made to him. It is quite clear that, had he known, Kerr would have immediately shut down his operation. This was a man who had his files taken off premises while he was on holiday, as well as after the initial *Guardian* story, so as to maintain security. Mary Kerr says that, when she later inquired why no-one warned Kerr, she received a solicitor's letter asking her to desist in her questioning.

It has now emerged that this was on the direct orders of Haden Young's parent company Balfour Beatty. A statement from Gerry Harvey, Balfour Beatty's TCA contact, seen by the authors, says:

❝I was aware from Paul Raby, the Group Human Resources Director, of the August 2008 ICO raid on HY's offices (as they are a Balfour Beatty group company). However, Paul Raby gave both Mr Johnston [Armar Johnston, another TCA contact] and me strict instructions that we were not to warn The Consulting Association and Mr Kerr about the raid and we were to have no further dealings with the Association.

❛ Both Armar Johnston and I both clearly knew the potential consequences of this decision. We both considered that it would be beneficial to forewarn Ian Kerr and we discussed whether this should be done. However, in the end we both abided by Paul Raby's clear instructions not to tell Ian Kerr as it was possible that the repercussions for BK [Balfour Kilpatrick] could be significant if we were thought to have "tipped off' Ian Kerr".❜

Failing to act on the warning signs was to prove catastrophic from Kerr's perspective.

In March 2009, the ICO issued a press release announcing it had seized the covert database of construction industry workers. Deputy information commissioner David Smith was quoted saying: 'Not only was personal information held on individuals without their knowledge or consent but the very existence of the database was repeatedly denied.'[19] As we have seen, those denials extended to the government but the raid led by Clancy had blown the covert operation wide open. The *Guardian* had been tipped off several days previously by the ICO as an exclusive and Chamberlain and experienced investigative journalist Rob Evans began piecing together the background. Kerr was tracked down but would only say that it was legitimate for companies to check on who they employed. 'There was nothing sinister about it. It was *bona fide*,' he said.[20]

The files, though, said differently. The ICO revealed only a small selection and each had a name, date of birth and National Insurance number. They included phrases such as 'will cause trouble, strong TU [trade union]'. Another was referred to as 'UCATT... very bad news'. A TGWU member was described as 'a sleeper and should be watched'. Other descriptions were 'ex-shop steward, definite problems' and 'Irish ex-Army, bad egg'. While it was claimed that the system was meant to identify people who could threaten companies because they stole items or had poor workmanship, the files suggested that being a union activist was the overwhelming criterion for inclusion. If there was nothing underhand about the way it operated then why was there a regular exhortation in the files that the source of information not be disclosed? Those sources were hidden behind a series of code numbers as well as by the initials of people. Kerr readily co-operated with the ICO in explaining that each number referred to a particular company. He also handed over the financial records to show who subscribed and how much they were invoiced for the checking of names.

The ICO identified 43 companies which, throughout the TCA's lifetime, had paid a subscription fee to become a member (£3,000 a year in 2009). Each name check cost £2.20. As one example, between October 1999 and April 2004 Carillion paid TCA £32,393 + VAT for its vetting service. That equates to checks on an estimated 14,724 people. The 43 companies are listed in an annex at the end of the book. This was a roll call of the biggest (and not so big) names in the business. The accounts showed that £478,000 passed through the small office between 2004 and March 2009.

The story breaks

Deputy Information Commissioner David Smith toured the media from morning until evening on the day the story broke. In an interview for BBC Radio 4's *Today* programme he added an important detail, saying: 'There are some indications that those who raised genuine safety concerns may have been prejudiced by this database.[21] In an industry where an average of one person a week was dying because of an accident, this caused particular outrage. UCATT general secretary Alan Ritchie told the *Today* programme:

> ❝UCATT members have been working to reduce deaths and injuries on sites and trying to work with companies to achieve these aims. We now know that those same companies have connived to dismiss them and block their future employment.❞

He didn't know it at the time, but Ritchie also had a blacklist file from his time working in the Upper Clyde Shipyards that also included information about his campaigning work for the Anti-Apartheid Movement. So far the media was working only from the select information released by the ICO on what the files contained. The organization then announced that it would operate an enquiry system so those who believed they might be on the list could find out and, if so, get hold of their files. From then on the information wouldn't be filtered by the ICO. Few realized at the time that this move would blow the scandal wide open and start to suck in all sorts of organizations and individuals.

Some of those who did realize the implications were the people closest to the blacklisting operation. Mary Kerr recalls her husband going down to the paper shop on the day the story broke to buy all the newspapers, aware that it was coming out. He took notes on the media coverage and hunted for a solicitor while outside his house journalists waited. David Cochrane and Alan Audley, respectively the chair and vice-chair of TCA, called him to discuss the situation. That evening the Kerrs left to spend the next few weeks at a relative's house and avoid media attention.

Weeks earlier, on the day of the raid, Mary had been at home laid up with a broken leg following a skiing accident. Ian had only taken the files back into the office three days before Clancy came calling. Kerr called David Cochrane, who was the head of human resources at Sir Robert McAlpine as well as TCA chairman. The construction firm's legal advisors confirmed the ICO raid was legal. Discussions started on how to minimize the fall-out for the prestigious building firm with its network of political and financial links. The authors have now seen Kerr's notes of phone conversations he had with Cochrane from this period. One note records Cochrane instructing: 'Ring everyone – Cease trading – Close down. We don't exist anymore – Destroy data – Stop processing.'

After the ICO had returned copies of the documents they had seized, Ian Kerr arranged for his brother-in-law to bring his large horsebox up to the TCA premises at night. Any unseized material from the office was loaded into it. The photocopier and some of the furniture was donated to a charity shop. The files were taken to his brother-in-law's property and a large bonfire was built. Afterwards they had to search around for all the paperclips to ensure the horses didn't eat them.

Now it was a case of waiting for the judicial process to work its way through. Kerr pleaded guilty through his solicitor before magistrates in Macclesfield to breaking data-protection laws. Magistrates were unimpressed by Kerr's absence at the court hearing and the limited information they were offered on how The Consulting Association was organized. Kerr had not wanted to reveal any more unless he was forced to. His solicitor tried to ring him to get that detail but he was showing his son around a prospective university and had his phone switched off. The magistrates described their sentencing powers as 'wholly inadequate' and referred the case to the Crown Court.

Weeks later, when Kerr appeared before Knutsford Crown Court, there was anticipation that he would be hit with a fine running into the tens of thousands. In court, sitting quietly in the public seats, was a representative from McAlpine. Nearby were Kerr's daughters and wife. The gallery was filled with angry protesters. When they asked Kerr's daughters what they were doing there, they said they were law students. They sat and listened while protesters and journalists took bets on the size of Kerr's sentence. To the surprise of all, and the disgust of many, Kerr was fined £5,000 with £1,187.20 in costs. Kerr told the court that although he had earned an annual salary of £47,500, he was now unemployed and had minimal savings. He didn't say that he had been advised not to start taking his generous pension package and therefore, as far as the court was concerned, it could only fine him on the basis of his disclosed income.

After 30 years working covertly to build a picture of perceived troublemakers in industry, Kerr was desperate not to have his picture taken. He came out of the court from a side exit and put

Outside Macclesfield Magistrates Court in 2009. L-R Tony Jones, Howard Nolan, Steve Acheson, Graham Bowker, Sean Keaveney

up an umbrella to hide his face from a photographer who had climbed on to a wall. With one of his daughters driving, a second daughter and his wife in the back, he kept his head hidden under a newspaper. Outside, dozens of blacklisted workers had been waiting all morning. For so long, they had been unable to point the finger at one person and say that it was him who had stopped them from working and Kerr was suddenly thrust into that role. His daughter edged their car out, her hand permanently on the horn. The car collided with blacklisted scaffolder Mick Abbott. The banging on the vehicle caused Kerr to look up momentarily and he was snapped by a photographer. It was clear that he would not be able to stay in the shadows.

A strong signal

Following this case the ICO issued enforcement notices against 14 companies which had subscribed to The Consulting Association. The companies were: Balfour Beatty Civil Engineering, Balfour Beatty Construction Northern Ireland, Balfour Beatty Construction Scottish & Southern Ltd, Balfour Beatty Engineering Services (HY) Ltd, Balfour Beatty Engineering Services Ltd, Balfour Beatty Infrastructure Services Ltd, CB&I UK Ltd, Emcor Engineering Services Ltd, Emcor Rail Ltd, Kier Ltd, NG Bailey Ltd, Shepherd Engineering Services Ltd, SIAS Building Services Ltd and Whessoe Oil & Gas Ltd.[22] Essentially these are warnings against their future handling of personal data. Deputy information commissioner David Smith said:

> ❛We have used the maximum powers available to us and this enforcement action sends a strong signal that organizations must take the Data Protection Act seriously.❜[23]

In private there was a feeling within the ICO that the case demonstrated that the regulations lacked teeth. The companies named responded with some shows of contrition but generally with a steadfast refusal to admit any significant wrongdoing. In public, an employment law professor commissioned by UCATT to write a report on the issue questioned the small number of enforcement notices, adding: "the list does not include some of the heaviest users, including McAlpine and Skanska, for reasons that are not revealed... this does not seem an adequate response."[24]

Meanwhile a pattern began to emerge of official resistance to releasing information which might implicate anyone with links to TCA. Responding to Freedom of Information requests from the authors, various police forces refused to confirm or deny that they held any information on either The Consulting Association or Ian Kerr. Quickly all those people and organizations which might have knowledge of Ian Kerr began to row back from any association.

The Knutsford hearing did confirm several details about Kerr and The Consulting Association. His solicitor admitted that Kerr had worked for a previous blacklisting organization called the Economic League and that, when that folded, The Consulting Association had been set up by construction firms to continue its secret vetting work. Kerr was paid to run the organization, which was not registered as a company but was described by his solicitor as an 'unincorporated trade association' – a meaningless term. So, although much remained a mystery, the process of breaking apart the conspiracy was under way.

By November 2009 some 230 files had been disclosed by the ICO and that started to produce a body of evidence for campaigners to look into. An analysis by the ICO estimated that over three-quarters of the files concerned trade unionists and activities associated with trade unions. Professor Keith Ewing, from the Institute of Employment Rights, studied a number of files after he was commissioned by the building union UCATT to write a report on the issue. 'I was deeply offended at the amount of intimate and personal detail so meticulously gathered,' he said. 'At the same time some of the files were hopelessly inconsistent.'

Inconsistent they may have been, but the effect they had had on individuals was clear. John Breen, a labourer from North Ayrshire, was blacklisted in the 1980s and told fellow GMB members at their Congress in 2016:

> My blacklisting hit my family hard financially. We couldn't buy anything and had to live day to day and scrimp and save. We couldn't have any savings and were stopped for a long time [from] having a family. It was too expensive for us to go out and do things. We only made ends meet by relying on my

wife's earnings. Not being able to be the breadwinner was frustrating and it hurt. The whole situation caused me a lot of stress and anxiety. I would sit awake at night and wonder what went wrong and how I ended up in this situation.[25]

John's wife, Elaine Breen, explained how blacklisting impacted on their family life:

> At first I resented my husband for almost losing me my job, as it was, as he went on strike. I blamed him even though it wasn't his fault. After that he wasn't able to find work. It was really hard for both of us. I was earning for the both of us so I had to do any job I could get. It made me feel quite resentful. As I had to be out working it meant for a long time we couldn't have a family. I had no choices. Because I had to be working it put a strain on both of us. We had our daughter in 1986. We had planned to have more children but without my husband being in work we couldn't afford to. After having my daughter I had to go back to work so we had a source of income, but this was through necessity, not choice. We were living on the breadline. We could never afford any holidays and weren't able to go out and do things. There were times we couldn't even afford the train fare to go and see my mother in Edinburgh. It was existence and only that.[26]

The wife of bricklayer John Jones told the authors:

> Things were really bad for us, around the Eighties. It was impossible for him to get a job, absolutely impossible. Soul destroying. Difficult for me with the three kids, I ended up having to go back to work.

Vic Williams' marriage didn't survive the blacklist which had affected him for decades:

> At the time, in 1985, it was commonplace for people to be able to buy their own homes but I was never in a position to be able to do that. It affected the old marriage. Eventually that ended in divorce. Obviously when you can't earn any dough, that has an impact and the missus don't like that sometimes. I've had a bit of heart trouble. There has never been any heart

trouble in my family. My old man and all the family are all in their eighties and nineties but I've got the cholesterol thing and that can be built up by stress – I had to have a stent put in, I'm on statins. All my brothers and sisters didn't have any heart trouble. You ain't never gonna prove that in a court of law but they are factors. I'm not going to cry in my soup, but it's worth a mention.❜[27]

Some of the files contained information that was bordering on the ridiculous. One file describes how a union activist organized a petition against homelessness, while others uncover equally serious malpractice:

> *very bad news – Buddhist*
> *talks like a young Alf Garnett*
> *wears Anti Nazi League badges and insignia and is suspected*
> *of being a supporter*

For decades, blacklisted workers had been fighting to expose the conspiracy. Union conferences had debated the issue, while rank-and-file activists had campaigned outside building sites. Following the discovery of the files, the workers felt vindicated but also frustrated that, after the initial media splash, the story had vanished from public view. Many of them contacted their MP

Only image from 2009 initial meeting of Blacklist Support Group in Westminster

and, on 21 July 2009, John McDonnell MP chaired a meeting for workers who had received copies of their blacklist files in the House of Commons. They established the Blacklist Support Group (BSG) for workers on The Consulting Association blacklist in order to disseminate useful information and ensure that the voice of those actually blacklisted was heard. Immediately *Hazards* magazine, which was respected for its coverage of health-and-safety issues, agreed to run an online blog and lawyers came forward to provide legal assistance.

McDonnell told an early Blacklist Support Group meeting that he wanted to see a public inquiry into what he described as 'one of the worst cases of organized human rights abuses in the UK ever'. Over the next five years, BSG campaigning would drag the blacklisting conspiracy centre stage. Blacklisted workers linked up with investigative journalists, trade unions, lawyers, academics, politicians and human rights activists. Far from going away, the scandal would lead to debates in parliament, a Select Committee investigation, prime-time TV documentaries, ground-breaking legal actions and historic industrial disputes. That was in the future – first the campaigners needed to delve back into the past to work out how they ended up with such an iniquitous yet widespread system.

1 Scottish Affairs Committee, *Blacklisting in Employment: oral and written evidence*, The Stationery Office Limited, London, April 2013, p168. 2 Interview with the authors. 3 theguardian.com/money/2008/jun/28/workandcareers – accessed 13 March 2014. 4 Interview with the authors. 5 Unless otherwise stated, Acheson quotes are from interviews with the authors. 6 Interview with the authors. 7 'Sacked electricians win tribunal ruling', *The Socialist*, 30 March 2007, socialistparty.org.uk/articles/2241 8 Interview with the authors. 9 Interview with the authors. 10 Interview with the authors. 11 Interview with the authors. 12 Interview with the authors. 13 Employment Tribunal, Acheson & Others v Logic Control Limited, written judgment. Case reference 2402599/2006. 14 https://ico.org.uk – accessed 10 March 2014. 15 Alan Wainwright, written evidence to Scottish Affairs Select Committee, nin.tl/SACevidence 16 'Lonely life of a construction industry whistleblower', *Guardian*, 15 May 2009, nin.tl/lonelywhistleblower 17 Ibid. 18 Interview with the authors. 19 'Do not touch – the covert database that kept union activists out of work', the *Guardian*, 6 March 2009, nin.tl/29xy8Ca 20 Ibid. 21 'Call for action over rampant blacklisting of workers', *Telegraph*, 6 March 2009, nin.tl/rampantblacklisting 22 https://ico.org.uk/for-the-public/construction-blacklist/ 23 'Blacklisting', *Construction News*, 4 August 2009, nin.tl/CNblacklisting 24 Prof Keith Ewing *Ruined Lives* August 2009 p 6. 25 Statement from GMB Congress 2016. 26 Statement from GMB Congress 2016. 27 Interview with the authors.

2
Conduct which kills freedom

Pauline was 18 when she took the job, which seemed like a simple secretarial position in a suburb of south London alongside three other women. Her role was to take phone calls, record the names given, check them against files and then report back if a file existed. Pauline (not her real name) recalls:

> ❝I was not that political when I started, it was just a job that was round the corner from where I lived. But I did become aware about what was happening in the country as a result of doing it, a lot more than my friends. I was very aware of left and right. It wasn't said explicitly but I knew I wasn't supposed to talk about what my job involved with anybody else.❞[1]

It was 1972 and Pauline was working for the Economic League's central records and research department based at 99a High Street, Thornton Heath. She would take phone calls from companies. They would give her a password to identify themselves and then the name, date of birth and national insurance number for an individual. Pauline would go and check a filing system and see if a record was held. If it was, she would report the information back. Two other women handled the invoicing of companies for their search requests and keeping the records up to date. Working in the same office were a group of men who liaised with corporations and the League's other offices. Several of these men, as well the husbands of some of the secretarial staff, were former or serving Metropolitan Police officers. One of those Pauline remembers regularly dropping by was Ned Walsh, who sported a trilby and a mysterious manner. 'He acted just like a spy, he was always very cautious,' said Pauline. Walsh's official post was researcher for the League, a job he held from 1961 to 1988. However, investigative journalists were slowly uncovering the shady operations of the League.

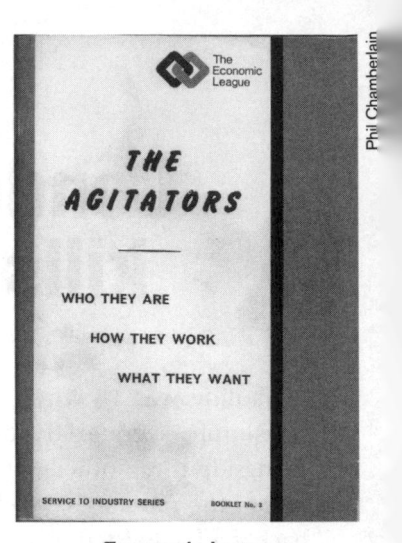

Pauline was right about the actual role of Ned Walsh, according to journalists Mark Hollingsworth and Charles Tremayne: 'His real job was to infiltrate trade unions, charities, research groups and anything else the League regarded as politically subversive.'[2] According to the *World in Action* reporters, Walsh infiltrated the Anti-Apartheid Movement and the Transnational Information Centre as a delegate from the Association of Scientific, Technical and Managerial

Economic League propaganda pamphlet

Staffs union as well as meetings of the Transport and General Workers' Union and the AGM of long-time League foe, the Labour Research Department. In the early 1970s, the League was getting more than £400,000 a year in subscriptions and donations and used that to employ around 160 staff and print some 20 million leaflets warning against the dangers of subversion.[3] The list of construction companies Pauline dealt with would all turn up years later as subscribers to The Consulting Association.

> ❛Kier, McAlpine, Bovis, Babcock, Balfour Beatty, I remember them all ringing. They were only supposed to ask for a certain number of names to be checked at a time but sometimes they would have quite a lot and so they would give some, ring off and then ring back straight away with the next lot.❜

And just as some companies were regular callers, so some of the names became familiar. Pauline said: 'If anybody rang up about Des Warren then alarm bells would go. He and Ricky Tomlinson had big files. I remember getting calls about them.' The League wasn't the only organization with an interest in Tomlinson. Special Branch had a file on him which branded the former plasterer, later to become a well-loved actor, a political thug prone to violence.[4]

Echoes of McCarthyism

The League's activities were mirrored in other countries. Over a five-year period from 1936, the La Follette Civil Liberties Committee, named after the senator who chaired it, investigated how companies dealt with trade unions in the United States. Chief executives and private detectives were called to give evidence. The result was to catalogue collaboration between the police, private security and corporations to sabotage meaningful industrial relations.

Edwin Smith, head of the US National Labor Relations Board, saw the impact on people marked out as union activists:

> ❝Here they were, family men with wives and children on public relief, blacklisted from employment, so they claimed, in the city of Detroit, citizens whose only offense was that they had ventured in the land of the free to organize as employees to improve their working conditions. Their reward, as workers who had given their best to their employer, was to be hunted down by a hired spy like the lowest of criminals and thereafter tossed like useless metal on the scrap heap.❞⁵

The hearings have a familiar ring to them. For instance, the head of the notorious Pinkerton detective agency was questioned about the reasons for spying on union meetings. He said it was to get: 'Information dealing with sabotage, theft of material, and other irregularities.' The actual reports produced by the agency showed no evidence of sabotage or theft but plenty of information about how unions were organizing. Asher Rossetter, the head of one company which employed Pinkerton, blustered: 'It might lead to sabotage if those people were the kind that I think they may be – Communists.'⁶

Fast forward 70 years and company director Cullum McAlpine is giving evidence to MPs about The Consulting Association. He is asked to explain how what McAlpine describes as a 'reference service' would work.

> ❝I was led to believe that the member companies would provide information to The Consulting Association on individuals who had acted in a disruptive way on building sites, had broken

some of the working-rule agreements, had sabotaged such things, or had committed criminal acts such as theft, vandalism or threatening behaviour – that sort of stuff.[97]

Setting aside the passive voice used to distance himself from an organization with which he was intimately involved, McAlpine's justification echoes that deployed by Rossetter. And that justification continues. On a corporate web page called *Mythbuster and FAQs*, construction firm Carillion explains its position in relation to blacklisting and its use of The Consulting Association. It says Crown House, a subsidiary which subscribed to the Association, was concerned about 'suspected or actually reported sabotage, threatening behaviour and intimidation' and when it attended meetings they would be about things like preventing theft.[8] An analysis of the files by the authors shows that only a tiny handful mention theft – the main criterion for inclusion was lawful union activity.

Rossetter at least had the grace, or perhaps the lack of ingenuity, to admit that the surveillance and disruption of union members was a political decision. In post-War America, the blacklist was to become an explicit political weapon.

The House Committee on Un-American Activities (HUAC) hearings and Senator McCarthy's campaign against supposed communist infiltration had some very public victims. The 2016 film *Trumbo* highlighted the case of the famous Hollywood Ten who refused to name names before HUAC. Dozens of other actors, directors and screenwriters all found themselves effectively barred from their jobs, while some were even sent to prison during this period of mass paranoia. Beyond that, though, an estimated 10,000 people without a public profile were blacklisted because of their supposed subversive views. The storm lost its focus once McCarthy was exposed for being a self-aggrandizing bully; but while the Cold War continued so would the hunt for reds under the bed.[9]

'Subversion in public life'

Back in the UK and in the 1970s an interdepartmental committee was set up, on the advice of MI5 director-general Michael Hanley, to advise the Cabinet on subversion in public life. It produced a series of reports looking at different sectors, including the construction industry. 'The papers included considerable background information on unions and industry from the Department of Employment, and some from the FCO [Foreign and Commonwealth Office]'s Information Research Department.'[10] The Information Research Department had for many years provided an outlet for government psychological operations and disinformation. We will meet them again later in this chapter in relation to the Shrewsbury trial. A request by the authors for the construction industry report to be released by the National Archives was refused on grounds of national security. The initials IRD appear on numerous blacklist files.

In 1974, the influential Institute for the Study of Conflict circulated a document suggesting the sacking and blacklisting of communists and subversives.[11] It was already happening, and Pauline, working out of her Economic League office, was involved in it on a daily basis. 'You have to remember these people were trying to bring the country to its knees,' she said. Having subsequently read the stories of those whose lives were blighted by its files, she does have misgivings about her work having targeted some people wrongly.

Retired bricklayer George Fuller was one of those whose file was started by the League and inherited by TCA, and whose life was blighted. Originally from Ipswich, with a soft East Anglian brogue, his initial experience was on the huge Barbican building project in London which began in the late 1960s and was the focus of a bitter industrial dispute.

> ❝The first job I got when I came to London was a Laing's job at the Barbican – and by the time I got home I had a telegram telling me not to start. And, you know, there were jobs where I'd start working and get the sack within a few hours. It affects your skills really. You keep going from one job to another rather than having 18 months on nice-quality particular work. Poor workmanship is not mentioned in my blacklist file. Up until then they never mentioned anything at all and then when you get elected as a union steward, they start talking about it.❞[12]

In 1978 it was revealed that two Glasgow-based companies maintained their own blacklists. On their second day at work with Lafferty Construction, two joiners handed in their personal details and were sacked 20 minutes later. Four days later a manager handed them the blacklist which contained their names, along with 13 others. The pair then got a job with a company called Whatlings, only to be sacked again once they handed in their personal details. This time a sympathetic manager handed them Whatlings' blacklist, which had 53 names. Out of the 72 names on the two blacklists, 67 were union members.[13] While this shows it had its rivals, the Economic League had a history, ideology and connections second to none, which made it 'one of the most powerful, most active and most durable of anti-labour employers' combinations in the 20th century'.[14]

Originally known as National Propaganda, it was formed over Christmas 1919 with financial support from engineering, shipping and mining associations. It eventually became the Economic League in 1926. Its guiding light was Sir Reginald Hall – a Conservative MP and director of Naval Intelligence during World War One. Hall was convinced that there needed to be a 'crusade for capitalism' to counter what he saw as the growing popularity of socialist ideas in the wake of the Russian Revolution and general unrest in the aftermath of war. The midwives to the League's birth made it unusual among the many anti-subversive organizations which sprang up at the time. The League combined what it called 'educative propaganda' with a covert strategy to ensure that all militant socialists, communists and other 'subversives' were denied employment in British industry. League speakers went out to the factory gates to preach the benefits of capitalism while printing presses churned out leaflets on the perils of socialism.

Less noticeably, names of those who would destabilize the British industrial elite were shared among League subscribers. In the General Strike of 1926 the League was quick to bring its propaganda and intelligence services to the aid of the government and demonstrate its value. That relationship, according to veteran League-watcher Mike Hughes, continued during the Cold War.

There is a persuasive body of circumstantial evidence of a

continuing connection between British Intelligence and the Economic League after the Second World War: an already established relationship, a common cause (anti-Bolshevism), a common tactic (the blacklist) and the League's employment of individuals with an intelligence background. It would be truly incredible if MI5 had not sought and received information from the Economic League and its nationwide network of contacts in personnel departments.'[15]

It has been described as big business's 'dirty tricks department'[16] but it didn't need to bug and burgle to gather its information. It took advantage of the open nature of many progressive organizations and turned it against them. Its officers attended meetings, they read the movement's press and, where possible, they made links with those as ideologically opposed to 'subversion' as they were. If those fellow patriots were union leaders as well, then all the better. Alan Harvey was an assistant director at the League based in Skipton, Yorkshire, when he met what he thought were two businesspeople in 1987. They were actually *World in Action* reporters. Harvey explained that the information flow included sharing details with the police and Special Branch – 'in return they're not exactly unfriendly back' – and tip-offs from trade unions. 'A lot of trade unions don't want subversives in their ranks any more than we want them in ours,' he explained.[17] As Harvey said: 'People like CND [Campaign for Nuclear Disarmament], Friends of the Earth, Anti-Apartheid, animal rights, they're very useful vehicles for subversives' and the League needed to know about the one in a thousand who 'want to bring the whole system to its knees'.[18] Bidding his new friends goodbye, Harvey said he was off to the nearby university. He explained: 'I take my jacket off, put an anorak on, wander in and buy a few subversive newspapers.' This example of the wide range of democratic campaigning organizations which are dragged into such political monitoring will be repeated with The Consulting Association.

As more League documents were uncovered and published by, among others, the investigative journalist Paul Foot in the *Mirror*, it became clear that the corporate paranoia of the Economic League meant that thousands of individuals were hoovered up in their spying operations. One was Syd Scroggie, a war hero from Dundee, blinded and left with one leg after standing on a landmine during the liberation of Italy in 1945. Scroggie went on to be the first blind man to climb Everest and appeared on the TV show, *This Is Your Life*. Scroggie, believe it or not, was added to the Economic League blacklist and branded a subversive after writing to a newspaper in support of Edinburgh District Council's decision to buy a portrait of Nelson Mandela.[19] According to exhaustive research by Mike Hughes, between 1975 and 1989 around 600 companies were connected with the League. Every sector was represented, from manufacturing to finance, newspapers to transportation. Hughes said: 'A very brief comparison of this list with the Times 1000 for 1986 reveals some interesting facts: 6 of the top 10, 20 of the top 50 and 37 of the top 100 UK companies occur in this list. Together, in 1986, these companies alone employed more than 2.1 million people.'[20]

The new recruit

The machinery of propaganda, blacklisting and the nexus of corporate interests and state security services was well-established when, in 1969, the League took on a new recruit. Ian Kerr was born in July 1942 in Leicester, the son of a master tailor. He trained as an art teacher and started his career in 1967 working at a primary and then a secondary school in Warley in the West Midlands and then the Lozells School in Birmingham. He left that career after two years 'ostensibly to earn enough money to get married'[21] and joined the Economic League as a training officer. While there was an explicit ideological drive behind the League's operations and it tended to attract people with a similar view on society, this didn't mean all were political activists. Mary Kerr spotted the advert for a League training officer in the *Birmingham Post* and showed it to Ian. He applied and was taken on. Mary says it was a financial decision.

> Ian earned about £850 a year as a teacher and to get a mortgage they multiplied your salary by two and a half and didn't take the woman's earnings into account. When Ian joined the League, overnight he started earning about £1,600 a year and there were perks like £25 a month expenses.[22]

That was in the spring. In the summer the couple were married, holding their reception at The Belfry.

It was also a big year for the League – 1969 marked its 50th birthday and as a present the Labour Research Department published a pamphlet: 'A subversive guide to the Economic League.' It showed an organization in good health, with an income of £266,000 and more than 150 firms subscribing to its services. Kerr was one of 39 speakers and trainers and its corps of propagandists organized 24,250 group talks and outdoor meetings, 6,340 courses for apprentices and 3,750 for supervisors. As Hughes puts it: 'The Economic League was a major operator in the class wars of the late 1960s and early 1970s'[23] and Kerr was stepping straight into the firing line.

Ian Vogler/Daily Mirror

Ian Kerr

Kerr was recruited by Jack Winder, who had joined the organization in 1963 and, like many in the League, had a military background. Winder, gregarious and always keen to promote his own skills, and the unassuming Kerr did not seem to have a lot in common. However, they lived close by each other in that well-to-do stretch of commuterland south of Birmingham and the families began socializing outside of work. Kerr's meticulous yet diffident manner made him valuable for the often laborious work the League required. Giving the same talks over and again to bored apprentices was not enough to interest the League's more self-regarding class warriors. For Ian, the conscientious worker and church-goer, it was the task he had been handed and therefore the one he would do his best to deliver. Mary recalls both of them preparing carefully the night before he was due to go out and address workers in his training capacity.

He might have been taken on as a training officer but he also undertook infiltration for the League. He was later to tell MPs at a Select Committee investigation:

❝A lot of these [union discussions] were held as public meetings in public places. I worked from the Birmingham office. They would hold them in Birmingham Town Hall, in the Digbeth Institute, which is a well-known meeting place in Birmingham, in upstairs rooms of pubs, and I would just go along and take notes. The briefing I would be given was to note who was speaking, who was he representing, how many were there, and what were the general points, ideas and themes that were being discussed. Then I would go back and make a brief summary. That sort of information would find its way into files, possibly, but equally into publications by the League that were put out publicly to newspapers in their attempt to get this particular view across to counter the anti-capitalist message, which was quite strong at the time.❜[24]

Mary laughingly recalls that Ian, thin, about six feet tall, who had large round glasses and who never felt dressed for work unless he was in a suit, 'must have stuck out like a sore thumb'. Despite this, Michael Noar, the League's director-general between 1986 and 1989, praised Kerr's work for the organization. Noar said he infiltrated 'a lot' of trade union and political meetings, recording who had said what and taking away documents such as attendance lists. 'He was a key guy,' Noar told the *Guardian*. 'He was one of our most effective research people – his information was genuine and reliable.'[25]

According to the Labour Research Department, at the end of the 1960s, construction and engineering firms made up 60 out of the League's 155 subscribers.[26] The interest in the construction sector grew even more in the 1970s. Most of the popular histories of the 1970s barely mention the 1972 building workers' strike, perhaps because there were so many other strikes to report on. The imprisoned Pentonville 5 dockers and the miners' strike of the same year have, for example, taken on mythic proportions. However, the building strike had just as profound an effect on both trade unions and on employers in the construction industry.[27]

The 1972 strike

It began when UCATT, which arose in 1972 out of the amalgamation of numerous craft unions, began renegotiating collective agreements. It knew it needed to establish its credibility as an effective negotiator. Within weeks a national strike was launched. Neither employers nor UCATT foresaw the ramifications. After two increased wage offers were rejected by unions, a series of targeted strikes started in June 1972. These quickly spread and a month later flying pickets were first used in Manchester to enforce the shutdowns. In July an estimated 160 sites involving 10,000 men were out, with many others affected by overtime bans and go-slows. The shrewd use of flying pickets wasn't just forcing employers to the negotiating table; it was undermining their whole industrial strategy. In August an improved offer was provisionally accepted by UCATT and the other unions involved. However, the strike had galvanized rank-and-file action and, when the deal was announced, thousands marched against the agreement. UCATT was forced to reverse its decision. The labour historians Ralph Darlington and Dave Lyddon explain:

> From early August to mid-September 1972, the last six weeks of the building workers' strike witnessed a massive assertion of rank-and-file control over the running of the dispute. Even in an exceptional year this was outstanding. It was more than a strike. It was a revolt.[28]

The rank-and-file revolt was co-ordinated by a movement called the Building Workers' Charter, which had been set up in 1970 following a meeting of shop stewards from London, Liverpool and Manchester and was heavily influenced by the Communist Party and other leftwing groups. The Charter's demands for greater union democracy and a wage policy of £35 for 35 hours quickly drew wide support among building workers.

Strikes were no longer targeted; whole cities shut down and Building Workers' Charter members were busy organizing further action. Employers claimed that a few militants were to blame and that the majority of workers were uninterested or bullied into taking part. This was faithfully reported by the mainstream media, which had otherwise generally ignored the dispute. However, unions estimate that, at its peak, 270,000 workers across some 9,000 sites were involved. In September, the employers' federation agreed the largest single pay rise ever won in the industry – though it was not the £1 an hour the Charter wanted. The unions called the strike off. The employers began preparing retribution.

Richard Clutterbuck was an influential rightwing theorist on political violence at the time and had developed his ideas while serving with the Army in numerous post-colonial wars. Later historians may have overlooked the battles in the construction industry but Clutterbuck's view at the time suggested it was as potent as the more celebrated miners' dispute. His analysis that the 1972 strike represented a major escalation in class war was widely shared amongst industry leaders. The characterization of the dispute as one of unbridled violence, and so ignoring legitimate grievances, would be rolled out repeatedly.[29]

A pamphlet produced by the Economic League quotes a National Federation of Building Trades Employers (NFBTE) report listing what it saw as a new militancy and violence in the industry:

> 'The end result of the incidents recorded in this file was that small but well-drilled groups were able to hold to ransom a whole industry employing a million or more men and thereby cause incalculable damage and loss.'

As a League pamphlet warned: 'The strike itself was an example of how extremist groups organize and plan their operations against British industry.'[30] Who better to keep an eye on these extremist groups than the experts from the League? The refrain was the familiar one that political cadres were manipulating reasonable workers into acting against their interests. Construction sites had been very difficult places for unions to organize in because of the casual nature of the work. The growing militancy from the late 1960s up to the 1972 strike showed that employers could not rely on this factor any more – and the fear this aroused lay at the heart of their response.

The Shrewsbury pickets

Firms had already been asked to compile dossiers on flying pickets to highlight what they characterized as extreme levels of violence. One particular incident took place in Shrewsbury and entered union folklore. On 6 September 1972, 250 flying pickets in six coaches from Chester and North Wales responded to calls for support to shut down sites in Shrewsbury. At the first site they were confronted by the son of the contractor, armed with a shotgun. He was disarmed and the gun given to the police. Dave Cooper, a young bricklayer from Chester, was one of the Shrewsbury pickets on the coach and recalls:

> ❝I was 23 at the time, I had hair down me back. Everyone was long haired and into the music; even if you were a building worker, you didn't look like one. When the guy pulled the shotgun out, I remember everyone moving forward, especially a couple of the big Welsh lads, to take the gun off him. I ran and hid behind the nearest wall thinking "what the hell have I got myself into?"❞[31]

Next they visited a McAlpine's site in Telford, which was well prepared to defend itself, and there were minor disturbances between some of the workers and pickets.

Ricky Tomlinson was one of the Shrewsbury pickets. 'Although it may have looked disorganized to an outsider, the picketing was good-natured and effective. Flying pickets were lawful and we were escorted by police to all but one of the sites. Afterwards, a senior policeman, Chief Superintendent Meredith, shook hands with Dezzie and me, congratulating us on a peaceful picket.'[32] No arrests were made on the day.

Shrewsbury was painted in a whole different light by the NFBTE dossier, which was sent to the Home Secretary Robert Carr and the press. It portrayed a scene of apocalyptic violence. Clutterbuck describes one picket being a 'giant' and 'like King Kong' ripping up trees by their roots. 'Those witnesses and victims to whom we spoke left us in no doubt as to the viciousness of the violence and the extreme degree of terror which they felt.'[33] Sir Robert Mark, commissioner for the Metropolitan Police, said:

Des Warren and Ricky Tomlinson

> ❝To some of us, the Shrewsbury pickets have committed the worst of all crimes, worse even than murder, the attempt to

achieve an industrial or political objective by criminal violence, the very conduct, in fact, which helped to bring the National Socialist German Workers Party to power in 1933. Conduct of that kind kills freedom, and there are still people who feel that freedom is more important than life itself.'[34]

It turned out that Robert McAlpine had written to Mark complaining that, while there was no problem with the law governing pickets, the problem was a lack of enforcement.[35] McAlpine could also call upon the support of the high sheriff of Denbighshire, who happened to be the ninth member of the McAlpine family in succession to have held that post.

In November, two months after the events, under pressure from the Home Secretary, police arrested dozens of pickets and 31 were charged. Even the then Attorney General, Sir Peter Rawlinson, considered the incidents so minor that a conviction was unlikely. In a letter to Robert Carr, the Conservative Home Secretary, dated 25 January 1973, Rawlinson stated that the strike had produced 'instances of intimidation of varying degrees of seriousness' but added that the Shrewsbury events 'consisted of threatening words and... there was no evidence against any particular person of violence or damage to property.' The Attorney General concluded by arguing, 'proceedings should not be instituted.'[36]

Nonetheless, the prosecutions continued and the jury in a trial at Mold Crown Court acquitted all 11 of those before them. At that trial, defence lawyers had exercised their right to challenge potential jurors. At Shrewsbury Crown Court, 24 were tried, with six facing additional charges carrying maximum terms of life imprisonment. In between the two trials the Lord Chancellor had decided to abolish the defence's ability to challenge the jurors. The courts were taking no chances and didn't want a repeat of Mold. The day that the prosecution completed its case, ITV screened an hour-long programme called *Reds under the Bed*, followed by a studio discussion. The programme had footage of two of the defendants as well as images of marches and supposed violence by pickets. The discussion was not broadcast in every region but it was in the area covering Shrewsbury. The final words of that discussion were from a Tory MP talking about violence in the building strike.

It seemed like blatant contempt of court but the judge dismissed complaints. Subsequently a government file revealed a memo from Thomas Barker from the government's Information Research Department, saying: 'We had a discreet but considerable hand in this programme. In general, this film, given national networking, can only have done good.'[37] The jury heard numerous claims of violence and that pickets had been screaming 'Kill, kill, kill' and had been armed. The defendants were astonished by the picture painted. However, files revealed in December 2015 that Home Secretary Robert Carr directed police evidence-gathering while inconvenient witness statements were destroyed. The picture was being painted quite deliberately.

Terry Renshaw, one of the Shrewsbury pickets, has a very different recollection of events:

> We were people from North Wales, we didn't know where the sites were. But the West Mercia constabulary were very obliging and took us one by one to the site. At the end of the day Detective Superintendent Meredith thanked the pickets for the way they had conducted themselves. Then the conspiracy started, between the government, the employers, the police, the judiciary and the secret service. We have the evidence of MI5 involvement.[38]

Renshaw later served as a county councillor, became mayor of the north Wales town, Flint, and a member of the North Wales Police Authority.

At the end of the conspiracy trial, John McKinsie Jones was jailed for nine months, Tomlinson for two years and Des Warren for three years. Not for committing any violence but for the amorphous crime of 'conspiracy'. In his famous speech from the dock Des Warren was defiant:

> Was there a conspiracy? Ten members of the jury have said there was. There was a conspiracy, but not by the pickets. The conspiracy was between the Home Secretary, the employers and the police. It was not done with a nod and a wink. It was conceived after pressure from Tory Members of Parliament who demanded changes in picketing laws. Of course, there

was a very important reason why no police witness said he had seen any evidence of conspiracy, unlawful assembly or affray. The question was hovering over the case from the very first day: why were there no arrests on the 6 September? That would have led to the even more important question of when was the decision to proceed taken. Where did it come from? What instructions were issued to the police? And by whom? There was your conspiracy.[39]

There were two subsequent trials arising out of Shrewsbury, which saw three more pickets – Brian Williams, Arthur Murray and Mike Pierce – jailed and others receive suspended terms. Terry Renshaw's suspended sentence meant the Preston College TUC tutor was later unable to stand as a Police and Crime Commissioner and still can't get a visa to travel to the US. His fellow defendant, McKinsie Jones, said:

Like a lot of the other pickets, I had never been in trouble in my life. We were completely innocent of these charges. We were branded as criminals by the media. We were blacklisted.[40]

The effect on Warren was far worse. Like Tomlinson, he considered himself a political prisoner, going on hunger strike and refusing to wear prison uniforms in protest. This resulted in his spending eight months in solitary confinement and at times being forcefully sedated with medication known as the 'liquid cosh'. His family say that it helped to bring about the onset of Parkinson's Disease, which killed him in 2004.

Ricky Tomlinson reflected on the effect Shrewsbury had on the defendants:

Many of them never worked again due to the blacklist, in particular Des Warren, who died in 2004. The prison sentences and fines we received for picketing completely wrecked our lives.[41]

Even campaigning for the release of the Shrewsbury pickets was sufficient to ensure a worker had information secretly held about them. Scaffolder Mick Abbott, who died in 2014, raised money for the families of the jailed union activists and in 1975 led a march by building workers from Wigan to London to protest against the miscarriage of justice. Following the release of Des Warren from prison, the pair became close friends at the time when Des was writing his iconic book, *The key to my cell*. Abbot's blacklist file starts in 1964, the first entry in which actually reads 'On building industry blacklist' and includes the following entries:

> *1974 Nov 28 (Workers Press) One of the signatories to an article saying 'All unions with members in the building and construction industries must be forced to call indefinite strike action until Des Warren and Ricky Tomlinson are released' (The Shrewsbury pickets)'.*
>
> *1975 Feb 4 (information for Mr ▮▮▮▮ – Bovis) This man is one of the leaders of the march from Wigan to London to protest against the gaoling of the Shrewsbury Pickets.*

Abbott's file records how he was repeatedly refused work by firms such as Tarmac, Bovis, Sir Robert McAlpine and Fergus & Haynes. Abbot later told *The Observer* newspaper:

❝ This nearly ruined my marriage and it meant my children were on free meals at school. My file goes back to 1964 and the last entry says that I rekindled the campaign for justice for the Shrewsbury pickets in 2006. They have been watching me all these years and passing this information around, blighting my life over four decades.❞[42]

The campaign Mick Abbott helped to rebuild to get the Shrewsbury convictions quashed has resulted in an application to the Criminal Cases Review Commission (CCRC). Eileen Turnbull, researcher for the Shrewsbury 24 Campaign, explains:

❝ The CCRC are looking at abuse of process. They are not looking like any other criminal trial about whether forensic evidence has been messed up or whether there was false identification. This is about whether the government interfered with the case. Our application was lodged on 3 April 2012 and since then the CCRC say that the evidence we have submitted is tangible. So, if you think about it, they have tangible evidence before them to show inference by government: this trial was political. And we are going to prove it.

Forty years ago Ricky Tomlinson and Des Warren made a speech at the end of their trial and, word for word, what they said was absolutely correct. The problem was that no-one at the time had the documents or the information to prove it. We have now got documents that show a link between the security services and the companies and those documents are in with the application.⁹

One of the documents linking the security services to the Shrewsbury trial is a letter sent to Downing Street from Sir Michael Hanley, Director General of MI5 in the 1970s. Large parts of the letter are redacted but sections that are visible state that Warren and Tomlinson must be kept in prison.[43]

Shrewsbury picket Terry Renshaw reflects: 'The question I have always asked is: were MI5 involved before the strike, during the strike or after the strike? And my belief is: all three.'

CCRC spokesperson Justin Hawkins has confirmed that 'the issues that have been referred to the CCRC required detailed further investigation.'[44]

The campaign to overturn the miscarriage of justice has resulted in a vote in the House of Commons in favour of releasing all the documents in the case. But, over 40 years after the events, the government files on Shrewsbury remain sealed on the direct order of the Home Secretary. The government says that only a handful of files have not been transferred to the national archives on the grounds of national security. Campaigners believe there are many more and dogged research has turned up a series of memos which cast serious doubt on the official narrative.

Andy Burnham MP revealed in a House of Commons debate on 9 December 2015 that Prime Minister Edward Heath was sent a transcript of the *Reds under the Bed* programme and he noted: 'We want as much of this as possible.' A further note from the PM's parliamentary private secretary alludes to a 'new unit' which Mr Heath hoped was 'in being and actively producing'. Mr Burnham told MPs: 'The documents I have revealed can only lead us to one conclusion – the Shrewsbury 24 were the convenient scapegoats of a government campaign to undermine the trade unions and the victims of a politically orchestrated show trial.'[45]

In May 2016 Amnesty International revealed that it had adopted Des Warren as a prisoner of conscience in 1975 but had then changed its mind after pressure from the UK government. The human rights organization said it now believed there was strong evidence the Shrewsbury trials were politically motivated and called on the government to release all the relevant files.[46]

A new spying section

It is clear that the response to the 1972 strike by the construction industry was both overt and covert and involved close liaison with the state. The Economic League, as ever in lock-step with these interests, joined the fray. A key contribution, which would establish a direct antecedent of The Consulting Association, was the formation of the Services Group (SG). This was a separate section within the Economic League dedicated to spying on the construction industry. Companies that were members of the Services Group paid an additional premium for extra support from the League. It was initially co-ordinated by David Laver, who was also the League's director for the Southeast Region. A bulletin was sent out to companies giving them sector-specific information. There would also be twice-yearly meetings between personnel and industrial relations managers and League officials. As journalists Mark Hollingsworth and Richard Norton-Taylor explained: 'The aim of these meetings is for the League to brief the firms about the industrial-relations scene in their area. If a major strike is taking place the League officials would identify trade-union activists involved by name and provide information on them.'[47]

This modus operandi would be replicated by The Consulting Association.

There were nearly 40 members of the Services Group, and more than 40 companies at one time or another subscribed to The Consulting Association. Of course as firms take over and sell each other, the list of company names was always likely to change. However, there is a large amount of overlap between the two lists. McAlpine, AMEC, Balfour Beatty, Edmund Nuttall, French Kier,

John Laing, Matthew Hall Electrical & Mechanical, Norwest Holst and Trafalgar House were among those who were members of both. According to Kerr, the Services Group:

> ●Operated within the Economic League on behalf of the construction companies. Economic League staff were given an additional role – or a role – which was to look after the construction companies' needs, which were very wide-ranging. I became party to that as the League's fortunes changed and the training activities wound down. I then moved across to being one of the co-ordinators. Each region of the League had a Services Group co-ordinator. I eventually became the Midlands region co-ordinator up to the point when the League ceased operating and the Services Group companies chose to continue as an operation. It, effectively, held a series of meetings with various chairmen. I was invited to some of these, at which point I subsequently was asked if I wanted the role of chief officer. It was then organized and set up by the steering committee as an unincorporated trade association. I was its main employee, with a contract of employment, PAYE and salaried.●[48]

Stan Hardy, former director general of the Economic League, gave evidence to the Select Committee investigation. He tried to convince MPs that the Services Group was very much run by Ian Kerr and that its records were not shared. 'It was a totally separate set of records. It was not in the generality of the League's records – it was totally separate. He was the only person who had access to it.'[49]

According to Mary Kerr, as the training work dried up, her husband was given an additional role working alongside Peter Thackeray, who had become the co-ordinator for the Services Group and was based in Alcester Road, Birmingham. When Thackeray retired, Kerr took over that job.

As well as responding to companies looking to vet workers, Mary Kerr said:

> ●Most of Ian's time was taken up reading articles in the press about topics that might be of interest to Services Group

members. Ian travelled around the country to various anarchist book shops as well as reading the far-left and rightwing press, finding out as much as possible about the problems construction sites might encounter. In addition, he monitored proposed employment legislation which was likely to affect the industry, he kept up to date with which full-time trade-union officials had moved positions and he reviewed what issues or agendas particular trade unions wanted to pursue. Ian also collected mainstream press articles that were of interest to the construction industry – relating to unions, legislation, court decisions and specific construction projects and these were copied and sent out to members in mailing lists.❜ 50

Kerr's name crops up in League documents obtained by the Labour Research Department. There are minutes of a meeting held in 1988 which, indirectly, make clear Kerr's central role in the Services Group. The Economic League records department was receiving 17,000 calls a month and 'the great bulk of these were from Services Group (SG)'. According to the minutes, the Services Group was consuming more than 50 per cent of the League's resources even though it contributed only about 18 per cent of the income (approximately £150,000).

Ian Leake, the now retired industrial relations boss from Taylor Woodrow, recalls meeting Ian Kerr on one occasion when he addressed a meeting of the NFBTE in the 1970s:

❝From what I can now recall, Ian Kerr's talk related to the threats posed to companies generally – not just construction companies – by groups of people on the far left who were looking to disrupt British industry in general, with some focusing on construction.❜ 51

Another of those who dealt with the League and The Consulting Association was Ann Cownie. She joined Balfour Beatty in 1979 as an industrial-relations assistant and one of her jobs was to contact the League to check on hourly paid employees from lists supplied by site managers.

❝As the checks could be done so quickly, I assumed that the EL had their own records to check against, but I did not know at the time what form these records took or the information contained in those records.'[52]

Once an individual had been cleared they were allocated a four-digit reference number followed by the letter 'A'. Without this they couldn't get on the payroll. Site managers were sent these as soon as the checks came through, which could be a day later, and according to Cownie, they would not have known it was related to vetting by the League. Although copies of these payroll numbers were kept, each time a list came through they were checked with the League again. Being cleared once didn't mean you would be cleared again.

Cownie, who is now a human-resources project manager with Balfour, carried on with the checks for years, including through the handover to The Consulting Association. She said: 'I am aware now that the EL was disbanded in around 1990 and that there must have been a transition in our use of the checking service from the EL to The Consulting Association. However, there was no real change in the way things operated from my perspective and I do not recall the time of any transition/changeover.'

Another person whose links covered the transition from League to TCA was Daniel O'Sullivan. He worked for Costain in human resources and rose to become the assistant to Dudley Barrett, who was head of industrial relations at the firm. O'Sullivan eventually held the chairmanship of TCA for a year.

The now retired manager said: 'At some point in the early 1990s, I attended a small number of meetings of the Economic League and it was at these that I first met Ian Kerr. Dudley Barrett would attend Economic League meetings as head of IR [industrial relations] and one of my colleagues and I were delegated to go to the Northeast Regional Economic League meetings. I believe I attended just two of those meetings, which were both held in Wetherby.'[53]

O'Sullivan explained that he didn't realize until the high-court action launched in 2015 that what he was actually attending were meetings of the League's Services Group.

'My understanding at the time was that the Economic League was an organization formed in the 1970s by major construction companies in response to significant industrial unrest. The construction companies were very worried at that time about the impact of political activism on construction sites. I now understand ... that it may have been the Services Group of the Economic League that was formed at that time and that the Economic League was already in existence, but I do not believe I was aware of the term "Services Group" or any other facets of the Economic League at the time.[9]

O'Sullivan, whose career started the same year as Kerr's in 1969, said that he can't now recall what was discussed at these meetings as he 'kept a low profile' because 'it was all relatively new to me'.

His boss Dudley Barrett worked his way up from labouring in the mid-1960s, including a spell as a TGWU shop steward, to become an industrial-relations officer with Costain. He was first introduced to the League while working for construction company Higgs & Hill as it handled the Southampton General Hospital contract. A call to the League was standard when it came to employing site workers. The vetting system didn't change when he eventually moved to Costain in the 1970s and he didn't notice a difference when the Services Group became the TCA. It was clear from the evidence of those who used it that this was a well-used and efficient system which operated whatever company was taking part and despite the upheaval of the League folding. It was just another part of the job and there seems to have been little thought about its impact. As Cownie said: 'At the time, I did not consider the legality of the EL [Economic League] or the question of individuals' privacy; the EL checks were simply something I undertook as a routine part of my role.'[54]

Barrett, who is now retired, said the rationale for the vetting should be seen in the context of events in the 1970s. 'This gave rise to concerns within the construction industry, which I shared at the time, that a number of politically motivated individuals saw construction projects (and other commercial activities) as appropriate means for placing pressure upon employers,' he said. 'I was told a number of times during that period, and subsequently, including by trade-union contacts, that one objective of such individuals (especially from the extreme left) was to cause such widespread disruption that it would enable workers' councils to bring about a change of government.'[55] As far as the construction firms were concerned they needed 'some way of ensuring that anyone who was thought to pose a risk of causing disruption, was not given the opportunity to do so'.

As well as relying on the League and then TCA, Barrett would also pass information the other way and kept his own personal set of records, By the time he left in 2002 he estimated they numbered several hundred. The postcards would contain information about workers who had performed 'unsatisfactorily' and that might include political detail. They were maintained by Barrett's secretary, Gayle Burton, who was also a regular contact for Ian Kerr. Barrett recalls:

> ❛Although much of the physical checking process was done by my secretary rather than me, Gayle Burton was always very thorough and I believe she would always have faxed the names to the Services Group or Consulting Association in addition to the checks of our internal record cards. I saw the record cards as a separate and different source of information and almost as a back-up; for example, if Ian Kerr was not available there would still be something to go on – though I do not recall his availability ever being a problem in practice,❜

It is not known what happened to this separate set of files, which he left with Costain when he retired.

The blight of 'lump labour'

Meanwhile, many of the fundamental problems that had led to the 1972 building workers' strike remained unresolved. It might have won the largest pay rise ever for construction workers but it hadn't abolished the hated use of 'lump' labour. Ricky Tomlinson saw at first hand how this prevented effective organizing on building sites.

> ❛The biggest stumbling block was known as "the lump". This was the colloquial name for self-employed contractors and sub-contractors, many who employed unqualified labourers and were notorious for cutting corners, doing shoddy work and ignoring safety. These weren't licensed builders or card-carrying members of the union. They were cowboys, who

disappeared as soon as the job was done, didn't pay taxes and didn't train apprentices. At the same time, they were undercutting proper tradesmen and forcing down wages to below poverty levels.'[56]

Instead of building workers being employed directly by construction firms with the benefits of holiday pay, sick pay, redundancy and other statutory entitlements, large contractors began to pay workers a lump sum to complete a certain amount of work. 'The lump' allowed employers to reduce costs but the workers lost all their employment rights and the Treasury lost tax revenue as well as employers' National Insurance contributions.

During the post-War boom, large building firms generally employed their workers directly and the labour force normally transferred from one project to another with the same employer. This changed from the 1970s onwards, with major companies now winning the contract for large projects but then dividing the work into separate packages for brickwork, electrical, engineering, groundworks and concrete structure. Each of these packages was then sub-contracted to separate specialist sub-contracting companies. The major contractors therefore employed fewer and fewer staff (effectively only the senior managers on site and those employed at head or regional offices). Lump labour went from being a minor part of the workforce to being endemic. By the 1980s, especially in London, many of these sub-contractors simply stopped employing any workers directly. Instead, the packages were sub-contracted multiple times until workers found themselves being employed on a supposed self-employed basis.

There are of course some situations where a building worker can be considered genuinely self-employed, such as when a small builder agrees to build your new extension, supplying all the materials, labour and plant, choosing their own hours, and taking time off whenever they choose, with their final remuneration depending on how profitable the project has been.

Most workers in the construction industry work for someone else. They are told what time to start and finish work and even when to take their tea breaks. They are told which section of a site to work in and are supervised by a company foreman. The company supplies all the materials and heavy plant. The worker is told to wear company-branded hardhats, high-visibility jackets and other safety equipment. The vast majority of these workers are paid by the hour or by the shift and will receive the same weekly wage regardless of the profitability of the project – a site-negotiated productivity bonus as an incentive does not make anyone a small businessperson. Yet for decades, employers, courts and the tax authorities reclassified them as self-employed independent sole traders without any employment rights. The trade unions in the building industry have campaigned on this issue for the past 40 years.

Major construction firms have funded and lobbied successive governments to maintain this profitable set-up. The obvious example is Lord McAlpine, who was chair of the Conservative Party and a confidant of Margaret Thatcher. In *The Servant*, his presumptuous reworking of Machiavelli's *The Prince*, Lord McAlpine wrote that the servant 'must have his own network of informants and men who will assist him. The servant must always know how to use the network of the State. Dealing in deceit, as the servant must, great caution must be required. Avoid small deceits: like barnacles on the bottom of a ship, they build in the minds of people whom you may need to convince in a large deceit.'[57]

Big business argued for construction to be treated as a special case because of the temporary nature of much employment and politicians have dutifully introduced a myriad of tax schemes that normalized self-employment in the industry. The lump started off as a cash-in-hand part of the black economy but, with HMRC construction industry specific tax schemes, has become prevalent across the entire industry. The tax schemes' names may change through the years, from 714 and SC60 certificates to CIS cards and offshore payments, but the outcome is the same.

Even on a major project with several thousand workers engaged on site, it is entirely possible that the principal contractor may only directly employ 10-20 people. These will almost always be the senior office-based staff.

Whether a worker is directly employed by a sub-contractor, employed via an employment agency or told that they must work nominally 'self-employed' is decided by the construction companies, not by the individual worker. The result is that most building workers involved in private-sector projects have worked on the basis of a variety of different payment methods during their working life. The actual relationship between the building worker and the company remains exactly the same, regardless of how it is labelled.

The advantage for the building companies of the official tax schemes is the saving in employers' National Insurance contributions and tax liabilities but also the associated costs of redundancy and other employment rights payments. For the average building worker, the opportunity consciously to choose to work directly for a major contractor simply never arose. If you wanted to work on a building site, especially in London and the Southeast from the 1990s onwards, you worked on a self-employed basis or you did not work at all. The impact was that hundreds of thousands of building workers over decades received no holiday pay, sick pay, redundancy pay or other statutory benefits such as being able to claim unfair dismissal – all rights enjoyed by employees.

Umbrella payroll

The latest blight in the industry is the use of 'umbrella' payroll companies. Many firms now only employ their workers if they agree to be paid through a limited company. The building company uses an employment agency, often wholly owned by the contractor itself, to set up all new starters as directors of their own individual limited company. At the end of the week, instead of being paid wages from the contractor, each worker has money paid into the account of their new company (with no income tax or National Insurance deductions). The worker's own company then deducts both employee and employer National Insurance and pays the worker (very often at the minimum wage). A variety of expenses are claimed, before an additional amount is paid as a dividend. All this is to avoid being paid wages by the contractors, which, with creative accounting, absolves them of any tax or employment-rights liabilities. Tax relating to companies is paid at a significantly lower rate than the 40-per-cent higher rate of income tax.

All of the administration and accountancy related to the new umbrella company is carried out by the agency, which charges the workers a fee for this service that would usually be carried out by a company wages department. Effectively, workers have to pay £30-40 a week for the privilege of receiving their own wages. Very often the agency administering the system is not only owned by the contractor but based in the same building. On the surface it would appear that 200 small businesses are flourishing on a project. But in reality it is one building contractor employing 200 workers via another tax scam. The potential for corruption on the part of those with influence in the industry is obvious.

UCATT estimates that over half of the construction industry is falsely self-employed and that the Treasury as a result loses £1.9 billion a year in lost revenue.[58] Construction accounts for around a quarter of the total number of self-employed workers in the UK, despite only making up about five per cent of the workforce.[59] Even on prestigious projects such as the 2012 Olympics, where a conscious effort was made to enforce direct employment, the figures for PAYE peaked at 70 per cent on the Aquatic Centre but only reached 30 per cent in the Athletes' Village.[60]

The unions have fought a rearguard action against casualization from the 1970s onwards. The National Working Rule Agreement that sets terms and conditions of employment for hourly paid workers on most building sites and the National Agreement for the Engineering Construction Industry (the 'NAECI Blue Book'), which covers major engineering construction projects throughout the UK, both have clauses restricting the use of self-employed or agency labour. But the spread of bogus self-employment has been relentless, regardless of the wording of these nationally negotiated collective-bargaining agreements between the employers' federations and the unions.

On 5 April 2014, the UK government changed the tax rules again, declaring that anyone working through an employment agency could no longer be classified as self-employed. The vast majority of agencies in the building industry immediately changed their systems, telling workers that the only payment option now available was to work under an umbrella company scheme. Some agencies were even telling the workers that because they were officially only earning the minimum wage, they might be able to claim housing benefit. Within weeks there were sit-ins and protests at major construction projects, with groups of agency workers demanding to be taken on directly.[61]

A new rail-signalling control centre by Romford station would became the scene of a significant dispute over bogus self-employment. Graeme Boxall, a young electrician new to union activity, held a meeting amongst the agency workers on site (the vast majority of the workforce). The aim was to discuss being taken on the cards by the main electrical contractor, T Clarke Electrical, rather than being employed via an umbrella scheme. Boxall was elected shop steward and two like-minded colleagues were elected as deputy and safety rep. Two days later, all three were sacked. The victimized union members refused to leave site. Boxall remembers his first-ever experience as a union rep:

> All we wanted was to be taken on the cards. They responded to that by the sackings. We got our tools and then walked round to the other fellas: "we're going to cabin up and were all gonna stand together. Are you gonna do it with us?" Three became six, became eight and by the end of it there was a large group of us. As we walked round, we explained to the cards in sparks [electricians] – because a lot of them were union members but not active at all. And they came out with us as well. Now we wanted direct employment for all 14 sparks and the reinstatement of the three of us who had been sacked.[62]

This was on the Friday afternoon. By Monday, a ring-round of rank-and-file activists resulted in a picketline in support of the sacked agency workers.

> In the morning we stopped the site dead: nothing moved. Management had a small heart attack. They capitulated, reinstated us and took us on the cards effective on 1 September.

Two and a half years after the new tax rules were introduced with much fanfare to end bogus self-employment, the umbrella scam has become the default method for engaging workers on building sites.

Mass self-employment has consequences beyond the formal

employment relationships within the industry and the loss of tax to the Inland Revenue. The loss of employment rights, which makes dismissing workers as easy as making a phone call to an agency, has meant that trade unions have been unable to win unfair-dismissal claims for their members. Combined with a systematic blacklisting of union activists, this means that trade unionism has disappeared on all but the largest construction projects. This is bad news for trade unions but the impact for issues such as safety mean the consequences for workers are even worse.

Some are fighting back; even in sectors which would have been thought very hard to organize. Bike couriers have become members of the new Independent Workers Union of Great Britain in an effort to gain better terms and conditions.

The union's president, Jason Moyer-Lee, told the BBC in 2016: 'Employers are taking advantage of the power imbalance and forcing the couriers to accept a job with zero employment rights. The couriers should be like all other workers and have the right to the minimum wage and paid holidays, among other things.'[63]

A campaign mixing old-fashioned protests and savvy social-media networking has seen one firm, eCourier, promise a 28-per-cent wage rise. The union is taking four firms to court over their employment practices. One of those joining the action is Andrew Boxer. He said: 'I am typical. I work for one company for around 50 hours a week. They tell me what to do, when to do it and how to do it. I am monitored, have to have company ID with me at all times, and can't take work from other companies. I get paid per delivery, not per hour. I am required to sign a contract which says that I am self-employed, which means I don't get any employment rights.'[64]

Maggie Dewhurst, another who is part of the action, explained that it is about more than just money. 'We have to sign contracts stating that we are independent contractors, we don't have any employment rights and often earn less than the minimum wage. This sector is unregulated free-market capitalism. We are trying to make vulnerable people feel safe. It is about dignity and respect: a collective voice.[65]

The constant battle between unions attempting to represent workers, construction workers trying to organize and employers in the construction sector has bubbled and flared since the 1972 strike. And sitting inside the Economic League was the Services Group – a ready-made organization able to take off on its own to help frustrate such efforts. When media exposure forced the League to collapse in 1993, the construction firms activated their creature.

1 Interview with the authors. 2 Mark Hollingsworth, and Charles Tremayne, *The Economic League: The Silent McCarthyism,* National Council for Civil Liberties, London, 1989, p 25. 3 T Bunyan, *The history and practice of the political police in Britain,* Quartet Books, London, 1977, p 248. 4 Peter Taylor, 'Tomlinson "gobsmacked" by secret files', BBC news, 27 October 2002, nin.tl/ **BBCtruespies** 5 Quoted in Leo Huberman, *The Labor Spy Racket,* Modern Age Books, New York, 1937, p 28. This book synthesized much of the evidence from the hearings and reported aspects newspapers had not found time for. 6 Huberman, op cit, p 14. 7 Evidence given to the Scottish Affairs Select Committee, 22 January 2013. 8 Carillion website nin.tl/carillionFAQ **(since deleted)** 9 Figures on the number of people who lost their jobs during the McCarthy witch-hunt are taken from Ellen Schrecker, *The Age of McCarthyism: a brief history with documents,* St Martin's Press, Boston, 1994, available from nin.tl/**McCarthyismdocs** 10 C Andrew, *The Defence of the Realm: the authorized history of MI5,* Penguin: London, 2010, p 597. 11 T Bunyan, *The history and practice of the political police in Britain,* Quartet Books, London, 1977, p 250. 12 Interview with the authors. 13 Mark Hollingsworth and Richard Norton-Taylor, *Blacklist: the inside story of political vetting,* The Hogarth Press, London, 1988, p 181. 14 A McIvor, 'A Crusade for Capitalism: The Economic League, 1919-39', *Journal of Contemporary History,* Vol 23, No 4, October 1988, pp 631-655. 15 M Hughes, *Spies At Work,* 1 in 12, Bradford 1994, p 247. 16 E Lubbers, *Secret Manoeuvres in the Dark,* Pluto Press, London, 2013, p 35. 17 Hollingsworth, and Tremayne, op cit, p 107. 18 Ibid, p 105. 19 Obituary, *The Independent,* 16 September 2006. 20 M Hughes, op cit, p 322. 21 Scottish Affairs Committee, *Blacklisting in Employment: oral and written evidence,* The Stationery Office Limited, London, 2013, p 142. 22 Interview with the authors. 23 M Hughes, op cit, p 199. 24 Scottish Affairs Committee, op cit, p 163. 25 'Man behind illegal blacklist snooped on workers for 30 years', *Guardian,* 27 May 2009, nin.tl/snoop30years 26 Labour Research Department, *A Subversive Guide to the Economic League,* 1969. 27 Dominic Sandbrook's *State of Emergency: The way we were: Britain 1970-1974,* Penguin, London, 2011, is typical. 28 Ralph Darlington and Dave Lyddon, *Glorious Summer: Class struggle in Britain 1972,* London: Bookmarks, 2001, p 179. 29 Richard Clutterbuck, *Britain in Agony: The Growth of Political Violence,* Faber & Faber, London, 1978, p 78. 30 Economic League (date unknown), *The Agitators: Who they are, how they work, what they want,* Service to industry series booklet number 3, p 22. 31 Interview with the authors. 32 Ricky Tomlinson, *Ricky,* Time Warner, London, 2003, p 113. 33 Clutterbuck, op cit, p 88. 34 Quoted in Alwyn W Turner, *Crisis? What Crisis?: Britain in the 1970s,* Arum Press, London, 2009, p 77. 35 Cited in a speech by David Anderson MP, House of Commons debate, 23 January 2014. 36 'Shrewsbury 24 case', *Guardian,* 11 October 2012, nin.tl/ **shrewsbury24** 37 Quoted in a speech by Tom Watson MP, House of Commons

debate, 23 January 2014. 38 Reel News video, *Blacklisted*, 2012. 39 Quoted in Des Warren, *The key to my cell*, Living History Library, 2007. 40 Quoted by David Hanson MP, House of Commons debate, 23 January 2014. 41 Shrewsbury 24 Campaign website, nin.tl/picketsspeak 42 'Blacklisted builders launch mass legal action…', *Guardian,* nin.tl/buildersaction 43 Ricky Tomlinson, Application to the CCRC, reference 00397/2012. 44 Interview with the authors. 45 'Spies rigged Shrewsbury pickets trial', Morning Star, 10 December 2015, nin.tl/StarShrewsbury 46 'United Kingdom: review of the case of Des Warren', Amnesty International, 9 May 2016, nin.tl/AmnestyWarren 47 Hollingsworth & Norton-Taylor, op cit, p 183. 48 Scottish Affairs Committee, op cit, p 142. 49 Ibid, p 210. 50 Witness statement seen by the authors. 51 Witness statement seen by the authors. 52 Witness statement seen by the authors. 53 Witness statement seen by the authors. 54 Witness statement seen by the authors. 55 Witness statement seen by the authors. 56 R Tomlinson,*op cit*, p 209. 57 Quoted in speech by Tom Watson MP, House of Commons debate, 23 January 2014. 58 *The Great Payroll Scandal*, UCATT-sponsored report by the Institute of Employment Rights. 59 Melissa Wickham, *Self-Employment in London,* GLAEconomics working paper 56, April 2013, nin.tl/GLApaper 60 Janet Druker and Geoffrey White, *Employment relations on major construction projects: the London 2012 Olympic construction site*, in *Industrial Relations Journal* 44, 2013, pp 566–583. 61 Reel News video, *Umbrella scam: sparks lead the fightback,* nin.tl/umbrellascam 62 Interview with the authors. 63 'Bike couriers launch legal fight over workers' rights', BBC news, 22 April 2016, bbc.co.uk/news/uk-36103978 64 Ibid. 65 Interview with the authors.

3
Blood on their hands

'I find it difficult to believe that I am standing here today talking to you with the utmost sadness about my father, Patrick O'Sullivan. He was a man of great talent, wit and dedicated to his family. On 5 January, our lives changed beyond recognition when my father was killed here, at Wembley... The last words my father heard were: Run, Patsy, run.' What kind of terror and fear must he have felt? No-one should have to die like that – to be treated like fodder, just another payroll number to be struck from the list. Surely a man's life is worth more than that? It has to be.

I had no real comprehension of the dangers he faced at work. He was a carpenter all his life, so too was his father and his father before that. It was a trade that was passed from father to son and he was proud of this tradition. You can see the buildings he helped build, homes where families are now living, landmarks like Canary Wharf, Wimbledon... so many... and now Wembley. Yet all these landmarks were built on the sweat and blood of carpenters, scaffolders, labourers, and the hundreds and hundreds of men who work and suffer within this industry.

How many men have to die? How many fathers, sons, brothers must be maimed or killed before governments say enough is enough? The level of complacency that exists within construction would never be tolerated in any other industry. And in this, the 21st century, men are injured and killed every day on building sites around the country – most going unreported by the press. It takes a high-profile site like Wembley to highlight the appalling safety record that these men are forced to endure. It's too late for my dad. His blood was spilt at Wembley and his blood is on the hands of those responsible for his death.'[1]

Margaret O'Sullivan

Although it accounts for only around five per cent of the UK workforce, construction accounts for 27 per cent of fatal injuries and 10 per cent of major injuries. Even with the decline in the industry's workload following the 2008 financial crisis, an average of 47 workers have died every year since.[2] Construction also has the largest burden of occupational cancer across industry, with over 40 per cent of all occupational cancer deaths and cancer registrations. Occupational diseases such as vibration white finger, carpal tunnel syndrome, occupational deafness and dermatitis are all significant issues and incidents of work-related muscular skeletal disorders are 60 per cent higher than in other industries.[3] Even the Health and Safety Executive acknowledges that workforce casualization is a factor, highlighting self-employment in its official statistics. In construction's flexible labour market, profits appear to be put before people every day of the week.

Safety has been a perennial issue for unions on building sites, where often the most basic welfare facilities are absent. Pete Farrell, chair of the Construction Safety Campaign and UCATT member, remembers when he first started work in the 1970s:

> Even as a teenager I remember thinking, sod this. Talk about degrading: there was one toilet with no seat, and it didn't flush either. The bucket, which was all we had to wash in, was used to swill down the toilet. Where you ate your sandwiches was disgusting and seats were upturned buckets and pots of paint.

Over 30 years later, in 2008, in the Channel Tunnel rail link between Stratford and St Pancras station, the situation had not got any better, according to testing and commissioning electrician Robert Smith.

> You could walk for miles down there and you would not find a portable toilet or anything. People used to take their food down there because you'd be working in the tunnel all day. They were taking babywipes because there was no water to wash their hands and also taking black bin bags down there with them, so if they wanted to go to the loo, you'd do it in the bin bag, tie it up, then chuck it down the tunnel and wipe

your arse on whatever you happened to find. Originally they used to have portable toilets, but they got taken away and so for the last year there were absolutely no facilities at all, which wasn't very good obviously, especially with the rat problem. There were some massive rats down there. The facilities in the tunnel were appalling really, atrocious, 'cause they did have them originally but took them out. Well obviously you know why – it saves a couple of quid.⁹

Old Bailey toilets action

Contractors saving money on welfare facilities is an all-too-familiar tale in the building industry. The Barbican luxury apartment and arts complex was one of the largest construction projects ever in the City of London when it started in 1962. Vic Heath, a scaffolder from Camden, was elected as a convenor for the Amalgamated Union of Building Trade Workers on the site. He remembers how the activists first built the union by organizing a meeting about the lack of toilets and welfare facilities. When the contractor refused to supply them, the men all walked a quarter mile to the nearest public facilities at the Old Bailey. After three days of lines of workers tramping along the main road to the court and back, the firm capitulated. The newly established union representatives linked up with another section of the Barbican project operated by Myton (a subsidiary of blacklisting firm Taylor Woodrow), forming a stewards' committee with Lou Lewis, Mickey Houlihan and Ralph Langdon. The Barbican was to become one of the best union-organized sites in the industry. A fitting legacy was a historic dispute where the workers refused to install asbestos despite threats of dismissal by the employers. Decades later, the Barbican is one of the few buildings from that era not riddled with the deadly substance. One of the site's elected UCATT convenors, Jim Franklin from East Ham, went on to be one of the leading lights in the Construction Safety Campaign. The Barbican stewards were to link up with other unionized sites such as Horseferry Road to form the rank-and-file Joint Sites Committee (JSC) movement, which brought together union activists from different unions and different trades. The government of the day was so worried about the activities of these union activists that a government inquiry was held to investigate it.[4] The JSC stewards were founding members of the Building Workers Charter and were to play a leading role in the 1972 national building strike.

Vic Heath remembers what happened following his role as elected union convenor on the Barbican:

> I couldn't get a job anywhere in the London area. I'd phoned a number of companies that were advertising for scaffolders in different parts of the country and on every single occasion they'd take my name, hang on a minute or something like that, come back and say no. Several jobs I'd be on for maybe a day and I'd be paid off, and they'd never give you a reason. That went on for a long time.[5]

Even on jobs where canteen and welfare facilities were of a better standard, building workers still saw their treatment as less than satisfactory. Francie Graham and Steuart Merchant are two blacklisted electricians who worked together at Aldermaston Atomic Weapons Establishment.

Now retired, Merchant remembers:

> The whole time we worked on Aldermaston I kept asking for these wee badges. You know, like them nurses' badges for radiation? Six times, during the wee spell I was there, they came over the tannoy: "Something has happened – if you're in the building, stay in the building. If you're outside the building, get in the nearest Portacabin and shut the windows."
>
> We used to look out the windows and these boys in the white suits with their Geiger counters would appear but then four hours later it would come over the tannoy: "It was an electrical fault, everything is fine."
>
> But the site next door, the MF Kent site, they never got this tannoy system, and between them and us was a wire fence. Now, I didn't know a fence stopped radiation going through.

Veteran campaigner Francie Graham from Dundee worked alongside Merchant at Aldermaston and remembers:

> 24 hours a day, 365 days a year, there is a "beep-beep-beep". You can hear it all over the site. They say to you, if that beep

stops, get yourself cabined up or stay where you are if you are indoors. It's a radiation leak. OK. You're in a smoking cabin – where people were complaining about the draughts in the cabin and you've got to shut your doors and then the radiation won't get through them. It's just a fallacy. It's idiotic.[9]

Graham's blacklist file has one particular entry that refers to that site:

Date not known: Aldermaston baddies!!

Last emerged September 1989. Possible EPIU.
1996 October: Date information received from source: 3223 (J.D.)
NOTE: 3228 (G.B.) may hold further details.
Do not divulge any of above – refer first.

3223 = Balfour Beatty (JD) = John Dangerfield
3228 = Costain UK Ltd (GB) = Gayle Burton

Building-site deaths on the rise

Their glossy PR brochures might highlight their concern for health and safety, but they omit the fact that, over the decades, many building companies have faced huge fines for criminal breaches of the Health and Safety at Work Act.[6] For safety to improve on building sites it cannot simply be left to the employers: the workforce needs to be actively engaged in the process.

Deaths and injuries in the construction industry have remained a stubborn blight accompanied by concern about the inability of the Health and Safety Executive to hold companies to account. In 2016 UCATT highlighted the fall in construction inspections. Brian Rye, Acting General Secretary of UCATT, said:

> The prospect of an unexpected knock on the door by a construction inspector is what keeps many employers on their toes. If employers believe that their safety procedures are not going to be checked this will lead to slackness and corners being cut. Workers could pay with their lives.[7]

As UCATT previously warned: "These dangers are being

exacerbated by the massive cuts that the government have made to the Health and Safety Executive's budget and their continued attack on safety laws and regulations.'[8]

The constant refrain from corporate lobbyists has been that safety regulations strangle growth. This is a message that has found a receptive audience in the government.

In a speech in 2012 at the rightwing Policy Exchange thinktank, the then Minister for Employment, Chris Grayling, declared that the government's aim was to 'remove as many of the barriers to employment and entrepreneurship as we can'. And the kind of barriers he had in mind were the employee protections which were already withering through poor enforcement.

Grayling said: 'Within two years, we aim to have rewritten all of our hundreds of health-and-safety regulations and guidelines to make them simpler, easier to understand and more relevant to business. And to have cut the number of regulations in half. We are also taking steps to exempt a million self-employed people from health-and-safety regulations altogether.'[9]

Grayling was merely following the lead offered by the then prime minster. David Cameron said in January of that year his new year's resolution was to 'kill off the health and safety culture for good'.[10]

Hazards, the respected workplace safety research organization, pointed out that Grayling appeared unresponsive to requests for action from families of people killed at work – and traced that back to his career before he became an MP.

'If Grayling's not interested in the views of the relatives, he's keenly interested in public relations,' Hazards reported. 'The former PR man [was] with top industry lobbyists and union-busting specialists Burson-Marsteller – he was director in "Employee communications practice" then European Marketing Director in the 1990s when it spearheaded a continent-wide campaign against action on passive smoking.'[11]

Blacklisted joiner and UCATT member Bill Parry said:

In the last 10 years there have been more deaths in construction than in the armed forces since the invasion of Iraq and Afghanistan. With such an awful death toll, it is a duty to raise health-and-safety issues and no-one should be afraid to speak out.'[12]

While fictitious media stories about health-and-safety laws are used to deform any rational debate on employee protection, there is actually a wealth of evidence that inspections and worker involvement make for safer, and indeed more profitable, firms.[13]

Regrettably, the blacklisting files suggest that speaking out about health and safety on a building site was more likely to get a worker victimized than to win them praise. Many blacklisted workers suspected they were being targeted because they raised concerns about safety issues, but their suspicions were always ignored by those in authority. Alan Rayner, an electrician from Hutton in Essex, said:

> I knew I was, but I couldn't prove it. I was on a job and I complained about safety. Sometimes it was even silly things. On another job I complained about asbestos, which is deadly.'[14]

Rayner suffered from being blacklisted for 45 years. According to another electrician, and one-time union safety rep, Jerry Murphy from Romford: 'My file said "don't employ under any circumstances". These companies are not worried if somebody dies, so health and safety goes out of the window.'[15]

Legislation allows union safety reps to carry out inspections on behalf of the workforce and HSE statistics consistently show that workplaces with union safety reps have fewer accidents and fewer days lost than those without. Safety reps allow a voice from the workforce to be heard within a company's safety processes. In a much-quoted speech from July 2000, Bill Callaghan, former chair of the Health and Safety Commission, called union safety reps a 'reality check' for employers.[16]

Unfortunately, employers in the building industry did not always value this reality check. Norman Chapman, a plater from Hull, was blacklisted in 1999:

> When I was being refused work I was told there was no start. I felt despair and not being protected because I was a safety rep. I thought the law would protect me in a situation like that. I felt like I was banging my head against a brick wall.'[17]

Howard Sharpe, a member of Unite the union, told delegates at the TUC in September 2015:

> ❝I stood up for trade union rights, for health and safety, for my fellow workers. In exchange, construction employers put my name on a list against employing me and said that I was someone not to be employed at all costs. From 1994 to 2007 I could not get a job with any large construction company or construction site. My working life was cut short because of my concern about health and safety. This hurt me and my wife and children.❞[18]

In the case of engineer Dave Smith, his 36-page blacklist file records how he repeatedly lost his job whenever he was elected as a UCATT safety rep. In July 1998 he was dismissed by Costain during the refurbishment of a Tesco store in Goodmayes, Essex. Costain supplied TCA with a copy of an official UCATT leaflet distributed by Smith about asbestos. Smith won the initial stage of his tribunal for victimization for health and safety reasons, which was seen as a landmark victory in the press at the time. The company offered a sizeable financial incentive for Smith to withdraw his claim. Smith's blacklist file records:

> *1999 May:*
> *Hearing date set. Above has said 'No' to settling out of court – intent on winning this as a test case. Danger is how H&S aspect was handled. If lost, unwanted precedent may be set.*

The company successfully appealed the judgment. The 1999 Employment Appeal Tribunal judgment found that because Smith was an agency worker and not a direct employee of Costain, he was not protected by the legislation.

A year later, Smith was working via an agency for a groundworks sub-contractor called Cinnamond on new British Telecom offices being project-managed by Schal, a wholly owned subsidiary of Tarmac. (Within a few months, Tarmac would change its name to Carillion). He was again elected as safety rep and his credentials were sent by the union to inform the contractor of his election.

This time the safety rep's credentials were photocopied with the Schal company stamp and added to his blacklist file, accompanied by the following entry:

> *1999 May 4th:*
> *Dave Smith has been appointed as UCATT Safety*
> *Representative (see copy of union credentials. Re. Dave*
> *Smith). Letter from UCATT signed by Lou Lewis, Reg Secr.)*
> *asking Schal as main contractor to 'facilitate D. Smith*
> *representing all our members on site'*
> *(Source: 3271/KC) (see copy)*

3271 = Tarmac/Carillion

But rather than the main contractor embracing someone prepared to act as a voice of the workforce on safety issues, they devised a method to remove Smith from the site and recorded their thoughts on his blacklist file.

> *Advice given by official of construction body is to establish*
> *if D Smith is employed by an agency, and not directly*
> *employed, write to UCATT stating that he is not thought a*
> *suitable person for this appointment, and/or if the company*
> *does not recognize UCATT, his appointment as safety Rep is*
> *inappropriate.*
>
> *1999 May 6th:*
> *Cinnamond Construction to refuse above's credentials (as*
> *safety rep) as he is not an employee of theirs. Cinnamond*
> *to tell Heffo agency supplying above to site, that D Smith is*
> *no longer required on site i.e. do not propose to pay him an*
> *engineer's rates to go around site as safety rep.*
>
> *Concern has been expressed that the route onto sites*
> *via agencies is not frequently monitored, and this needs*
> *addressing as similar tactics by D Smith are almost certain to*
> *arise in the near future.*

The experienced engineer was dismissed from site soon afterwards and, in the middle of a building boom, his income in the next 12 months fell to just £12,000. Ron McKay, the UCATT regional official at the time, recalls:

> ❝I held meetings with management on site concerning Smith's dismissal. They refused point blank to reinstate Mr Smith. Instead they tried to buy him off but he refused the offer. Worryingly, it is my experience that when someone took on this safety representative's role, their days were numbered and they would usually be dismissed from site at the earliest opportunity.❞[19]

The companies which used the blacklist have, however, steadfastly maintained that it was not a tool for targeting those who raised safety concerns.

Cullum McAlpine, director of Sir Robert McAlpine Ltd, told the Scottish Affairs Select Committee: 'Reporting health and safety would never be disruptive. It is entirely right and proper that health and safety opinions – constructive ones – should be heard in the right way.'[20]

Mike Peasland, CEO, Balfour Beatty Construction Services UK, reassured MPs on the same committee: 'We would never discriminate against people for genuine health and safety grievances.'[21]

1999 picket to reinstate sacked safety rep Dave Smith.

Harvey Francis, executive vice-president, Skanska UK, which was one of the biggest users of the Association, declared a few months after the scandal broke: '[We] subscribed to the list to ensure the safety of people working on our sites. Health and safety in construction is of paramount importance. While I'm not excusing [using the blacklist], this was also a way of trying to keep the sites safe.'[22]

Meanwhile Ron McKay has subsequently been sent a copy of his own TCA blacklist file.

Targeting safety reps

Simon Hester, Prospect union rep for HSE inspectors and himself an HSE construction inspector who investigates deaths on building sites, has witnessed the effects of targeting safety reps.

> Good health and safety on construction sites is dependent on high levels of communication and openness – and trade union organization is officially recognized as beneficial. Blacklisting of trade union reps is a disaster because it creates a climate of fear.[23]

One GMB welder from Wales who wishes to remain anonymous describes how standing up for safety caused him to be blacklisted:

> The work for Cleveland Bridge on the Avonmouth Bridge was the most brutal and physically demanding I have ever done, including underwater, and there was no proper ventilation or extraction anywhere on the site. Four men died on the Avonmouth Bridge on 18 September 1999. I believe that the deaths of the four men were avoidable and that Kvaerner Cleveland Bridge bore responsibility for the deaths. I raised this with management at the time. I believe that my involvement in raising these issues led to me being blacklisted. As I was the shop steward I felt it was my responsibility to counsel the workers and to be strong to them. My wife knew that my role as shop steward was affecting me and so she felt that I should step away from the role as it was having such an impact on me. Of course I couldn't do that. I felt a loyalty to the workers and to bring those responsible for the accident to account. On my

final day on the Avonmouth Bridge the workers lined up and applauded me as I walked off site. I still feel traumatized by the deaths of my friends and colleagues on the site. It appears now that I've been punished for standing up to show how their deaths were preventable. I believe that I was blacklisted in a vindictive and malicious way for standing up for the right thing.❜[24]

Even on building sites where safety reps had patently improved safety conditions, their names were still forwarded to The Consulting Association, as Mickey Guyll, a blacklisted crane driver from Billericay in Essex, explained:

❛I worked for Edmund Nuttall on the Docklands Light Railway where it went underground from Tower Hill to Bank station in 1989 and there was a death on that site and loads of major accidents. We got organized as workers and I was elected safety rep. After I was elected safety rep, we had no more deaths on site and no more major accidents. My thanks for that was to be placed on a blacklist by Edmund Nuttall at 24 years of age. I've never drove a tower crane again, although I'd love to. Life was very hard. I went from being a tower crane driver to making concrete posts at about 20 per cent of the wages. I'm a clapped-out cabbie now.❜

Mickey Guyll's first entry on his blacklist file reads:

1992 source 3246: Worked at their docklands job. Was shop steward involved in safety issues.

3246 = Edmund Nuttall (now BAM Nuttall)

The more TCA documents that were released by the ICO, the more apparent it became that union safety reps were regularly targeted for raising concerns about safety on site, as entries from dozens of blacklist files demonstrate, among them the following:

UCATT activist concentrating on health-and-safety issues

> *After taking on showed signs of militancy over safety*
> *Involved in safety strike*
> *Elected safety rep on site*
> *While at Stansted, drew H&S issues to the attention of site*
> *manager*
> *He was a T&GW safety rep first class troublemaker.*
> *Spoke at TUC conference on Health & Safety*

Despite the mountains of documentary of safety reps being victimized, those at the heart of the blacklisting conspiracy claim both that safety was a priority and indeed that problems may have been the fault of workers themselves. Stephen Quant, former TCA chair and prolific user of the blacklist, said: 'It would have been counter-productive for anyone to "punish" someone for raising a valid health-and-safety query or concern. However, there was another aspect to this in that, given the increasing importance of health and safety from the late 1990s, bogus health-and-safety concerns became an easy issue for individuals to latch on to in order to disrupt a project. Although I cannot now recall any specific examples, one had the impression that sometimes health-and-safety issues were raised by certain individuals primarily for this purpose, rather than in response to a genuine concern.'[25]

None of those involved in the blacklisting operation have been able to produce evidence of a single example of a bogus safety issue.

The hostility to any interference with employers' absolute authority was such that many safety reps were targeted as soon as they were elected. As the building boom started to take off in the mid-1990s, Bovis was the main contractor on a £30-million casino and luxury flat complex on the Isle of Dogs, close to Canary Wharf. The project had six tower cranes and 600 workers and UCATT had received a number of complaints about safety. UCATT official Jerry Swain held a union meeting in the site canteen and George Fuller, a bricklayer working for sub-contractor Irvine Whitlock, was elected:

❝ When Jerry gave his speech about building workers being safe at work, he asked for a safety rep and I volunteered. On a show of hands I was elected but immediately people were saying things like "you'll be gone by the end of the week, mate" or "bye bye".[26]

Fuller recalls Irvine Whitlock management interrupting the meeting to tell the bricklayers that all overtime would be stopped if the union came on the job. Fuller was separated from the rest of the bricklaying gangs and made to work on his own. When the UCATT safety rep went to the site office he was repeatedly sworn at and threatened. Fuller claims to have received a death threat from one of the Irvine Whitlock managerial staff and so started carrying a small recording device.

> A whole squad of them came up to me. This labourer gave me the whisper: "watch out, George, they're on their way".
>
> One came up to me and called me a "cunt" – and he had a director standing with him, and I was like that bloke in *The Bridge on the River Kwai* saying "Under the Geneva Convention", I was saying "Under the Working Rule Agreement".

The company was making the bricklayers build the internal blockwork at the same time as the external brickwork, with a danger of bits of block or tools dropping on the people working below, especially in high winds. Despite Fuller's safety reports, this is exactly what happened.

> About 60 blocks – big blocks – got blown from the sixth floor down to the second floor where some bricklayers were working fixing these metal ledges. Luckily, most of them had gone inside of the building. I didn't have a camera – but I made some witness statements, writing down a description of it and I went to report it. It's what I'd been saying was likely to happen. I went into the office with this safety rep's report form. All he was interested in was how much time I'd spent away from my place of work. Wall-to-wall effing and blinding.

Because of the earlier threats, the UCATT safety rep secretly recorded the exchange and the voice recording was broadcast on a BBC TV documentary. The incident gained considerable media attention and two east London Labour MPs, Tony Banks and Jim Fitzpatrick, both intervened on the bricklayer's behalf.

Directors of Irvine Whitlock were contacted by the authors but declined to comment. However, director Geoff Irvine told *Building* magazine: 'I gave Mr Fuller a verbal apology [for the way the foreman had spoken to him].' Irvine denied that Fuller had ever been victimized.[27] But UCATT official Chris Tiff, quoted in the same article, responded: 'The matter is far from resolved, until we get a written apology from Irvine Whitlock.'[28]

Sometimes the employer's response to workers who complained about safety on site went further than just threats.

George Fuller and another UCATT member, John Keane, were employed on a housing site in Hammersmith, London. Both had refused to be registered as self-employed and had asked to be put on 'the cards' – paid through PAYE. Fuller then records what happened when they were elected as a steward and safety rep.

> ❝The firm put us on an isolated part of the job, brought in four strangers to the job who hardly did any work and cleared off early to breakfast: you could tell they weren't really there for the building. We came back from breakfast and all our walls had been pushed over and one of them started trying to rough us up. As it happened I got hold of one of them round the neck and I sort of got him on the ground. Surprised myself really, was thinking, "what have I done?" One of them had a metal lintel and said "let him go or I'll whack you". John Keene and a foreman came along and then they both let go and run off. I've still got a cauliflower ear from it.❞[29]

The police were called but Fuller says the main contractor dismissed the incident as: 'Six of one and half-a-dozen of another'.[30]

Keane and Fuller both found themselves blacklisted. The attack was just one incident in a wave of violence against union activists on building sites in the mid-1980s. Most went unnoticed but the George Fuller confrontation appeared in the press, as did a much more serious incident.[31]

In 1984 two brothers, John and Garry Churton, along with another bricklayer, John Jones, were building retirement homes in South London. There were a number of sub-contractors on the site. Jones remembers what the site was like when they first started:

> ❝The health and safety and welfare conditions were atrocious. The changing room, you wouldn't let your dog in it, so bad, dingy, dirty, filthy to eat your sandwiches. So we set about asking them for better conditions.❞[32]

Jones was elected as UCATT shop steward and, with support from the Churton brothers, negotiated brand new toilets, a large canteen and new changing huts. But the employers on the site made it obvious that the union was not welcome. The union men were given the worst jobs, John Jones' car was repeatedly damaged, Garry Churton's shoes were nailed to the floor and attempts were made to sack the union men. But when that failed things suddenly got worse.

Garry Churton remembers what happened:

> ❝The employer didn't want any union organization. I don't know why. I don't know what they thought we were doing wrong. We went there, did us job, like all the others, but they just wanted to get shot of us. I think they were having enough of it and the employer thought they'd get someone to sort us out. And they did.
>
> It was just a normal day. Me and me brother normally worked together but they split us and put us on different parts of the site. And the bloke who did it. He'd only started the day before. He'd come from nowhere. Sort of cocky lad – but he came up to talk to us and find out things, which was a bit unusual. He was working for the subbie. He said he was a hod carrier but he didn't seem to do anything. He didn't seem to know the trade, what to do. He was struggling with the hod. He must have been 30 years old. The foremen said they knew him but when he did what he did, they said they didn't know him.
>
> They split us up on that afternoon. The real annoying part about it was I wore my safety hat all the time but because they put me in a certain place where there was nothing above me in a small alcove, I took it off.

He came up to me with two blokes from the office. And there was th`ree of them all around me. And he's got this hod and I was thinking – what's he doing with them and why's he holding the hod like that? I thought, he's not gonna hit me with the hod is he? And then he clouts me with it. He hits me with the hod and the only thing I could do, I didn't go down, I just grabbed hold of the hod and wrestled it off him. I had it in my hand and he just ran off. It annoyed me, why didn't I hit him back with it? I threw the hod down. This was a metal hod, aluminium.

As I went to go up to the canteen, I saw my brother, he was walking up staggering. Blood gushing from his head. What's happened to him? The same thing that had happened to me. He did my brother first and then he came round and done me.❜[33]

Garry Churton had 10 stitches in his head; his older brother John wasn't so lucky.

❛My brother ended up with a fractured skull and he has never worked since. He moved back to Stoke-on-Trent and he's been on medication ever since. He's diagnosed as a multiple schizophrenic. Paranoid and depressed. He's on medication, some sort of liquid cosh to keep him sedated. Not completely sedated but to keep him calm and stop him getting aggressive. He was quite an activist my brother was. To be quite honest, I looked up to my brother when he did what he did. Going on marches and organizing things – quite good. Now it seems he's just lost the plot because of his age and the drugs all that time.❜

The police investigated but no-one on site had any details for the assailant.[34] It became something of a *cause célèbre* that was reported widely in the radical and trade press.[35] UCATT provided legal representation and the two brothers received compensation from the criminal injuries scheme. John Churton received £66,000 and Garry was awarded £600. But, as *Construction News* reported: 'The anonymous male attacker, described as having a "military appearance", was never found.'[36]

However Garry says he later bumped into the man responsible for ordering the assault in a pub in London.

> ❛To be honest he was quite pleasant. He said: "I paid that bloke £500 to do it." I said: "That's not proof, is it? I can say you said it and you could say you didn't. I'm not gonna get into anything. It'll be no good to me."
>
> I've sort of brushed it under the carpet. I don't talk about it – or not as much as I could do. It's not that I want to forget it: I've just forgot it. At that time, I didn't feel like a martyr. I felt like I was doing what activists do. Standing up for their rights. You've got to stand up or else nothing will get done. I feel, alright then, it was a hod, it could have killed me to be quite honest, but 'cause I survived I feel that I done good for some reason. It just proves a point that this is the kind of stuff that goes on and we are always accused of being the aggressors.❜

Jones and the Churton brothers were all added to the blacklist after that dispute. John Jones and Garry Churton both found it difficult to find work in contracting but eventually found work in local authorities. John Churton never worked again in the next 30 years.

Construction Safety Campaign

According to the industry, safety is of paramount concern. Even those most closely involved in the operation of the blacklist say that health and safety was not something they ignored. David Cochrane from Sir Robert McAlpine, who was subsequently to play a controversial role in TCA, was employed as a safety officer with the firm from 1976. He recalled:

> ❛From the time that I began to specialize in safety to my promotion to Safety Manager, the recognition by the industry of the importance of safety on construction sites increased significantly. In the early-mid 1970s there was relatively little in terms of written safety rules and procedures in the construction industry. However, by the mid-1980s, a large part of the role of Safety Officers was implementing procedures

and carrying out practical risk assessments of site operations. In this role, I saw at first hand the importance of safety on construction sites.[37]

The experience of members of the Construction Safety Campaign paints a different picture. During the late 1980s, the Thatcher government was fighting the unions while a boom in the building industry saw deaths in the construction sector rise to an average of three a week. It was against this industrial background that rank-and-file workers decided to set up the Construction Safety Campaign (CSC). Two UCATT bricklayers, Tony Holding from Liverpool and John Keane from Islington, complained about the safety conditions on a building site in west London. Holding, now an experienced trade union tutor, remembers:

> They were still demolishing on the scaffold above our heads when we were laying bricks in the footings. We didn't think it was very safe but they didn't take it very seriously. So we walked off the job. The next day the scaffold collapsed and we saw it on the news. Two young lads from Ireland were killed. That was the beginnings of the Construction Safety Campaign. We had complained about the safety – that was the first time a rank-and-file building workers' group had picketed a coroner's court.

George Fuller remembers that the incident galvanized worker action.

> We distributed leaflets around all the local building sites. It got on TV and the *Irish Post* came along. And then we carried on doing that for two more coroner's courts and then the CSC grew out of that. The jury delivered an open verdict and it gained a lot of publicity in the press. The CSC had all the ingredients – us, the lawyers, the media, the relatives – it was broad based.
>
> There was another one where an Irish labourer called Patrick Walsh was killed in a trench collapse, so our union branch hired the Red Rose Club in Seven Sisters Road to put on a benefit do. Instead of three or four people turning up like usual, we got a really big crowd and it set a precedent.

It showed other people that there was a model of activity for building workers to campaign.❜

The activity coalesced and two meetings were held in parliament attended by Labour MPs Mildred Gordon and Eric Heffer. Activists from UCATT, TGWU and different leftwing groups came together to build a rank-and-file campaign to take up the issue of deaths on building sites. Tony O'Brien was elected as Secretary, Andy Higgins as Treasurer and ex-Barbican steward Jim Franklin as the first Chair of the Construction Safety Campaign.

Mick Holder, currently national health-and-safety officer for the train drivers' union ASLEF, was formerly a carpenter and, for a short time, the full-time worker for the CSC. He said:

❛We took an aggressive stance against the deaths, protesting at sites where workers were killed, outside inquests, outside the law courts if there was a prosecution following a death. It was a very busy few years, especially in the City of London, which became the construction killing fields and the unions were barred from many of the major sites.❜[38]

According to Tony O'Brien, blacklisted painter and CSC secretary from its formation until 2013:

❛From its inception, the CSC has said that workers' safety is both a political and industrial struggle, and that this struggle could only be won by the workers themselves getting organized

Construction Safety Campaign vigil 1989.

and advancing their ability to take control of their own safety. While construction workers have carried out thousands of mainly individual acts of resistance to poor health and safety on sites, the CSC gave a political campaigning expression to this resistance.[939]

For more than quarter of a century, the CSC has been the premier grassroots safety campaign in the building industry. The profile of deaths on building sites has been raised and made into a political issue. The CSC was at the forefront of the campaign to ban asbestos in the UK and the establishment of International Workers Memorial Day on 28 April. CSC activists have gone on to play leading roles in the Hazards movement and in asbestos victims' support groups. But campaigning for better health and safety, protesting outside coroner's courts and assisting bereaved relatives was enough to get someone blacklisted. The well-respected union-funded safety magazine *Hazards*, edited by one-time CSC activist Rory O'Neill, was one of the publications purchased by The Consulting Association. Articles about building workers were cut and pasted into files.

Leading figures in the CSC such as Andy Higgins, Tommy Finn and Tony O'Brien were all blacklisted for their roles in the Campaign. O'Brien's blacklist file is filled with cuttings and reports from his years of campaigning. The Consulting Association held a separate file on the Construction Safety Campaign, which unfortunately the ICO failed to seize, but press cuttings and entries relating to the CSC appear on blacklist files decades apart.

The Pfizers dispute

One of the safety disputes to become part of industry folklore took place in 2000 at the new Pfizers pharmaceutical factory being built to manufacture Viagra at Sandwich in Kent. The sudden upturn in demand for the drug meant that there was a desperate need for skilled workers by the main contractor AMEC and electrical contractor Balfour Kilpatrick. One of those that went there was Steve Acheson, who had recently finished two years as a supervisor on the Channel Tunnel for Balfour Kilpatrick. Met Office weather reports later used as tribunal evidence show that the area had experienced the worst rainfall since records began; the effect was to leave the site awash with slurry. Acheson describes the conditions:

❝For a multimillion-pound project, what a disappointment. It was reminiscent of the Somme – the old battle scenes you watch on TV. Walking through six inches of soaking wet mud to your workface. Such was the size of the site, it was 20 minutes for me to get to my workplace. We were walking through a sea of mud, no separate pedestrianized walkways, no nothing. We were followed at all times by these big American-type load haulers where the wheels were twice the size of a human, about 15-foot massive tyres on them. We noticed articulated lorries were pulling up and when they were reversing, no banksmen were being used or anything. I knew that this was an accident waiting to happen.❞[40]

The presence of vermin on site meant that there was a clear risk of workers contracting the potentially fatal Weils disease from rat urine contaminating wet overalls. Between AMEC and the other contractors, there was a large team of company safety officers on site. The workforce had repeatedly raised the issues highlighted by Acheson but nothing had been done. Workers on site had contacted the HSE and eventually tarmac roads were laid but still no drying rooms or Wellington boots were provided.

The rain kept falling and a deluge left the site completely flooded, with orange road cones floating away in the fast-flowing water.

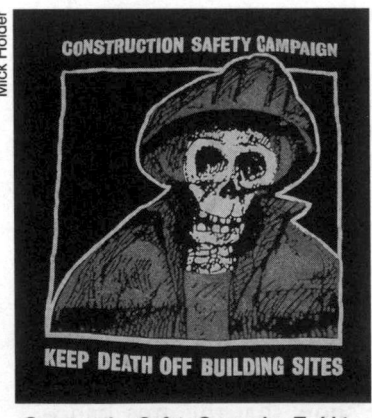

Mick Holder

CONSTRUCTION SAFETY CAMPAIGN

KEEP DEATH OFF BUILDING SITES

Construction Safety Campaign T-shirt

The workers faced the prospect of having to walk through the flood but with no facilities to dry their clothes at the end of the shift. Exasperated, the workers wanted to walk off the job but union activists argued instead that they should exercise their legal rights and remain on site but stay in the canteen until the employer provided mandatory Wellington boots and the workplace was made safe. The company response was to dismiss around 200 workers without notice.

Using a Working Men's Club in Dover as a base, the locked-out workers picketed the plant for seven weeks. Eventually workers were forced to reapply for their previous jobs. Many of those not reinstated won successful employment tribunal claims. During the tribunal hearing, a Health and Safety Executive inspector apologized to the sacked electricians because, despite his best efforts, it had taken their actions to improve conditions on the site.

Rab Campbell, the Amalgamated Engineering and Electrical Union steward, had worked for one of the contractors, Balfour Kilpatrick, for nearly 35 years. He could have gone back to work at any time but stood out on principle with the rest of the sacked workers. He was blacklisted after the dispute but died before receiving any legal redress. Another long-term Balfour Kilpatrick employee sacked and then blacklisted was Frank Matthews. He was to tell the BBC TV *Panorama* programme,

> ⁶The site was flooded and we didn't want to work out there in the rain and the soaking wet because we had nowhere to dry our clothes. So they decided to sack everybody. They'd just employed me for 15 years and gave me full rein of looking after jobs and managing sites responsible for millions of pounds. It just doesn't add up, does it? I was never a troublemaker.⁹

Matthews, along with 50 other workers from the Pfizers building site, was added to the Consulting Association blacklist. Jill Fisher is another of those named and is one of a handful of women with a blacklist file, which has the following entry:

> *2000 June 21 the following were not re-employed by 3223/F following the unofficial action at Pfizer, Sandwich between April and May 2000: these were regarded as followers rather than leaders of the unofficial action*
>
> *One of the main troublemakers during the dispute*

3223/F = Balfour Kilpatrick

The blacklisted workers were exercising their legal right not to be forced to work in unsafe conditions – as was proven when many of them were successful in subsequent employment tribunal claims. Yet Balfour Kilpatrick is happy to secretly smear them as being 'troublemakers' involved in 'unofficial action'.

For Fisher, now teaching electrical engineering in Glasgow, those secret smears got very personal and have followed her around ever since.

> It says on my file that I'm a "nasty piece of work", with exclamation marks, which I was a bit surprised about. I was only 20 at the time. It says I was phoning people up and threatening them, which is a lot of nonsense. It's actually slander, complete lies.
>
> I had virtually nothing to do with the union but was dismissed for no fault of my own. These people tried to sabotage my working life and deserve to be punished for their actions. It was the start of the building boom but I found it impossible to get a decent job. I couldn't progress my career in any way because I couldn't get a job with any of the big companies. So I ended up leaving the trade, paying myself through college and university and starting as an electrical engineer. That's what I had to do, basically. Four years, HNC, HND, then I was up at Cali Uni getting my BEng. I just managed to get work in November.[41]

Jill Fisher was talking in 2013, a decade after the Pfizers dispute.

Gerry Harvey, TCA main contact for Balfour Beatty, remembers the dispute and its consequences:

> A decision was taken to dismiss the entire Balfour Kilpatrick workforce on the Pfizer project for what was perceived at the time to be another unofficial stoppage (but which was later found by an Employment Tribunal to be an official stoppage and justified on health and welfare grounds).[42]

Harvey helped with the production of the dismissal letters for the operatives sacked at Pfizers and describes how the company felt a number of workers 'had slipped through the net' and claims that afterwards a strict policy was introduced by the Director of Personnel. 'Armar Johnston made clear that it would be a disciplinary offence if we were found to have taken on somebody without running a Consulting Association check on them first.'[43]

Harvey also admits that the names of the workers dismissed from Pfizers were shared with other companies.

Gerry Harvey remains employed in a senior HR role at Balfour Beatty's Glasgow head office to this day.

The information on the blacklist files is very often incorrect. Sometimes, after a worker had raised genuine concerns about safety issues, they were dismissed and then false information subsequently placed on their blacklist file. Blacklisted electrician Steve Kelly from Essex is well known in the industry – always smartly dressed in a mod style and riding a vintage Lambretta. He worked on the redevelopment of the Colchester Barracks in 2007. He lasted one day. The following entry appears in his blacklist file:

13th December 2007. applied to 3239 via agency Hays Montrose for Colchester garrison project along with ▐▬▬▬▬▌

Main contact DC given details both were removed from site on the day of application for poor quality of work

3239 = Sir Robert McAlpine Ltd
DC = David Cochrane, head of HR at McAlpine's and the last Chairman of The Consulting Association

Kelly has a slightly different recollection of events.

> ❝Total bollocks! We refused to work on a moveable mobile scaffold tower as we had been instructed to following the health-and-safety induction by McAlpine, where McAlpine's safety officer said: No-one works on my site without the training – if you haven't got the right ticket don't go on them towers. It's down to your employer to give you the training.❞[44]

It would appear that the company's desire to keep Kelly off the project took priority over its own safety officer's stated desire for a safe site. David Cochrane now recalls the incident:

> ❝Two individuals I do remember speaking to Mr Kerr about were Fred Cook and Stephen Kelly. Their cards record that both individuals applied to SRM [Sir Robert McAlpine] for the Colchester Garrison project. This was a large and sensitive Ministry of Defence project. I recall calling Jack Robinson,

who was SRM's site office manager for the Colchester Garrison project and telling him to keep an eye on both of them.[945]

Cochrane claims that the two had already left site and that 'at least one of them had simply walked off site', a claim that is rejected by the electricians. Cochrane, like Quant, also believes 'there were occasions when individuals used bogus health-and-safety issues to disrupt work'[46] and similarly no evidence has been produced for this claim.

On 9 December 2009, Shaun Scurry, a 39-year-old fire installation worker from Kirby, was crushed to death during the construction of the Westfield shopping centre at Stratford. He was trapped between ducting and the mobile platforms handrail. A work colleague who was untrained in the use of the lifting equipment was unable to release him. The HSE investigation found lack of training was a factor in the death. Firesafe Installations Limited was later fined £30,000 for a single breach of health-and-safety regulations.[47]

Safety on offshore oil rigs

On 6 July 1988, 167 oil workers were killed when the Piper Alpha oil rig was engulfed in flames due to a massive gas leak after a safety valve had been deliberately removed. In the wake of the disaster, the North Sea saw a wave of industrial action over the issue of safety, including occupations of oil and gas rigs. The activists who led the occupations in the North Sea coalesced around a rank-and-file organization called the Offshore Industry Liaison Committee (OILC).

One of those OILC members was Lee Fowler, a young electrician from The Wirral who was working on the construction of Piper Bravo, the platform built to replace Piper Alpha. There were 1,500 workers living and working 120 miles north of Aberdeen on an accommodation barge next to the new rig, itself only 500 yards away from the burnt wreckage it was to replace. In March 1992, snow caused a white-out and helicopter operations were cancelled. Further north, near the Shetlands at Shell's Cormorant Alpha rig, a Bristow Helicopters Super Puma crashed, killing 11 men.

The tragedy had a big effect on the 22-year-old electrician, who put himself forward and was elected safety representative for the 200 electricians on Piper Bravo. For a few months, safety appeared to be given a high priority by the Offshore Installation Manager, who held weekly meetings with the safety reps. But towards the end of the project the pressure was on to get the job completed and supervisors started to ignore the concerns raised by the reps. Fowler remembers that, in exasperation, all eight safety reps simultaneously put in a letter of resignation. The company building the rig flew in a senior executive from America and Fowler remembers a tense meeting but the situation improved slightly.

Once the contract had finished, however, Fowler, still in his early twenties, was put on the blacklist and never secured a job working offshore again. Some time later, he managed to find employment on a gas terminal in North Wales, where he bumped into a supervisor who was on Piper Bravo, who asked: 'How the fucking hell did you get on this job? You're blacked.'

Concerns have been raised repeatedly about the treatment of health-and-safety reps in the offshore oil industry. In 2010, the House of Commons Energy and Climate Change Committee produced a report looking at the UK implications of the Gulf of Mexico oil spill. The report says that the industry body Oil and Gas UK 'tried to assure us [the Committee] that the offshore workforce are "free and able to intervene on issues of safety, and without fear of retribution"'. However, the Committee also noted an HSE report from 2009 that rig staff were subject to 'bullying, aggression, harassment, humiliation and intimidation' from offshore management. And the Committee heard from Dr Jonathan Wills, independent councillor for Lerwick South and a freelance environmental consultant, who said: 'Whistleblowers are not able to call a halt to things and the managers are obviously trying to make money for the company.'

The Committee's report concluded: 'We find some conflict in the reports from the HSE about bullying and harassment on rigs and the assurances of the industry that sincere whistleblowers will be heard and protected. We recommend that the government should discuss with the industry and unions what further steps are needed to prevent safety representatives from being or feeling intimidated into not reporting a hazard, potential or otherwise.'

Many of the OILC union activists and participants in the wave of occupations never worked in the sector again, becoming blacklisted by use of what is known as 'the NRB system'. At the end of any stint offshore, the rig manager writes comments on the worker's personnel card. NRB stands for 'Not Required Back'; it appeared on the offshore industry paperwork for hundreds of OILC activists and has been described as an open blacklist for many years. Fowler explains what a culture of fear NRB created on the rigs:

> ❝NRB was a big deal. You basically kept your head down and kept your mouth shut because if you didn't do exactly what they wanted you to do, you weren't working in the North Sea again. We had the OILC stickers on our hats and they didn't like it. They frowned upon that. Unions weren't mentioned. The only ones I really knew were in the union were those with the OILC stickers on their hard hats – they were brave enough to say "Yes, I am in the union".❞

That The Consulting Association took an interest in the offshore industry is undoubted. The large number of blacklisted workers from Aberdeen and Aberdeenshire that appear on the blacklist, including some of the OILC leading lights such as Ronnie McDonald and Jake Molloy, are testimony to that. TCA kept a separate file on OILC, which the ICO again failed to seize.

It was not only union activists who were added to the blacklist due to raising concerns about safety in the offshore industry. The Consulting Association also opened a file on Professor Charles Woolfson, the aforementioned leading academic in oil industry safety and industrial relations. His blacklist file includes the entries:

Woolfson, Charles (Professor) – senior Lecturer in Industrial Relations, University of Glasgow.

See also file: OILC

1995 December: Author of contradictory findings on health and safety after Piper Alpha tragedy. Saying standards laid down since are not being adhered to.

Radio: 1.12.95 – headline: 'Academics: saying North Sea is most dangerous place to work'

> *From S & NW Meeting: 20th June 1996*
> *His activities now being felt by ACOA. Funding from oil*
> *industry to Glasgow University may be cut if aboves [sic]*
> *activities continue, or there may be a reduction in his activities*
> *to prevent this happening.*

The file even records a speech the academic made at the Royal Society for the Prevention of Accidents conference. Professor Woolfson continues to undertake research into oil-industry safety at Linköping University in Sweden. He recently wrote about the effect of blacklisting in the international oil industry today:

> What is remarkable, and in my view undeniable, is that many of the same lethal ingredients that led to Piper Alpha 25 years ago appear to be still present in today's offshore industry in the US. These include reckless cost-cutting that compromises safety, the undermining of regulatory control and enforcement mechanisms through industry lobbying, ongoing "regulatory capture", and above all, the systematic exclusion of worker voice in the safety process. None of the proposals for post-disaster reform in the US address the crucial missing ingredient of securing the legitimacy of employee voice in the safety process, and the need for collective protection and support for those who speak out on safety issues. In this sense, the shadow if not the reality of the blacklist remains offshore.[48]

Only a handful of heavily redacted financial documents seized during the ICO raid have so far been released into the public domain but amongst them is a sales-book entry that records an invoice for 'AMEC offshore ser' on 14 May 2001. What this offshore service was is so far unknown. But what is known is that a number of individuals involved in blacklisting in the building industry have subsequently moved to senior human resources (HR) posts in the offshore industry. One is Kevin Gorman, who was Alan Wainwright's boss at Tarmac and then moved to senior HR roles in Bristow Helicopters and Subsea 7, before taking up his current role of Vice President HR for the offshore inspection and maintenance company Harkand.

The RMT union, of which OILC is now part, has said that North Sea oil workers are still fearful of speaking up about safety concerns in case they are blacklisted by employers and that unions are still denied access to their members working offshore. In August 2013, following the deaths of four more workers in a helicopter crash in the Shetlands, the late RMT general secretary Bob Crow said: 'There is a lack of trust and it's not surprising given a history of blacklisting by employers. The use of NRB labelling has left some petrified that their careers could come to an end.'[49]

Even the employers were forced to admit that blacklisting of those that raise safety issues in the North Sea is ongoing when Oil & Gas UK, the employers' federation, issued a statement saying:

> The whole question of NRB is one we have been working to address and stamp out. We have produced guidelines which seek to give procedures to be followed about how safety issues are raised and addressed.[50]

Following the BP Deep Water Horizon tragedy in the Gulf of Mexico Judith Hackitt, chair of the HSE, told an oil-industry conference that senior managers needed to work with safety reps and trade unions to ensure that safety standards did not decay, but indicated 'that this will only happen if senior managers learn to ask the right questions and respond appropriately when concerns are raised. Blame hunts – or, in this industry's case, NRB – is not an appropriate response to genuine safety concerns.'[51]

This was in February 2011. The head of the UK's safety watchdog was telling the oil industry to stop blacklisting workers who raised safety issues. Just like in the construction industry, everyone knows it is going on but no-one in authority appears to want to do anything about it. In the spring of 2016, the HSE launched its strategy entitled Helping Britain Work Well. Judith Hackett introduced it, saying:

> Too much complexity and bureaucracy has built up around health and safety. We heard many people say that we already have the knowledge to make the themes of the strategy a reality. The message that this is about being smarter – not simply doing more – resonated with our audiences. By keeping

things as simple and straightforward as possible we can ensure that all businesses see this as enabling them to be successful and productive.*[52]

A failure to investigate

Safety remains a central issue for construction workers. Despite the assurances of those at the top, when safety impacts on profits, the mask of compassion is often dropped to expose naked gangsterism. The almost pathological dislike of anyone who dares to criticize the way safety is managed has resulted in the voice of the workforce virtually being extinguished. Construction continues to have a fatality rate far in excess of other industries: victimization of workers prepared to raise concerns about safety is without doubt a contributory factor.

Blacklisting union safety reps costs workers' lives. The Health and Safety Executive has powers under the Health and Safety at Work Act 1974 to issue notices and even take criminal prosecutions. Yet, despite making the right noises, the HSE has not issued a single improvement notice or prosecution against a company for mistreatment of a safety rep since 2004. More than seven years after the discovery of the blacklist and all the subsequent revelations, the HSE still has not carried out an investigation against any firms involved in the systematic blacklisting of union safety reps.

1 Speech made to a Construction Safety Campaign vigil outside Wembley Stadium on Workers Memorial Day 2004. 2 Health and Safety Executive, 19 February 2016, nin.tl/HSEresponse 3 Health and Safety Executive, nin.tl/HSEsafety2014 4 Public Records Office (1967) *Court of Inquiry into construction disputes involving Myton Ltd and certain workers at the Barbican Development Site in the City of London; submission of Report to the Minister,* Ref: LAB 10/3158 5 Interview with the authors 6 Health and Safety Executive Prosecutions History – construction, nin.tl/HSEprosecutions 7 UCATT, New figures reveal fall in construction inspections, 7 March 2016, nin.tl/fewerinspections 8 UCATT press release, 3 July 2014, nin.tl/UCATTpress – accessed 13 December 2014. 9 Speech delivered on 18 April 2012 at the Policy Exchange, London, nin.tl/graylingspeech – accessed 13 December 2014. 10 'David Cameron: I will kill off safety culture', *The Independent,* 5 January 2016, nin.tl/Cameronsafety 11 'Dark Hearts', *Hazards* issue 118, April-June 2012, nin.tl/hazards118 – accessed 13 December 2014. 12 Reel News video: 'National blacklisting day of action sends shock waves through the building industry'. 13 See, for instance, David I Levine, Michael W Toffel, Matthew S Johnson, 'Randomized government safety inspections reduce worker injuries with no detectable job loss', *Science,* vol 336, no 6083, pp 907-911, 18 May 2012. 14 Interview with the authors. 15 Interview with the authors. 16 Keynote speech to 'Partners in

Prevention' conference in London, July 2000, nin.tl/LGCHandS 17 Quoted at GMB Congress 2016. 18 Speech at TUC 2015. 19 Witness statement to Employment Tribunal, 1 August 2011. 20 Evidence to Scottish Affairs Select Committee, 22 January 2013. 21 Evidence to Scottish Affairs Select Committee, 12 March 2013. 22 Quoted in *People Management*, 20 November 2009. 23 Interview with authors. 24 Quoted at GMB Congress 2016. 25 Witness statement seen by the authors. 26 Interview with the authors. 27 'MPs called in after alleged threats on site', *Building*, no 45, 1999, nin.tl/allegedthreats 28 The authors put all these allegations to Irvine Whitlock but received no comment. 29 Interview with the authors. 30 Written evidence to Scottish Affairs Select Committee, nin.tl/Scotcomm 31 Duncan Campbell, 'Boys from the Black and Blue Stuff', *City Limits*, 25 May 1984. 32 Interview with the authors. 33 Interview with the authors. 34 Duncan Campbell, op cit. 35 Ibid. 36 *Construction News*, 8 April 1993, nin.tl/churtonredress 37 Witness statement seen by the authors. 38 Interview with the authors. 39 Quoted from Construction Safety Campaign: over 20 years fighting for workers' health and safety. 40 Interview with the authors. 41 Interview with the authors. 42 Witness statement seen by the authors. 43 Witness statement seen by the authors. 44 Interview with the authors. 45 Witness statement seen by the authors. 46 Witness statement seen by the authors. 47 *Construction Enquirer*, nin.tl/liftdeath 48 Charles Woolfson, 'A cruel conspiracy in international union rights', *Journal of the International Centre for Trade Union Rights*, vol 21, no 12014. 49 'North Sea oil culture needs to change', *Guardian*, 30 August 2013, nin.tl/Crowonoilculture 50 Ibid. 51 Speech 2 February 2011, nin.tl/Hackittspeech 52 HSE, nin.tl/29uVFie

4
Angry – so angry

A number of well-established collective-bargaining agreements exist in the construction industry. The most significant is the National Working Rule Agreement to which UCATT, Unite and GMB are signatories and which covers most building trades. The National Agreement for the Engineering Construction Industry (the 'NAECI' or the 'Blue Book'), which is signed by Unite and GMB, applies to larger engineering projects such as oil refineries and power stations. Electricians are covered by the Joint Industry Board (JIB), under which Unite are the only recognized union. In excess of a million construction workers should be covered by the three collective-bargaining agreements, which would entitle them to minimum standards of pay, rest breaks, overtime payments, welfare facilities and lodging allowances. The agreements even go into detail on such issues as provision for a safe place to store tools on site and who is to pay if those tools are stolen from the lock-up.

All the national collective-bargaining agreements have clauses within them that attempt to stem the flow of self-employed or agency labour, in favour of direct employment. But having a collective agreement is one thing: enforcing it is quite another. Mass false self-employment has meant that the terms and conditions for the vast majority of private-sector construction workers are no longer negotiated by the national unions but individually on a company-by-company, site-by-site basis. Without direct employment and collective bargaining, pay rates are determined by supply and demand: in times of recession, wages and conditions deteriorate. The self-employed workforce, denied legal employment rights and without union representation, ends up in a dog-eat-dog fight with each other, having to work for whatever is offered.

Dave Ayre, a well-respected bricklayer from Crook, County

Durham, was sacked repeatedly and blacklisted because of his union activities and forced to work on a self-employed basis to provide for his young family. Ayre recalls how the reality of self-employment in the winter of 1971 helped to mould his trade-union consciousness:

> About a week before Christmas, our labourer was ill, and we were working double on the "top lift" of a scaffold, building a tricky double chimney-flue in a blizzard. Being self-employed, we could get no dole, so we got soaked through and frozen solid. It was a hard lesson. I knew nothing about Adam Smith or Karl Marx, but I learned that a shortage of work and an abundance of labour power equalled excessive exploitation. I'd been sacked so many times at Christmas that my kids thought it was part of the Father Christmas story, except that the "sack" was empty. It was then that I truly learned where my politics lay.[91]

Construction is an intrinsically itinerant sector and holding onto the even limited terms won by collective bargaining becomes an important goal for union activists. Veteran activist Willie Black became a YouTube sensation when caught on TV cameras heckling government minister Iain Duncan Smith and calling him a 'ratbag' during a speech about dismantling the welfare state. The blacklisted electrician from Edinburgh notes the constant struggle to keep the gains of the past:

> Travelling guys knew that, if they went to Wales, Bristol or Kent, they had this Blue Book agreement, they had decent terms and conditions. When there were big sites, the push would come for the workers to improve the agreement. When the sites were closed or there was less activity, in what was termed the Blue Book area, the employers would push. They would get back some of the concessions that they would make. So there was a constant battle on the sites between the employers and the union.

And that battle is made considerably more difficult if the best union activists are excluded from building sites because of blacklisting. John Hendy QC told blacklisted workers: 'They are blacklisting people not because they don't like your faces but because they are scared stiff of collective bargaining.'[2]

But the fight to defend collective-bargaining agreements in construction has been a rearguard action. On Teesside in 2015, union members demonstrated weekly for more than 12 months outside Sita Sembcorp UK sites in Wilton and Haverton Hill over claims the company is exploiting cheap foreign labour rather than sticking to a national pay agreement for construction workers. Government statistics indicate that only 18 per cent of the workforce is now covered by any kind of collective agreement, with union density down to 15.5 per cent.[3] On the vast majority of small building sites, there is almost no union presence at all. The only areas where the unions retain any cohesion are the ever-dwindling public sector and the large prestige projects. Longevity of contract and substantially better terms and conditions, along with the sense of pride all building workers take when working on a famous development, mean that most workers aspire to work on the major projects.

Importing the JIB

The most controversial national agreement between a trade union and the employers is the Joint Industry Board (JIB), set up by the electricians union, the EETPU. It still operates in the construction industry and some see its mode of operation as contributing to the climate from which blacklisting emerged – certainly there have been disproportionate numbers of electricians blacklisted over the years.

In the 1960s, EETPU general secretary Frank Chapple led a union delegation to New York to discuss an alternative industrial relations model for the electrical industry. For more than 20 years, a model agreement known as the JIB (the Joint Industry Board) had been in place between the New York electrical employers and the International Brotherhood of Electrical Workers Local Trade Union 3. The EETPU delegation was so taken by the scheme that the JIB was imported into the British electrical contracting industry.

The British version of the JIB was established on 1 January 1968 and consisted of the Electrical Contractors Association (ECA employers) and the EETPU. The JIB was not a standard collective-bargaining structure where unions negotiate with employers but a legally binding social partnership agreement between the leadership of the EETPU and the bosses. Every electrician working for a JIB company was automatically signed up to be a member of EETPU, with the membership fees being paid by the employer.

In order to maintain standards of safety in the industry, it is JIB policy that electrical contracting work should only be carried out by qualified electricians working for a JIB company. Rule 17 of the JIB actively encourages direct employment and lays out supposedly strict conditions that need to be met before any self-employed or employment agency staff can be engaged. No sub-contracting is allowed, except to another JIB member firm. And except under exceptional circumstances, no directly employed electrician should be made redundant if there are any agency electricians still working on a site. If all JIB companies played by the rules, this would virtually ensure that the entire sector remained directly employed, with work carried out by qualified labour.

During the 1970s and 1980s, all the major electrical companies signed up as JIB companies, with the result that virtually every qualified electrician in UK contracting became a JIB electrician. The JIB rate became the industry-recognized rate of pay and provided an agreed package of pay, welfare benefits and training.

JIB rules meant that, whenever a worker was employed by a JIB company, whether they wanted to join or not, they automatically had their EETPU union subs paid. The employers, by paying union dues on behalf of union members, were able to give the union up to £1 million every year through the JIB 'check-off' scheme. A consequence of the JIB was that union density among electricians directly employed by JIB firms was close to 100 per cent. In return for these guaranteed benefits and guaranteed income streams, the union agreed to discipline its own members, improve productivity and eliminate strikes.

The friendly relationship between the ECA and EETPU grew ever stronger and in 1979 the Conservative government's employment minister Patrick Mayhew granted a unique dispensation. This exemption allowed the JIB to substitute its own dismissal procedure for unfair dismissals; it is the only such exemption order granted in any industry. The result was that any electrician registered with the JIB lost their legal rights to take a claim for unfair dismissal to an Employment Tribunal but instead was legally obliged to use the JIB procedures.[4]

Paul Corby, former head of the EETPU construction section and current national chair of the JIB, told the authors: 'I believe in social partnership, I make no apology. I want to work with employers and make things better. I think that is more important than being an oppositionist.'

Despite attempts by major employers to pull out of the agreement, the JIB continues to provide the terms and conditions framework for the electrical contracting industry to this day.

The Joint Sites Committee

Whether among electricians, bricklayers or carpenters, to improve conditions on building sites the process has been the same: fight to get on the job in the first place, fight to get the job unionized, fight to get the national agreements adhered to. It is an ongoing guerrilla war. By the early 1990s the London Joint Sites Committee (JSC) had been resurrected by two Scottish building workers, Michael Dooley and Chris Clarke, attracting a new generation of union activists. For more than a decade the JSC and its fanzine-style magazine *Builders Crack* was to play a significant role on building sites across London. In one famous incident, the JSC turned up with a van full of thermolite building blocks. Harrow-based bricklayer and JSC secretary Paul Crimmins proceeded to build a six-foot-high wall across the front entrance of the Construction Employers Federation headquarters while the national pay talks were taking place inside. Unsurprisingly, the JSC was of particular interest to both the Economic League and The Consulting Association, and the latter kept a separate file on the rank-and-file body. The following entry appears on a number of blacklist files:

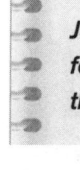

JSC is an unofficial grouping, without formal union backing, formed to fight what it sees as poor pay and conditions where those exist on sites during the present recession.

Reports and press cuttings of JSC disputes over unpaid wages,

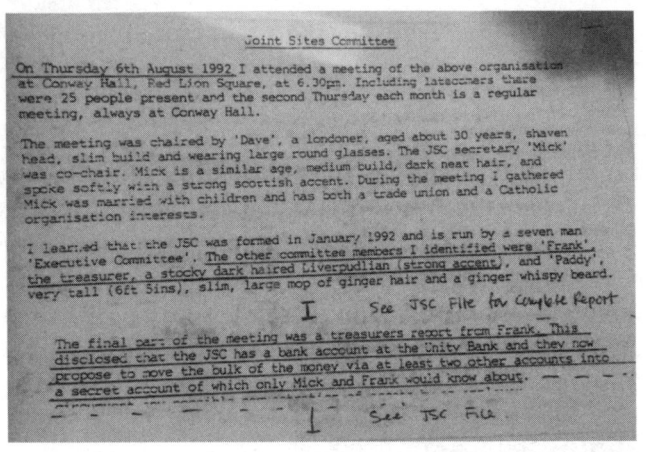

Extract from Consulting Association files describing spying on JSC in 1992

victimization of union reps and safety appear on dozens of blacklist files. But the blacklisters were not content with simply acquiring their information from the media and industrial relations managers. As we have already seen, Ian Kerr would spy on union meetings while working for the Economic League. One of the documents seized by the ICO is a report of a spying mission against the JSC.

> *Joint Sites Committee*
>
> *On Thursday 6 August 1992 I attended a meeting of the above organization at Conway Hall, Red Lion Square at 6.30pm. Including latecomers, there were 25 people present and the second Thursday each month is a regular meeting, always at Conway Hall.*
>
> *The meeting was chaired by Dave, a Londoner aged around 30 years, shaven head, slim build and wearing large round glasses. The JSC secretary Mick was co-chair. Mick is a similar age, medium build, dark neat hair, and spoke softly with a strong Scottish accent. During the meeting I gathered Mick was married with children and has both a trade union and a Catholic organization interests.*
>
> *I learned that the JSC was formed 1 January 1992 and is run by a seven-man 'Executive Committee'. The other committee*

> *members I identified were 'Frank', the treasurer, a stocky*
> *dark-haired Liverpudlian (strong accent) and Paddy, very tall*
> *(6ft 5ins), slim, large mop of ginger hair and a ginger whispy*
> *[sic] beard.*
> **See JSC File for Complete Report**

The four people named in the report are Michael Dooley (bricklayer), Dave Smith, Frank Smith (bricklayer) and Paddy Little (joiner). The rest of the executive were hod carrier Chris Clarke, electrician Tim Loverage and bricklayer Alistair McQueen. Paul Crimmins, Steve Kelly, Jim Grey, Jim Lafferty, Carl Linkson and Steve Hedley were all to take on leading roles in the JSC during the next 10 years. All of the rank-and-file leaders and virtually all of the building workers who regularly attended the JSC meetings and protests have blacklist files.

In 1992, the JSC unionized workers on the construction of a new hotel in Kensington. Only a stone's throw from the museums and Harrods, the Vascroft site became a famous industrial-relations battleground. It was the depths of the early 1990s recession and labourers on the site were working for as little as £23 a shift.[5] There was no canteen on the job and the workforce shared three toilets without doors that were still functioning in the basement of the semi-demolished rubble of the previous building.

Chris Clarke was already working on the job:

> The conditions with regard to health and safety were atrocious, literally the worst I had ever seen in 15 years in the industry at the time. When I became a steward, one of the labourers came to me and complained about the demolition work. When they were demolishing this nine-inch wall, the foreman had told them to "kick it and run!"[6]

On returning from the Easter break, the JSC organized a two-hour sit-in until conditions on site were improved. The effect was immediate: wages were increased, hours were cut and a new toilet block arrived before the end of the week. It was a smash-and-grab victory for the JSC and the workers on the site. Union officials visited the site the day after, recruiting members and agreeing recognition on the site. Three union stewards were elected, Michael Dooley, Chris Clarke, and Dennis Falvey, and they were issued with accreditation by the TGWU and UCATT.

The elected stewards raised a number of issues with management and, within two weeks, all three were sacked. This time the workers walked off the job in support of their reps and production on the job ground to a halt. Strikers sent flying pickets to other major construction sites to build support. This was long before security checks and turnstiles on building-site entrances and the strikers simply walked onto the sites and addressed impromptu meetings in the canteens. This resulted in the hard hat being passed around to allow for strike pay.

When one squad of flying pickets discovered another Vascroft site and managed to persuade workers from that job to down tools and walk out in support of the workers in Kensington, the company caved in and reinstated all three of the victimized union reps, agreeing to pay lost wages to everyone who participated in the strike as part of the settlement.

The company bided its time and prepared the ground before taking any more action. After a few weeks of relative calm, the elected UCATT and TGWU stewards were sacked again. This time the workers didn't have to go on strike as Michael Dooley arrived on site early the next morning and occupied the tower crane. In the centre of London, with limited access and storage space, every delivery was unloaded by use of tower cranes. The logistics of building in the centre of a major city simply do not allow for an alternative. For 10 days the occupied tower crane and the JSC picket brought the site to a standstill. As the jib of the crane swung around in the wind, there were times when the furthest point was hanging over the road; at this point a long rope would hurriedly be lowered and JSC supporters would tie provisions to the rope before Dooley quickly pulled it back up again.

The crane occupation caught the attention of the national press when Vascroft applied for a High Court injunction to the value of £250,000, naming both UCATT and the TGWU in the legal papers.[7] After 10 days, Dooley was forced to come down from the crane. Although the stewards went on to win claims for unfair dismissal for trade-union activities, the TGWU and UCATT had been driven off site.

After Vascrofts, Dooley and Clarke were both added to the Consulting Association blacklist and found it almost impossible to gain employment. Dooley went to Ruskin College in 1993 and later became a union official. There are entries on his blacklist file that relate to his time at Ruskin. Clarke had long spells of unemployment and suffered ill health. He said:

> ❝ My health collapsed and I nearly died in 2005 from an arterial fibrillation attack, when your heart goes out of rhythm and speeds up dramatically. In 2008, it was touch and go, I nearly drowned in my own blood when a blood clot stopped the flow of blood to and from my lungs. I believe the blacklisting played a significant part in my ongoing illnesses. Blacklisting has severely damaged my health, damaged my relationships and damaged my everyday life.❞

Roy Bentham is a softly spoken joiner from Merseyside. He is a keen supporter of Liverpool Football Club and over the years has been involved in the Hillsborough campaign and the fans' group *The Spirit of Shankly*. In 1995 Bentham worked on the Connah's Quay power station on the north Wales coast, which was one of the biggest civil-engineering projects in the country. There were a number of grievances on the site, including safety and welfare facilities, but the main bone of contention was companies deliberately trying to circumvent paying the Working Rule Agreement rates of pay by only employing their workers on a self-employed basis. Six hundred workers voted to go on strike. They stayed out for nearly a month. It was a major victory for the unions, which managed to secure direct employment for many workers, better wages, better terms and improved welfare and drying facilities. Bentham, who was voted in as steward for the joiners, recalls the aftermath:

> ❝ I was then targeted. I was made to work alone from the men and, after a further three weeks of isolation, I was then dismissed. Three fellow stewards – a scaffolder, steel fixer and concrete finisher – were also trap-doored on the same day.❞[8]

The following entry appears on Bentham's blacklist file:

1995 June: Involved in dispute at Connah's Quay, Deeside, April-May 1995.

Bit of a sheep but elected steward at Connah's Quay
SOURCE: Main Contacts: SP / DA 3271/35

Connah's Quay Dispute Power Station:

Dispute centred originally in Lancsville, the labour supply agent to construction management company Henry Boot. Whereas the men returned to work on agreement to pay them WR [Working Rule] rates the attention is now returned to 3271/35, who are still on site with a self-employed workforce. Little is known about Lancsville – thought to be a Southern England based company with little more than a book of names and telephone numbers. Two sources state that Henry Boot have on site a number of militants from North West.

3271 = Tarmac

SP = Sandy Palmer – senior manager at National Construction Service (NCS) employment agency – wholly owned by Tarmac (later renamed as Carillion).

DA = Dave Aspinall – senior manager at NCS employment agency.

The bottom entry on the blacklist file appears on the files of dozens of people who worked at Connah's Quay and is likely to be part of the fortnightly summaries of industrial issues Kerr circulated to select HR officials.

Having his name added to the blacklist had almost immediate consequences for the joiner, who had only ever been on strike once in a perfectly legal dispute. Bentham, who had previously found no difficulty in getting work close to his home, commented:

❝I just couldn't get any work in the Northwest. I had to go working around the country for a number of smaller builders and in between that I had to pick up short-term work with agencies, a little self-employed graft allied to long and frequent spells of unemployment. In 2004, one of the biggest jobs in Europe was Liverpool One, and I couldn't get work on there at all over four years. They were crying out for skilled men. The strain of being kept out of work and having to scrap for any bits around the country took its toll. I was broke and the usual things you'd do in relationships went by the wayside. Being apart from my long-term girlfriend also put a strain on me and her emotionally. We have subsequently split up. It does impact on your home life – and it's still impacting now. **9**

The Jubilee Line Extension

The end of the 1990s saw the start of an unprecedented building boom that was to last until the global financial crash in 2008. Prestige projects such as the Millennium Stadium in Cardiff, the Millennium Dome and the Royal Opera House in London created a shortage of skilled labour and a resulting increase in wage rates. The pages of the trade press during this period are peppered with reports about industrial action on building sites amongst tower-crane drivers, steel erectors, shuttering carpenters and caravan builders.

But the project that cast the biggest industrial relations shadow at the time was the Jubilee Line Extension, known as the JLE. The low-intensity war hidden behind scaffolding on the high streets was about to go underground. The extension to the underground railway system went from Green Park in the west to Stratford in the east. The project was too large for one contractor, so was divided into a number of smaller contracts, with most of the blacklisting firms having a section of the work. The main electrical contractor on the project was Drake & Scull, which was a TCA subscriber.

The first Drake & Scull shop steward to be elected on the JLE was Steve Kelly, who was based at Stratford station in 1996. Again, poor welfare facilities would be the spur to build union organization on the project.

6 Drake & Scull gave us what they deemed as a facility to have a tea break. But what they gave us was a steel container like you'd have on the back of a lorry for transporting goods around in. In Drake & Scull's eyes that was suitable accommodation

for 20 guys. You'd open up the container, freezing cold, no lights in there and to me that just wasn't a place to get changed in or have a tea break. We discussed it amongst ourselves and agreed that if we were gonna change things then we needed a union and it ended up that I was asked to be the steward. The AEEU officer, Frank Westerman, then came down and met us outside work, because you've got to be careful what you're doing. If the construction-company bosses get wind of it they'll try and get you off the job.[9]

After being elected steward, Kelly successfully negotiated a proper canteen facility and that first small victory established the union. After the breakthrough at the Stratford site, workers at other stations quickly elected their own representatives and the JLE 'shop' was born. Starting with a handful of activists, union organization grew as more and more workers joined.

A new generation of activists were to cut their teeth on the underground tunnelling project, including Jim Turner, who was originally employed as a chargehand but after discovering the union was later elected as an AEEU safety rep. Turner is not his actual name, as he fears for his employment prospects.

I've never ever had any confrontation with an employer before. I have been disgruntled like everyone else who has seen unfairness at work but doesn't really have the tools to deal with it. But going onto the Jubilee Line I realized there was a thing called a shop. I didn't know what this was, who it was responsible to or what the mechanisms were. But the penny started to drop with all things union. The shop is basically an elected group of workers who take on trade union roles. It morphed. It started off as just one safety rep and one steward and they would come along to any of the 15 or so sites, with just one monthly meeting, but it wasn't too long before we started going to bigger union meetings. There was a massive sense of empowerment. We were going to work on an organized job, straight away there were issues and we were winning. We weren't on the back foot. We had seized control and they had no redress.[10]

When, in May 1997, the Drake & Scull electricians elected four new shop stewards to their shop committee, including Keith Knight and Tony Miller, who were to take up the role of convenors, management attempted to seize back control. An article written in *Builders Crack* by one of the Jubilee Line electricians explains what happened:

> ❝The firm refused to recognize our committee and a week later the stewards' committee and seven others who had spoken out at the meeting were the ones chosen to get the bullet. The lads voted to hit the gate until all 11 were reinstated. With two years' work left on the job, how could there be any redundancies? It was obvious victimization. We picketed all the JLE sites on Tuesday and Wednesday. Drake & Scull then sacked the entire workforce on Thursday for taking unofficial action. But we knew if we stuck together we could beat the bastards. We kept up the pickets. On Friday we went to ACAS and the firms agreed to reinstate the 11 men. A week later they said there would be no redundancies.❞

The JLE went on to become one of the best union-organized sections in British industry, leading to a number of high-profile disputes. One famous incident occurred in December 1998 after a fire alarm went off at London Bridge station. When the fire brigade evacuated the station they found the workers in the new tunnel were completely unaware of the emergency because there were no working fire alarms installed. Ten years earlier, 31 people had been killed when fire engulfed Kings Cross station and strict new procedures had been introduced to protect people. The workers quite understandably protested about this situation. David Hyndman, a thick-set electrician from Manchester, was one of those who complained. He said: 'We raised it with the management and they disagreed. They wanted to sack or transfer certain individuals and I was one of them. They considered me a troublemaker.'[11] Hyndman has since been struggling to gain employment due to being blacklisted, and so supplements his earnings through acting.

Drake & Scull dismissed 12 workers, including the elected AEEU safety rep. A hastily arranged meeting in Westminster Hall was organized using the then new technology of mobile phones and the workers voted to strike until their colleagues were reinstated and the safety issues had been rectified. The strike lasted two weeks in the run-up to Christmas. Eventually all the workers were reinstated on their original sites and, as part of the settlement, AEEU national safety officer Malcolm Bonnett was allowed to carry out a safety audit.

In 1997 and again in 1999, during the JIB pay negotiation between the AEEU and the ECA, the Jubilee Line electricians played a leading role in building a national rank-and-file network. The electricians were campaigning for a better basic rate of pay but primarily in opposition to the employers' demand for the introduction of a new semi-skilled electrical grade of 'Skilled Mechanical Assembler' (SMA). The electricians saw the SMA grade as an attempt to deskill the trade because of the cyclical skills shortage.

The powerful rank-and-file network had contacts on major projects across the country and organized a series of one-day strikes and demonstrations outside Downing Street and the JIB headquarters in Sidcup, involving over 10,000 workers in total. Blacklisted JLE shop treasurer Jim Grey explained:

> The whole of the Jubilee Line came out – you're talking 400 sparks [electricians] there. Another 3-4,000 in London came out with us. We took out the whole of Sellafield, Methylls in Scotland: a total day of action that the AEEU had never seen before. This was just solidarity, stewards talking to each other, sticking together. In the end we made the AEEU take out the SMA grade in the pay deal. Obviously this was a big slap in the face for the employers because that was the thing they wanted to get through. That's the first day of action by sparks for ages and shows what solidarity can do.[12]

The massive penalty clauses for failure to open the JLE by Millennium Night, and the fact that Drake & Scull had been awarded the electrical contracts on all the stations, gave the electricians bargaining strength. And they exploited that to its fullest potential. Towards the completion of the contract, the stewards' committee was able to negotiate a 'finishing bonus' of up to £4,000 per worker. The news of a finishing bonus was spread by *Builders Crack* and taken up by building workers across London, with action spreading to the Opera House, Millennium Dome and other trades on the JLE. Afterwards Stephen Quant, one-time chair of The Consulting Association and experienced industrial-relations manager at Skanska, was forced to concede that the union's tactics on the JLE had been astute.

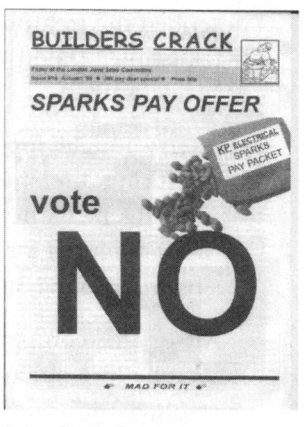

Joint Sites Committee fanzine Builders Crack produced for JIB pay dispute

The empire strikes back

There might have been grudging respect for the tactics – but employers were making sure they gathered information to identify those responsible. That appears to include covert video recording of JLE and JSC activists during this time. The evidence comes from the blacklist file for AEEU scaffolder Glen Jones.

> **1999 September 2nd:**
>
> **Worked with 3221 / 3223 Joint Venture London Bridge section of the Jubilee Line Extension for 6 months. Problems arose with severance pay. Very supportive of Joint Sites Committee, regarded as a possible member. Possibly a 'sleeper'.**
>
> **Video record shows him being very close to JSC members when problems arose on contract earlier in 1999. Was a workers' representative during this time.**
>
> **SOURCE: 3221/M (DC) originated from D&S**

D&S = Drake & Scull

The employers' story, which was repeated by the media, painted the JLE as an appalling example of industrial relations. One union activist, Terry McBride, was targeted by the press. The tabloids tried to discredit him, using doctored photographs, and published smear stories about him as an activist in the 1980s. This put him and his family under the most unbearable pressure and without doubt contributed to his early death. Union official Frank Westerman described the treatment of Terry McBride as 'deliberate, conscious blacklisting'. David Hyndman, a friend and co-worker of Terry McBride, said:

> ❝Terry fought for better pay, terms, and conditions all his working life, both as a shop steward and a spark. An intelligent, hard-working man, and a first-class tradesman, he never shirked a challenge. He was blacklisted when most of us were taking our 11 plus.❞

All of the companies on the project made a profit and the new Tube line opened on time, with the Queen making the first ever official journey when visiting the Millennium Dome on 31 December 1999. That did not stop the employers taking revenge. When the Jubilee Line Extension was over, hundreds of workers found themselves added to the blacklist. The following entry appears on Steve Kelly's file and similar comments are repeated on many other files:

> *December 1998: involved in series of disputes which culminated in the 2 week walk out of electricians at the jubilee line extension in December 1998. militant minded and involved in the organisation of disputes relating to rates of pay, WTD, hours, bonus rates, severance pay etc...*
>
> *25th Feb 1998: one of 15 electricians employed by Drake and Scull all are of militant nature and regarded as troublemakers active during this period 97-98 involved in a series of strikes over electricians pay offer. Went on strike at the drop of a hat involved in sabotage on site, graffiti on walls, and threatening behaviour towards supervision. source would not advise taking any of the 15 on above is very militant and involved in the TU side*
>
> *(3221/E (DC)*
>
> *November 20th 1998: Shop steward on JLE singled out as one of the agitators during current electricians dispute source 3245/T (HP)*

> **Worked at Jubilee Line Extension 1997 to 1999**
> **UNDER NO CIRCUMSTANCES WHATSOEVER**

WTD = Working Time Directive; 3221 = Morgan Est;
3245 = Vinci / Norwest Holst Group

It is hardly surprising that Steve Kelly and some of the other JLE workers found themselves virtually unemployable.

Carl Linkson was 24 years old when he started working on the Jubilee Line. He played guitar in a rock band and his youth and long hair made him stand out at union meetings but by the end of the project he was the elected Bonus Steward and chair of the Amicus London Contracting Branch. He has the following entry on his blacklist file, credited to Danny O'Sullivan of Kier, who in 2000 went on to become TCA Chair:

> **1997-98 Worked on the Jubilee Line Extension. Not in the front line of action. Allowed himself to be drawn along by the course of events at the JLE**

Blacklisted electrician Paul Gledhill has the following entry on his Consulting Association file:

> **1999 April 19th:**
> **Confirmation from D&S Electrical LIFO sheet that at this date was in the employment of Drake & Scull.**
> **Start date was 29.9.97**
> **Location: WES**

LIFO = Last In First Out, used as a selection criteria for redundancy on large construction projects and often helps to protect union activists from unfair selection. WES = Westminster station.

This one entry on a blacklist file related to the JLE would have enormous consequences. In the two-and-a-half years after being made redundant from the JLE in November 1999, Paul Gledhill's file records eight separate occasions when he was name-checked against the blacklist and refused work. The sites including Pfizers, projects for Vinci and a Ministry of Defence project in Whitehall for Skanska. In October 2000, Gledhill's file records his dismissal after just two days by Shepherd Engineering when working via the JIB agency ESCA. Gledhill applied for work at least four times via the Carillion-owned employment agency Sky Blue in 2002-2003 and each time his blacklist file records how HR manager Liz Keates was given the details and the company refused to employ him. Carillion also refused to employ him at Gatwick Airport in 2000.

In an attempt to overcome the vetting process, many simply 'forgot' to mention the JLE when applying for new jobs. Unfortunately the blacklisting firms had thought of that too:

> *Employed by Drake & sculls at Jubilee Line. Was actively involved in the issues which arose during the term of the contract.*
>
> *Advice is to take up references on previous employers on application.*
> *NOTE: Known to have worked at the Jubilee Line should this not appear on his application form.*

It was obvious to the JLE electricians that they were being blacklisted. Danny Regan from east London was one of the electricians who had first raised concerns about the lack of running water on the JLE. He recalls how building-site managers were completely open about blacklisting:

> ❝There were years and years of threats from them: "you will never work again", "we will make it hard for you to work in London", "you will not have any friends in the construction industry, we will make sure of that".
>
> I used to get 25 phone calls per day asking me to work for them and now I get zero, and no-one wants me to work for them. To say this has ruined my career is a massive understatement because it has totally finished my career. I have spent more of my children's birthdays and Christmases out of work than in work. We all have, in black and white, files from the ICO showing how they systematically kept us out of work.❞

And it was not just those in the front line of action who were targeted, as retired Manchester electrician Ray Morris remembers:

❛I worked on the Jubilee Line for just over a year. The only strike that I actually took part in was a health-and-safety issue, the fire-alarm system at London Bridge station. When the job was over, everyone who worked on the Jubilee Line was blacklisted.❜

'Please keep this information confidential'

Morris' suspicions were well founded, as the JLE electricians were not only being blacklisted by The Consulting Association. Group Personnel Director for Drake & Scull at the time was Sheila Knight, one-time Assistant Director of the government arbitration service ACAS. On 8 August 2000, she sent a memo to a number of labour managers in other companies on major projects with a list of the names and national insurance numbers of every Drake & Scull worker on the Jubilee Line, adding in the text of the message 'Please keep this information confidential'.

One of the recipients of the email was Alan Wainwright, who was employed by Haden Young Limited (a subsidiary of Balfour Beatty) at the time. Wainwright says that Michael Aird, labour manager and TCA main contact for another subsidiary, Balfour Kilpatrick, reciprocated by sending Knight a list of the names and

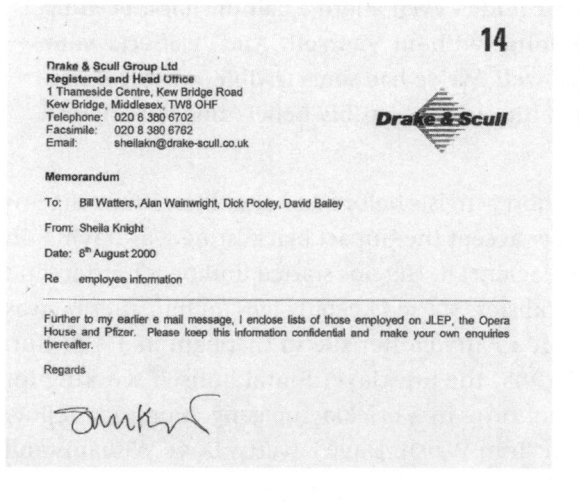

Memo sent by Sheila Knight with a list of electricians working on Jubilee Line

national insurance numbers of every Balfour Kilpatrick employee at the Royal Opera House and Pfizers.[13] It was these lists of electricians circulated by Knight that were used as evidence by the ICO to convince a judge to grant the warrant that allowed the raid on TCA.

The Sheila Knight list is separate to that held by The Consulting Association but both Balfour Kilpatrick (now Balfour Beatty Engineering Services) and Drake & Scull (now Emcor) were amongst the most active subscribers to TCA. It is therefore hardly surprising that many workers from Pfizers, the Royal Opera House and JLE appear on both lists and suffered continued difficulties in their career progression. At least two workers from the JLE have committed suicide. Whether difficulty finding work was a contributory factor will probably never be known.

Glaswegian bricklayer Brian Higgins has the stamp of a heavyweight boxer and, set in front of an audience, his speeches pull no punches. He is secretary of Northampton UCATT branch and of the Building Worker Group, a rank-and-file group that attracted many activists during the 1980s. His 49-page Consulting Association file is the largest on the database. His long-suffering wife Helen recalls holding down three jobs at once to try and bring money in to make sure their two girls had what they needed while Higgins was on strike. She said:

> I've seen myself putting cardboard in my shoes when Brian was on strike. I couldn't even afford a pair of shoes. Feeding the kids and doing without yourself. And it affects your relationships as well. We've had some terrible, terrible times. I never did ask him to give up his beliefs but I'm angry – so angry.[14]

But, like other union activists before and after him, Brian Higgins did not just passively accept the impact blacklisting was having on his family: he raged against it. Higgins started finding it hard to find work when the blacklisters started keeping tabs on him after he was elected convenor on a Fairweather site in Clapham in 1978. But, in the summer of 1985, the bricklayer found himself working for a company called Jonoroy in a bricklaying gang, alongside fellow union-minded men: Tom Walsh, Dave Laverty, Dave Williams and two hod carriers, Ray Mills and Jim Whitegaze.

With 200 houses for the subcontractor Jonoroy on the Laing's site in Surbiton, there was potentially two years' work in front of them. Everybody kept their heads down because they needed the money but a month into the job a Jonoroy manager told them he was letting them go because 'Laing's have told me you're union men'. Higgins recalls:

> ❝We were just so fucking angry, pissed off and fed up with getting blacklisted. But you knew it was all tied up with the right to belong to a union and democratic election of a shop steward on site, it was all part of that general fighting, and we were conscious that it wasn't just about us individually, it was a collective thing.❞[15]

And so started the Laing's Lock Out dispute. The six started off picketing their own site in south London but within a few days the picketing had spread to the biggest Laing's job in London, the British Library. The dispute became a focal point for other unemployed builders and flying pickets stopped lorries and disrupted production on a total of 14 Laing's sites, including at Hays Wharf near London Bridge. A conciliation panel was convened under the National Joint Council for the building industry, which eventually agreed that the workers would be temporarily employed on a site at Banstead before returning to Surbiton in January 1986.

The Laing's Lock Out is recorded on Higgins' blacklist file:

> *1985 October 30 'Lockout Committee Chairman' – at Laing's Superhomes site. Currently chairman – Eastern Region of UCATT*

Despite the conciliation panel's decision, when the bricklayers returned to Surbiton, the main contractor refused to take the workers back and the Laing's Lock Out Committee again visited sites across the capital. In February 1986 a High Court injunction was granted to six companies within the Laing group, naming the four bricklayers and two hod carriers as defendants with the threat of hefty fines or imprisonment if they did not desist from their actions. Instead they stepped up picketing and used the injunction as a means to address mass meetings of print workers and at the Ford plant in Dagenham. Refuse workers declared that they would park their dustcarts outside Pentonville Prison if the building workers were jailed. The dispute lasted six months, during which Albert Williams, then UCATT general secretary, repudiated the action and Higgins' claims to have received death threats. Eventually the workers were forced to 'give it up and walk away to fight again another day', as Higgins describes it.

Afterwards all the participants found it virtually impossible to find any long-term employment. Higgins got a few weeks' work for an employment agency but that dried up very quickly. Higgins says,

> After the lockout, as you can imagine, the blacklist intensified industry wide. After defying the High Court, I couldn't get work anywhere, any industry – nothing.

The secret war uncovered

Blacklisting was rife across the building industry and industrial disputes to defend victimized stewards and safety reps were commonplace over decades. But it was not until 20 years later in Manchester, when another group of workers took a principled decision to take a stand, that the issue of blacklisting would again have such a high profile.

Industrial relations in the building industry do not constitute a cosy discussion around a table: this is a war. A war in which some people are bullied, assaulted and lose their lives, while others make a lot of money. A war between big business and a dedicated nucleus of union activists trying to build a safer workplace and better living standards for their families. It is a war that occasionally explodes into the public consciousness during a big strike but most of the time is carried out in secret by both sides. Businesses hide their dirty secrets in order to protect their corporate brands. Union activists organize clandestine meetings in order to protect themselves from persecution. The discovery of The Consulting Association blacklist in 2009 was the first hint to the outside world of what that secret war between big business and union activists was really like. When campaigners dug deeper, they would discover the unprecedented scale of this abuse of workers' human rights.

1 Quoted in Ayre, Barker, French, Graham, Harker, *The Flying Pickets: The 1972 builders' strike and the Shrewsbury pickets*, The Des Warren Trust Fund, 2008. 2 Speech to the Blacklist Support Group AGM in 2013. 3 Dept for Business Information & Skills, **nin.tl/unionmemb2012** 4 John McAllion MP, Hansard, 26 October 1999. 5 *Enough is Enough: It's time to fight* and *support the Vascrofts Strike* (1992) – A5 and A4 leaflets produced by the JSC during the three separate Vascrofts disputes. 6 Interview with the authors. 7 'Contractors plan legal moves over JSC', *New Civil Engineer*, June 1992. 8 Interview with the authors. 9 Interview with the authors. 10 Interview with the authors. 11 Interview with the authors. 12 *Builders Crack: The Movie*, Unionfilms, 1999. 13 House of Commons Scottish Affairs Select Committee, Blacklisting in Employment – Written & Oral Evidence. 14 Interview with the authors. 15 Interview with the authors.

5

Out of time and out of order

Despite all the media coverage when The Consulting Association (TCA) was raided in 2009, few realized that, shockingly, it was not against UK law to blacklist a worker because of their trade-union activities. Back in the 1997 General Election, Labour had promised to make the practice illegal. UCATT Executive Council member Tony Farrell addressed the first union conference after the election of the Blair government. He said:

> One of the greatest things as far as I am concerned, they are going to outlaw the blacklisting of trade unionists. I can tell you, comrades, there were times when I could not go with my mates on the job because they got the sack as I got the sack as soon as I gave them my National Insurance number.[1]

In 2009, Farrell found out the reason for his continual loss of employment: he was one of those on the TCA blacklist.

True to their word, in 1999 the government drafted a set of regulations to make blacklisting illegal as part of the Employment Relations Act. During a debate in the House of Commons on 30 March 1999, Stephen Byers, the Secretary of State for Trade and Industry, laid out the government view: 'We believe that it should be a criminal offence to use such a list for the purpose of blacklisting individuals.'

The distinction between blacklisting being a criminal rather than civil offence is important. If civil employment rights are granted by legislation, it is up to an individual to enforce those rights by gathering the evidence themselves and raising the issue with their employer or bringing a claim to an Employment Tribunal. The only sanction in court for a civil claim is compensation (in most employment law this is limited to loss of earnings). In criminal law, it is the state that enforces the legislation. The police, Health and Safety Executive or other enforcing authorities have the powers to investigate an offence and, if found guilty in court, the perpetrators can be jailed.

Byers told the authors: 'One of the most formative events for me personally was the 1972 building workers' strike. I was in my late teens and living in the Northwest. Many good men lost their jobs and experienced a lifetime of being denied work due to being blacklisted.'[2]

Unfortunately, despite the many fine words and personal experience of Labour MPs, the draft regulations signalled by the then government were never implemented. In 2003, a Department of Trade and Industry review of the Act was published and the regulations were put out for consultation once more. The official government line was clear:

> There has been no known case of blacklisting – covert or overt – since the 1980s. In part, these changes reflect the improved state of employment relations today. In line with good regulatory practice, the government considers it inappropriate to introduce regulations where there is no evidence that a problem has existed for over a decade.[3]

There was considerable lobbying by employers' trade associations during the consultation. The Confederation of British Industry, Engineering Employers Federation and Newspaper Society all formally voiced their opposition to implementing the regulations. The TUC, Unison, Association of University Teachers, Graphical, Paper and Media Union, Northern Ireland Public Service Union, the Work Foundation and Thompson's solicitors all supported immediate introduction. UCATT, TGWU and GMB all supported the government's position that no regulations needed to be introduced until 'evidence emerged of the problem reoccurring'. Amicus did not make any submission to the consultation. The ICO response was: 'We have no specific comments to make on the draft regulations.'[4]

This was an opportunity to present the numerous examples of

ongoing blacklisting in the building industry and influence the government. Yet the government records: 'No respondent reported any evidence or knowledge of blacklisting taking place in recent years.'

This was in 2003, when hundreds of union members remained unemployed, especially those who had worked on the Jubilee Line, Pfizers and Royal Opera House and when the DAF dispute at Manchester Piccadilly over blacklisting was being supported by the local union movement.

In 2005, following calls by Tameside and Manchester Trades Councils, the National Conference of Trade Union Councils passed a motion against ongoing blacklisting in the building industry. But the motion did not move the Labour government, which considered that evidence of blacklisting was only anecdotal.

After the consultation, the draft regulations were forgotten about until The Consulting Association scandal broke. An adjournment debate was held almost immediately and Mick Clapham MP told the House of Commons: 'Now that evidence has emerged that blacklisting is taking place, it is time to bring them [the regulations] into effect'.[5] So the Labour government launched yet another consultation process – except that any mention of blacklisting being a criminal offence had now vanished from the draft proposals.

As part of its submission to the new consultation, UCATT commissioned Keith Ewing, President of the Institute of Employment Rights and Professor of Public Law at Kings College London, to carry out research. The result was published in August 2009 as *Ruined Lives: Blacklisting in the UK construction industry*. At the time it was the only academic paper on the scandal and remained the foremost investigation until the Scottish Affairs Select Committee's first interim report in 2013. *Ruined Lives* provides a legal overview of the scandal and critiques the inadequacies of the government proposals.

The Blacklist Support Group (BSG) submission highlighted a major shortcoming in that blacklisted workers could only make a claim against the company that refused to employ them. In The Consulting Association situation, it was the major contractors that orchestrated the blacklist but these companies hardly ever employed carpenters, bricklayers or electricians themselves. As the BSG submission said:

> Even if the proposed Blacklisting Regulations were introduced today, as they stand, most of the current Consulting Association claims would be no better off. The proposed regulations are only an improvement on the current situation if they are enforceable against those guilty of blacklisting.[96]

UCATT general secretary Alan Ritchie's response to the limited protection offered to those involved in union activities was a lot stronger than his union's supine effort in 2003 had been:

> Blacklisting took place on the basis of raising health-and-safety concerns, press comments, and even alleged political affiliations. These and a number of other factors fall outside the regulatory protections. The proposed regulations will therefore not stop blacklisting... Given the narrow definitions in the proposed legislation much normal trade-union activity will fall on the wrong side of the line.[97]

Another loophole was that any worker who was blacklisted after raising concerns about safety would only be protected if they were a member of a trade union. Whistleblower protection in the UK is notoriously poor despite the introduction of the Public Interest Disclosure Act 1998, yet these regulations would do little to bolster that support.[8]

One industry body's consultation response argued that 'vetting of prospective employees was necessary to weed out troublemakers, criminal elements and other undesirable people'. The government reassuringly responded: 'Virtually all vetting activity, which should normally have nothing to do with trade-union matters, is left unaffected.'[9]

The Employment Relations Act 1999 (Blacklists) Regulations 2010 was one of the last pieces of legislation passed by the Labour government. It bans the use of blacklists of trade unionists, makes it unlawful for an employer or employment agency to refuse employment, to dismiss or cause detriment to a worker for a reason related to a blacklist and provides for a minimum £5,000 compensation award at tribunal.

Despite these headline changes, the lobbying had paid off and, although the new regulations were a step forward, the failure to make blacklisting a criminal offence was a major flaw. Professor Ewing said: 'The blacklisting of construction workers because of their trade-union activities is a vile practice, which the current government has, to its eternal shame, done next to nothing to eradicate, and even less to compensate the victims.'[10]

Further, the small legislative step was enough to give future employment ministers a ready-made answer to requests for greater workplace protection. Unions had asked for blacklisting to be outlawed and now it was – what more did they want? To some extent, Labour's fag-end piece of legislation did more harm than good by shutting down the debate on legal safeguards.

Employment Tribunals

Even if blacklisting wasn't expressly against the law, the details in the files seemed to offer clear evidence that could be used in Employment Tribunals. However, as we shall see, having evidence of being blacklisted was not enough to gain legal redress and this exposes fundamental problems in the current tribunal system. Indeed, in one case, as we shall see, a company proudly submitted the blacklisting evidence as its justification for sacking a worker.

Almost immediately after the scandal broke blacklisted workers and their unions started submitting Employment Tribunal claims. Some claims were submitted after receiving legal guidance from solicitors, while others were rapidly sent in by the workers without getting advice. The result was that every conceivable claim was put in, from unfair dismissal and trade-union victimization to discrimination on the basis of religion or belief and human rights. By the autumn of 2009 there were in excess of 60 claims being heard across the country by different judges.

Prior to 2009, blacklisting cases were unheard of at a Tribunal. The Consulting Association threw up many complex and unusual points of law. The President of the Employment Tribunal, Judge David Latham, therefore made a decision to transfer all of the blacklisting cases to the Manchester Tribunal, where Judge Jonathan Brain would hear all the cases.

The joint Case Management Discussion (CMD) covering all

the claims took place on 24 November 2009 in Manchester; blacklisted workers travelled from around the country to attend the hearing. CMDs are the first stage of the Employment Tribunal process, before any witnesses are called or evidence is heard. It is a short meeting arranged to sort out certain technical issues – what the claim is actually about and whether the tribunal has the jurisdiction to hear it – and for the judge to place orders on both sides to submit certain documents by particular dates. They are very low-key affairs without the need for a claimant to be present and no press.

The Manchester CMD lasted a whole day with over 60 people in court at one point. Nick Toms acted as lead barrister for the claimants, supported by David Renton as counsel. The Court allowed four claims already under way – Michael Dooley, Phil Willis, Steve Acheson and Paul Tattersfield – to continue at their original locations. All other claims were to be heard at Manchester. At the time, blacklisted workers were very upbeat about their chances. In an attempt to get the Tribunal claims thrown out, lawyers for the employers raised a number of issues. The Case Management Order issued by Judge Brain stated that, prior to going to a full Tribunal, all cases would be required to go through a Pre-Hearing Review (PHR). One of the main issues he highlighted was: 'Whether or not the claims as pleaded have been brought in time or, where they have not, whether the Tribunal should exercise its jurisdiction to extend time to hear the claim.'[11]

The employers' lawyers had rightly spotted that the claimants were up against the clock. To be able to go to an Employment Tribunal, any claim needs to be submitted within three months of the date of the incident being complained about. This is a well-known rule and union training courses make a big point of highlighting to new shop stewards the dangers of missing this time limit. The rule is very strictly interpreted and there have been cases disqualified because an email was sent before the deadline but not delivered until a few minutes after midnight on the cut-off date. Under exceptional circumstances, for example if an incident resulted in a claimant being hospitalized, the Tribunal is able to extend the time limit. How much additional time is allowed in these exceptional cases is not specified in statute.

What then of the blacklisting cases? Some of the incidents identified on the files relate to incidents not three months earlier but three decades. It was obviously not possible to complain about being refused work due to your trade-union membership in 1992 if the evidence only came to light in 2009. But when a blacklisted worker received their file in the post from the ICO; how long did they have to submit an Employment Tribunal claim?

Blacklisted workers didn't have long to wait to find out the answer to that legal question. Between July and October 2010, three claims were heard at the Manchester Tribunal that would set the pattern for virtually every other case.

Howard Nolan's blacklist file has entries that record how he was refused work on two separate Balfour Beatty sites: Pfizers in Kent in 2001 and in Newcastle in 2006. One of the applications for work was via the employment agency Beaver Management Services Limited (BMS). After receiving his blacklist file on 14 May 2009 and contacting his union, a solicitor and the Citizens Advice Bureau, Nolan completed the ET1 form himself on 28 July 2009. This was 11 weeks after receiving his file, well within the three months that he believed he had to make an application.

By the time he reached court, Nolan was supported by Unite and was represented by Nick Toms – but his arguments as to why the case should proceed were rejected, although Judge Brain admitted that 'it is, of course, impossible not to have sympathy with the difficult personal circumstances in which the claimant found himself'. He ruled in favour of Balfour Beatty, finding the claim was 'presented out of time and the time will not be extended to enable me to consider them'; the stated reason being that the claimant had 'sat on his hands for too long'.[12] An appeal by Unite was also rejected.

Balfour Beatty was back in Manchester for another Tribunal in August 2010, again in front of Judge Brain. This was the case of East London electrician John Cullinane. This time the written judgment describes how the claimant had acted 'reasonably quickly' and agrees that 'these cases are complex and it would be unreasonable to expect the claimant to present the claims himself without the benefit of trade union or legal assistance'.

Within four days of receiving his file, on 30 March 2009,

Cullinane had contacted Unite, who had forwarded his file to their solicitors. The application was submitted on 14 May, only seven weeks after the file had been received. Yet the inflexible judgment found that:

> This is an unfortunate outcome for the claimant who, I find, did all that he reasonably could himself to put in hand steps to have his claim determined. However, I find that a seven-week delay is simply too long to be reasonable.[13]

In October 2010, an identical decision was reached in the UCATT-sponsored case of *Phil McNeilis v Balfour Beatty*. Judge Brain dismissed the claim by the carpenter and former shop steward, saying he and his solicitors had 'slept on his rights'.

This harsh interpretation of time limits was to be repeated many times over the next three years, with Unite and UCATT members still having their claims dismissed as late as 2012. Of course, there do have to be time limits in legal procedures but legislation does not specify how much additional time should be allowed when it is not 'reasonably practicable' to bring a claim within the original three-month period; the decision rests entirely with the court. An excessive delay would supposedly place a terrible burden upon any employer. But when the blacklisting firms had deliberately hidden their illegal activity for decades, it is difficult to see how they would suffer any burden whatsoever by waiting a few days.

The lawyer Nick Toms reflected:

> Ultimately, it was unfortunate the decision was taken to case manage all the blacklisting cases in Manchester. There seemed no good reason for this given each case depended on its own facts. Elsewhere in the country some judges had shown a great deal of sympathy for the claimants. However, it rapidly became clear that the Manchester Tribunal was going to take a hard line on whether the claims were presented in time. It was a very unusual situation but little leeway was offered and many cases were struck out without the merits ever being considered.

Experienced lawyers consider the rulings by Judge Brain particularly harsh. He had stated that his overriding objective in looking at the cases was to ensure that they were dealt with justly, which meant

> ❛ensuring that the parties are on an equal footing; dealing with the case in ways that are proportionate to the complexity and importance of the issues; ensuring that it is dealt with expeditiously and fairly; and saving costs.❜[14]

But it is difficult to square this when on one side were retired or ex-building workers with only the most rudimentary (if any) knowledge of the law; on the other side blue-chip construction giants with expensive legal teams.

On a number of occasions the written judgments identify delays by unions and their solicitors. Someone untrained may not appreciate the nuances of employment law but lawyers are paid handsomely for their expertise. Where solicitors gave incorrect advice, those blacklisted workers who lost their opportunity to be heard in court have every right to feel aggrieved. However, the decision on whether or not to allow the blacklisting cases to continue was entirely at the discretion of the judge. These particularly unsympathetic rulings resulted in every single case heard by Judge Brain being denied the opportunity to have that evidence aired in court.

The Dooley case

In addition to the time-limit issue, another major legal hurdle stood in the way of blacklisted workers. This was employee status: a crucial issue in UK employment law. You can only claim unfair dismissal, redundancy and other breaches of employment law if you are a direct employee. What then of a situation where an individual was blacklisted by a major contractor but was employed via a sub-contractor?

Michael Dooley v Balfour Beatty was one of the few claims allowed to proceed after the Manchester CMD. It became the first unfair dismissal claim to reach a full hearing at the Central London Employment Tribunal in January 2010. A majority decision found in favour of the company. This was despite documentary evidence showing that Balfour Beatty had supplied information to the blacklist database being shown to the Tribunal (which

Judge Charlton described as 'ghastly' in court and 'an abuse of people's rights' in the written judgment).[15] Balfour Beatty did not dispute the blacklisting evidence. With commendable chutzpah, the company had provided the blacklist file as part of *their* bundle of documents. It argued that the information on the file was justification for Dooley's dismissal from a West London building site in early 1993. The Tribunal decision turned on the question of employee status and found that Dooley was working for a sub-contractor called Bansal Building Company Limited and was not an employee of Balfour Beatty. Since only 'employees' are covered by unfair dismissal legislation, the claim was lost.

The Dooley scenario is typical of many of the blacklisting cases because most construction workers are employed by sub-contractors, employment agencies or are nominally 'self-employed'. The reality of how the blacklist operated in the building industry is that the major contractors set up The Consulting Association to co-ordinate the sharing of information about trade unionists. It is the major contractors who exercise control on large projects. It was the major contractors who used the blacklist to deny employment to trade unionists who appear on The Consulting Association database. Even when they are not employing the workers directly themselves, they use their influence with the sub-contractors and the employment agencies to achieve the outcome of refusing employment to trade unionists and activists. The blacklist files are clear evidence of this. But as the major contractors did not directly employ the workers they blacklisted, they become removed from the legal remedy of unfair dismissal.

Another disturbing element of the Dooley decision relates to the truthfulness of the entries on the blacklist files. Much of the information held on the TCA database is wildly inaccurate or constitutes little more than malicious smears. Incidents are exaggerated out of all proportion. Terms such as 'troublemaker', 'communist' and 'unlawful' are used like confetti and without evidence. One file accuses a safety rep of arson, while another claims a blacklisted electrician attacked a site agent with a hammer. Both allegations are untrue. Hundreds are accused of participating in unofficial strike action or violence without the slightest shred of evidence. The lawyer for Balfour Beatty argued that 'it is not an issue of whether the contents of the blacklist dossier were accurate or not' but that after reading the information on Dooley's file 'any employer would be concerned' and this would make the dismissal fair in law.

While the Tribunal found that Dooley's claim for unfair dismissal failed because he was not a direct employee of Balfour Beatty, Judge Charlton mused on the information in the file:

> If we had found that Mr Dooley had been directly employed by Balfour Beatty, we would have no doubt that Balfour Beatty as a subscriber to the blacklist would have consulted it with regards to his appointment... the correct test was to consider what was in the mind of the person making the decision to terminate employment when he took the decision. We would have decided that it was the contents of the dossier... and that the dossier principally refers to activity not within the protection of the statute but unlawful activity and whether those allegations were true or not it is the majority view that this would have given rise to the decision to dismiss.[16]

So having checked Dooley against an illegal blacklist, even where information was completely untrue, if the term 'unofficial' was written on the file, the company would have acted within the law to dismiss. The judgment clearly identifies a weakness in the Blacklisting Regulations 2010, which only cover the narrowly defined 'official union duties'. Even if they had been in place at the time, they would not have protected Dooley.

During 2010, there was a noticeable change of attitude by the unions and their solicitors. The original positive outlook altered as Thompsons and OH Parsons began receiving letters from the companies quoting the Dooley, Nolan and Cullinane decisions and threatening the claimants with costs. Solicitors started to telephone their clients to tell them that the union was no longer prepared to represent them because they were likely to lose on either time-limits or employee status. The blacklisting cases were being assessed purely on the legal merits of the cases rather than as an element of a wider campaign to expose the wrongdoings of the companies. What appeared to be lacking in the original evaluation of the Tribunal cases was any overarching strategic plan. In some cases there was a hastily agreed compromise agreement signed (the average settlements for these were around £1,000) but in most cases the claims were simply dropped.

For UCATT member John Jones, legal representation was withdrawn only a few days before his hearing was set to take place. The retired bricklayer was left with the option of representing himself, with the danger of costs being awarded against him, or dropping the claim. Like many others, he reluctantly agreed to withdraw his complaint, even though he had already paid for a hotel and train ticket to Manchester from his home in Kent (eventually reimbursed by the union). As it was the union lawyers who had submitted the Tribunal claims in the first place, there was considerable criticism by the disgruntled claimants.

Of all the Tribunal claims submitted, a grand total of five cases actually had their day in court, each time with more unredacted evidence disclosed by the ICO and the employers. To date, only three claimants have been successful at Employment Tribunal: Phil Willis, Paul Tattersfield and Steve Acheson. All three were successfully represented by Nick Toms and Unite.

Phil Willis v CB&I

The *Phil Willis v CB&I* case was based around the refusal to employ the steel erector on the Isle of Grain power station site in Kent in September 2007. The Unite member from Kent was one of the workers that erected the iconic yellow masts of the Millennium Dome and is a prominent trade unionist, having been the shop steward on both Canary Wharf and Heathrow Terminal 5. His wife Cathie is a well-known union activist in her own right.

Willis applied to CB&I by submitting an application form but also had his CV given to Ron Barron, the senior HR manager and Employee Relations manager responsible for recruiting labour on the site. Willis received a letter from the company saying that they were recruiting in the next three months but he was never contacted again. When his blacklist file was disclosed in 2009, it transpired that entries had been added from CB&I at the time of his application, even though he had never worked for the company.

The written judgment in the case shows how Ron Barron, the

Phil Willis

Phil Willis at Canary Wharf

CB&I main contact for The Consulting Association, was a regular user of the blacklisting database. In the six months between April and September 2007 he had made 984 name checks at the cost of £2,164.80. Barron had actually introduced the blacklisting procedure to CB&I and is quoted as the source of the information added to The Consulting Association about Phil Willis in October 2007.

The judgment recorded its annoyance that despite being a key witness who used the blacklist as a matter of routine, Barron refused to attend the court case, even though he lived in Ashford, the very town where the case was being heard. The Tribunal 'concluded that the sole purpose of TCA database was use as a blacklist'[17] and Phil Willis became the first person to win an employment tribunal specifically for having been blacklisted by The Consulting Association. Willis was awarded £18,375 compensation for loss of earnings and hurt to feelings, of which £2,000 was for 'aggravated damages' – a pay-out almost unheard of in UK employment law. Ron Barron will appear again in this story when we look at allegations of blacklisting on current projects such as Crossrail.

Paul Tattersfield v Balfour Beatty

Aggravated damages were also awarded to Paul Tattersfield following his successful Employment Tribunal decision against

Balfour Beatty Engineering Services in February 2011. Tattersfield had been denied work by Balfour Kilpatrick (now BBES) at the Lindsey Oil Refinery, close to his home in Hull, in September 2008. The key company witness in the case was Gerry Harvey, director of human resources at BBES and the firm's main contact with The Consulting Association. The written judgment records Harvey's evidence that he had personally attended a number of TCA meetings and that the company recruitment process was based upon 'whether The Consulting Association holds any records relating to the applicant'.

A document seen by the authors records Harvey's description of how TCA checks worked once he took over from Armar Johnston in 2005. He delegated the role of Main Contact first to Brenda Connor and then to Elaine Gallagher in the Human Resources team. It demonstrates that people's livelihoods were being decided in a secret, unaccountable and arbitrary manner.

> ❛I made it clear to both ... that if information came back from Ian Kerr that indicated an individual had been involved in a previous industrial dispute, they needed to use their own judgement to decide whether or not BK should employ the individual. For example, whether the individual had been a leader or a follower in a dispute and the nature of the dispute would be relevant to the decision.
>
> Given her time in the role and experience, Brenda Connor did not often discuss her decision making with me whereas Elaine Gallagher would generally discuss issues with me before making a decision whether or not to employ an individual, but this was not the case on every occasion that there was a match. No other people in the Human Resources team at BK had contact with Mr Kerr or The Consulting Association to discuss any information held by The Consulting Association on an individual.❜[18]

The written judgment records that 'at no stage in these proceedings has the respondent led any evidence that the claimant was anything but a good electrician'. The judgment reprints extracts from the TCA blacklist file, which it describes as 'direct evidence of trade-union discrimination':

> *2007 December: above applied to 3221/M in North East and was not furthered. 3221/M main contact states that 'serious concerns' have been expressed. An active member of UNITE-amicus. A member of the North East J.I.B. committee. He has been around for some time.*
>
> *Source: 3221/M main contact (SMcG)*
>
> *Further note via 3293 M.C. BMcA states 'He's alright, a good electrician. Ex rugby league player – gave up due to serious injury. Could be a handful if he wants to be.' Assumption from this is that B.McA would have indicated if above was sided either with D Simpson or EPIU faction. However, view was 'he'll be in the know and be demanding of everything that's due and possibly more'.*
>
> *Source: 3292 main contact (I.C.)*
>
> *2008 September 25th: Applied to 3223/F directly for Lindsey Oil Refinery Project, Immingham, NE Lincs. Main contact EG given details. Co has not furthered.*

3233/F = Balfour Kilpatrick (now BBES)
EG = Elaine Gallagher who worked in the human resources department for Balfour Kilpatrick and was managed by Gerry Harvey.
3292 = Emcor Rail (previously Drake & Scull)
I.C = Iain Coates, previously Labour Manager at Haden Young and served on the national council for the Heating and Ventilating Contractors Association.
3221/M = Morgan Est
SMcG = Steve McGuire, head of Human Resources, previously with AMEC and currently owner/director of McGuire Construction based in Preston.
BMcA = Bernard McAulay, current Unite national officer for construction.[19]

The Tribunal commented on Harvey's evidence:

❛It was only in the course of cross-examination that we discovered that Mr Harvey had attended regular meetings of The Consulting Association and he must, by this fact alone, have been considerably more aware of its activities. Mr Harvey told us that, although he attended a number of these meetings, there were no agendas nor minutes. This raises questions for us and again we are not satisfied with Mr Harvey's evidence.❜[20]

Mary Kerr, the bookkeeper for TCA, has told the authors she personally typed up the minutes from TCA meetings. She has described how there were not just meetings of the principal members but also those involved in particular sectors such as the Industrial Relations Group or Environmental Group. Up until January 2015, despite numerous requests in court and Parliament, not a single blacklisting firm had put any minutes into the public domain and all have claimed that they do not exist.

In his evidence, Tattersfield told how he had suffered long periods of unemployment since 2009 despite having made a very large number of applications. 'These companies will have long memories and this will affect my future employment,' he told the Tribunal; a sentiment with which they fully concurred.

Steve Acheson v Beaver Management Services

Following the Manchester Royal Infirmary dispute, Steve Acheson, Tony Jones and Graham Bowker continued to apply for work but were repeatedly turned down, even though it was the height of the building boom. One of the applications Acheson made was to a company called Lindhurst for work on the Fiddlers Ferry Power Station site in Warrington, Cheshire. At 8am on Friday 11 July 2008, some 12 months after he originally applied, he received a phone call and was offered employment on site to start the following Monday with at least three months' work. Acheson remembers the phone call vividly: 'Told the missus, even woke the youngster up, "guess where your dad's going on Monday?" Typical teenager, had all morning and the day off. She said, "where are you going, Dad?" I said "work". So made up, she even got out of bed. The missus was chuffed.'[21] Four hours later, Mr Ambrose, the site manager, telephoned to say the job offer was withdrawn.

Mick Holder

Steve Acheson outside the High Court

Lindhurst was a small electrical company with no connection with The Consulting Association but labour was being engaged via the employment agency Beaver Management Services Ltd (BMS), whose industrial relations manager was ex-Amicus official Jim Simms. The Unite legal department and Derek Simpson personally intervened on Acheson's behalf with the result that, at the end of August, Simms offered Acheson a job as a supervisor. Simms denies that BMS, which was not a subscriber to TCA, had any involvement in blacklisting but rather contends that it was the main contractors that vetted all staff. He said:

> ❝I'm the only person who gave Steve a job in 12 years! What would happen is someone like Carillion would need 20 electricians but would ask us to send them 40 names and they would screen them themselves.❞[22]

In the intervening six weeks since the original job offer, hundreds of workers had started on the project but Acheson had finally found himself with 12 months' work ahead of him on a unionized site under national agreements. He worked for 16 weeks before he was made redundant. There is a matrix for redundancies under a national agreement. Over 300 workers made redundant on Fiddlers Ferry Power Station project were dismissed using that matrix. Acheson claims that, when it came to him, the national agreement was temporarily suspended and an 'otherwise agreement' made which led to his early redundancy, the matrix being immediately reinstated after the redundancy was issued.

After his dismissal, Acheson submitted an Employment Tribunal claim against BMS but before the case came to court the ICO raid took place and Acheson received his blacklist file, which included detailed surveillance of him at Fiddlers Ferry. This contained the following entry, which appears in the familiar smaller font size indicating that the information was sent out to companies as part of the 'two week note' service provided by Ian Kerr. Two former Consulting Association chairmen, Stephen Quant and Trevor Watcham, have both confirmed that Acheson's name came up during discussions at TCA meetings.[23]

Stephen Acheson, EPIU Activist – Fiddlers Ferry Power Station, The Wirral

A verbal job offer was made to Stephen Acheson by a small on-site electrical sub-contractor. This was for a night shift which was later abandoned. Following this, Acheson is understood to have gathered support from fellow workers for strike action. At the request of Alstom, the project managing agent, he was transferred onto the books of BMS, acting as labour-only supplier to the site. After attempts to divert him to several smaller local sites failed, Alstom resolved matters whereby BMS offered him a senior foreman's role on site. This was effective from 18 August when Jim Simms [sic] of BMS was to go over his job specification with him.

Comment is that Acheson will keep his head down, provoking from a distance and letting others lead on confrontation. His aim continues as before, to end up in tribunal as part of a claim for trade-union activities to further the ongoing EPIU grievances against employers.

An alternative view is that BMS has knowingly taken Acheson onto their books and are confident that in the role of foreman he will find difficulty in representing the men on site. Further thoughts suggest this may be a manoeuvre to contain in the north west the EPIU activist element of Unite, weakening any EPIU actions on major projects in London and the south east.

Of interest will be his overt or covert response if fellow EPIU colleagues apply to Fiddlers Ferry and receive no offers of work.

Simms is adamant that this information did not come from him but was put together by the industrial relations officer from the contractors. Simms said:

> Alan Audley was a gobshite. What he'd do is he used to go to all the trade association meetings and say to someone "what's going on?" Someone would say "Steve Acheson is on as a foreman at Fiddlers Ferry".

> But he would fabricate something and add something on like... oh, that is to keep him quiet.[24]

Audley, who in retirement lives only a few miles from Fiddlers Ferry, refused requests by the authors to comment.

Finally, on 12 March 2013, Acheson won his claim for the original refusal of employment by Lindhurst due to his previous trade-union activities and was awarded £11,728.60 (after being out of work for four-and-a-half years).[25]

Smith v Carillion

The only remaining blacklisted worker that made it to Tribunal was Dave Smith, whose blacklist file arrived on 23 April 2009. Within days of receiving it, he supplied UCATT with a copy for use in publicity. However, his former union declined to provide any legal representation for his claim. At the time, this appeared to be a major setback. Subsequently it proved extremely fortuitous.

Smith submitted the ET1 forms against three companies that were all part of the Carillion group: Carillion PLC, Carillion (JM) Ltd (formerly John Mowlem) and Schal International on 15 July 2009, 12 weeks after he received his blacklist file. On a summer afternoon in an Italian café opposite Congress House, Smith sat down to discuss his case with David Renton. They are an unlikely pairing. Smith is from a council estate in east London. He went to a comprehensive school where he failed his O-level English. All of the male members of his family work in the construction industry. Renton, meanwhile, went to Eton and one of his uncles is Lord Renton, a former Conservative Chief Whip and the man 'in the grey suit' who told Thatcher when it was time for her to go. At the time Renton was a member of the Socialist Workers Party and a pupil barrister at the leftwing legal enclave Garden Court Chambers as well as being an active member of the socialist lawyer group, the Haldane Society.

This lunchtime meeting set the strategy for the entire case. Both agreed that the claim was unlikely to win in the British courts because of the employee status issue but viewed Keith Ewing's *Ruined Lives* document as a route plan for manoeuvring a test case into the European Court of Human Rights. It is only possible to submit a claim to the ECHR once all domestic remedies have been exhausted. On the basis of running a test case to change the law as part of a broader political campaign, Renton agreed to represent Smith on a *pro-bono* basis via the legal charity, the Free Representation Unit (FRU).

Looking back, Renton remembers:

> Dave told me "I'll be representing myself. The case is quite straightforward really. All I'm looking for is a barrister to bounce a few ideas off before I get to court." And then we discussed the time limits and how they work, and how many respondents he was suing. I knew immediately that this was something that was going to take hours and hours of work.

Other members of the Haldane Society assisted and after a few months Declan Owens, a softly spoken solicitor from Ireland who read law at Trinity College Dublin, agreed to act as solicitor via the FRU. Owens remembers why he got involved:

> When I first saw the files, I was shocked by the level of detail involved and the epic scale of the conspiracy was really brought home to me. The phrase "the banality of evil" also came to mind when I considered how TCA operated. I was dismayed how casually employees and directors of these companies could conspire to prevent people from working to feed their families.

Smith overcame the time-limit difficulty by requesting that the case be heard not in Manchester but in Central London, where the Employment Tribunal proved to be more sympathetic. The Tribunal granted a Third Party Disclosure Order allowing access to all the unredacted documents held by the ICO that referred to either Smith or the three Carillion companies. This would entail painstakingly sifting through the Consulting Association database held in the ICO offices near Manchester and identifying every page where the reference numbers for Carillion or Mowlem were recorded.

The ICO did not have enough staff to do this and the *pro-bono* lawyers suggested that Smith did it himself. This turned out to be another piece of good fortune. Four hundred pages of unredacted documentation were disclosed, including blacklist files, invoices, pages from the sales book that recorded dates of meetings, the Consulting Association constitution and the handwritten list to identify the code numbers for each company. The unredacted files meant that, for the first time, it was possible to read the names or the initials of the individuals who had supplied the information to the blacklist files. In addition, Smith was able to identify dozens of activists who had not previously applied for their files, including individuals who did not work in the construction industry, such as journalists, academics and even elected politicians.

One of the journalists with a blacklist file is Molly Cooper, one-time Executive Council member at the National Union of Journalists and secretary of the NUJ freelance branch. Cooper was shocked when she discovered she had a file.

> As a photographer you are just there to cover stories, so I cannot understand why they should open a file on you.[26]

Cooper was never aware of losing any work because of the file and now works in Higher Education.

Michelle Stanistreet, NUJ general secretary, said:

> The union is very concerned that NUJ members carrying out their legitimate work as journalists have been targeted by blacklisting companies. People targeted because of their journalistic work or trade-union activity is illegal and deplorable. The NUJ totally condemns blacklisting and the union will take action in support of journalists who fear their personal details were unlawfully recorded.[27]

At Smith's tribunal hearing in January 2012, before any witness eveidence was heard, Carillion provided a written statement to the judge that admitted blacklisting the former UCATT safety rep. They also agreed that their managers had supplied information to his blacklist file, that the reason was because of his trade-union activities and because he had raised health and safety issues. They also admitted that the blacklist had caused him a detriment.

. Dave Smith still lost the tribunal. This is because he had never been a direct employee of any of the Carillion companies but had been engaged via employment agencies when the blacklisting

Dave Smith with his legal team: (from left to right) Declan Owens, David Renton, Dave Smith and John Hendy QC.

took place. As UK employment law only protects employees, the case was lost. The written judgment from Judge Snelson concludes by stating:

> ❝ We have reached our conclusions with considerable reluctance. It seems to us that he has suffered a genuine injustice and we greatly regret that the law provides him with no remedy. ❞[28]

Smith, Renton and Owens were jubilant. This was the very outcome they had hoped for.

At the Employment Appeal Tribunal (EAT) John Hendy QC volunteered to join the FRU legal team. Hendy represented the NUM during the miners' strike, Unite in the British Airways dispute and pretty much every progressive and trade-union cause in between. He is a campaigner as well as a lawyer, just as much a regular at union conferences as the Supreme Court. In 2013, he was awarded Employment Silk of the Year at the Legal 500 Awards. At a time when he could be naming his price, he decided to act *pro bono* in the *Smith v Carillion* case.

In the appeal heard in October 2013, Hendy argued that blacklisting breached Articles 8 and 11 of the European Convention on Human Rights (ECHR) and that the original Employment Tribunal had a duty under the Human Rights Act to interpret

UK legislation in such a way as to uphold Convention rights. The written EAT judgment by Mrs Justice Slade acknowledged the human rights violations and expressed concern that Smith 'suffered an injustice from blacklisting' but again found in favour of Carillion because the claimant was not directly employed by the construction transnational but by an employment agency.[29]

The decision was appealed again with Hendy asking the Court of Appeal to issue a *Declaration of Non-Compatibility* with the ECHR as Smith's human rights under the Convention were patently not being protected by UK employment law. In June 2014, lawyers acting on behalf of then Secretary of State Vince Cable intervened in the case and provided a written submission, which, for the very first time, presented the UK government's legal position on the human rights issue. Paragraph 58 reads:

> The Secretary of State accepts that the Appellant's Article 8 rights were engaged by the conduct of the Respondent. There has been an interference with his right to respect his family life due to covert collection of data on him.

Paragraph 61 reads:

> The Secretary of State accepts that the Appellant's Article 11 rights were engaged by the activities of the Respondent, insofar as they would have breached s.146 TULRCA (but for the issue of his employment status).[30]

This is the UK government admitting that blacklisting of trade unionists is a breach of Articles 8 and 11 of the European Convention on Human Rights and that the only reason that Smith did not win his case was because of his employment status. Despite this massive legal admission, the UK government intervened in the case in order to fight against Smith and argued that the Court should not issue a declaration of non-compatibility.

Following the Secretary of State's intervention, Hendy and Renton responded:

> The European Convention is to be considered in the light of the fact that it was drawn up in the aftermath of the Second World War to prevent in future the development of totalitarian

regimes such as that of Nazi Germany by forestalling the incremental abuses of human rights which lead such regimes ultimately to the grotesque atrocities for which they are responsible. Blacklisting of workers was precisely one of the early abuses by which the Nazis suppressed opposition to their rule from the labour and trade-union movement.'[31]

Smith lost his appeal and the case is now lodged at the European Court of Human Rights in Strasbourg.

The *Smith v Carillion* legal decision does not just concern blacklisted workers. It has an impact upon the millions forced to work through agencies or on zero-hours contracts. It makes them second-class citizens when it comes to employment rights.

Even where evidence of bosses' wrongdoing is overwhelming, it is impossible for any agency worker to win Employment Tribunal claims of this kind because of a legal decision known as the 'necessity test'. This legal precedent, handed down by unelected judges, makes it all but impossible for anyone working through an employment agency ever to be considered to have a contract with the end user (ie: the company they are actually working for). At a stroke, this excludes agency workers from a raft of legal protection, including unfair dismissal.

There is a term in employment law called 'automatic unfair dismissal', reserved for the claims where an employee is sacked after standing up for their basic legal rights, such as making a complaint about not receiving the minimum wage. In ordinary unfair-dismissal cases the claimant needs to have been employed for two years, but this is not applicable in these most serious cases. Employment law provides this 'day one' protection in case of reprisals from vindictive employers. But even in these examples that are considered to be 'automatically unfair', agency workers are still excluded.

This is most blatant in the case of trade-union victimization, which is a basic human right enshrined in Article 11 of the European Convention on Human Rights, and is supposed to apply to 'everyone'. But as the Carillion test-case demonstrates, in UK employment law, Article 11 only really applies to direct employees.

The legal loophole that allows agency workers to be unfairly dismissed, blacklisted and victimized for raising health-and-safety concerns with no legal redress whatsoever needs to be closed. Hendy, Renton and Owens worked *pro-bono* for many years precisely in an attempt to break the log jam of the 'necessity test' ruling. However, the Supreme Court has slammed the door shut. Therefore, any change will require statutory provision.

The Supreme Court letter announcing the failure of the appeal arrived in the same week that two agency workers working at Canary Wharf and Oxford Circus were dismissed within hours of being elected as Unite shop stewards. So long as the 'necessity test' denies full equality before the law, employers will continue to sack agency workers with legal impunity. This has got to stop.

Smith v Carillion is a vivid example of how the expense of litigation stacks the system in favour of big business rather than ordinary working people. The *pro bono* team have spent far in excess of a thousand hours on the case and the legal fees alone would bankrupt most people if fully realized. Without *pro bono* legal support, the claim would have had little chance of achieving anything tangible within the justice system. After the final Supreme Court refusal, Carillion even tried to claim £3,500 legal costs against Smith, incurred for writing a letter and including £600 for one hour's work by a QC reading the draft. The bill was never paid.[32]

The European dimension

Of the five blacklist cases that reached the full employment tribunal hearings, the three Unite-backed cases of Willis, Tattersfield and Acheson won their claims. The two remaining cases of Dooley and Smith lost on the employee status issue. The increasing piles of unredacted TCA documents used as evidence in each case brought another small piece of the jigsaw puzzle into the public domain. It is without doubt that if the remaining ET cases had passed the time-limit test, a high proportion would have been successful in court. Even if they had failed, they would have generated publicity to highlight the inequities of the UK employment law system and provided cases to take forward to the European Court of Human Rights (ECHR).

The Consulting Association cases are not one-off incidents of unfair dismissal but centrally orchestrated prolonged victimization.

The blacklisting files provide documentary evidence of deliberate systematic breaches of the European Convention on Human Rights, which has now been publicly acknowledged by the UK government. However, the Human Rights Act (HRA) is only applicable to public bodies. As the organizations that are breaching the convention are private companies, it is not possible to make a direct claim against them under the HRA. Once claimants have exhausted legal redress, however, they can take a case to Strasbourg because the respondent becomes the government for not giving them legal protection.

Only two blacklisting cases have been lodged with the ECHR. The first was for Terry Brough, a retired bricklayer from St Helens. Supported by UCATT, John Hendy QC prepared the submission and *Brough v The UK Government* (case number 52962/11) is now being pursued.

Brough, though, remains sceptical about whether a change to the law would actually stop the practice:

> You hear many times about blacklisting going to be resolved by legislation. It will never be resolved by legislation. You can't get boots off an employer, that's legislation, that's lawful. There's only one way to beat the blacklist and that's traditional strong trade-union organization.[33]

At the time the Brough claim was submitted, it was hoped that dozens of others would be added to his case against the British government on a variety of different issues. The BSG even organized a meeting in July 2011 at John Hendy's Old Square Chambers, chaired by Professor Keith Ewing, with legal representatives from OH Parsons, the Free Representation Unit, Guney Clark & Ryan and Unite to discuss this issue. Unfortunately, because of the Employment Tribunal decisions, it seems likely that Brough and Smith will be the only human rights claims taken to the ECHR.

Howard Beckett, director of legal services at Unite, sums up the attitude of many:

> The legal system of this country has been weighted against victims of blacklisting. No-one should be in any doubt that the Tribunals had the discretion to allow those cases to proceed and

for claims to be heard on their own merit. Instead Tribunals ruled cases out and looked to turn members against their union. That the establishment again sided with employers is no surprise.[9][30]

The tribunal system had certainly failed the blacklisted workers but there were moves to try a different legal tactic – one which would hit the companies on their bottom line. The full story would not be played out until the spring of 2016 and is covered in the final chapter. For the moment, attention switched to how Parliament was investigating the scandal,

1 UCATT Conference speech, June 1998. 2 Email correspondence, 12 May 2013. 3 DTI, Review of the Employment Relations Act, February 2003, p 66. 4 DTI, Review of the ERA, 1999 – government response to the Public Consultation, December 2003, p 42, nin.tl/DTIresponse 5 Adjournment Debate in the House of Commons, 23 March 2009. 6 The Blacklisting of Trade Unionists: Consultation on revised regulations, submission from Blacklist Support Group. 7 Letter sent to members of the Joint Committee on Statutory Instruments, 15 January 2010. 8 For statistical data on whistleblowing, see the annual report from Public Concern at Work: nin.tl/whistleblowingrep 9 BIS – government response to the Public Consultation, The Blacklisting of Trade Unionists: revised draft regulations, November 2009. 10 Quoted in Blacklist Support Group press release, 8 March 2010. 11 Anthony Jones & others v BMSL Limited & others, Case Management Order, 26 November 2009. 12 Howard Nolan v (1)Balfour Beatty Engineering Services (2) Beaver Management Services Limited judgment on Pre-Hearing review. 13 J Cullinane v Balfour Beatty Engineering Services Limited, judgment on Pre-Hearing Review case, No 3202023/2009. 14 (1) P Willis v CB&I (2) P Tattersfield v Balfour Beatty Engineering Services Limited (3) S. Acheson v Beaver Management Services Limited, Case Management Order, 23 April 2010. 15 Dooley v Balfour Beatty judgment 5 March 2010. 16 Ibid. 17 Willis v CB&I judgment, 30 November 2010. 18 Witness statement for the High Court seen by the authors. 19 Bernard McAulay was contacted by the authors but declined to comment regarding any issues raised in the book. 20 Tattersfield v Balfour Beatty reserved judgment 1 March 2011. 21 Interview with the authors. 22 Interview with the authors. 23 Witness statements for High Court seen by the authors 24 Interview with the authors. 25 Acheson v Beaver Management Services Limited judgment, 11 November 2010. 26 'Senior journalists' union activist named on notorious blacklist', Union News, nin.tl/journolisted 27 'Senior journalists' union activist named on notorious blacklist', Union News, nin.tl/journolisted 28 Smith v Carillion judgment, 19 March 2012. 29 Smith v Carillion EAT judgment, 17 January 2014. 30 Smith v Carillion – written submissions on behalf of the intervener, 9 June 2014. 31 Smith v Carillion – Appellants Addendum Skeleton Argument, para 37, 18 July 2014. 32 nin.tl/Carillionsorry 33 Interview with the authors. 34 Email to the authors, 8 April 2014.

6
The gift that kept on giving

The last time he had been seen was in the dock at Knutsford Crown Court in 2009. In the three years since, Ian Kerr had stayed where he preferred: quietly at home with his family. The companies that had employed him for 16 years had clinically severed all connections. Unknown to them, he had given an interview to *The Times* but for various reasons this had not yet been published. It was a hand grenade with a delayed fuse which would be some payback for those who had cast him adrift. That period of purdah was about to end. A committee of MPs was to give the investigation new momentum.

Astonishingly, this would be the first time anyone involved in the blacklisting scandal would have faced anything like serious questions. Companies had batted away queries via their press offices, with short, carefully crafted statements or no comments. The Tribunal process had put a handful of firms in the dock to be cross-examined. The media, aside from the trade and radical press, had pretty much ignored the story. Trade-union stories, when covered by the mainstream media, usually involve industrial action. It's a simple story of barons versus bosses over better pay. Complicated issues such as health and safety, at the heart of many of the blacklisted stories, didn't fit this narrative. Honourable exceptions were the *Morning Star*, *Private Eye*, *Guardian*, *Observer* and *Mirror*, with the last focusing on the related issue of the lack of rights for agency workers.

A comparison with the phone-hacking scandal is instructive. The scandal had been rumbling on since 2006 when the first reporter had been arrested. Then, in July 2009, four months after the ICO raid, the *Guardian* revealed that News International had made huge out-of-court payments to several celebrities over phone hacking. A further 3,000 people were suspected of being victims of tabloid intrusion. The timing and numbers are uncannily close to the blacklisting figures but the difference was that the victims in this case were generally celebrities. The results of the phone-hacking scandal were mass resignations, criminal cases and a public inquiry.

This is in no way meant to underplay the significance of the phone-hacking scandal or the excellence of its reporting.[1] However, no-one had paid a similar price for intruding into the personal lives of safety representatives working on building sites. So far the scandal had been contained, despite the efforts of campaigners. Some of the companies involved had hired PR firms skilled in managing reputation damage but an expected counter-attack never materialized.[2] The likely deliberate policy was to create a vacuum and let the campaigners blow themselves out. It had taken three years but Kerr was about to fill that vacuum and the Select Committee was about to force the story on to the front pages and the front benches.

The Select Committee

The Select Committee was the most intense scrutiny that Parliament had offered so far. When the activities of The Consulting Association were revealed it was natural that questions would be raised there. Unions quickly mobilized their sponsored MPs and an Early Day Motion was lodged on the Monday, the story having broken the previous Friday. A fortnight later Labour MP Mick Clapham secured an adjournment debate. It got half an hour and veteran campaigners on the issue such as John McDonnell, who was to raise this issue repeatedly in the House, and Jim Sheridan, whose brother Joe Sheridan appears on the blacklist, spoke. All were searching for ways to make sure it could not happen again and that those responsible could be suitably punished. Responding for the government was Pat McFadden. He started off by apologizing for the weakness of his voice and then said that the government took the matter very seriously and would look at it in detail. Wolverhampton MP Ken Purchase witheringly responded: 'It is not the weakness of your voice that concerns me, but the weakness of the response that our government are making.' McFadden's holding statement did reveal that officials in his department had liaised with the Information Commissioner's Office 'at an early stage' when they became aware of its investigation. It seems that liaison did not include passing on the name of Ian Kerr, which had been given to them back in 2007.

While Early Day Motions and adjournment debates were the time-honoured way of raising issues, it was clear that something more substantial would be required. Ian Davidson was elected in 1992 for the old Glasgow Govan seat and, after boundary changes, now represents Glasgow South West. Davidson has had close support from trade unions – particularly those associated with Govan Shipbuilders, which remains a major employer in his constituency – and two of his election agents were full-time UCATT officials. One of the people Davidson beat to retain his seat in 2010 was Tommy Sheridan, who would subsequently find he had a blacklist file. Davidson became chair of the Scottish Affairs Select Committee in 2010 and the issue of health and safety was already something he wanted to investigate.

Sources have suggested that the inquiry was agreed to by Liberal Democrat and Conservative members as they guessed it would be no more than a rehashing of ancient history and in return they could get inquiries into areas that interested them. As it started to break new ground on the scandal, and as the press and public benches began to fill, the Labour members were joined by MPs from other parties as ever more high-profile witnesses gave evidence. As Davidson said: 'It just kept on unravelling. It was the gift that kept on giving.'[3]

The Committee began taking evidence on 22 May 2012 from former Glasgow MP Maria Fyfe. She spoke about her experience investigating the activities of the Economic League. Three weeks later, Dave Smith gave lengthy evidence on his experience of being blacklisted and the issues raised by the Blacklist Support Group. Though Smith was from Essex and had no direct experience of blacklisting in Scotland, Committee chair Ian Davidson said it was useful to provide some national context. A fortnight later the Committee announced it was mounting a formal inquiry. Senior figures in the construction industry, along with past members of the Economic League and representatives from the human resources sector, were about to face one of the most damaging investigations into their involvement in blacklisting.

After Smith, two Scottish electricians – Francie Graham and Steuart Merchant – gave evidence to the Committee. The Committee could have heard from all sorts of people first – but it was the tales of those who suffered who were allowed to set the agenda.

Merchant, from Dundee, has the aggravation of not knowing what exactly was held on file about him. The ICO seized a list of names and a card index – but there are more names than cards and Merchant is one of those without all the evidence. He never expected to see his name on such a list.

> ❛I have never, in my whole working life, been disciplined for poor workmanship or poor timekeeping. In fact I have never been disciplined in my working life. To get something back saying that I was on a blacklist, I can't even point at a company and say, "They must have put me on it for some reason". But there's nothing.❜[94]

Graham, in contrast, had been able to recover his file, which ran from 1975 to 2000. The effect of his blacklisting, he said, was devastating.

> ❛I think it has had a massive impact on my family. As a matter of fact, I lost my wife seven years ago. I found it hard to get work in Dundee. Therefore, I had to move out of town, and I was out of town for a lot of years. We had no family; so my wife was left on her own in Dundee. That had a massive impact on her – a massive impact. She was in the house on her own. I couldn't get local work. I had to work away. I have worked in England and Wales for years and years. I am near enough talking about the whole of my working life, maybe getting home every four weeks or six weeks for what they call a long weekend, but it is not a long weekend. You are just home and you are back on the train again. That had a massive impact on my life and on my wife's life.❜[95]

Merchant highlighted the impact upon his self-confidence:

Steuart Merchant & Francie Graham (2nd-3rd left) protesting outside Balfour Beatty HQ in Glasgow

❝There were two years during the Eighties when I couldn't get a job at any place… it begins to get you down and you begin to wonder, "Why's he getting a job? Why can't I get a job? I'm as good as him." Then you begin to get personal doubts, and you think, "Am I any good, or is it because I'm useless that I cannot get a job?" It does get you feeling… I am not suicidal but… I do know that I couldn't get a job for two years for some reason or other. I still can't get a job with any of the big companies like Balfour Kilpatrick, Baileys.❞[6]

Merchant's evidence shows that the blacklist was a blunt tool that couldn't be disclosed and whose deployment could only be guessed at. In these cases it didn't stop the men carrying out their legitimate union activities. Since neither were classed as poor performers – and since they judged themselves, and thought others did too, on their skill as electricians – it made no sense to them that they were on a blacklist. The disruption it caused them personally was never explained – they took it as part of the vagaries of the job.

Also giving evidence was whistleblower Alan Wainwright. He confirmed the secretive nature of the operation. At Carillion, he said, knowledge of the checking procedure was tightly controlled, with all name checks being co-ordinated centrally through the office of personnel director Frank Duggan. Although Wainwright submitted names to be checked, even he wasn't aware that TCA held regular meetings with representatives from companies. This climate of secrecy was backed up by Ian Kerr, who said:

❛The information wasn't just swimming around in an HR department. It was in the hands – very tightly controlled – of one individual, who, because of his or her experience in the industry, would know how to deal with that information.❜

On TCA documentation this is the 'main contact' but on the files, the full names are not divulged, only their initials.

Between Ian Kerr and Alan Wainwright, the Select Committee was provided with a list of the company directors and human resources professionals that were intimately involved with blacklisting (listed in Appendix I).

Chairs of The Consulting Association (named by Ian Kerr)
1993-96 Cullum McAlpine (Sir Robert McAlpine Ltd)
1997-99 Tony Jennings (Laing O'Rourke)
2000-01 Danny O'Sullivan (Kier)
2002-03 Stephen Quant (Skanska)
2004-05 Trevor Watcham (Balfour Beatty)
2006-09 David Cochrane (Sir Robert McAlpine Ltd)

Ian Kerr's wife Mary has told the authors that, despite the number of names coming through from subscriber companies, only a fraction ever matched a file. Her recollection is that on average only about eight names a month ever scored a hit. 'You actually got a little thrill, a little bolt of adrenalin if one of them matched,' she said.

In his evidence to the Committee, Wainwright suggested a similar 'hit rate'. But he also said that at least one company was operating a parallel list that saved it the expense of having to check with TCA. He told MPs:

❛If a name came back as a "no", then a marker would be put in the database to save us redoubling a check. I think that then makes Carillion a data controller legally. If you look at when I left, as I say, there were at most probably only five noes... Carillion are holding the data in that database, if they continued using it after I left, and I can't see any reason why they would stop.'

Each evidence session was pulling back the curtain that little bit further. It was to prove vital, along with evidence from others, in union campaigns to target those responsible. A sign of the kind of revelations the Select Committee would provide came during the evidence from David Clancy from the ICO, who was one of the earliest witnesses to be called. A casual question from the Committee elicited the fact that the ICO had only seized between 5 and 10 per cent of the material from Kerr's office. The ICO maintained that its warrant restricted it to seizing the information on the construction blacklist. The warrant issued by Manchester Crown Court authorized the ICO to seize material to achieve three objectives. The first was to 'to inspect and seize any documentation that may provide evidence of the existence and operation of the blacklist in breach of the data protection principles'. The second was 'to inspect and seize any documentation or materials relating to telecommunications service providers whose systems may have been used to facilitate the transmission of communications relating to the blacklist'. Finally it authorized the investigators 'to inspect and seize any electronic media that may contain evidence of the operation of the blacklist'.

Under repeated questioning as to why they had left so much material, Clancy said:

> 'I was just satisfied at the time. We went in there and looked for the information. We had spoken to Kerr and were satisfied that that was what we had gone in for. That was what was covered by the warrant.'

It failed to convince the MPs. Iain McKenzie said:

> 'Forgive me, gentlemen, but it seems a strange raid. I am trying to put it in the context of what the police would do. If the police did a drugs raid, they wouldn't go in, find a pill and say: "Right, that's enough, let's go", and leave it at that. They would assume that that room had additional things to look at and so on.'

When Kerr came to give evidence a month later it would be clear that potentially vital material that would have been used as evidence in court cases had been left behind, allowing him to destroy it.

Ian Kerr takes centre stage

Kerr was accompanied by his wife Mary when he sat down to give evidence. Several police officers remained in the room to prevent any disturbance and Davidson came over to the public benches to warn against any disruption of the proceedings. It made for a tense start in the gilded committee room. There were to be fireworks – but they all came from Kerr. Over nearly four hours he set out calmly how the Association had operated, the names of those who had been his main contacts and the kinds of projects involved. McAlpine's strategy from the day of the raid onwards to keep the fall-out focused on Kerr was in tatters.

Kerr revealed to MPs that McAlpine, Balfour Beatty 'and possibly Skanksa' had used the Association for their Olympic contracts. Other schemes for which companies had checked employees were the headquarters for GCHQ, hospital PFI projects, power stations and the Jubilee Line Extension. The ongoing multi-million-pound Crossrail project had been discussed by companies that subscribed to the Association, Kerr said.

MPs heard that the Association was established after Sir Robert McAlpine Ltd paid £10,000 to two of the Economic League's directors for a list of names. Those directors, Stan Hardy and Jack Winder, would find themselves giving evidence before the MPs in the months to come. Like the scenes of the senate committee hearings from *Godfather II*, the names of the *consigliori* from the big construction families who took turns chairing TCA were all unveiled by Kerr. The last to hold the post was David Cochrane, McAlpine's head of human resources. As an example of how close an interest McAlpine's took in the Association, Kerr revealed that the company had paid his court fine. The money was paid to his daughters with instructions that they pay it on to their father in small batches to obscure its origin.

As Kerr continued to explain his role, it was clear that a number of leads had been established that would require further investigation. Speaking afterwards Justin Bowden, the GMB National Officer, said:

> ❛He blew off the lid which the construction companies like Carillion, Sir Robert McAlpine and Balfour Beatty had tried so hard to keep from coming off. They were clearly in it up to their necks.❜[7]

The other witness who helped flesh out the conspiracy, albeit with a lawyer sitting by him and remarks calibrated not to prejudge pending legal action, was Cullum McAlpine. A director of the eponymous building giant, McAlpine generally works out of offices in Bristol. Described in one profile as 'quite sharp, quite bright; quick on his feet',[8] he maintains impeccable social credentials with his membership of the Merchant Venturers – an exclusive club for Bristol businesspeople originally founded by slave traders.[9] McAlpine previously lived in a manor house in South Gloucestershire, 15 minutes from the M4. According to Mary Kerr, it was a place her husband had visited once when he needed to deliver some items to the construction boss. McAlpine has certainly attempted to portray his own role with TCA as hands-off. But MPs, in their interim report, said they were 'not persuaded'. Indeed, documents seen by the authors show McAlpine's signature and handwritten notes on agreements for how much Kerr should be paid each year right up to 2008. Former TCA chair Stephen Quant described McAlpine to the authors as the organization's 'patron'.

Between them, Kerr and McAlpine gave the clearest explanation yet of how The Consulting Association operated. Kerr, under McAlpine's patronage, made secret plans to put in place the successor to the Economic League's Services Group – taking on the same clients, using the original files as a base, bringing to the new office the same filing system, as well as an administrative assistant from the League.

Everything was ordered around colour-coded files. As Kerr explained to MPs:

> ❛Each company had a main contact. Their details were kept in what was called a red binder – a red book – per company. It was by company reference number and by name. There

was sometimes a second contact should that first contact not have been there for any reason. In addition to that, there was a blue book, which consisted of the personnel departments' users, who were the day-to-day clerical users, who would be in charge of amassing those names for whichever trades the company was putting together for a particular project. Say they wanted 100 names or, say, 20 people; they would probably put an advert in and accept an application from 50, out of which they would probably eventually take 20. Part of the process of deciding who to take was to put those names through The Consulting Association.**⁹**

It was a two-way operation, with companies supplying information to Kerr, which supplemented his own research, as well as receiving names and information. One main contact told the authors that he never knew what was in the files – he just got a confirmation if a name matched a record.

Also colour coded were the indexes to the files. The orange folder was for mechanical and electrical, black was for industrial relations, green covered environmental groups and blue was for older names. A joke by Ian Davidson about the significance of orange and green to a Glaswegian passed Kerr by. Indeed, the by turns gruff, sardonic and penetrating questioning by the Scottish MPs appear to have unnerved a number of English witnesses. One of the most dramatic moments in Kerr's evidence came when MPs returned to the issue of the files. It was almost by chance that Ian

Davidson wanted to clarify why some of the names in the indexes didn't have corresponding files. Kerr dropped the bombshell that files on around 200 environmental and animal-rights activists were among the material not seized by the ICO.

Those files in the green folder were subsequently destroyed by Kerr, along with the computer hard drives and the memory sticks used to hold material. There are also references in the files to others covering groups and these would have been general portraits

Ian Davidson MP

of organizations or publications of interest to the subscriber companies. One example is the OILC, which represents workers in the oil industry. Another was for the rail union the RMT which had a number of people on the blacklist. None of those files were recovered. Former Special Branch officer Peter Francis told the authors that the set-up mirrored the way it managed its own intelligence files.

The Association had a clear structure, with a constitution. Its accounts were audited by a chartered accountant and it paid a quarterly VAT bill. Only company directors were allowed to attend its regular meetings. Companies received copies of the minutes, according to Mary Kerr, who would sometimes type them up. Despite numerous court cases and questions in parliament, the companies have all repeatedly claimed that they held little or no documentation from their 16-year involvement with TCA. Although Harry Pooley, the main contact at Rosser and Russell, told the authors:

> ❝I've been retired nearly 12 years now and I've got a new life now and really don't want to get into it. There were many, many other people involved. I destroyed most of my records when I retired.❞

TCA had a finance committee, chaired by McAlpine, which met in February and October each year in McAlpine's Bernard Street offices near Russell Square. It also had separate regional industrial-relations meetings. In London these would take place at the exclusive Stafford Hotel close to Buckingham Palace, owned in succession during the period by two of the blacklisting firms: Costain and Trafalgar House. Discussions at these meetings would be on a range of issues of current concern to members. Those who attended the meetings say that individuals were rarely discussed – though the names of well-known activists would come up. Minutes were sent out after each meeting but to date not a single set has been found by any of the blacklisting firms (although many of the blacklist files have entries that read exactly like part of a set of minutes). However, some topics were apparently off limits at meetings. Former TCA chairman Stephen Quant told the authors:

⁶We never, ever discussed commercial issues because it is against the law. That would be criminal. You would normally discuss if you had trouble with disputes; you see, there were some nasty disputes.**⁹**

Dudley Barrett, Costain's former industrial-relations chief, told the authors he attended the quarterly Services Group and TCA meetings. He repeats Quant's claim:

⁶Very rarely did names come up at those meetings. It was people in the same kind of job discussing what was going on on their contracts. It wasn't specifically finger pointing at anybody. Sometimes you would have someone say, "I had so and so and he's on your job now. He causes a few problems, be careful about putting him on". Other people would say "so and so is a carpenter but he's not a very good one".**⁹**

Yet in the same interview, Barrett admits the meeting entailed,

⁶all the people at my level going through a whole box list of names, saying "you can take him off now because he has passed the age or you can take him off because he has been on my site for so long. I can recommend him, he has been no problem whatsoever". It was very clearly vetted along the way as well. There wasn't anyone on there who didn't deserve to be on there is the simplest way of putting it.**⁹**[10]

Kerr was well chosen for the work. A lot of trust was placed in him to ensure it operated efficiently and the bureaucratic procedures gave everybody clear rules to operate by. Kerr told MPs:

⁶It was a system that was understood clearly by all. Part of my job was to ensure, for instance, to any new company came on board that I explained very thoroughly how it worked. Each of them was aware of the need, because it was, if you like, a secret organization, to keep its information. People were very good and very thorough in keeping to the rules and regulations that it had in its constitution, for a start.**⁹**

Kerr tried to maintain neutrality when it came to reporting back to companies: 'I didn't embellish. I didn't put emphasis on certain things. I didn't interpret. You could have dialled the office like the speaking clock, in a sense.' There were, though, flickers of independence. Kerr said that some companies were more 'hard-nosed' than others; Balfour Beatty and Skanska were named. Kerr said:

> If they sent a list of, say, 20 names in to us and we could quite clearly say, "No, we don't know 19", but there was one name where we had partial identifying features, like the name, the area they lived, and maybe a bit of the address and a bit of their date of birth but we couldn't be positive, some companies we perceived over a period of time would think, "That's good enough for us" and not employ them. We ceased to give that bit of information on that particular name back to the company, so we would say that we had 20 clearances.

Documents recently seen by the authors give a clearer picture of the structure of TCA. There were meetings around the country for various interest groups within The Consulting Association. These groups were the main Industrial Relations Group, the Environmental Group and even a Healthcare/Facilities Management Group for companies with contracts in the newly privatized sections of the NHS.

The Industrial Relations Group (or Construction Industry Group – shortened to 'CIG') was the largest group, focusing on industrial-relations issues within the construction industry. The meetings would discuss various site problems, labour shortages, wage demands, trade unions and their officials – in terms of change of positions, appointees, objectives/agendas and disputes.

According to Mary Kerr: 'From what I understood from Ian and from typing up the minutes, seldom were employees discussed, except for the well-known activists where they had written articles or where it was known that they were campaigning at a particular site.'

The Industrial Relations Group, comprising about 40 people, would also receive a fortnightly mailing of information. This was the 'Two-Week Note' described by Mary Kerr thus:

> Ian would also circulate a "Two-Week Note" to Mr McAlpine,

the Chairman, past Chairmen and other senior IR/HR individuals every two to three weeks. The note was intended to be a short summary of what disputes, IR issues and union issues had been going on within the construction industry. It was always in a smaller font to other documents (9 or 10 compared to font 12 for meeting agendas and minutes) and it was limited to one side of A4 paper, with the objective that it could be read quickly to bring the reader up to speed with the bigger issues affecting the industry. Sometimes items from this "Two-Week Note" were copied and pasted on to reference cards. I understand that these items (in a smaller font) have been mistaken for minutes of meetings.[11]

The admission that there was a 'Two-Week Note' totally explodes the façade erected by the companies that information about activists was kept strictly within TCA filing cabinets and never disseminated. The authors found the tell-tale smaller font size on multiple occasions, especially on the blacklist files of leading activists, including Steve Acheson, Tony Jones, Graham Bowker, Chris Murphy, Steve Hedley, Dave Smith and Roy Bentham, as well as virtually all of the workers blacklisted from the MRI and DAF disputes in Manchester, Pfizers, Connah's Quay and the Jubilee Line electricians. On every occasion individuals are specifically identified. Sometimes individuals are named as the ringleaders of disputes, sometimes the two-week note lists names of workers who participated in a strike, which in most cases were perfectly legal. It is little wonder that these activists found it almost impossible to find long-term employment, as their names had been circulated (in some cases on numerous occasions and over many years) to virtually every industrial-relations manager in the country.

The Environmental Group originally met at Tarmac's offices in Wolverhampton, before moving its meetings to The Bear pub in Woodstock, Oxfordshire. According to Mary Kerr, the 'Woodstock Group' of about 20 people, often comprising senior security managers as well as industrial-relations managers, would also be sent mail-outs about once or twice a month, which updated them on targeted projects.

The Healthcare/Facilities Management Group met irregularly

and focused mostly on the developing and changing commercial issues arising out of PFI projects as well as the availability of labour and the unions' positions on specific projects. There were two other groups: the Rail Group of about 10 members who were sent information about once a month; and a Mechanical & Electrical Group, which met from the early 2000s to discuss issues specific to that sector.[12]

All TCA files relating to these specific groups have been destroyed.

Mary Kerr has subsequently given a picture of how the office was laid out that held all these files:

❛There were two rooms within the Droitwich office separated by a narrow corridor. In Ian's room would be his desk, the safe (in which the green and pink record cards were kept), the copy Monodex white ringbinder file. a cabinet with a drawer of current financial year bills, the files for company invoices and acknowledgements for each company, current year's meeting files, historic meeting minutes and agendas, the red book which listed contact details for day-to-day HR contacts (as they changed over the years) and the blue book which listed contact details for the Main Contacts, files of copy correspondence. A drawer of articles on construction projects and boxes of historic mail-outs, old magazines and newspapers, historic rent bills and receipts, plus old bills for electricity and telephone.

In the other room would be two desks and a table, the Monodex itself, the computer, the record cards stored in a filing cabinet, the Sales Day book which recorded all the invoices sent to the companies, the ring binders on the various trade unions (gleaned from the press and from union publications) and the red ring binders containing the usage figures for each company. In addition, there would also be the photocopier, further old magazines and newspapers, the fax machine, the typewriter, stationery cupboard and shredder. In the corridor would be a metal cabinet containing some historic files of usage figures and also boxes of paper and stationery, envelopes and an old photocopier.❜[13]

Asked by Pamela Nash MP if, given his time over, Kerr would do it again, he said:

> ❝I wouldn't. Absolutely not. Is there anything that I regret, did you say? I would be truly sorry if we had ruined somebody's life permanently but, as I pointed out, they were all in a position to seek employment for their trades and skills elsewhere in the industry. If it caused genuine hardship, then no, that's not right. It was felt that these companies had a right to protect themselves, and by refusing employment they were not flagging them up openly to stop them getting work elsewhere. That is what I would come back to all the time. I would equally say that where it had ruined lives and it could be genuinely shown to have done that, then that would be a concern and a matter of regret for me.❞

Ian Davidson said Kerr's evidence was important because it made the process of blacklisting 'real' to people who otherwise couldn't grasp how it operated. As for Kerr, Davidson said:

> ❝He was loading the train. Other people told him who to put on it, how to do it. He was hostile to the left but basically he was just operating the machinery. It was a job. He was not all that apologetic. He did think people deserved it.❞[14]

Kerr, knowing that behind him sat men whose lives he had monitored for years, slowly broke the habit of a lifetime and revealed name after name. And then he was done. He and his family had been told they could leave by a side entrance but they were taken the wrong way and had to turn back and walk through many of those in the public seats. The day ended as it had begun, with Kerr forced to run a gauntlet.

Two weeks later Kerr was dead from an existing heart condition. He was at home correcting his evidence on the day he died.

Mary remains bitter about how her husband was treated – and that includes the Select Committee, which she says knew that he was ill. Kerr was due to have heart surgery in January 2013. Davidson said: 'I think it was probably true that it was the writing of the evidence for us to clear his name that possibly kept him alive as long as he did.'[15]

Only two former TCA contacts, Alan Audley and Danny O'Sullivan, sent their condolences to Mary Kerr. Cullum McAlpine did, three months later. No TCA members attended his funeral.

A ruthless focus

Kerr's evidence was dynamite but the Committee had to tread a careful line to make sure it did not stray outside the borders of its remit. Too much of a focus on blacklisting operations unconnected with Scotland could raise questions about the legitimacy of their work. However, it is clear that a carefully thought-out strategy kept the Committee heading in a particular direction. Former UCATT general secretary Alan Ritchie, now working as an adviser to the Committee, was one of a number of senior union officials, including Justin Bowden from the GMB and Gail Cartmail from Unite, who regularly met Davidson and other committee members to discuss this strategy. They agreed that certain aspects of the scandal were not going to be covered. One was any involvement by trade unions. Union officials were called but the question of collusion barely raised. Another was the involvement of the police or security services. That also meant no real analysis of why environmental or animal rights campaigners had been targeted.

Davidson told the authors:

> We were quite ruthless in focusing on working-class people rather than being diverted into these issues. It took us into a whole range of other issues and there is already an industry there to pursue these matters and the danger is that they would hijack the question of blacklisting. Similarly, the question of the greens. I mean the whole middle-class constituency would love to think they had been blacklisted and would see it as a badge of honour and they would get in the television studios and be far more articulate and presentable than building workers and therefore the attention would be diverted.

It didn't mean that these issues were not raised. Ian Kerr and former Economic League members Stan Hardy and Jack Winder were all asked about their links with Special Branch.

The evidence given by David Clancy from the ICO to MPs was crucial in establishing the likelihood of police collusion. However, no representatives from the police were called and nor were any environmental campaigners. Uncovering those links would be down to a network of journalists and activists working outside of Parliament, who later on would expose a whole other murky side to the scandal. The Labour Party at its most senior levels has long had a troubled history on how to deal with the police and security services. The evidence that Labour officials have been spied upon since the Party's formation is barely contested. Nor has that stopped members who had MI5 files obtaining senior positions in government; Harriet Harman, Patricia Hewitt and Peter Mandelson among them. However, the party, at least up until the election of Jeremy Corbyn, was always sensitive to allegations that it undermines the work of those charged with protecting the state – and often overcompensates to try to destroy this canard.

If the Committee was going to produce a unanimous report then it didn't want to raise issues which might drive a wedge between members. A strategy was identified early on that kept the blacklisted inquiry in the industrial sphere and framed it as one where companies operated iniquitously, for whatever reason, and had to be 'shown back towards the path of righteousness', as Davidson put it. As the investigation proceeded, the witnesses and questioning tended to confirm that interpretation of events.

The strategy behind the Select Committee approach was outlined in a report it issued on 14 March 2014. This said that it was up to the state, at a national, devolved or local level, to ensure blacklisting does not recur by using its leverage as a contractor. Unless firms implicated in the scandal demonstrated that they had 'self-cleansed', and any bidders could show best practice, then they would be disqualified from publicly funded work. It defined self-cleansing as:

> Various activities, including an admission of guilt, full compensation and other appropriate remedial steps. We believe that the levels of restitution should not be solely for the companies themselves to determine, but must be agreed after negotiations with the relevant trade unions and representatives of blacklisted workers.[9]

As for best practice, it suggested that the model should be the contracts agreed between unions and French energy firm EDF for the construction of the Hinkley Point C nuclear power plant.

> ❛We support their mechanisms for ongoing monitoring and reporting procedures for health and safety, as well as the commitment to direct employment and the establishment of an employment brokerage for all jobs on the site. We will be urging the UK and devolved governments to implement these standards on all publicly funded contracts in future.❜

Perhaps the key change here is the one on direct employment. False self-employment had been identified by the unions as a major obstacle to maintaining wages and conditions and to workers asserting their rights at Employment Tribunals. However, the government rejected the main proposals in the report, citing European procurement rules and the need for 'flexible employment structures'. Employment minister Jenny Willot said: 'Our view is that an effective regulatory regime, along with the promotion of the benefits of best practice and a culture of transparent and responsible businesses, should guard against individuals being blacklisted from the outset.'[16] The wearily familiar line was trotted out that the blacklisting regulations would be reviewed if evidence of the practice was produced. Davidson immediately announced that his Committee would carry on its investigations.

The scandal goes national and local

The tactic of targeting public-sector contracts as a way of putting pressure on the companies involved in blacklisting had been pioneered by the GMB. Although this is the union with the smallest number of members affected by the issue, it has mounted an incredibly effective campaign, backed by an astute media team led by Steve Pryle, to embarrass construction firms. Many of the blacklisting building firms are now providing all sorts of different services as the public sector has been opened up to private providers. Carillion's expansion into the public sector includes supplying cleaning staff to the NHS. Carillion and the GMB were already locked in a dispute over the treatment of hospital workers in Swindon and in June 2012 the union issued a 26-page report with the unwieldy title *Blacklisting – illegal corporate bullying: endemic, systematic and deep-rooted in Carillion and other companies.* The report used documents from Dave Smith's Employment Tribunal against Carillion to turn the issue from one involving an unidentifiable mass of people into something that resonated at local level. An analysis of the postcodes of 224 blacklist files enabled the GMB to create a perfect story for media dissemination across the UK. The postcodes covered most of the country's regions, so that suddenly the blacklisting scandal broke out of the industrial heartlands. It gave an obvious hook for local media to write a story and for local activists to campaign for action.

The campaign to bar blacklisting firms from publicly funded contracts took on a life of its own when GMB general secretary Paul Kenny sent a copy of the report and a covering letter to every Labour councillor in the country. The first council to agree not to deal with blacklisters unless they could show they had reformed was Knowsley, followed by Hull. Tower Hamlets council in London became the first authority in the capital to say that it would not deal with companies involved in blacklisting. Shortly after, the Welsh Assembly announced that it was instructing 103 public-sector bodies, including local councils, NHS trusts and police organizations, that they can exclude such companies from public contracts unless the firms have taken measures such as compensating victims of blacklisting. It is estimated that annual public procurement spending in Wales is £4.3 billion, with around £1 billion a year spent on construction.

John Wheeler was a rigger at Fawley refinery in Southampton but found himself unable to get work for 20 years. He had a blacklist file – one of an estimated 50 people from the Hampshire area on the TCA list. Unite general secretary Len McCluskey visited the city to highlight his case. Subsequently local councillor Andrew Pope pushed through a motion that saw the City Council pledge not to deal with blacklisting firms. More than 24 councils followed suit, including major authorities such as Bristol, Manchester and Islington. The London Borough of Islington is one of many where the blacklisting firms are already providing services to the local authority for building maintenance. Kier, for example, had set up separate subsidiary companies for various public-sector contracts of this kind. The blacklist file for Chris Murphy, who was the elected

UCATT convenor for building workers employed by the council, includes insulting personal comments added by a manager when the council building maintenance contract was privatized and awarded to Kier Islington. Chris Murphy is another blacklisted worker who, sadly, did not live to see justice.

In February 2013 MSP Neil Findlay organized a summit on blacklisting in Scotland, where more than 400 people are estimated to be on TCA files. Findlay was one of several Labour MSPs, including Drew Smith, who had been pressing for the SNP-led government to stop public contracts going to firms implicated in blacklisting. In November of that year the Scottish government issued a procurement policy note to public-sector bodies saying they could end contracts if firms were found to be blacklisting or discriminating against trade union members. In March 2014 the Northern Ireland Assembly agreed similar rules.

Almost 100 public bodies have taken the symbolic step of passing a resolution opposing contracts going to blacklisting firms, with the movement even encompassing Tory strongholds such as Royal Tunbridge Wells. The authors have been told by a number of councillors that firms, including a number of subsidiaries, have been denied public contracts because of their involvement in blacklisting. But, in autumn 2014, the London Borough of Islington became the first local authority to throw a blacklisting construction firm off a public contract when they took the contract for council-house repairs back in-house from Kier. The £16.5-million-a-year contract had been carried out by Kier for the previous 14 years. In all, 140 former Kier employees are now directly employed by Islington Council. Islington resident Chris Clarke, blacklisted since being a TGWU steward at Vascrofts, responded to the announcement: 'Marvellous decision! Not just the loss of the contract for the blacklisters but 140 taken on as direct labour. A good day for Islington. A bad day for blacklisters! Bye bye, Kier.'[17]

Labour councillor Gary Doolan said:

> As an elected councillor there are times when doing the right thing is easy. There was no other way to deal with this, but to send a message loud and very clear to any contractor wishing to bid for work in our borough, in that those contractors who are

guilty of blacklisting or using the services of The Consulting Association, that unless these contractors can satisfy the council that they have now satisfactorily cleansed themselves, they will be excluded from any tendering for work. Islington is the first local council that's made this statement. However, it should be made by the Local Government Association on behalf of every council, not just a minority. If it's right for one council to stand up for workers, it's good enough for all the others to take the same stance. Perhaps that way blacklisting will finally be eradicated.[18]

An attempt to stop firms involved in blacklisting winning public contracts had been made decades earlier, when bricklayer John Bryan was elected to Southwark Council in London in 1982. At Bryan's instigation the Housing Committee began vetting companies that bid for work. Poor safety, lump labour and blacklisting were criteria for removal from the preferred contractors list. The response of the firms was not always positive. Bryan remembers what happened when one company was removed: 'A few days later two big fellas come knocking on my door saying to me, "You're Johnny Bryan, ain't you? There are a lot of people really unhappy".' Despite this veiled threat, the contract compliance scheme continued for several years.

Decades later, John Bryan found that he had been blacklisted himself. His TCA file starts in 1979; the first entry records a speech he made at a Labour Party meeting and covers his years as a UCATT activist, elected councillor and parliamentary candidate. Bryan says:

I thought by being a councillor I could help that fight for building workers, for working people in general to improve our conditions and now I found I was being blacklisted for that as well.[19]

Scotland has seen a fierce debate on whether public contracts should be off limits to firms who had engaged in blacklisting. With millions in potential procurement schemes on offer it was a debate with the ability to have a real impact on the industry. Initially the noises were positive with the Scottish government in 2013 issuing a 'procurement note' which would allow construction firms who blacklist workers to be banned from public contracts. Unfortunately, implementation has been less than universal. Sir Robert McAlpine Limited had been awarded major contracts as part of the £1-billion Dundee Riverside redevelopment, with Dundee City Council coming under pressure over BAM's £45-million job to build a new V&A Museum.[20]

From 18 April 2016, it became a legal requirement for public bodies in Scotland to exclude businesses which are found to have breached the Blacklists Regulations 2010, or which have admitted to doing so. The exclusion remains in force until the business has taken appropriate remedial measures, or a period of three years has elapsed since the blacklisting occurred, which is the maximum timescale allowed under EU law. However, this exclusion only kicks in if there has been a breach of the 2010 regulations, thereby allowing the historical TCA blacklisting to go unpunished.

As Scottish Rank and File committee member and councillor Jim Harte said:

> The inclusion of the maximum timescale of three years is a real kick in the teeth to those who found themselves in the Consulting Association's files. In recent months, Unite The Union, Neil Findlay and others have been raising questions around the amount of public-sector contracts that have been awarded to blacklisting companies since the publication of the Scottish Procurement Policy Note on blacklisting in November 2013. With recent additions, this has amounted to over £1.5-billion worth of contracts. This provision lets these companies off the hook and legitimizes the inclusion of them in the procurement process.[21]

The row in Scotland over public contracts gained extra focus in the summer of 2016 when Kier was named as the main contractor for the restoration of the Mackintosh Building at the Glasgow School of Art which had been destroyed in a fire. Unions lined up to condemn such a prestigious contract being awarded to a firm which had been proven a blacklister. In a letter, the Scottish Artists Union, which represents more than 1,400 professional artists, urged the art school to review its decision.

'The "Mac" building was renowned throughout the world for its craftsmanship; innovative use of materials; its functionality and its commitment to the values of the arts and crafts movement,' it said. 'It's therefore incongruous that the GSA have awarded £25 million of government funds for its restoration to a company that has engaged in blacklisting activities.'

It added: 'The Glasgow School of Art is a world leading institution, known as innovative and progressive. This contract undermines the distinct values of the institution.'[22]

The political campaigning amongst elected politicians was beginning to make headway. The more direct-action approach adopted by the Blacklist Support Group – which involved everything from halting traffic on Oxford Street to handing out blacklisting 'awards' at construction industry events and at one point even attempting to perform a citizen's arrest on Cullum McAlpine – had a mixed response from union leaders, being seen by some as useful and by others as counter-productive.

Union leaders' strategy, exemplified in the Select Committee's report, was to go for the contracts and establish a new relationship with the companies. The then UCATT general secretary Steve Murphy said:

> If we politically get Labour into power we can then say [to the companies] that if you blacklist workers, as part of procurement exercise, you won't get the job unless compensation is paid to blacklisted workers. Now, from my perspective, we can jump up and down, we can do all the demonstrations, but the only way you are going to hit them is in the pocket and procurement hits them in the pocket.[23]

Murphy's faith in the potential of a future Labour government to take action in this area was shared to varying degrees by his fellow union leaders and by MPs who had long campaigned on the issue. Since the government had failed to implement what it had promised in 1999 and then brought in what was widely seen as ineffective stop-gap legislation in the dying days of the Brown administration, there was understandable caution among many others. Nonetheless, hope was bolstered when shadow business secretary Chuka Umunna went on Radio 4's *Today* programme in

January 2013 to demand a full investigation into blacklisting.

> To date, nobody has been properly held to account about what happened. We need a proper investigation as to the extent of blacklisting across the public sector and finally we also need to look at the law to see whether that is sufficient to actually protect people who could be victims of this or have been victims of this in the past.

What was becoming clear was that Labour could count on a growing cross-party consensus. When Panorama screened its *Blacklist Britain* programme in June 2013, including allegations that the practice had been used during the building of the Millennium Dome and the Olympic sites, it offered political cover for those who wished to raise the issue but didn't come from the left. Suddenly it wasn't just activists who were making these claims. Actually, much of that programme's material had been revealed previously by campaigners and journalists. However, as with Umunna's appearance on *Today*, it took a flagship mainstream programme to make it acceptable for politicians to take the issue seriously. Suddenly campaigners found some unusual supporters. While at an awards night organized by the civil liberties group Liberty, where the Blacklist Support Group had been nominated for its work, the campaign was congratulated by Tory MP David Davies. The former Home Secretary and now, at the time of writing, 'Brexit' minister, revealed that his grandfather had been blacklisted for his communist sympathies while working in the mines.

Support also came from Caroline Murphy, anointed successor to the construction giant of the same name, who tried to turn it into a co-operative venture and eventually left the family firm.[24] Murphy, a member of Unite, has become a respected commentator on various issues. She wrote:

> The 20th November [TUC] national day of action on blacklisting saw hundreds of events nationwide and those personally affected spoke powerfully at meetings held in Parliament. It was heartbreaking to hear first-hand the way in which this has impacted the lives of the men on the blacklist and their families. As an immigrant my father was turned

away from accommodation in London by the sign "No Dogs, No Blacks, No Irish". He was excluded from workplaces in this city with notices that "No Irish Need Apply". Barring people from work on the grounds of race was wrong then, just as it is wrong now for the brave workers who have raised their voices to make building sites safer for everyone.�9[25]

The most evasive and potentially dishonest witness

Keeping a cross-party consensus was a key part of the strategy for the Select Committee so that companies would see no option but to accept the recommendations for action and Labour would feel emboldened enough to make this a manifesto commitment.

It also helped that the Select Committee had been treated to a series of woeful performances by witnesses from the construction and human resources sectors. Of particular note was the appearance by Stephen Ratcliffe, director of the UK Contractors Group (UKCG), one of several industry trade bodies. Described variously during his testimony as 'shifty' and 'evasive', Ratcliffe gave an insight into the blankly amoral approach of his organization and its members. According to its website, one of the UKCG's principal objectives is: 'To encourage contractors to work together (especially in health and safety and environmental issues) to promote change and spread best practice.' Ratcliffe has run the UKCG since it was formed in 2009 and earns £120,000 a year. Before that, he headed another trade body called the Construction Confederation. Despite having been a civil servant in the Department for Trade and Industry in the 1970s and involved in construction for decades, he said that prior to 2009 he had never heard any hints about blacklisting. Of the 32 members of the UKCG, 11 had been subscribers to TCA but Ratcliffe told MPs that blacklisting had never been raised at its meetings. It had been mentioned informally in an email to members but only because the Chartered Institute of Personnel and Development had been in contact suggesting a meeting about the issue. Despite allegations raised subsequently about blacklisting on the Crossrail project that would contravene UKCG's ethical principles, it had not asked the consortium involved, BFK, for an explanation.

When asked why nothing had been discussed about blacklisting generally, Ratcliffe said it was still early days – though it was four years since the TCA raid had taken place. Ratcliffe agreed that blacklisting contravened its code of conduct but there was no automatic sanction for members who broke that code – indeed it appeared the code itself is pretty much whatever companies decided it to be. Ratcliffe did say, however, that he was sure the companies were embarrassed by what had been revealed by the raid and subsequent investigation. It turned out under further questioning that this assumption was based on reading the transcripts of evidence given by companies to the Select Committee because it had never come up at the UKCG. In fact Ratcliffe was not convinced that blacklisting had actually occurred. According to him, dealing with The Consulting Association 'was clear evidence that there was a breach of the Data Protection Act. I don't think there is yet clear evidence that they were blacklisting.' Ratcliffe also told MPs that his member companies had apologized for what happened but it turned out he had emailed this statement to them all and 'five or six' had replied and he assumed the rest agreed. Conservative MP Simon Reevell said:

> Can I say that you are the most evasive and potentially dishonest witness I have encountered at this Committee – and, frankly, in 20 years of practising at the Bar?

The UKCG does not have a regulatory function. Construction companies abide by various pieces of legislation drawn up by Parliament or from Europe. In some cases they might have agreements with unions on how they should operate. They may also have their own internal codes of conduct. The Select Committee exposed the weakness of these codes, which appear to be applied as a company sees fit and breaches of which provoke few, if any, sanctions. Only one person was removed following the raid. Stephen Quant left Skanska when it began investigating its links with The Consulting Association. Quant described the move as 'mutually advantageous' but was unable to say more because of a gagging clause.

Because of documents disclosed in litigation, we now know of a number of other employees who were subject to investigation by companies as they scrambled to deal with the fallout from the ICO raid. Geoff Hughes was the divisional HR manager for Costain from

2004 to 2010. Hughes took over the HR role from Sean Mobbs who said it would be up to Hughes if he wanted to continue subscribing to TCA. Hughes had never heard of The Consulting Association but, after being advised by two directors, continued to use the checking service on behalf of the company.

When, in 2009, Kerr called Hughes to tell him about the ICO raid, Hughes passed on what he described as 'the very limited number of documents that I had' to Tracy Wood, who was Costain's HR and Legal Director. Hughes, who had joined Costain as a graduate in 1974 and, except for five years, spent his entire career with them, described what happened next.

❝Shortly afterwards, Costain began disciplinary proceedings against me regarding my connection with The Consulting Association. I found these disciplinary proceedings very distressing and, ultimately, I believe that Costain made me a scapegoat for simply continuing to oversee a procedure which I had not set up, which had been operating for some time before I became involved and which I had authority from Costain directors to use.❞[26]

Eighteen pages of notes from his disciplinary and appeal that took place in April and May 2009 are now in the public domain. The hearing notes indicate that two company directors, Symon Taylor and David Jenkins, who sat on the Costain Executive Board, reporting directly to the CEO, were fully aware of TCA and had told Hughes to continue using the vetting procedure. At one point the record of the hearing reads: 'It was a routine action and one targeting trade union members.'[27]

Another Costain manager who checked names and attended a number of TCA meetings was Ken Ward from Costain's oil and gas division. He has stated that he was instructed by ex-HR director and Executive Board member Alex Vaughan to use The Consulting Association and that its continued use was discussed at a meeting of Costain's senior HR managers in March 2004. When, in April 2009, he was asked to attend a disciplinary hearing over his role in the blacklisting operation, he claimed: 'I had no faith in the service and thought it unethical.'[28] But, just like many others who in hindsight claim unease, the Costain manager did nothing at the time.

However, we can now reveal that at least one individual would end their employment with a blacklisting firm following the ICO raid and he did act on his ethical dilemma. Paul Field was the in-house lawyer for Laing O'Rourke and had represented the company in tribunals more than 20 times and applied for union injunctions at the High Court, including during a dispute at Terminal 5. On 9 March 2009, just three days after the discovery of the blacklist was the lead story on the TV news, the solicitor handed in his letter of resignation, explaining:

> ❝ My decision has been prompted by the company's actions in breaking data protection laws by subscribing to… an illegal blacklist. I cannot in all conscience continue acting for the company as its employment solicitor in light of these damaging revelations and Laing O'Rourke's public response to them. I believe that the press statement issued is misleading and inaccurate.❞

Field refers to the company saying it had mistakenly continued paying the £3,000-per-year subscriptions for Laing and Crown House Technologies following their acquisition by Laing O'Rourke, while having no real involvement with The Consulting Association. But Field claims that senior managers up to director level, including Tony Summers, Dianne Hughes, Chris Hale, Sylvia Smith and Karl O'Mahoney, all had knowledge of and participated in the blacklisting operation.

O'Mahoney has worked for Laing O'Rourke for over 26 years and is currently head of Forensic and Group Administration. He has revealed that it was the company deputy chair Bernard Dempsey who personally asked him and Sylvia Smith, director of payroll, to check all new starters with The Consulting Association. O'Mahoney and Smith both spoke to and corresponded with Ian Kerr, although it was Chris Hale who attended TCA meetings. From June 2007 onwards, the company also set up an internal database of workers who had been checked via TCA.[29]

Paul Field's resignation letter said that the revelations had put him in an impossible sitation regarding his professional integrity:

> ❝ I can only assume that information about some of the claimants

that I have acted against in the last three and a half years has been passed on to Mr Kerr. That being the case, then I have almost certainly negotiated and signed settlement agreements on behalf of LOR containing confidentiality and non-disparaging remarks clauses which LOR never had any intention of abiding by.⁹

And Field said there was no legal justification for the secret operation:

Legal powers exist to deal with any form of misconduct by workers or unions without resorting to this form of third-rate McCarthyism to unjustly deny people employment without any more legitimate reason than they happened once to be active in their union or complain about conditions on site.⁹

Field said he found the idea that people were denied work simply because they had joined a safety committee as 'repugnant' and he described Kerr's operation as 'Orwellian'. In further documentation dated 14 April 2009, Field states:

I could not in good faith and as an officer of the court continue acting for a client which was guilty of such systematic dishonesty and which was tainted by its association with such a corrupt practice as blacklisting.⁹³⁰

Field's assertions appear to be borne out by an email later disclosed during litigation and dated 18 April 2007, which was sent by Laing O'Rourke's labour manager Mick Connolly and titled 'STRICTLY PRIVATE & CONFIDENTIAL – NORTH STAFFS'. It referred to the need for HR clearance and implicitly acknowledged the need to keep blacklisting secret:

An activist does not generally declare any industrial unrest on his CV... all agency and subcontract operatives supplied to the project need to be cleared through myself and HR prior to engagement / employment on site. To disguise our vetting (recent Alan Wainwright case) I suggested that all operatives (direct /subcontract / specialist / agency) will need to be IIF trained and therefore all suppliers would need to submit their name, NI, DOB and Residential Location. I gave the recent examples of how similar high-profile projects are currently being targeted by activists at Manchester MRI (55 miles away) and stressed the importance and adhering to procedure, coupled with the fact that the Manchester and Liverpool activists will now be applying for work beyond their surrounding counties.'[31]

In October 2014, around 30 members of the Blacklist Support Group visited the Dartford head offices of Laing O'Rourke with the intention of handing out leaflets highlighting the involvement of the company in The Consulting Association. Some of the blacklisted workers were assaulted by security and managers when attempting to enter the building, an assault viewed by thousands around the world after Reel News posted video footage on YouTube. Unable to hand out flyers to staff in the canteen, BSG blockaded the car park entrance and climbing an external fire escape unfurled a large banner from the side of the building which read 'LAING O'ROURKE BLACKLISTING SCUM'.[32]

Paul Field may have had the decency to break with his employer because of the ethical issues relating to blacklisting but the company main contacts who orchestrated the victimization of trade union members had no such pangs of conscience. Many of these HR senior managers were members of the professional trade body the Chartered Institute of Personnel and Development (CIPD).

Peter Cheese, chief executive of the CIPD, was asked to give evidence to the Select Committee and told MPs that, as a result of the raid, his organization was investigating a number of its members to see if they had broken its new code of conduct. He said that it had voluntarily begun investigations into 19 members relating to blacklisting as a result of information in the public domain. By coincidence, the Blacklist Support Group contacted the CIPD on the very day its new code of conduct was published, asking it to investigate members named as being blacklisters. According to Cheese, the organization was going to do this anyway. The CIPD carried out its investigation in secret but by mid-2016 the findings had still not been published; nor had a single HR professional involved in the blacklisting scandal been expelled or publicly disciplined by the organization.

The professional body introducing a code of conduct after a blacklisting scandal has a sense of *déjà vu* about it. In 1988, when the Economic League was being exposed, the authors Hollingsworth and Norton-Taylor noted: 'The Institute of Personnel Management, which represents most personnel directors, does have guidelines on "Standards of Professional Conduct" and a "Recruitment Code" for its members... one highly experienced former Personnel Director, an IPM member for over 20 years, did not even know the IPM had a code of conduct! There is no indication at all that the IPM is going to do anything about the practice of blacklisting by its members. Unless the government introduces rigorous reforms (an unlikely prospect), it will be up to officials themselves to take a stand.'[33]

However, while construction companies have said separately that they have improved their internal practices, it turns out that none of them have consulted the CIPD on this. The Select Committee report said:

> All the information available to us suggests that most of the firms involved would have continued to use TCA and its sinister and odious practices had they not been caught.[34]

Indeed, Mary Kerr recalls one company main contact ringing her husband several months after the raid to see if he would continue, as 'there was a need for this checking'. Understandably, Kerr declined to carry on.

Taking the campaign to Europe

When asked whether he thought that companies engaged in activity that is morally wrong should be debarred from public-sector contracts, the response of the UKCG's Ratcliffe was: 'This is governed by the EU procurement rules.' This suggests that if the EU has authorized it, or not forbidden it at least, then that is all construction firms need to guide them on their behaviour. As part of its campaign, the Blacklist Support Group had been out in Brussels since September 2011 talking to MEPs about what role the European Parliament could take. Initially it was to prove a successful new front. At the time there was no specific EU-wide legislation against blacklisting of individuals for 'safety reasons'. However, many of the firms involved in blacklisting in the UK either had parent companies in other European countries or operated across the continent. These include Swedish firm Skanska, Bam from the Netherlands, Vinci from France, Ireland's Laing O'Rourke and UK-based transnationals, including Sir Robert McAlpine, Balfour Beatty, Kier, Costain and Carillion. Two of those in that initial BSG delegation were Steve Acheson and Brian Higgins who had been dogged in pushing the issue with MEPs. They were able to present the files to the EU Commissioner for employment, social affairs and inclusion, László Andor. The visit had been arranged by Labour MEPs Glenis Willmot and Stephen Hughes, and the blacklisted workers also had backing in their European lobbying efforts from employment lawyer Professor Keith Ewing and the GMB.

In 2013 the European parliament voted in favour of an amendment to the draft data protection regulation that would make blacklisting on the basis of trade-union activity a breach of EU law. It was only draft legislation and it took another year before it came to a vote. In March 2014, MEPs passed amendment 192 of the General Data Protection Regulation. This states that workers' personal data, especially sensitive data, such as political orientation and trade-union activities, may not be used to compile blacklists and 'the processing, the use in the employment context, the drawing-up and passing-on of blacklists of employees shall be prohibited'.

The GMB's European officer Kathleen Walker Shaw was one of those who had worked hard to get the amendment through. At the time she said: 'The measures require governments to adopt adequate sanctions and penalties to enforce these measures.'[35]

However, subsequent negotiations saw the word blacklisting deleted and the new Article 88 on processing data in the context of employment is weaker than the original one voted on in the European Parliament. A separate report on health and safety at work also had a clause about workers not being blacklisted for raising such concerns that did not make the final draft. Political developments in 2016 make it very hard to predict how, if at all, European rules on data handling and health and safety will have an effect on UK legislation.

1 The exemplar of such reporting is Nick Davies' book *Hack Attack*, Chatto & Windus, 2014. 2 For instance, Carillion employed the PR firm Spada, named after a Greek sword, which continually monitored social and mainstream media activity and the Blacklist Support Group in particular. That included sending pictures of BSG protests. Spada has since merged with another company to form Infinite Spada. Laing O'Rourke was given a profile of author Phil Chamberlain by its media-monitoring outfit. 3 Interview with the authors. 4 Oral evidence given to Scottish Affairs Select Committee on 19 June 2012 5 Ibid 6 Ibid 7 Interview with the authors. 8 'The Family', *Building* magazine, 1999. 9 merchantventurers.com/about-us/membership 10 Interview with the authors. 11 Witness statement prepared for the High Court. 12 Witness statement prepared for the High Court by Mary Kerr. 13 Ibid. 14 Interview with the authors. 15 Ibid 16 'Government "unlikely" to bar blacklist firms from public work, *Building*, 20 May 2014, nin.tl/unlikelytobar 17 Council boots blacklisters off contract, *Morning Star*, 4 Aug 2014, nin.tl/29Vu9MC 18 Interview with the authors. 19 Interview with the authors. 20 BBC news, nin.tl/BAMTayside 21 'SNP and blacklisting', Scottish Rank and File website, 23 Dec 2015, nin.tl/rankandfile 22 *The Herald*, 2 July 2016, nin.tl/artistsdemand 23 Interview with the authors. 24 *The Irish Examiner*, 5 April 2014, nin.tl/carolinemurphy 25 Caroline Murphy blog, 24 Mar 2014, nin.tl/murphyblog 26 Witness statement seen by the authors. 27 'Key documents disclosed pursuant to July Disclosure Order': exhibit in High Court trial. 28 Ibid. 29 Ibid. 30 Ibid. 31 Ibid. 32 Reel News video youtube.com/watch?v=9mdqRxxpTE8 33 Mark Hollingsworth and Richard Norton-Taylor, *Blacklist: the inside story of political vetting*, Hogarth Press, 1988, p 229. 34 Scottish Affairs Select Committee, Blacklisting in employment: interim report, 26 March 2013. 35 'EU Parliament vote on blacklisting', GMB, 12 Mar 2014, nin.tl/GMBonEU

7
Blacklisting the Olympics and Crossrail

B lacklisting was being fought in the courts by lawyers. It was being fought in council chambers and parliaments by elected politicians. But these were attempts to deal with historic blacklisting. Many were arguing that blacklisting was still going on even after the ICO raid. Blacklisting is first and foremost an industrial-relations issue and, if it was ever to be defeated, it needed to be fought industrially on building sites. And that's just what happened.

Building the Olympic Park

Back in 2006, London started preparing for the Olympics. The redevelopment of former industrial wasteland in Stratford, east London, into the Olympic Park was to become the most high-profile construction project in the world. By autumn 2008, more than 2,700 workers were already on site, building the infrastructure for the 2012 Games. The multi-billion-pound project, paid for by public and Lottery funds, was too large for one contractor, so every major construction firm in the UK was awarded contracts. Spread over 70 individual projects, virtually every subscriber to The Consulting Association was part of the action.

Sir Robert McAlpine was building the 80,000-capacity Olympic Stadium that would host the gold-medal exploits of Mo Farah and Usain Bolt. Balfour Beatty won the £303-million Aquatics Centre, while Carillion and Skanska were working on the Media Centre. Laing O'Rourke was part of the CLM consortium, with a £400-million contract as project consultants, with overall control of the day-to-day industrial relations on the project.

For building workers who had been hit hard since the global financial crisis, TV images of hoardings being erected around the Olympic site were bright spots in an otherwise dismal industry. Unfortunately, those hoardings were to prove impenetrable for almost every worker on the blacklist.

Only weeks after the ICO revealed its raid on TCA, unions were warning that blacklisting was happening on the Olympic site. Alan Ritchie told London's *Standard* newspaper: 'It is especially deplorable that blacklisting appears to have taken place on the Olympic Stadium, the showpiece structure for the whole Olympics.' This was a direct accusation against Sir Robert McAlpine Limited, which robustly denied it was blacklisting workers. A spokesperson was quoted as saying: 'No-one has ever been denied employment on any of our sites, including the Olympic main stadium site, on the basis of their beliefs or background.'[1]

It certainly seemed that construction firms were trying to play fair.

In 2007, prior to major construction works and to much fanfare, the government, the unions, the Olympic Delivery Authority (ODA) and CLM had signed a *Memorandum of Agreement*, which established an Industrial Relations Code of Practice on site. The Memorandum called for an 'ethos' of direct employment and union involvement in safety. Five convenors from UCATT and Unite were appointed on various contracts, including the enabling works, the Stadium, the Aquatic Centre and the Athletes Village, and these carried out the site safety inductions for new starters. Although far from universal, levels of direct employment undoubtedly showed major improvement on the project, reaching a maximum of 70 per cent in the Olympic Park and 30 per cent in the Athletes' Village (still significantly higher than the industry norm). Safety figures on the Olympic Park, meanwhile, are some of the best ever recorded in UK construction, with not a single fatality in 81.6 million working hours.[2] Where workers were directly employed and unions were involved in safety issues, the improvements were obvious for all to see. What, then, of blacklisting?

Paul Corby is currently Chair of the Joint Industry Board (JIB) – the special employer-union body for electricians described in

Chapter 4.[3] The former head of the construction section within Amicus left the union on a voluntary redundancy package in 2005 after the election of Derek Simpson as general secretary. On leaving the union, Corby started working as a consultant providing strategic industrial-relations advice for a number of major building companies, including TCA subscriber AMEC.

In 2007, Corby was hired as the main industrial-relations consultant by the ODA, where the Director of Construction was Howard Shiplee, who would later be honoured with a CBE and placed in charge of the Conservative government's Universal Credit programme. Soon after taking up his new role on 12 June 2007 and at the time the Memorandum was being negotiated, Paul Corby sent Shiplee an email about industrial relations on the Olympic site. The email starts 'Hi Howard, STRICTLY PRIVATE AND CONFIDENTIAL' and then goes on to make personal comments about the blacklisted electrician Steve Kelly, describing him as a 'well-known electrical militant and co-ordinator of the militant rank-and-file body'. Corby describes the suggestion that the GMB union should be allowed as signatories to the agreement on the project as 'idiotic' and 'beyond belief', adding:

'I must warn you that this is a very serious development as militant electricians would now have the option of linking up with the laggers' [traditionally represented by the GMB].

The Corby email was only discovered in 2013, when it was anonymously forwarded to Paul Kenny of the GMB. The union's lead construction organizer, Phil Whitehurst, subsequently said:

> We all knew blacklisting was happening on the Olympics, but never expected it, as the email suggests, coming from our side of the fence, with regard to Steve Kelly.[94]

In response, Corby told the authors:

> I had no interface with any contractor on the Olympics. I had a contract with the ODA to advise the Director of Construction on strategic stuff. I sent a private and confidential email to Howard Shiplee. That email is nothing to do with blacklisting. What it says about Steve Kelly is a fact. At the time that email was sent, he was a GMB official. I have no problem with Steve

Kelly, I have no acrimony, he was a capable organizer, if he was on there for the GMB he would have made gains. That would cause an industrial-relations risk.

I sent a confidential email to the Director of the ODA, not to anyone else. I haven't circulated that email about Steve Kelly; it's other people who have done him a disservice. I haven't deliberately or inadvertently colluded with blacklisting. I have fought against it. Do I regret sending that email? Of course I do. But I didn't do it to do Steve Kelly any harm. It was about the GMB. I offered to go and see Paul Kenny but he wouldn't even discuss it.⁹

Steve Kelly worked temporarily as a GMB organizer between March 2004 and March 2006, going back on the tools 15 months before the email to Howard Shiplee. Following Corby's email, Kelly, currently secretary of the Unite London Contracting Branch, said:

⁶ I tried to get on the Olympics. I applied for a job with T Clarke Electrical. I had a long conversation with the labour manager, he was asking me various questions. Then he asked me what jobs had I been on, had I been on the Jubilee Line?

He obviously had my name and they were actually looking for electricians because a friend of mine, Chris, was on there at the time. He said they'd let me know and eventually a letter came through saying my application for employment was unsuccessful but they'd keep me on file.

About a week later, Chris rang me up and told me, "The supervisor on this site is constantly talking about you, seems like he's obsessed. He's never gonna work again in London. He's the biggest troublemaker going. He was down here a couple of days ago handing out leaflets telling people to join the union."⁹

Other workers targeted

Kelly was not the only worker to have suffered what appears to be a post-TCA version of blacklisting on the high-profile construction project. By mid-2010 three electricians who had previously worked together on the Jubilee Line had managed to get through the defensive shield, working for an electrical company called

Daletech Services on the Media Centre, where Skanska and Carillion were in charge. Frank Morris had been an apprentice while working on the Jubilee Line but Dave Auvache and Jim Grey had both been shop stewards, Grey also taking on the role of shop treasurer.

Frank Morris said at the time: 'When I started in August 2010 at the Olympics I was overjoyed, I bought into the Olympic dream and was proud that I could be part of the building of it. I was also guaranteeing myself a reasonable weekly wage in the worst recession since the Great Depression, which was a lifeline to me and my family.'

But after only a few weeks all three of the union members were to be removed from the job. Jim Grey remembers:

> God knows how we got on there but we did, they were desperate for anyone. We found out there was a shop steward in place and we thought "good, everything is hunky dory". It turns out he was appointed by management and not really doing a lot. There were deals being thrown out left, right and centre. The whole job was on price, even though we were on the cards. So people were agreeing their own little deals and we said if there is going to be a bonus, it should be shared out across the board, which didn't go down too well. We forced the steward to hold a meeting and in the end I got elected as deputy steward with Frank and Dave backing me up.

Immediately afterwards, Dave Auvache was sacked for no apparent reason, despite hitting a productivity bonus and having a 100-per-cent attendance record. Frank Morris was shocked at the sacking but even more so by what happened next:

> Later that day I was speaking to my electrical supervisor and I asked what was the reason behind the dismissal. His reply was astonishing. He stated he was dismissed because his name has come up on a list; he was a union man, a known troublemaker. He confirmed this again the following day.

Dave Auvache was appealing his dismissal through the JIB procedures, so Morris quickly passed on the information and remembers, 'that was the end of my Olympic experience'.

Auvache had lasted a month. Frank Morris was transferred by Daletech from the Olympics to another Skanska job at Belmarsh Prison a week later. Jim Grey was transferred 30 miles away to Southend, just three weeks after becoming an elected union rep. Auvache and Grey both appear on the Consulting Association blacklist. Entries relating to Daletech appear in a number of the blacklist files. All three electricians appear on the Sheila Knight list circulated after the Jubilee Line Extension. The Olympics may have been high profile, with a full union recognition agreement and five appointed union convenors – but the habit of blacklisting appeared to be hard to shake.

After being transferred to the Belmarsh Prison project, Frank Morris was forced to work in isolation from the rest of the workforce and alleges constant intimidation from the management team on site. On 16 December 2010, he presented a grievance to the company about the alleged bullying but later that day had to call the police for his own protection after a senior electrical engineer threatened him with violence. Morris' grievance was heard on 4 February 2011 and on Valentine's Day he received notice that he was being dismissed for gross misconduct.

Normally these sackings would have gone unnoticed but the Blacklist Support Group immediately mobilized over 60 trade unionists to an early-morning protest outside the Olympic site. The protests continued over a number of weeks, blockading the main goods entrance to the project when protesters repeatedly crossed a zebra crossing while carrying their banners. When the International Olympic Committee visited London in the spring of 2011, supporters of Frank Morris and Dave Auvache were assaulted by armed plainclothes security guards when they attempted to hand out leaflets to IOC members outside the Park Plaza Hotel at Westminster Bridge.

On one occasion the protesters visited the ODA offices with the intention of explaining what had happened and to ask why the ODA was continuing to make public announcements that blacklisting was not taking place on the project. The ODA locked the doors and refused entry to both Frank Morris and Steve Hedley, the RMT organizer who was representing the dismissed workers. Hedley said:

❝It's not very often that managers put in their own witness statements that they offered to take the employee off the site and sort it out man to man!❞[95]

Employment Tribunal claims were submitted for whistleblowing, unfair dismissal and blacklisting under the new blacklisting regulations, although due to the vagaries of UK employment law and the lack of evidence at the time, the cases were later withdrawn. Frank Morris was to remain unemployed for nearly 12 months. Despite the furore around the blacklisting issue, the press refused to run any story that might disrupt the pre-Olympic media love-in. It was not until the Scottish Affairs Select Committee called the blacklisting firms to give evidence that the truth was slowly uncovered. In June 2012, Dave Smith first told the Scottish Affairs Select Committee about the blacklisting of the three electricians at the Olympics.

In October 2012, UCATT gave evidence to MPs and Steve Murphy highlighted the issue first raised by a previous general secretary three years earlier. Murphy stressed the central role of Sir Robert McAlpine Ltd and drew attention to the fact that invoices showed a spike in the number of name checks made by the Olympic builder. From July to September 2008 McAlpine was invoiced for £12,839.20, equating to a total of 5,836 individual name checks. The UCATT general secretary told MPs:

❝That is 65 checks being done per day, seven days a week. Robert McAlpine's surge in blacklisting checks corresponded with the large-scale recruitment on the building of the Olympic Stadium. My union would therefore suggest that taxpayers' money meant to be spent on the building of the Olympic Stadium – the centrepiece of the Olympic Games in 2012 – was instead spent on blacklisting construction workers.❞

Kerr confirms Olympic blacklisting

Despite the denials by the ODA, all speculation about possible blacklisting was eradicated in November 2012 when Ian Kerr gave evidence and was asked outright about blacklisting on the Olympics.

'Bearing in mind that we went out of business in 2009, the earlier stages of preparation for the keynote buildings – the Velodrome, the swimming pool and all the rest of it – hadn't got very far, but with the groundworks, the preparation of the sites, yes, we were involved,' he said.

Kerr named McAlpine's, one of Balfour Beatty's subsidiaries and possibly Skanska as carrying out Olympic blacklisting checks. 'This was the early stages, so they may well have been building up bodies of people whom they were going to be asking to work for them further down the line,' he said.

Coming only weeks after the Olympics closing ceremony, the UCATT and Ian Kerr revelations about blacklisting on the project gained considerable media coverage. Having repeatedly denied the conspiracy against Olympic job applicants, the ODA came under pressure to explain itself. Despite the Blacklist Support Group protest in support of Frank Morris outside the Stratford offices of the ODA, chief executive Dennis Hone told the Budget and Performance Committee of the London Assembly:

> ❛The ODA did not receive any evidence or could [not] find any evidence of blacklisting on the Olympic Park during the construction phase or otherwise.❜

It later transpired that the ODA had never actually asked any of the companies but, a month after his optimistic statement, Hone finally wrote to the major contractors asking them whether they

Cullum McAlpine gives evidence to the Scottish Affairs Select Committee

used the Consulting Association blacklist on the Olympic site. Balfour Beatty responded and became the first company to admit having used The Consulting Association, confessing to vetting applications made by 12 workers on the Olympics. Only days after the Balfour Beatty admission, Cullum McAlpine was a Select Committee witness and revealed that the ODA had raised the issue of blacklisting – but only once all the work was complete and only then in response to political pressure. Since the ODA had never explicitly asked, McAlpine's hadn't volunteered that it had checked thousands of names with TCA, but under pressure from MPs he was more forthcoming.

> Cullum McAlpine: 'In 2008, when we were starting on the groundworks of the Olympic Stadium, we did check the workers who came on to the site. There were no references, so nobody was affected. By the time the main project started, The Consulting Association had been raided by the ICO, so that was not an issue.'

> Ian Davidson MP: 'But had somebody's name been flagged up by The Consulting Association, you might very well have refused them the job.'

> Cullum McAlpine: 'I do not think I can answer that question.'

> Ian Davidson MP: 'No, I do not think you can either.'

Less than six months after the Olympics had finished, the builders of the Olympic Stadium and the Aquatic Centre had both admitted blacklisting on the site but the supposed tiny number of prospective workers affected was in stark contrast to the vast number of name checks indicated in the invoices. As Dave Auvache, Jim Grey, Frank Morris and Steve Kelly had all worked for or applied to smaller subcontractors on the project, there were some who still doubted the allegations. It did not take long before a bit more light was shone on the dark conspiracy.

Harvey Francis, Skanska executive vice-president, told the Select Committee: 'Many of the people who were checked were not actually people Skanska was going to employ. They were subcontract workers we were looking to have placed on our sites.'

Ian Davidson then suggested the most likely course of action was that a worker employed by a sub-contractor was flagged up by The Consulting Association.

> Ian Davidson: 'Presumably, there were cases where you refused to allow subcontractors' staff on to your sites, which could very well result not in you yourselves sacking them but in the subcontractor doing so.'
>
> Harvey Francis: 'Hypothetically, yes, I guess.'

Francis had admitted that it was absolute standard operating procedure for Skanska to check all sub-contracted and agency workers on major sensitive projects. This is borne out by the vast number of entries on blacklist files ascribed to Skanska's main contact, Stephen Quant. But, according to Francis, an internal investigation came back with assurances that The Consulting Association was not used on the Olympics. This was despite Skanska being identified by Ian Kerr as 'possibly' using the blacklist on the Olympics and their having paid in excess of £28,000 for blacklist checks in the period they were working on the Media Centre – the largest invoice to any company. The MPs were unconvinced.

After hearing the evidence at the Select Committee, Jim Grey, the Unite union rep electrician transferred from the Skanska-built Media Centre, said:

> ❝All the jigsaw pieces fitted into place then. They always denied that there was a blacklist on the job, denied there was a list of names, but obviously there was all the way along. I think I've been blacklisted off the Olympics. I was transferred off the job but I believe I would have been sacked if there wasn't so much stink thrown up when Dave got sacked.❞

The BESNA sparks dispute

On a hot Saturday afternoon in August 2011, a meeting was held at Conway Hall, Red Lion Square, in London. The meeting had been arranged via text messages by a handful of union activists in the electrical contracting industry. Originally the meeting was to be held above a pub but it soon became obvious that this wouldn't be large enough for the numbers likely to attend. In the end it was standing room only as 500 building workers crammed into the large wood-panelled Victorian hall to discuss a rumour that was circulating through the industry. This was the start of the biggest industrial battle seen in the UK building industry for decades. The rank-and-file-led 'sparks dispute' transformed blacklisting from being a fringe issue to centre stage at national building industry negotiations.

The rumour was that eight of the largest mechanical and electrical contractors had decided to withdraw from the JIB agreement; this turned out to be true. The eight renegade firms had announced their intention to leave the long-established partnership agreement and unilaterally set up a new set of terms and conditions for the industry called the Building Engineering Services National Agreement (BESNA). The new agreement to cover electricians, plumbers and heating and ventilation engineers allowed unqualified workers to carry out the work currently undertaken by electricians. The JIB rate of pay for electricians would be reduced from £16.25 per hour to as low as £10 per hour under BESNA: a 35-per-cent pay cut. The companies were: Balfour Beatty, Crown House Technologies, T Clarke, SPIE Matthew Hall, Gratte Brothers, NG Bailey and Shepherd Engineering Services. Six of these were also subscribers to The Consulting Association. The chief executive of the newly formed body was Blane Judd, a Conservative Party councillor in Essex.

Union activists immediately saw BESNA as an attack on their pay and an attempt to deskill the industry – a virtual rerun of the late 1990s SMA dispute. The deskilling of the industry was not simply an issue of jobs: it was about safety. This was particularly the case for Stewart Hume, a young electrician working at the Grangemouth Oil Refinery for Balfour Beatty Engineering Services (BBES), who had never been involved in any union activity before.

> This is a big issue. It's putting electricians out of work for a start but it's also the potential health-and-safety issue, with these people not qualified to carry out electrical work. My dad back in 1984 worked for South of Scotland Electricity Board. He was working on a substation literally two miles from the house. It was July 1984, a really warm summer day, when he got electrocuted and killed at his work. I got into the

trade to understand more what had actually happened to him. Obviously what happened to my dad was a tragedy. That was one of my driving forces for getting involved with the BESNA, the deskilling. If somebody as qualified as my dad could be electrocuted on site and some of these guys are walking about who have never worked in the electrical industry before, there is the potential there for more fatalities.⁹

The initial Conway Hall meeting elected a national rank-and-file committee made up of Steve Kelly and Kevin Williamson from London, Steve Acheson from Manchester, Jim Harte, a Labour councillor from Renfrewshire near Glasgow, Pete Shaw from Leeds and Russ Blakely to represent pipe-fitters. The meeting agreed to co-opt onto the committee the blacklisted Rolls Royce convener Jerry Hicks from Bristol, a prominent leftwing activist and former candidate for Unite general secretary (who, although never having worked in the construction industry, also had a Consulting Association file). The sparks (the popular term for electricians) unanimously voiced their total opposition to BESNA and left the meeting preparing for war.

Kevin Holmes, a twenty-something electrician from Blackburn working for SPIE Matthew Hall at Ratcliffe Power Station, recalls that first meeting:

⁶Five hundred people, that first ever rank-and-file BESNA meeting. Electrifying, honestly, I can't describe the buzz in the room, to feel part of something so massive. We were going to stand together to defend our rights. It was phenomenal.⁹

The rank and file started organizing 6am early-morning protests, the first being at Blackfriars in London, where Balfour Beatty were rebuilding the Underground station. A week later the sparks mobilized in Glasgow, Manchester and Lindsey Oil Refinery. Veteran leftwinger Tony Benn joined the protests on the steps of Stratford station to give out leaflets to workers on the Olympics. Within weeks the sparks' dispute had turned into a major industrial battle. The early-morning demonstrations were spurred on by fireworks, dhol drummers, rappers and bagpipes. Routine protests escalated into occupations of building sites, company head offices and wildcat walkouts on major blue-book sites. All of this was organized by an increasingly emboldened rank and file rather than via a top-down centralized leadership structure: within a few weeks, regional rank-and-file committees had been elected in London, Scotland, Wales, the Northwest and the Northeast. Younger electricians new to union activism such as Ian Bradley, Dan Dobson, Jason Poulter, Kevin Holmes, Stewart Hume and Greig McArthur were encouraged to take on leading roles.

This new generation of union activists were considerably more social-media savvy than the old guard. One electrician in his twenties under the pseudonym of JIB Electrician set up a Facebook page and a blog called *Electricians against the World* that was to co-ordinate much of the action during the dispute. Within weeks the blog was receiving 800 hits a day and the Facebook group rapidly went to over 2,000 members. Software showed that the IP addresses for Balfour Beatty, NG Bailey, ECA, JIB, the Houses of Parliament and the police came up almost every day.

YouTube videos were to become another major propaganda tool, with the *Reel News*[6] indie media collective uploading a new film every week throughout the dispute and electricians posting straight off their iPhones onto the web. At 6am picket lines people would show each other video clips posted onto YouTube that very morning at the other end of the country. One memorable moment that became a hit on social media was when Ian Bradley, a young electrician from Dagenham, was caught on video telling the electricians blockading Oxford Street, 'The TUC have called for civil disobedience, well, we've given them civil disobedience,' at the very moment a snatch squad of the Metropolitan Police attempted to grab his microphone and seize the spark's sound system. When workers outside a building site in London saw their Scottish counterparts had occupied site offices and the BBC Scotland building in protest at the media blackout, it was a matter of pride not to be outdone.

The YouTube videos also had the effect of spreading the news of the dispute to a global audience. The dispute received messages of support and financial donations from the Teamsters in America and the Construction, Forestry, Mining and Energy Union in Australia. In addition, Dean Mighell, Troy Grey and other leaders of the militant Victoria branch of the Electrical Trades Union (ETU) met leading rank-and-file activists in London and Melbourne and spoke on platforms when visiting the UK. Financial backing from the ETU to the tune of tens of thousands of dollars virtually bankrolled the rank-and-file action, paying for room hire, PA systems and the new *Site Worker* newsletter.

BESNA and blacklisting

The picket lines at Blackfriars were visited by Occupy activists who were sleeping in tents just around the corner at St Paul's Cathedral. The sparks returned the compliment by marching to St Paul's in solidarity with the anti-capitalist protesters. The links between the two groups were to become stronger as time progressed. Paul McKeown, a young electrician from Northern Ireland working in London, said:

> At that time there was a lot going on about social justice. You had the Occupy movement in New York, a similar thing happened at St Paul's. Revolutions were breaking out all across the Middle East, things were happening in Brazil as well. There was a lot of excitement in the air that things will turn in favour of the masses instead of the bosses: that was what people were demanding around the world. That spurred people on.[97]

BESNA had started as a dispute about a 35-per-cent wage cut and the deskilling of the electrical contracting industry but almost immediately 'End the Blacklist' became a central slogan of the dispute. The rank-and-file *Site Worker* paper flooded building sites across the country and blacklisting was mentioned in every edition. Electrician Kevin Loughran explains how blacklisting became part of the dispute:

> They thought they could just walk all over the trade by introducing this BESNA but they didn't realize that the backbone of the electricians' union, certainly the rank-and-file part of the union, were the blacklisted lads. Blacklisting came on because we thought, we can beat you, we can beat you at anything now.

It was a thought echoed by Jason Poulter, an electrician from Accrington with a young family. The Unite safety rep said:

❛They thought they would walk BESNA in because they thought they had already blacklisted all of the union activists: the people prepared to fight. They created an element of fear in this industry. But we went to a meeting and we were asking, why are these lads not stewards on our jobs if they are all electricians? The answer was that they can't get on sites. So then lads were saying, well, if these lads were on site, we wouldn't be in this pickle because it would have been nipped in the bud. So that's another reason why blacklisting got brought into it because the best stewards had been blacklisted off these jobs and when they do that they are gonna start worsening your terms and conditions and imposing horrible contracts.❜

Following a national day of action on 9 November 2011 in which thousands of workers walked out across the country, Unite balloted its members in Balfour Beatty for official strike action – they turned out to be 81 per cent in favour. The company obtained a High Court injunction declaring the ballot illegal on a technicality but the rank and file simply ignored the injunction and on 7 December organized nationally co-ordinated mass walkouts in Newcastle, Glasgow, Manchester, Cardiff, Wales and major oil refineries and power stations, including Grangemouth and Ratcliffe.

At Blackfriars station, over 300 pickets spilled into the main road, physically blockading the site entrance while their sound system pumped out high-volume drum and bass. Sheets of ply were nailed across the site entrance with the words 'CLOSED BY THE RANK & FILE' painted on them. The pickets were joined by the Unite EC member for construction John Sheridan and many more of the executive, John McDonnell MP and the late RMT union leader Bob Crow. Balfour Beatty sites in Aberdeen and Dunfermline walked out when young electricians, following the day's events on Facebook, organized impromptu meetings in the canteen, leading to whole sites walking off in solidarity.

Unite reballoted their members and again Balfour Beatty sought an injunction. In February 2012, over 300 electricians and their mobile sound system this time blockaded rush-hour traffic on Park Lane outside the Grosvenor Hotel where the Electrical Contractors' Association awards dinner was taking place. The great and good of the industry, in their black ties and dinner jackets, were forced to walk to the venue and run the gauntlet of the sparks jigging to *The Irish Rover*. The very next day the High Court threw out the Balfour Beatty injunction request and the company withdrew from BESNA.

A few days later, on 24 February 2012, Blane Judd of BESNA issued a statement:

> ❝Despite the best efforts of the Association and the significant progress that has been made in recent months, all seven companies who instigated the development of the BESNA have now withdrawn from the initiative.❞

BESNA was dead. The combination of rank-and-file militancy and official union action had buried it. Talks started at ACAS between Unite and the big electrical contractors and, for the first time ever at national negotiations, blacklisting was a key agenda item. In another first, the Unite national negotiation team included Steve Acheson, as representative of the rank and file.

But that, of course, was not the end of the story. Once the sparks' dispute had ended, electrical firms tried to victimize union activists who had played leading roles in the return of industrial militancy to the construction industry. Kevin Holmes and Jason Poulter, respectively Unite steward and safety rep at Ratcliffe Power Station, were both investigated on what the union regarded as trumped-up charges by the blacklisting firm SPIE Matthew Hall. Jason Poulter was eventually suspended for seven-and-a-half weeks and faced dismissal. Gail Cartmail raised the case in her Select Committee evidence but again it was the rank and file that resolved the issue.

Rob Williams, secretary of the National Shop Steward Network, remembers the day that dozens of rank-and-file sparks from London, Liverpool, Manchester and Scotland tried to get Jason his job back:

> ❝The guys working with Jay and Kevin had decided not to go to work. So we were outside the plant and the cars were going in,

everybody's head down. Most of the guys were going in at half six, seven o'clock. We were talking to them and encouraging them not to go into work but if they were, at least to have a meeting to discuss it. We were in constant contact with those inside the plant and we started getting word that there were meetings taking place from about eight onwards and from about 10 onwards the word started to come out that different groups of workers had agreed that they were going to come out of work. Some say 800 came out, some say 1,500. But what I will never forget was the different demeanour: guys were going into work with their heads down a little bit but when they came out, it wasn't a walk out, it was a drive out. They drove out in long lines of cars beeping their horns, absolutely ecstatic. What a day!⁸

Jason Poulter was reinstated the very next morning.

However, a few weeks after the dispute, Balfour Beatty Engineering Services (BBES) decided to carry out a redundancy process, across the entire country – yet only one worker was to lose his job. That individual was leading anti-BESNA activist Stewart Hume, who had worked for the company for 17 years since he joined them as an apprentice.

Again, Gail Cartmail of Unite raised the victimization with MPs:

> One of our members, Stewart Hume, was interviewed by a manager called Gerry Harvey who, if I can put it in the vernacular, has form on blacklisting. Gerry Harvey is the man who interviewed one of our leading representatives at Grangemouth for Balfour Beatty Engineering Services. I remember that Stewart Hume had a personal interview with him, and the result was Stewart's unexpected redundancy.⁹

Blacklisted workers travelled to Glasgow to protest outside BBES offices. Colin Trousdale drove up to Scotland in a VW campervan especially to highlight the role of Balfour Beatty HR director Gerry Harvey, who in a 2008 Tribunal had denied that blacklisting existed in the building industry. Only a year later, when the blacklist was discovered, the same Tribunal was recorded on Trousdale's Consulting Association file. Trousdale told the protesters: 'Being a trade union member is not a crime: perjury is.'

Glasgow Labour MP Jim Sheridan, whose brother appears on the blacklist, directed a message to Balfour Beatty:

> ❝It is a long time since the days when trade unions and trade unionists were seen as the enemy within. You don't have to get into blacklisting.❞[9]

Despite being transferred 50 miles away from Grangemouth, fellow workers didn't forget Hume. He had more than one reason to remember that period:

> ❝I'd just found out that Nikki, my partner, was pregnant again, so it was a bit worrying. I couldn't tell anybody but in the back of my mind, I'd just lost my job and another baby on the way but I thought I'm just gonna go for it. Nikki was behind me the whole way.
>
> If I hadn't known I was getting the backing of the guys it might have been a totally different story. I might have just rolled over. It was unbelievable, all these guys, some that I had never even worked with, they were willing to put themselves on the line to save my job. That's what solidarity is all about.❞[10]

Hume's case may have been raised in Parliament but it was when the Grangemouth workers voted to walk out over it that he was miraculously reinstated. Hume has since been elected as shop steward and onto the Unite national construction committee.

From being ignored on the Olympics, the sparks' rank-and-file action had dragged blacklisting centre stage with the BESNA dispute. But the biggest industrial dispute ever to take place on the issue of blacklisting had not yet even begun.

Crossrail

Crossrail is the largest publicly funded project in western Europe and, when finished, will allow train passengers to travel from East to West through central London without having to change onto the tube network. New tunnels run under the capital and major station redevelopment is taking place through the West End. The blacklisting firms – Costain, Laing O'Rourke, Carillion, Balfour

Beatty, Skanska, Cleveland Bridge, NG Bailey, BAM and Kier – all have significant contracts on Crossrail. And Kerr told MPs:

> ❝ There was an awful lot of discussion at our meetings about Crossrail because it was perceived as going to be a problematic contract, similar to the Jubilee Line. We thought that similar sorts of problems would probably arise. In relation to Crossrail, Balfour Beatty had a lot to say on that.❞[11]

Crossrail was the client and Ron Barron, the former industrial-relations manager at CB&I, was employed as head of employment relations across the entire project. Ron Barron's intimate involvement in blacklisting had been exposed during the Phil Willis employment tribunal. The new HR boss at Crossrail had been the main TCA contact at CB&I and actually took the company into the Association in the first place. Having participated in the Crossrail discussions described by Ian Kerr, he was now in overall control of industrial relations on the project and in day-to-day liaison with his previous co-conspirators who were still responsible for labour on different contracts across Crossrail.

One such contract was the £250-million C300 contract to dig two tunnels from Royal Oak through Bond Street and Tottenham Court Road, finishing at Farringdon, which had been awarded to a newly formed joint venture between BAM, Ferrovial and Kier (BFK). BAM and Kier were both subscribers to The Consulting Association; Ferrovial, meanwhile, is a Spanish transnational that made its fortune during the Franco dictatorship. BFK also won the contracts to build two stations at Bond Street and Tottenham Court Road.

Ron Turner, a highly experienced tunnelling engineer who had previously supervised work on the Channel Tunnel, Jubilee Line Extension and Heathrow Terminal 5, was part of the BFK tender team securing contracts on Crossrail. Due to his experience within the tunnelling industry, after 10 months' preparation it was Turner who actually did the final presentations to Crossrail on behalf of BFK during the tender submission process.

After winning the contract, Ron Turner was made plant manager for all the tunnelling activities, responsible for procurement and the erection of the conveyor-belt systems, the gantry cranes and the Tunnel Boring Machines (TBMs). The mechanics and electricians needed for the job were entirely under his jurisdiction and were all supplied via the company he owned, called Electrical Installations Services Limited (EIS). At the peak of the job, EIS had 45 workers, on a two-shift system, based at Westbourne Park station, near Paddington. The work had been carried out well and in June 2012 the EIS contract was extended by 15 months until September 2013.

A year after being dismissed from the Olympics, it was with EIS Ltd that Frank Morris finally managed to get a new job. Originally working on a small tunnelling job in Tower Hill, he was transferred into Crossrail, running temporary electrics in the tunnels. Looking back, Ron Turner remembers nothing remarkable:

> ❝Frank's CV came in. I didn't know Frank at that time. I read it. Frank had industrial experience working on the Jubilee Line on the installation. He was obviously a competent electrician. Frank started on 17 February, mild mannered, turned up for work on time, I got no reports from the supervisors that he was a problem. Frank was just another one of the lads: simple as that.❞

But not for long. In May 2012, when Morris had only been on the site a few weeks, Turner had a discussion with a BFK manager, who showed the EIS owner a list of his employees working on site. Turner said:

> ❝I got challenged by BFK that one of my employees was a union activist. I said, "Who is he?" They went down the list and said, "It's Frank Morris."
>
> I said, "Are you sure about this?" because Frank would not say boo to a goose in my opinion and I questioned whether they had got the right guy because it didn't seem to stack up.❞[12]

Ron Turner saw no reason to dismiss a good electrician and refused to take the hint but remembers:

'Some days later I was questioned by Pat Swift, the HR manager for BFK, as to why I had employed Frank Morris. And my reply was "Why not?"

'I had not and still do not have an issue with Frank but obviously his history from the Olympics has unfortunately followed him about.'

Pat Swift was identified by Ian Kerr as the main contact for BAM Nuttall and as someone who sought information on a regular basis from The Consulting Association. On the establishment of the BFK joint venture, he was appointed as head of human resources for the BFK consortium on Crossrail. The group HR manager for Kier was Kathy Almansoor, another main contact with The Consulting Association, as identified by Ian Kerr. Frank Morris was working for a small electrical sub-contractor on the most prestigious construction project in the UK since the Olympics and proven blacklisters were all in charge of labour in the section of the project he was working on. Unsurprisingly, he didn't last very long.

But, despite having been told to remove the union man from site, having a sense of fair play, Ron Turner still refused to sack Frank Morris, who in his eyes had done nothing wrong. Morris had never mentioned the union while working on the site, yet during the summer BFK managers suddenly for no apparent reason began asking the electrician questions about trade unions. He realized that BFK had discovered that he was a trade union activist and, from painful experience, knew what the likely outcome would be. Morris decided immediately to protect his position by formalizing a trade union role. He sought the support of his co-workers and, within 24 hours, Unite official Harry Cowap held a meeting in the site canteen. The majority of the EIS workers joined Unite and Frank Morris was elected as shop steward, with another EIS electrician elected as safety rep.

Tunnelling is a dangerous job. All workers are inducted about the dangers and strict controls are kept on access to and egress from the tunnel. The Crossrail Tunnel Boring Machines are fitted with refuge spaces, which are to be used in case of fire. There are 20 spaces in the refuge and therefore only 20 workers are allowed in the tunnel at any time. On one occasion when Morris was in the tunnel, he counted 24 people and reported this to the BFK safety manager. Morris was immediately isolated from the rest of the workforce, forced to make up extension leads in a cabin on his own, and banned by BFK from entering the tunnel and even the canteen. A few weeks later, Garry Gargett, an experienced electrical supervisor, saw a dangerous situation where a section of 11,000-volt electrical cables was covered by scaffolding and debris thrown on top of it. The engineer quite responsibly took a photograph of the cables being buried. He printed it off and was going to take it to his supervisor. He was intercepted by a BFK manager, removed from site and dismissed. The excuse that BFK gave for this dismissal was that he had taken photographs without having a permit. Ron Turner describes this as 'absolutely ridiculous'.

Garry Gargett was dismissed after raising a safety issue and Frank Morris was working in solitary confinement after raising a safety issue. But that did not mean the newly elected shop steward stopped raising issues with the BFK management. It became obvious that certain groups of workers on the project were being paid a productivity bonus based on how many concrete rings were installed as the TBM progressed. Tunnelling is very much a collective activity; everyone plays a role and the TBM only progresses if all workers do their job properly. Like countless union reps across the world, Morris consulted his members and then raised the issue of a collective bonus for all workers with BFK management. Ron Turner, Frank's employer, actually agreed: 'He'd every right to be disgruntled about it. I'm not a member of the trade union but I know what's fair and what's not.'

In September 2012, only weeks after extending the EIS contract for another 15 months, the EIS contract was terminated with one week's notice. The 28 EIS workers on site, including Ron Turner's daughter, were told to collect their tools before being escorted off by security. Ron Turner was not allowed back on site to try to settle the final accounts. After 12 years' trading and having a good reputation in the tunnelling industry, EIS Limited was liquidated by HMRC. The extension of the EIS contract with BFK was issued seven days before Frank Morris was elected as a shop steward and the notice to terminate the EIS contract was issued just 36 days after Frank Morris had submitted a formal grievance about the bonus.

And so started the UK's biggest-ever industrial dispute to get a blacklisted shop steward reinstated. Coming eight months after the

BESNA victory, the sparks' rank and file and the Blacklist Support Group mobilized nearly 100 people to Westbourne Park at 6am, stopping all deliveries into the project. Initially many of the dismissed workers attended the picket line but, as the work formerly carried out by EIS still had to be done, within days virtually all of the other EIS workers had transferred to other companies working on Crossrail. Frank Morris, of course, was not transferred to a new employer.

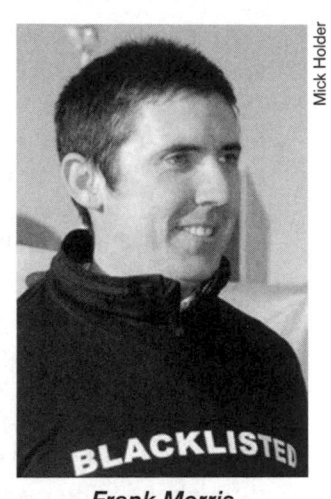

Frank Morris

The Crossrail dispute quickly developed a new tactic of flashmob picketing. Without warning, hundreds of building workers and supporters would appear out of nowhere and blockade the main roads outside Crossrail sites. The stations at Tottenham Court Road and Bond Street were hit repeatedly by this tactic, often stopping huge concrete pours mid-pour and always bringing West End traffic to a complete gridlock. The huge 12-feet-high, 40-feet-long hand-painted banners took on an iconic status as they were unfurled across Oxford Street junctions in front of red London buses. Tourists used to take selfies with the banners as the backdrop. The space in between the banners became mini celebrations once the sound system and the flares had their full effect. The traffic chaos meant that it often took the police over an hour to arrive, and even then in small numbers.

On 28 September 2012, only a few days after the sackings, the Westbourne Park site was closed by the Health and Safety Executive following the collapse of a metal gantry when a conveyor transporting spoil from the TBM became overloaded. The gantry ended up overhanging the London Underground train network, closing two lines out of Paddington station. In December a worker suffered 60-per-cent burns, having cut through a high-voltage live cable while working on the Crossrail project. Supporters of Frank Morris responded by occupying the Office of Rail Regulation, only leaving after securing 30 minutes of private negotiations with two directors of the rail industry safety watchdog.

An Employment Tribunal claim was submitted, naming EIS, BFK and Crossrail as co-respondents. Frank Morris had contacted Ron Turner beforehand to advise him that, even if he won the claim, he had no intention of claiming any money from EIS, his sole intention in making the claim being to have Crossrail and BFK in court on the charge of blacklisting. Turner even agreed to act as a witness on behalf of the claimant, despite the fact that the company he owned was the lead respondent.

In December 2012, when snow was on the ground and Morris was alone on the picket line, BFK managers taunted him, saying, 'What are your kids getting for Christmas, Frank?' But, as 2013 started, the rank-and-file flashmob protests continued.

In March 2013, 170 mainly blacklisted workers fought their way through the winter weather to attend the Blacklist Support Group AGM in London. Frank Morris received an ovation when he told the meeting what had happened at Crossrail:

> ❝They cancelled the contract for the entire company. They sacked 27 people and the day I was leaving the supervisor on the site was going, "We've all lost our jobs because of you". So I said, "Right, if I'm the issue then I'm just gonna stand outside here." That was in September and I've been there ever since.❞

The next speaker was Unite general secretary Len McCluskey, who said:

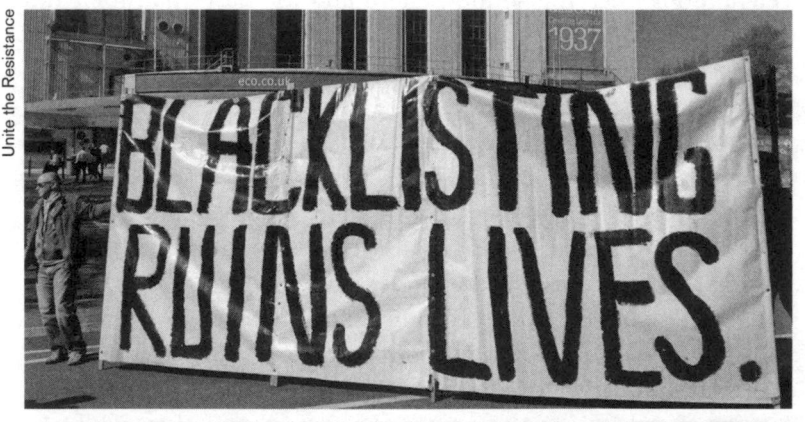

Protesters use giant banners to stop traffic outside Earls Court during the Crossrail dispute.

❝We intend to make Crossrail understand, if they believe that unions are a problem if they are recognized, then they are going to find out that by not recognizing us we are a bigger problem.❞

From that point on, Unite threw its full weight behind the battle to get Frank Morris reinstated on Crossrail. It was the rank-and-file sparks and BSG who took up the fight but it was without doubt the Unite leverage campaign that would land the killer blows. The Crossrail dispute suddenly went into overdrive. BAM, Ferrovial and Kier were targeted anywhere in the country they had contracts. From Bristol to Aberdeen, local authorities, hospitals and universities were targeted and there was an upsurge in councils passing motions banning blacklisters from public contracts. Over a period of six months, protesters with vuvuzelas and a giant inflatable rat called Scabby welcomed guests attending industry awards ceremonies, passengers at airports, and first-time buyers visiting housing developments. The offices of corporate investors in the City were occupied by protesters.

The response from Crossrail was to dig in its heels. Frank Morris was assaulted on the picket line and his giant banners were slashed to ribbons with a knife. The next day Unite called a mass picket where Guy Langston, the union's officer for construction, commented:

'Frank was abused by one of the security guards, I've asked Crossrail to have him removed because he was quite vicious to me this morning, he threatened to punch me, to find me and come and get me. They're just rent-a-mob, to be honest.'

Unite organizer Mick Duncan told the huge show of solidarity: 'We're here to tell Crossrail, "enough is enough". You can't sack our members, you can't blacklist our members and you certainly do not beat our members up.'[13]

With snow still on the ground, the first ever blacklisting march was held in Dundee. Jim McGovern MP told the marchers:

❝Blacklisting has been compared to McCarthyism. I think it is worse than that – it is secretive, it's behind closed doors. Many people who are on a blacklist don't even know they are on a blacklist. I refer not to McCarthyism, but to McAlpineism.❞

A second march was held in Glasgow during the summer and flashmob pickets continued to spring up across the country.

In May, the Crossrail campaign descended on BAM's £100-million redevelopment of Manchester City Football Club's stadium and training ground. During the protest a car collided with George Tapp, a 64-year-old electrician. Tapp was taken to Manchester Royal Infirmary, where friends and comrades staged a vigil. Tapp told the *Morning Star*:

> ❝When I came round, I was in hospital having an MRI scan. My head is still swollen, still bleeding. I have got two broken kneecaps. One of them is shattered and I have to have reconstructive surgery with steel rods.❞

The former Labour councillor from Salford was hospitalized for eight weeks, followed by months of physiotherapy. He will never work again. Originally a Greater Manchester Police press statement blamed Tapp for the accident, claiming that CCTV footage showed he had deliberately stood on the bonnet of the car. Tapp is now walking again with the aid of crutches and has even been back on protests. Despite the driver being cleared in court of a charge of dangerous driving, Tapp's union perused a compensation claim and the Unite member was awarded £80,000 for the horrific injuries suffered.[14] In December 2014, George Tapp won the Robert Tressell Award for services to working people.

As the leverage campaign gathered momentum, the dispute spread its wings and generated newspaper and radio interest across Europe. Working alongside the Dutch unions, Unite protested outside the AGM of Royal BAM in Amsterdam, while GMB worked with the Swedish Byggnads construction union to highlight the issue at the Skanska AGM in Stockholm. Meetings were arranged with corporate investors and financial analysts in Sweden, France and Spain, and questions were asked in the Dutch parliament.

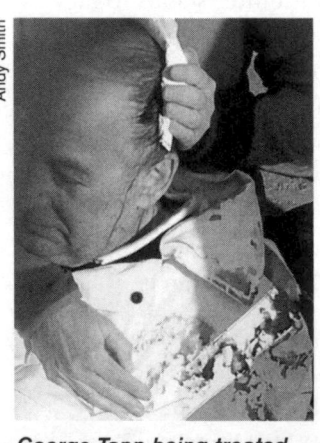

Andy Smith

George Tapp being treated.

In June 2013, the blacklisting

story finally broke in the mainstream media when the BBC *Panorama* programme broadcast *Blacklist Britain* on BBC One.[15] The documentary told the story of the Consulting Association blacklist, interviewing Mary Kerr and four blacklisted workers: Frank Matthews, Howard Nolan, Roy Bentham and Frank Morris. Crossrail was presented as proof that blacklisting was still a contemporary issue. Frank Morris told *Panorama*:

> There were times we ran out of food: cupboards were empty, Missus just bawling her eyes out. We had no money to pick the kids up from school and she was just screaming at me: "What have you done? What have you done?"

Crossrail told *Panorama*:

> It vigorously denies unsubstantiated allegations made by Frank Morris. It had seen no evidence of blacklisting of any kind by the contractors involved in the Crossrail project.[16]

But Unite assistant general secretary Gail Cartmail had seen the evidence and was recalled by the Select Committee investigation to be a witness for a second time, specifically about Crossrail. She told MPs categorically:

> Frank Morris was the victim of a blacklist. He was certainly discriminated against as a trade unionist, but we believe he was a victim of a blacklist. We believe that, as Ian Kerr stated in his evidence to this Committee, blacklisting is a contemporary issue. We believe the industry is unrepentant: it regrets only that it was found out.

Cartmail quoted the witness statement that Ron Turner had given to Unite in which the EIS Managing Director says: 'I firmly believe that the decision to cancel my contract was driven by BFK wanting to remove Mr Morris from the project.'

According to Cartmail, EIS and its workforce were 'collateral damage'. After hearing the evidence, the Scottish Affairs Select Committee referred the Crossrail blacklisting case to Vince Cable, calling on the Business Secretary to set up a government investigation into the events on the publicly funded project. That inquiry never happened.

Connections in Canada and the US

In Canada, Ferrovial had bought the rights to operate the Highway 407 Express Toll Route during a privatization spree by the Ontario Conservative government back in 1999. This has been described as Ferrovial's 'biggest cash cow'. In July 2013, Unite flew in a team of organizers to link up with the UFCW Canada and United Steelworkers unions in a rash of protests at the toll road, Ministry of Infrastructure and other contracts.[17]

By August 2013, executives of BAM and Ferrovial were flying in from Holland and Spain to participate in meetings at ACAS. The companies offered eye-watering amounts of money to settle but were not prepared to have Morris back on the job. Instead of calling off the leverage campaign, however, Unite organizer Erkan Ersoy, Frank Morris and Steve Acheson flew to Chicago, where Ferrovial were bidding to win the lease to run the Midway Airport – this was being put out to tender by the Mayor of Chicago, President Obama's former Chief of Staff, Rahm Emanuel. The Unite delegation met leaders of the IUF and UNI global union federations as well as having meetings with Chicago aldermen who had influence over the airport decision. IUF general secretary Ron Oswald warned:

‘Blacklisting has been illegal in the United States since 1935. Chicago should not allow Ferrovial, a company whose hands carry the stain of this illegal practice, to profit from a major contract such as the one at Midway Airport. Ferrovial must be told in the clearest terms you cannot act like that in the UK without consequences elsewhere.’[18]

Joe Hansen, UFCW president, added: 'We will do all we can to help our British sister union in its fight against blacklisting. Ferrovial clearly has serious questions to answer about the human rights issue of blacklisting in Britain.'[19]

During the visit, the blacklisted workers also had a private meeting with Dick Durbin, Chief Whip for the Democratic Party in the US Senate and a close ally of President Obama, with whom he had come through the Chicago political machine. Rank-and-file activists may have kick-started the Crossrail dispute but it is only the global political influence that a union like Unite can exert that swings a private meeting with a US Senator so close to the top of the Democratic Party.

After a full year in dispute, Frank Morris returned to work on the Crossrail project on 9 September 2013. The agreement was negotiated in late August but Morris refused to sign it without the consent of the Blacklist Support Group and the rank and file. The consultation meeting took place in the offices of Sharon Graham, the head of organizing and leverage at Unite. It lasted five minutes and then people retired to the pub to celebrate.

The BSG press release the same day virtually punched the air with delight:

> **The reinstatement of Frank Morris is a kick in the teeth for the blacklisting firms. This is a historic union victory.**

Frank Morris has subsequently been elected as the Unite EC member for construction, the highest lay union position for the UK building industry.

Postscript on Crossrail

In December 2013, Pat Swift, the head of human resources for BFK, was called as a witness by the Select Committee. In an evidence session lasting nearly two-and-a-half hours, Swift admitted being the main contact with The Consulting Association between 2004 and 2009 when he was director of HR for BAM Nuttall. He admitted staff in his department were in 'constant communication on a weekly basis' with the blacklisting organization. Swift admitted that the names of every applicant for hourly paid positions were checked on all projects undertaken by the company during his time in charge, including on the Olympics. Swift claimed The Consulting Association was simply a 'general referencing service' but when challenged as to why the entire operation was carried out in secret he responded 'because it was probably a dubious practice', later adding 'it was certainly illegal'.

It was questions about the dismissal of Frank Morris from Crossrail that caused the most consternation among Select Committee members. Despite all the denials throughout the year-long Crossrail dispute, Swift finally admitted that he did have a conversation with Ron Turner about Frank Morris. When

Pat Swift prior to giving evidence to the Scottish Affairs Select Committee

pushed, he told MPs: 'I said to Ron Turner he had raised trouble. I pointed out to him that he had caused trouble at the Olympics.'

When pressed on what this trouble was, Swift replied: 'This guy had been on a demonstration.'

Graeme Morrice MP responded: 'A perfectly legal demonstration against an illegal blacklist?'

Finally the Committee chair Ian Davidson MP asked directly: 'Did you ask Ron Turner to sack Frank Morris?'

Sheepishly, Swift replied: 'I may have.'

Meanwhile, in April 2014, documents leaked to the *Observer* and reports from a whistleblower showed a culture of spying on and intimidation of Crossrail workers. An internal report said that 'individuals cannot move and work freely as they are constantly looking over their shoulders and in fear of reprisals'.[20] This targeting of those raising safety concerns was particularly egregious since, in March 2014, a 44-year-old worker, Rene Tkacik, was killed after concrete sprayed onto the top of the tunnel fell on him.[21] The 'vastly experienced' Tkacik, originally from Slovakia but living in east London, was working more than 80 feet underground when the fatality occurred. He had been working in the UK partly so that he could pay for his daughter Esther to go to university. A year later, an inquest jury recorded a narrative verdict highlighting that the exclusion zone boundaries, where his body was found, were not clearly marked and that Crossrail safety briefings solely presented in English were a contributory factor with such a multilingual workforce.[22]

Helen Clifford represented Tkacik's family at the inquest and has submitted claims on behalf of numerous workers injured on the rail project. The 2016 Personal Injury Lawyer of the Year, from McMillan Williams solicitors, commented:

> The death of Rene Tkacik occurred as a result of falling shotcrete. The whistleblower confirms that the men were told to work under freshly applied shotcrete to remove the excess and this is something that he did on many occasions. Crossrail/BBMV were aware of shotcrete falls, but continued to require men to work in those conditions. Had they implemented a safe system of work, Rene's death might have been prevented.[23]

Crossrail has denied any culpability in Tkacik's death. Yet still the allegations came that raising safety concerns at Crossrail was dangerous for your employment prospects. In February 2015 a young electrician, Dan Collins, was working via an employment agency on the Bond Street section of the project. On the Monday morning he was told there was three years' work with the offer of unlimited overtime and weekend working. Two days later the Unite member complained about an unsafe raised walkway across exposed steel reinforcing without a handrail. Collins recalls what happened next:

> It was obvious that if someone carrying something had fell off there would have been a serious accident, so I put an observation card into my supervisor. It's a letter-box scheme Crossrail have set up for highlighting safety but you have to put your name on it, so obviously not many people put them in because they know they will be highlighting themselves for doing so. On the Wednesday evening when it was time to wrap up, my supervisor says to me, "They have been chewing my ear off about you putting in an observation card. We've been here for a year now. We haven't had any politics – let's keep things peaceful."[24]

On Friday morning Collins received a phone call from his agency telling him there had been a sudden downturn in work and he was no longer needed. Collins seethes:

> ❝On Monday I had three years of work with the foreman showing me round. I'm here on site and I can see the work that needs to be done and all of a sudden there's no more work for me! I got escorted to the welfare cabin with a security guard and the supervisor to get my tools. Both of them stood there watching me while I got changed and packed away all my stuff. It was like being escorted by a prison guard. Took my card off me and escorted me out the door.❞[9]

Unite and BSG blockaded Oxford Street and Park Lane on a number of occasions and Collins spoke to MPs in the Westminster parliament about his dismissal. He was quickly reinstated but on 'gardening leave'.[25] Over the next 18 months Collins was repeatedly dismissed from building sites across London, the anecdotal evidence being that he is another victim of ongoing blacklisting.

1 nin.tl/stadiumBL 2 nin.tl/Olympicslessons 3 JIB website: jib.org.uk/the-jib-committees 4 Interview with the authors. 5 Reel News video: Blacklisted, 2012, nin.tl/blacklistedyoutube 6 reelnews.co.uk 7 Interview with the authors. 8 Interview with the authors. 9 Hazards blacklist blog, nin.tl/barblacklisters 10 Interview with the authors. 11 Evidence to Scottish Affairs Select Committee, 27 Nov 2012. 12 Interview with the authors. 13 Reel News, 'The workers fight back', nin.tl/reelnews2013 14 *Morning Star*, nin.tl/courtawards 15 'Blacklist Britain', BBC TV Panorama, nin.tl/Panoramalink 16 Ibid. 17 nin.tl/UFCWCanada 18 IUF website nin.tl/Chicagosupport 19 Unite website, nin.tl/unitestateside 20 'Crossrail managers accused', *Observer*, 26 Apr 2014, nin.tl/crossrailaccusation – accessed 16 Jun 2014. 21 'Worker dies in Crossrail tunnel', BBC news, 7 Mar 2014, nin.tl/workerdies – accessed 16 Jun 2014; TUC website, nin.tl/TUCconcern 22 nin.tl/Crossraildeath 23 Quoted in *The Observer*, 2 Aug 2014, nin.tl/Crossrailsafety 24 Interview with the authors. 25 YouTube video: nin.tl/Crossrailsacking

8
How much did the unions know?

'I've spent about 11 years unemployed on and off. Four kids and a wife. The thing that gets me the most, is when the unions are mentioned.'[1]

Blacklisted Liverpool joiner Tony Sweeney

For as long as rumours of a blacklist had circulated, so had suggestions that some union officials were somehow involved in the process. That had always been denied. But when the blacklist files started landing on doormats in the spring of 2009, the speculation of a union connection ended. As well as press cuttings and the information added by companies, there were entries that named a trade union or a union official as the source of the information. Unsurprisingly, the workers with these entries on their files went berserk. Activists expected the employers not to like them – but if individuals from their own side had been in any way involved in blacklisting, that would be seen as treachery.

The files released by the ICO were heavily redacted, so while the comments were visible, it was impossible to know for certain which official had made the comments (although in some cases it was possible to make a pretty good guess). Amongst themselves, and drawing on their experiences on building sites over many years, the blacklisted workers came up with lists of the most likely candidates who might have provided information. However, as more unredacted files were slowly released, there came more questions than answers.

A name on a blacklist file is not proof of deliberate collusion, and employers' representatives may well have relied on hearsay and gossip, but a proper investigation should at least take place whenever a name appears. If someone chooses a career path that leads them to become an officer for a trade union, they often have a history of activism themselves. Why would they provide information about their own members to the employers?

The blacklist files were documents produced by the employers and their version of events is very often at odds with how a union will interpret the same incident. Even if every single union official whose name appears on blacklist documentation is completely innocent of any wrongdoing, why is their name mentioned as a source of information? How did the information get from the union official to the employer and on to the blacklist?

Two models of union activity

It is impossible to simply view the entries on the blacklist files in isolation. Any evidence that might suggest collusion needs to be placed in context. Only by understanding the history of industrial strategies adopted by the leadership of some trade unions is it possible to comprehend how a union official might have come to be named on a file.

Within trade unions there are differences of opinion about strategy. One current of opinion believes that the best way to advance the interests of members is to work in partnership with employers. If the company prospers, then the workers will benefit. The task of trade unions is to work collaboratively with management on issues where interests overlap; safety and learning are much-touted examples. Building close relationships with the employers is seen as central to this approach and anything that upsets that relationship is seen as divisive: detrimental to employer and union alike.

This model sees the union as effectively providing a service, in the same way that the AA provides a service to stranded motorists. A member pays their fees and hopes they never have to meet anyone from the AA but, if there is a problem, they expect an expert to come in and solve it for them. Once the car is fixed, the member thanks the mechanic but hopes they never have to meet them again. The union variant of this 'servicing' approach also views members as passive recipients of services such as individual representation provided by union experts, often external from the actual workforce.

The alternative 'organizing' model argues that union strength is not based upon someone coming in to save the day but upon workers acting collectively. A union has real influence when it is able to encourage workers to recognize their own strength and stick together in the workplace. Emphasis is placed upon building grassroots networks of activists who can mobilize workers in support of union aims rather than relying upon a union official or a benevolent employer.

In practice, every trade union, regardless of political outlook, employs both strands. However, it is safe to say that the organizing/mobilization approach tends to be supported by the left, while the partnership/servicing model is championed by the more rightwing people within the movement. Internal union politics are not for the faint hearted, especially in an industry like construction. Political differences can sometimes spill out into naked hostility on building sites. Talk to any experienced union representative and you'll hear talk of physical confrontations between reps and employers – and among union members themselves. It is hardly unusual for union officials to adopt a more conciliatory approach to certain issues than the members and activists they represent.

Ian Kerr was asked about the information attributed to union officials when he gave evidence to MPs:

> ❛I can sympathize with the union officials in that they represent their members... One or two people chose to disrupt a site. The poor union official had to resolve the two sides. Sometimes he didn't want an unnecessary problem, nor did his union often, of an outbreak on a site of unofficially generated action. It was in the interests of the HR manager to know who he should speak to in a particular union to try and resolve such an issue without it costing the company.❜[92]

The fact that some in the movement were prepared to work with blacklisting organizations to the detriment of individual members of their own union was confirmed during evidence given to the Scottish Affairs Select Committee by Jack Winder. The former director of information and research at the Economic League and, following its demise, director of Caprim Limited, told MPs: 'While I was with the League we had very good relations with certain trade-union leaders, who were concerned about problems caused by the far left.' He then named Leif Mills, from the banking union; Terry Carroll, from the engineering union; Eric Hammond, from the electricians; Dennis Mills, from the midlands region of the transport union; and Kate Losinska, from the Civil and Public Services Association.

Eric Hammond OBE was general secretary of the Electrical, Electronic, Telecommunications and Plumbing Union (EETPU) from 1984 until 1992, when the union merged with the engineers to form the Amalgamated Engineering and Electrical Union (AEEU). Hammond's open support for Rupert Murdoch during the 1986 Wapping dispute caused outrage amongst trade unionists. News International closed down the offices of the *Times*, *Sun* and *News of the World* newspapers in Fleet Street and moved their entire operations to a new complex in Wapping. The printers were dismissed en masse and the print unions derecognized. Hammond had negotiated a secret single-union/no-strike agreement with News International. To the horror of the trade-union movement, the mother of all sweetheart deals meant that all the new printers and even the journalists were now members of the EETPU. Wapping and other pro-business single-union agreements that the EETPU signed resulted in its expulsion from the TUC. The fall-out led to a split within the electricians' union as a section broke away in disgust, to form the Electrical Plumbing Industrial Union (EPIU).

Scabby the Rat: part of the unions' campaign against blacklisting

This was not an aberration but just one of many examples of the rightwing pro-business policies adopted by the leadership of the electricians' union over many years. The biggest jewel in the crown of Hammond and the EETPU leaders was not Wapping but the Joint Industry Board (JIB), set up by the previous electricians' leader, Frank Chapple. The JIB social-partnership model undoubtedly delivered high union membership levels and a steady stream of cash for the union machinery. Building friendly relations between the union and the employers was the key to the JIB's success and such overt moderation, including its famous hostility to the 1984-5 miners' strike, resulted in the union leadership receiving New Year's honours from successive governments. From top to bottom, EETPU officials were expected to follow the leadership line. But even EETPU officials such as former London area official Frank Westerman admit:

> The biggest contradiction in the industry is the JIB. We all know the history of how the union contributions used to be paid. Since its inception, it was opposed by the left but anyone involved knew it was definitely the best agreement.[93]

While the JIB clearly has benefits for the union in terms of membership density and guaranteeing financial security, many electricians viewed it with suspicion. They argued that the prospect of assured subscriptions (without the need for active recruitment), so long as there was no disruption, meant that the union machinery tended to side with the employers, sometimes against the best interests of its own members.

Andrew Alison, a blacklisted electrician from Dundee, recalls the attitude of one EETPU union official following a dispute about pay at the Anchor Steel works in Scunthorpe in 1973:

> I was called a professional industrial hijacker by the area official of the EETPU at the time. It was in the papers, he was on TV, this area official. I thought I was an electrician. We weren't on strike, we were working normal, just not working any overtime and he wanted people to work 7 days and 12-hour shifts.

EETPU officials supporting employers in their desire for

electricians to work excessive hours is a theme that emerges from talking to workers. Steuart Merchant, from Dundee, was a shop steward while working for MF Kent under a JIB agreement at Aldermaston. The blacklisted electrician remembers a conversation with a site manager after the workforce agreed to stop working overtime during a dispute. Merchant recalls that he was told:

> ❝"Your union official is on the telephone for you, we phoned him on your behalf. You better talk to him." The official says: "You're in a serious situation, Steuart, they're gonna sack you." "It's JIB rules – 39 hours a week – what's serious about that?" "Do you want me to come to the site?"
>
> I says, "If you're coming to the site to tell us we have to work 66 hours then don't bother." He says, "OK – I won't come down." So I go back to the cabin and in 10 minutes' time I got sacked. They sacked 50 of us.❞[94]

The friendly relationship between the Electrical Contractors' Association (the employers' group within the JIB) and the EETPU grew ever stronger and in 1979 the Conservative minister Patrick Mayhew granted a unique dispensation. This exemption allowed the JIB to substitute its own dismissal procedure for unfair dismissals – this is the only such exemption order granted in any industry. The result was that any electrician registered with the JIB effectively lost their legal rights to take a claim for unfair dismissal to an Employment Tribunal but instead was legally obliged to use the JIB procedures. This exemption was no mere paperwork exercise, it was invoked on numerous occasions, especially when union activists had been dismissed or victimized, and it was condemned in parliament by Labour MPs.[5]

The widely held belief amongst union activists was that the EETPU leadership was on the side of the employers. In private it was even bragged about by senior managers. Mike Shakespeare, managing director of Warwick Electrical Services, recalls:

> ❝I was sitting in a hotel in Russell Square during the early Eighties. Two members of NG Bailey's Major Projects Team turned up, one a main board director by the name of David Tunnicliffe, one a senior quantity surveyor. As we were

discussing matters relating to a big job, the name Frank Chapple suddenly came up in conversation; this was at a time when he was General Secretary of EETPU. The director turned to me and said, "Frank Chapple? He's been in our pocket for years. I would have thought you would have known that, everybody else does."[96]

Evidence of similarly close relationships comes from Trevor Watcham who worked for Balfour Beatty and was an Economic League contact and TCA chair from 2004 to 2005. Watchman recalls:

> The Economic League certainly had some considerable significance within UK industry as a whole in the 1970s and 1980s... I also met a number of union officials through the Economic League. During the 1980s the Economic League used to run a number of informal lunch meetings in the Midlands called "The Chairman Speaks" and I recall one meeting where I sat at a table with both Leon Brittan of the Conservative Party (who had been the main speaker) and Eric Hammond of the electricians' union together with some members of his union executive.[97]

Despite its shortcomings, one of the positive outcomes of the JIB was that the electrical contracting sector of the industry remained predominantly directly employed, unlike the rest of the construction labour force. Yet, despite the avowed policy of the JIB in support of direct employment, in 1987 the EETPU and ECA set up their own employment agency, ESCA Services, co-owned by the employers and the union. The industry has seen widespread casualization since the late 1980s, with electricians forced to work for agencies that undercut the JIB rate. ESCA was at the forefront of this process, becoming one of the largest agencies supplying temporary labour to the building industry.

According to blacklisted Dundee electrician and veteran campaigner against the abuses of the JIB, Francie Graham:

> This ESCA agency made a lot of money, a lot of money. The organization, they had a national agreement and they had an agency. So they've now got the best of both worlds basically within their grasp.[98]

Without direct employment with JIB companies, many electricians were often forced into working for the agencies, which made it easier for companies to dismiss those who stood up for their rights. Graham said:

❝You then had other agencies coming into the field of electrical contracting employment. A tap on the shoulder was enough to see you finished and on many occasions I've had that.❞

The conflict of interest was obvious for all to see and this suspicion was only fuelled when blacklisted electricians discovered entries on files such as 'is on ESCA's books'. After decades of criticism, in 2002, Amicus and the Electrical Contractors' Association sold ESCA Services to a newly incorporated company called 20-20 Recruitment based in Hampshire.[9] In its last set of accounts ESCA recorded a turnover of £24 million.

Unions mentioned in blacklist files

The EETPU was not the only rightwing union in the industry at the time. UCATT, under the leadership of Albert Williams, was also seen as a voice of moderation in the TUC but behind the scenes faced serious allegations of corruption and ballot rigging. Full-time officials receiving payments in kind from building companies, including free holidays and numerous golfing days, were exposed in the trade press; even the *Daily Mirror* ran unfavourable stories.[10]

The Channel 4 *Dispatches* TV documentary, 'The Ballot Fixers', broadcast in May 1991, exposed how Taylor Woodrow and Costain had invited UCATT general secretary Albert Williams and other senior officials to Thames river cruises, social evenings and overnight accommodation at Tower Hotel, London. Now retired, Dudley Barrett was industrial relations manager for Costain at the time and admits footing the bill for a group of union people, but claims that he was asked to do so by one of the senior union figures:

❝I took him out and a whole group of his people out on a boat when I was on the Thames Barrier, treated them very nicely, including a very nice meal afterwards that cost us the best part of £1,000. Next thing I know I'm on television, although my name wasn't mentioned, but Costain's name was mentioned for spending over £1,000.[9][11]

Barrett also claims to have subsidized the overseas visit of a senior UCATT official, paying for his hotels, meals and drinks bill.

Dispatches accused the UCATT leadership of 'crudely fraudulent techniques to keep a stranglehold over the union' and claimed that ballot rigging exposed 'a network of corruption extending to the highest levels in the union'.

Albert Williams told the programme: 'You show me some proof and we will act on it. Knowledge is one thing, proof is another but fine words butter no parsnips.'

When the blacklist was discovered, Albert Williams was recorded as the source of derogatory remarks on the TCA file of the respected and recently deceased UCATT executive council member Chris Murphy.

In the 1991 UCATT elections, an anti-corruption slate stood for the executive council. John Flavin, Peter Lenihan and Ron Doel stood against incumbents Jack Henry, John Rogers and Brian Veal – and beat them all. George Brumwell won the general secretary election. The UCATT executive council set up an inquiry under John Hand QC with a remit to investigate dubious practices of the recent past. The Hand Report was never published but a number of full-time officials resigned from the union prior to giving evidence or its completion. Many immediately took up positions within the EETPU, including Bernard McAulay, Roger Furmedge and Paul Corby, who was to head up the newly formed construction section.[12] This was at a time when the EETPU was still expelled from the TUC and openly making sweetheart deals with employers. Paul Corby recalls:

> I supported Jack Henry in the election. Eric Hammond rang me personally and offered me a national official's job in the EETPU. I went after *Dispatches* but that had no consequence. Nothing to do with Wapping; that had happened before I joined. They were expelled because they refused to kowtow to certain TUC rules.

It is hardly surprising that many blacklisted workers feel disquiet about information that appeared to come from EETPU officials. The electricians who joined the breakaway EPIU feel that they were particularly targeted. Every electrician working on a JIB contract was automatically signed up as a member of EETPU with their union subs paid by the employer. EPIU membership fees were paid via the branch or by direct debit, meaning that the employer did not need to know, yet entries relating to EPIU membership repeatedly appear on many blacklist files, even where no disputes ever took place.

The EETPU returned to the TUC fold when they merged with the rightwing engineers' union to form the AEEU and later on became Amicus – but with the same core of full-time officials in the leadership of the construction section. After a few years the EPIU merged with the Transport and General Workers' Union (TGWU). Both sides are now reunited since the merger of Amicus and TGWU to form Unite. Despite the name changes, entries on blacklist files continued to appear that raise questions about the role of some union officials. An analysis by the authors has discovered numerous examples, with those below representing just a small selection.

> *'EETPU says NO' [this appears on several blacklist files]*
>
> *'Reported by local EETPU official as militant'*
> *'All suspected of being EPIU members'*
> *'AEEU describes as f. evil as far as internal union dealings are concerned. Active at branch level.'*

The Select Committee specifically asked Ian Kerr about these entries.

Ian Davidson: 'The "EETPU says no" would seem to suggest that there had been some input from a trade union.'

Ian Kerr: 'Yes; I agree with you. That would have been the case. It would have been a particular relationship with an HR manager in a particular area and that regional officer of the union or the union. I don't know how you want to phrase it, but somewhere along the line that would have been discussed and somebody would have decided that that was information that we should have in our system.'

Graham Bowker is a Manchester electrician who was blacklisted by numerous companies. He describes how Amicus union official Roger Furmedge behaved towards EPIU activists on the flagship Marks and Spencer site in Manchester. Bowker and Steve Acheson had been elected as safety rep and shop steward. Bowker said:

> ❝ Furmedge drafted a letter about the elections of me and Steve and gave it to every operative to sign it to say that they weren't happy with our elections. This is a union official! Just after we'd been elected! He turns up, about 80 bloody A4 pieces of paper with word for word the same and just for the operatives to sign the bottom that they were unhappy with our elections. At the time, I had dual membership on there because I was cards in as a JIB member, which gave me Amicus status. At the time I was also a member of the EPIU. I think he was under orders. Because there was a history between the old EETPU and the EPIU which is very deep rooted the hatred from them to us. ❞

Entries relating to the appointment or election of union stewards appear on a number of files and often quote a union official. Some files simply record a situation and name a union official within the employers' interpretation of events, such as the file entry for the current chair of the Unite national construction committeee Billy Spiers when working at Heathrow:

> *2003 August*
>
> *Put Forward by* ▨ *to T5 Employers' representative body as a nominee for new position under recently agreed Major Project Agreement (MPA) of Designated site Representative (DSR) at Heathrow Terminal 5 for mechanical and electrical trades. Under the MPA unions have a duty to put forward their nominees CVs to the employers side of the project in question that then makes a decision whether to accept the persons nomination. The union (*▨ *for amicus) state that he is*

> *well versed in union procedures and has a good command of negotiating situations. Above is still an Amicus Executive Council member*
>
> *3221/W main contact (████████) given details ████████ will update on outcome.*
>
> *NOTE: Also put forward by ████████ for T5 were: ████████ (mechanical fitter) as nomination for DSR*
> *3221/W (████████) comments that ████████, to protect his reputation with employers, would not knowingly put an unsuitable (far left activist) person on site*

3221 = AMEC

Paul Corby reflects:

> ❝I am absolutely satisfied to have nominated both Russ [Blakeley] and Billy for the roles upon the T5 project. They co-ordinated the election of other shop stewards on site. I have no comment regarding any employer comment made, as I had no discussions with John Conner over this and cannot be responsible for any second-hand employer comments made on these strange files. But there was absolutely fierce employer opposition to getting Billy Spiers placed on site.❞[13]

Other files are open to a wider interpretation, such as the following entry relating to a major project in Liverpool:

> *8th Dec 2006 above put to 3288 as designated site rep (on basis that this was) preferable to 'someone known with local credibility – could get anyone if done by an election'.*
> *T Hardacre of amicus 'didn't feel an election would be in their interests'.*

3288 = NG Baileys

Tommy Hardacre was national officer for the construction section of Amicus, having replaced Paul Corby in 2005. Hardacre told the authors he is disgusted that secret files should be held containing second-hand information – he had not seen them until shown them by the authors. He disputes that he would not have wanted an election, saying the quotation is taken out of context.

Blacklisted workers turned away

The mid-1990s saw the start of an unprecedented 25-year building boom that was to last until the global financial crash in 2008. Millennium projects such as the Millennium Stadium in Cardiff, the Millennium Dome, Royal Opera House and Jubilee Line Extension (JLE) created a shortage of skilled labour and a resulting increase in wage rates. But for skilled workers on the blacklist, even during the building boom, it was proving difficult to find work. Bowker explains what happened when he contacted Roger Furmedge after repeatedly being turned down for work:

> ❝He asked me a question, "Would you like to go on Manchester City Stadium?"
>
> So I said, "Yeah, what about Steve Acheson?"
>
> He said, "Well, between me and you, even if I wanted to, I couldn't place him anywhere in the Northwest."
>
> Well, that set the alarm bells ringing. Something is totally wrong here. That simple statement by Roger Furmedge about Steve Acheson tells you there's collusion going on.❞

Later Bowker, Acheson, Tony Jones and Sean Keaveney were to meet up with Roger Furmedge again when the electricians were employed by DAF Electrical on the Piccadilly Gardens site in Manchester. The main contractor was Carillion, and Crown House (Carillion's mechanical and electrical section) had subcontracted an electrical package to DAF. The very first entry on Graham Bowker's blacklist file appears a week after he started working on the Carillion site:

> *EPIU*
> *2003 April 22: During w/c 14th April 2003 above was on site with sub-contractor Daf Electrical (Gloucester based) at 3271/81s Piccadilly Gardens redevelopment in Manchester.*

Two weeks later the following entry appeared:

> *2003 May 6*
>
> *Applied to 3271/81 at Piccadilly Argent Redevelopment,*
> *Manchester along with Stephen Acheson, Sean Keaveney,*
> *Tony Jones and Jonathan Russell. (see separate refs for all).*
> *Main contact (LK) given details. Co. already has the above*
> *plus the other 4 on site.*

3271 = Carillion. LK = Liz Keates, Head of HR for Carillion Group.

On 16 May 2003, DAF sacked 11 electricians from the Piccadilly site: Sean Keaveney, John Russell, Terry Moran, Mick Shortall, Kevin McGowan, Andy Hardman, Chris Donahue, Andy Baxter, Graham Bowker, Steve Acheson and Tony Jones. They then spent between four months and a year picketing the site in an attempt to win reinstatement with the support of local trade unionists, including Brian Bamford and Derek Pattison. All of the sacked workers applied to an Employment Tribunal. All of their names were added to the blacklist. An entry on Acheson's blacklist file says:

> *2003 June*
>
> *Amicus – AEEU*
> *Piccadilly Gardens, Manchester dispute*
>
> *Involves EPIU members*
> *Roger Furmedge of amicus-AEEU was required to support the*
> *5 union members. DAF then issued Redundancy Notices to the*
> *5 and the men went on strike. Roger Furmedge repudiated the*
> *mens' [sic] actions – DAF sacked the men.*
> *Current situation: Picket on gate still*

Thirteen months after their sacking some of the blacklisted electricians won claims for unfair dismissal for trade-union activities, while others were again defeated by the vagaries of the employment law system. One memorable cross-examination by Sue Machin, representing the electricians, was reported in the rank-and-file union newspaper *North West Cowboy* at the time:

❝"Amicus is our union!" cried Michael Fahey from the witness box.

This had Ms Machin on her feet. "Your union? The employer's union?"

"Yes, we pay the dues for the men," replied Fahey.❞[14]

The four workers weren't just sacked for being trade-union members but specifically for being EPIU/TGWU members. The written judgment goes on to state on more than one occasion that the reason that the company was aware that the electricians were union activists was because of information supplied to them by Roger Furmedge. The written judgment pours scorn on the evidence of DAF director David Fahey that he was unaware that the electricians were TGWU members by finding: 'It was more likely than not that Mr Furnage [sic] told him that Mr Acheson, a well-known "troublemaker" and TGWU member, was on site.'

At the remedies hearing to decide the level of compensation, DAF director Michael Fahey's written witness statement says:

❝I attended a meeting with Dave Fahey on 9th May [2003] at which Alan Swift from Crown House Engineering and Liz Keates [from] Carillion's HR department were also present. Alan told us that nobody from my site would be allowed onto CMMC [building site] and that the claimants were well known in the Manchester area as militants who had caused massive problems on other sites.❞

When Michael Fahey was pressed by Judge Keevash, he admitted that Roger Furmedge was also at the meeting.

Following the 9 May meeting between the contracting companies and the Amicus official, DAF wrote to Crown House and Carillion on 21 May 2003 stating that:

❝As a consequence of the action on site we are looking at ways of tightening our selection procedure and can confirm that, with immediate effect, any potential employee will be thoroughly screened before any offer of employment is made.❞

Both Carillion and Crown House were then major users of The Consulting Association. The Tribunal's written judgment interprets this letter as DAF informing Crown House 'that it would in effect screen for trade-union membership'. This was in the public domain five years before The Consulting Association was raided. Roger Furmedge has been repeatedly contacted by the authors to provide an explanation about the various incidents noted above but has declined to make any comment.

That the EPIU was targeted by officials of the EETPU was not disputed by two ex-officials. Jim Simms was a former national secretary for construction within the Manufacturing Science and Finance union before it merged with Amicus, and was a signatory to the NAECI agreement. He currently sits as a panel member on Employment Tribunals and is employed as the industrial relations officer for Beaver Management Services Limited (BMS). His current role as an industrial-relations officer for a major employment agency means that some in the union movement have questioned the reliability of his testimony.[15] Simms told the authors:

> The EPIU was more or less blacklisted *en bloc* – they'd never admit it but it was civil war between AEEU and EPIU. The employers obviously supported the EETPU and AEEU because they were business friendly. The London scene was notorious and everyone just let them get on with it. The argument was that with the agency branch and working rule 17, there were thousands of people where the employer paid their contributions and so therefore millions of pounds were coming into the union on subs and whatever the arrangements were, it was like Dodge City and the Wild West.

The full-time official responsible for the London area within the EETPU and later the AEEU was Frank Westerman. He has a blacklist file which was started by the Economic League in 1972 when he was an elected convenor on the Tate and Lyle HQ beside the Thames. His file finishes in 1986 when he became a union full-time official. Westerman considered the JIB the central reason for the dispute with the EPIU:

> The EPIU opposed it, even tried stuff in Parliament with MPs, so there was a constant to and fro. As an officer of the union, I would oppose the EPIU, I would oppose the T&G and UCATT.

The important thing for us was always the agreement.**9**[16]

In 1992, Westerman was the union official responsible for the Vascroft site in Kensington on behalf of the EETPU. At the very moment that TGWU and UCATT reps were dismissed from site, Vascroft cut a deal with the EETPU, who appointed a 'steward' from outside the job who wouldn't cause the company any trouble. Chris Clarke, the sacked TGWU shop steward, won his claim for unfair dismissal due to trade-union activities and said: 'That business with Westerman was as cynical an operation as I have seen in 40 years in the labour movement.'

Westerman remembers what happened at the time of the Vascroft crane occupation:

6 One of the trade suppliers had an agreement with the EETPU and Vascroft said they would have an agreement too. At the time it was open warfare, there is no other way to describe it. There were lots of things that went on at that time that people should not be proud of. That was nothing to do with blacklisting. All that fraternal stuff that goes on at conferences, when you get out on site it's a different ball game. Vascrofts was high profile but there were loads of things like that. It used to happen but it was more about membership. I didn't do anything deliberate. There were things that happened that shouldn't have happened, dozens of naughty things that went on.**9**

Jubilee Line and Terminal 5

Another group of workers who had good reason to demand answers were the electricians blacklisted after the Jubilee Line. The main electrical contractor on the project was Drake & Scull, which subscribed to The Consulting Association. The Jubilee Line was to become one of the most successfully unionized construction projects of the past 20 years. When the project was completed, the names and national insurance numbers of every electrician working for Drake & Scull were circulated by the head of human resources, Sheila Knight.[17] Scores were also added to the Consulting Association blacklist. But it was an identical entry that appears multiple times on the blacklist files of union activists who worked on the JLE that caused the most outrage:

> *Employed by Drake & Sculls at Jubilee Line. Was actively involved in the issues which arose during the term of the contract.*
>
> *Advice is to take up references on previous employers on application.*
>
> *NOTE: Known to have worked at the Jubilee Line should this not appear on his application form.*
>
> *NOTE: BUT DO NOT DIVULGE*
> *Above information arose from liaison between union, contractor and managing agent at J/L*

The entry is credited to Alan Audley, main contact for Vinci, who was vice-chair of The Consulting Association when it was raided in 2009. Audley, now retired, lives a few miles from the Fiddlers Ferry power plant site – a scene of many industrial disputes. When visited by the authors, he looked tanned and trim, having just come back from an ocean cruise. He refused to answer any questions about his role with TCA.

The full-time union official for Drake & Scull electricians was again Frank Westerman. He is adamant that he had never heard of TCA nor of any employers being involved in an organization like it:

> ❛I never knew of that Association, I never knew of their existence. I never had any contact with them. As far as the union is concerned, I don't think anybody was involved in helping this Association. I don't know what I said to Alan Audley. I had hardly anything to do with him. He was on the employers' committee. He might big himself up by saying Westerman says "he is a bag of shit" or something. At the end of the day, someone still has to go and meet the employer and make the deal – and that was my job.❜

After the JLE, Westerman went on to be the Amicus union official on the two biggest projects in London: the new Wembley stadium and Heathrow Terminal 5 (T5).

Michael Anderson was an electrician from northwest London

with a young family at the time and, having worked on the JLE, found it virtually impossible to find work on Wembley and T5, despite gaining support from his local MP. Anderson's redacted blacklist file has the following entry:

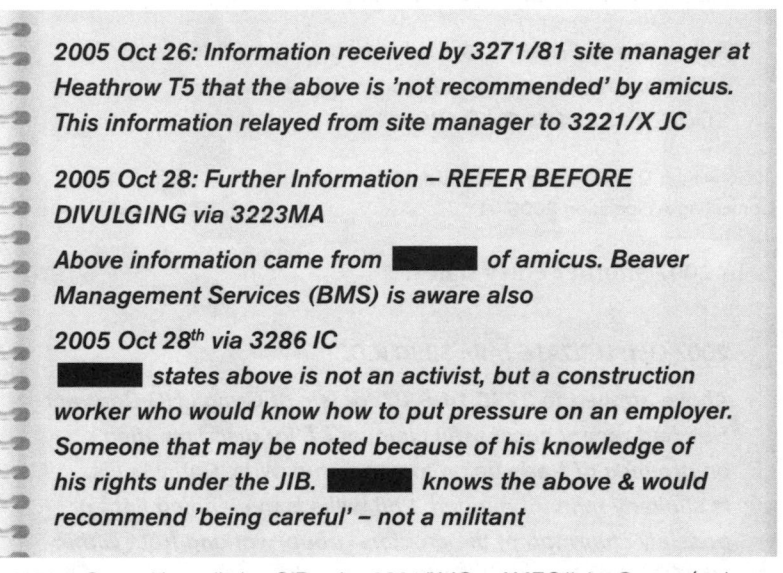

2005 Oct 26: Information received by 3271/81 site manager at Heathrow T5 that the above is 'not recommended' by amicus. This information relayed from site manager to 3221/X JC

2005 Oct 28: Further Information – REFER BEFORE DIVULGING via 3223MA

Above information came from ▮▮▮▮ *of amicus. Beaver Management Services (BMS) is aware also*

2005 Oct 28th via 3286 IC

▮▮▮▮ *states above is not an activist, but a construction worker who would know how to put pressure on an employer. Someone that may be noted because of his knowledge of his rights under the JIB.* ▮▮▮▮ *knows the above & would recommend 'being careful' – not a militant*

3271 = Crown House/Laing O'Rourke; 3221/X JC = AMEC/John Conner (main contact); 3223MA = Balfour Kilpatrick/Michael Aird (main contact); 3286 IC = Emcor/Iain Coates (main contact)

In just two days in October 2005, four separate blacklisting firms operating at T5 forwarded information about Anderson to The Consulting Association and all four main contacts name the Amicus union official as the source of the information. Anderson suffered prolonged periods of unemployment in the wake of this and eventually emigrated to Ireland with his young family. Frank Westerman was the Amicus official responsible for T5 and when questioned about these entries by the authors, claims that he was attempting to assist Anderson in finding a job on the project.

Phil Willis, a blacklisted steel erector, was elected as Amicus shop steward at the Terminal 5 project. The following entry appears in his unredacted blacklist file, which was used as evidence in his successful Employment Tribunal:

> *June 2003: With Severfield Reeve (owner Watson Steel) at*
> *Heathrow terminal 5 as a shop steward / convener. Sacked by*
> *Severfield Reeve and subsequently reinstated. Claimed unfair*
> *dismissal for Trade Union activities.*
>
> *According to Frank W: will sit in background & 'wind up' in*
> *other forums, is very clever, covers himself well.*
> *SOURCE: 3231 M.C. (D.O'S)*

3231 = Kier; D.O'S = Danny O'Sullivan, Kier main contact and chair of The
Consulting Association 2000-01

In 2007 another entry states:

> *2007 Oct: UPDATE from 3290 R.B.*
>
> *Above applied to 3290 14-9-07 for Isle of Grain LNG Contract.*
> *Has had recent successful claim at I.T. for discrimination*
> *on grounds of trade union membership. Wife, Cathy Willis,*
> *is similarly militant minded. Phil Willis is the leading light or*
> *possibly chairman of the erectors group, working from within*
> *UNITE – amicus at present.*
> *This information from a T.U. officer source within UNITE –*
> *amicus (FW)*

3290 = CB&I; RB = Ron Barron

Whether deliberate or not, the entries suggest that Frank
Westerman was having conversations about the union activities of
Willis and Anderson with construction employers.

Frank Westerman now lives in Canada and carries out industrial-
relations consultancy work for major construction firms, some of
whom subscribed to TCA. When questioned about the reason why
his name appears as the source of information on so many blacklist
files, he replied:

> ‘You've got to put this in context. If you see that and you
> didn't know how the industry operated you'd have a lot of
> concerns. I'm meeting people day in day out, year in year out,
> for 25 years. I was the main lead official in the London area.

Anything that happened, I was in the middle of it.

Them conversations happened all the time. I'm involved with talking to people about people and if they write it down what can I do about it? I'm quite upset about it because I was blacklisted myself and my family suffered in the Seventies and Eighties.[9]

Phil and Cathie Willis said of Frank Westerman:

❝We settled on the belief that he wouldn't knowingly do any harm to his members. There were often times when he trod a very shaky path between representing members and keeping the employers on side but I don't think he ever went so far as to deliberately give information away that could be damaging. The reason we do not believe that Frank handed over any deliberate information on members, is that the information contained within the blacklisted person's files was very inaccurate. If the information had come from Frank it would have been spot on.❞[18]

Michael Anderson was less inclined to give the ex-Amicus official turned industrial-relations consultant the benefit of the doubt:

❝If a union official makes statements like these to employers he knows exactly what's going to happen to the union member's job prospects. An apprentice would know not to drop names and details of who said what at union meetings to management, yet here was an experienced full-time official doing exactly that. He wasn't naive, he knew all about blacklisting, so what were his motives?❞[19]

How do union names get into the files?

Brian Higgins is another worker who has union officials quoted on his blacklist file. Some of the last entries in his redacted file state:

2002 Jan 17ᵗʰ:
Report by ▮▮▮▮ *that the above is to be a delegate at 2002*
UCATT Biennial Conference in Bournemouth

> ████████ *further commented: 'but people don't take any notice of him now'*
>
> *2003 Dec:*
>
> *Comments from another union's official is [that] B Higgins and colleagues are involved in the site issues at Wembley*

The entry dated 17 January 2002 relates to elections that took place in December 2001. The results were circulated to UCATT branches in January 2002. They were not published on the website or in the union magazine at the time. When Higgins' unredacted file arrived, the name of a current senior UCATT official was disclosed as the recorded source of the information. Higgins complained to the UCATT General Secretary, Steve Murphy, who personally visited the retired bricklayer's house in Northampton.

This meeting led to an internal investigation into the conduct of UCATT London regional secretary Jerry Swain. The details were never made public but it found that there was no case to answer and the UCATT executive council took no action. Higgins said:

> ❝The response of UCATT has been a downright disgrace. They should hold an independent inquiry conducted by a legal expert, who has no connection to any union, into all aspects of The Consulting Association, including and especially the collusion of some union officials with the blacklist.❞[20]

In September 2013 Murphy wrote to Higgins, stating:

> ❝The Executive Council once again reiterated its view that unless there is some concrete evidence that UCATT officials were implicated in blacklisting building workers it would be futile to have an independent inquiry.❞

In researching this book the authors made numerous written and verbal requests to UCATT over many months, directly and via intermediaries, for a response to questions raised by information on blacklist files and concerned union activists. The then general secretary Steve Murphy gave an interview, but subsequently both the union as a whole and its officials individually have refused to provide any substantial comment for publication.

Although there is no evidence that some rightwing union officials deliberately provided information with the intention of blacklisting some of their more leftwing members, information has undoubtedly found its way from union officials to the TCA files. The blacklist was an open secret in the building industry. Stewart Emms, a UCATT official between 1992 and 2002, recalls: 'I was quite sure that blacklisting was going on; other officials did too: without a doubt.' Emms' own blacklist file even contains a copy of a letter he wrote to the *Morning Star* in 1999, which observes:

> ❛I have been finding over the past few years that there has been a general move by employers to sack shop stewards and safety representatives, because they know they can get away with it. The union will probably threaten the employer with an industrial tribunal – which will get the sacked steward or safety rep a few bob. But the employer will gladly pay this to break trade-union organization and, ultimately, the steward concerned will be blacklisted.❜

Everyone knew it existed and union conferences regularly discussed it; so who did union officials think was actually responsible for the blacklisting? Blacklists do not compile themselves; information needs to be gleaned from somewhere by someone. Who would be doing all this, if not the industrial-relations managers of the big contractors?

Paul Corby admits he was aware that some industrial-relations managers were involved:

> ❛When it was the Economic League we knew who they were. Dudley Barrett from Costain used to boast about blacklisting people. I used to sing Irish rebel songs at conference. I was put on the list by Dudley Barrett. He told me about it.❜

But Corby mirrors the response of many officials the authors have spoken to:

> ❛I never blacklisted anyone. I haven't deliberately or inadvertently colluded with blacklisting. We knew about the Economic League but it was a secret society. I'd never heard of

> The Consulting Association until the day I heard about the raid.
> We didn't know they were doing that. Not in a co-ordinated
> way. We thought it might be a company basis.⁹

A witness statement seen by the authors from Daniel O'Sullivan, former TCA chair and industrial-relations official at Kier, says: 'I used to have general meetings with senior officials of trade unions, including Unite and UCATT, as part of my job at Kier. Our discussions would cover any recent developments at the relevant trade union and I believe the document dated 19 February 2002 that I refer to above contains my notes of one such discussion. These discussions also made clear to me that the union officials were also concerned to prevent unnecessary disruption on site. Occasionally, union officials would give me information concerning a particular individual.'[21]

The authors do not accuse any union official of any illegality or deliberate collusion with blacklisting members of their own or other unions. But the names of officials do appear as the source of information on TCA documentation and to ask how those names arrived on the files is a perfectly legitimate question to which blacklisted workers deserve an answer.

A knife and forker

Union officials in every industry need to have some kind of working relationship with their opposite number on the employer side. It may involve occasionally having a working lunch to discuss issues – a 'knife and forker' in the jargon. But there is a big step from professional courtesy to accepting hospitality such as evening meals, hotel accommodation and tickets to major sporting events.

The Goring Hotel in Belgravia is adjacent to Buckingham Palace. The luxury hotel has welcomed heads of state, presidents and royalty. Its own website describes how 'the great and the good, the famous and the infamous have walked the corridors and enjoyed the sophistication and discretion of this great hotel'. Perhaps it was the 'discretion' that was the attraction, because, despite having their own offices, this opulent venue is also where the JIB held its functions and where directors of blacklisting firms met union officials from the EETPU, AEEU, Amicus and UCATT for formal and sometimes less formal negotiations. Paul Corby, Frank Westerman and Jerry Swain among others have all attended meetings at the Goring, although all claim to have only visited in an official union capacity.

The Naval and Military is a gentlemen's club for military personnel. It is a few yards from Chatham House and round the corner from the Institute of Directors. A cannon greets you at the entrance, while its walls are lined with pictures of generals and admirals. The dress code is 'formal and conventional, business suit' or 'military dress'. One of its

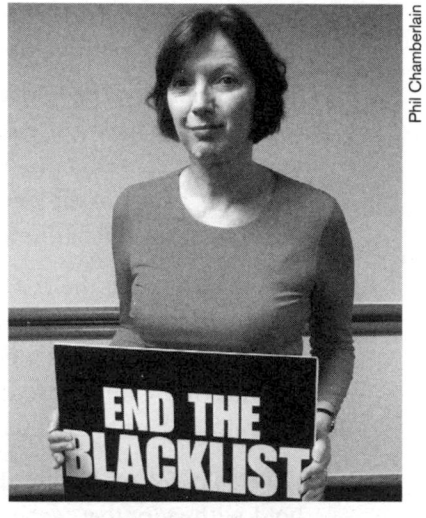

TUC general secretary Frances O'Grady

members is Stephen Quant, a former British army infantry officer and one-time TCA chair while employed by Skanska. Quant is quite open about the fact that he invited union officials to dine at his club. He explained to the authors how he used to develop friendly relationships with union officials.

> Quant: 'You can normally make a deal with anybody provided those people had what you would call a constructive manner. Outside factors are often what caused people to take stands. If you had a relationship with people that is ongoing, they are less susceptible to outside friends and outside influences.'

> Authors: 'Did people on the trade union side have that same view?'

> Quant: [long pause] 'Some people were reasonable and some people were unreasonable. Many of the people on the trade union were very reasonable and it was very easy in the days when there was Amicus and before that the EETPU. They were quite sensible.

> 'I had close relationships with UCATT, particularly a bloke called Jeremy Swain in London. I first met Swain in 1991, when he was just a regional officer, so I've known him for 20 years.'

251

Authors: 'How does that relationship work? Is it always just professional or over time does it become more than that?'

Quant: 'There are people who it is just business. There are people you can have quite sensible relationships with. Many of the people I .... Well, I don't need to go into that [laughs a little nervously]. Many of the people I have no problem about them. I've brought several of them here for a meal, for instance.'

Immediately after the ICO raid, Harvey Francis from Skanska held a number of conversations with various people about its impact. His personal notes were later disclosed and have been seen by the authors. One summarizes a telephone conversation with Jerry Swain on 5 March 2009 which says:

> Gerry [sic] Swain London Regional Secretary, UCATT. Doesn't hold with story that we've been blacklisting. Has always had good relationship with Skanska. Generally, if asked, right up at top of good, if not the best. Stephen [Quant] has provided good access to Skanska sites for UCATT. Grateful for being informed.[22]

Despite requests for an interview, Jerry Swain was not prepared to provide a public response to questions from the authors.[23]

It should be noted that at the time Stephen Quant had been named in a High Court legal action taken by UCATT. The union issued a statement to the authors via their solicitors, saying: 'We are surprised that the account of a serial blacklister is given credibility.'[24]

It was not just in London that the cosy relationships appear to have flourished. Barry Scragg, a UCATT official in the Northwest for over 20 years and himself a blacklisted ex-bricklayer, identified two officials who attended social events in the evening and weekends with industrial-relations officers.

> Jimmy Woods over the years has accepted hospitality from national and regional companies, such as weekends away at the Rugby League Cup Finals as a guest of AMEC. Likewise he has been the guest of regional companies in their hospitality suite at Aintree races. George Guy was also taken out for dinners or for drinks by a number of companies. This practice, in my opinion, was unhealthy. Alan Audley of Vinci, formerly Norwest Holst, was a regular visitor and host.[25]

George Guy held the position of Northwest regional secretary before taking on the role of general secretary (pro-tem) and then national officer for the union before he retired in the summer of 2014. Jimmy Woods took over the position of UCATT Northwest regional secretary from Guy and has also recently retired. Woods has a TCA blacklist file and there is no suggestion that he was involved in blacklisting, nor does his name appear on any documentation relating to TCA. However, the fact that even activists who were themselves blacklisted when working on site were prepared to socialize with employers once they took up the role of full-time union officers is an indication of how pervasive the practice was.

Neither officer was prepared to provide a direct quotation about these specific allegations but both strongly rebut any suggestions of acting illegally or against union rules.

Not all union officials agree with the need to hold meetings with company industrial-relations managers in fancy restaurants. Lou Lewis, blacklisted carpenter from the Barbican dispute, eventually became UCATT London regional secretary and on one occasion told the regional committee,

> Don't let anyone ever tell you that's just how the industry operates. I have never been for a meal with any of these people in over 20 years working for the union.

Former UCATT official and blacklisted joiner Stewart Emms reflected how his refusal to accept hospitality from managers often caused a stir:

> My problem was that when I had to negotiate with employers and their industrial-relations officers, I could never get into this going out and having a free beer with them. If I ever met them it was always, "I'll get this, Stewart."
>
> "No, you won't!"
>
> I never wanted any of my members to think I was accepting stuff from the employers. I remember George Brumwell once told me, "sometimes you get more from sugar than salt".
>
> Some officials went out for meals with the bosses but I never wanted to accept anything.[26]

Emms, who won a claim for unfair dismissal after being sacked by UCATT, claims that some union officials from Yorkshire Region attended cricket matches at Headingley with employers, while accepting bottles of whiskey and attending Christmas meals with employers was an annual practice in which he also refused to participate. Emms reflects: 'I'm not surprised some officials' names are on the files. I think some of the officials got too close. Did they ever go out socializing in the evening with their senior stewards?'

It may be that union officers believed they were invited to these hotels and social events because they were genuine friends of these company directors. In fact, Dudley Barrett, who attended blacklisting meetings on behalf of Costain, claims to have been a close personal friend of ex-UCATT general secretary Albert Williams and says he still regularly plays golf with ex-UCATT executive council member Jack Henry.

A document seen by the authors records Barrett saying:

> ❝ It was clear to me from the things that the officials said to me from time to time that a large number of unions within the construction industry knew about the existence of the Services Group and The Consulting Association. For example, I can recall officials from UCATT, TGWU and the AEEU each talking to me on separate occasions about the Services Group and the checking process.
>
> I also had a number of good friends within UCATT and the TGWU who would occasionally tell me names of individuals who they thought should not be employed on sites, on the basis that there might be a risk of these individuals using the opportunity to cause trouble to undermine a project and the official trade-union activities on that site.❞[27]

It is noticeable that Barrett cannot recall the actual names of his good friends who consciously provided the names.

If it was not genuine friendship, perhaps going out socializing with employers was just how the system had always worked. Even if the entries on many of the blacklist files attributed to union officials are due to loose tongues rather than deliberate collusion, this smacks of massive naivety. The industrial-relations managers were doing their job. They were playing the union officials in order to glean information on behalf of the company. Not to realize what was happening was, at the very least, inept.

From the point of view of blacklisted workers with a union official named on their file, the evidence of after-hours socializing in plush hotels demands an explanation. Failure to come clean at least gives the impression of potential collusion.

Bulk membership

However, the issue of potentially dubious practices by some union officials is not something only raised by disgruntled activists. In 2000, George Brumwell, UCATT general secretary, told his union conference:

> ❛Alan Ritchie [UCATT Scottish secretary at the time] took a big subbie [subcontractor] from London to the airport and he threw a brown envelope full of notes and said, "My office has slipped a couple of grand in here." Alan thought he was joking but when he saw the envelope he nearly passed out. He took it back. Now I wonder how many don't take it back.❜[28]

While rank-and-file activists were repeatedly dismissed and refused work by the industrial-relations managers, the relationship between the higher echelons of the unions and the same individuals was often somewhat different. Developing a friendly relationship with contractors was seen as part of the job role for union officials. When these relationships became very friendly, union officials were able to increase membership by recruiting the whole workforce of the companies en masse rather than just relying on recruiting individual workers.

Jonathan Jeffries, currently a TUC tutor, originally worked for TGWU in Gibraltar before joining the London region UCATT office team in the 1990s. He explains how, at the time, union recruitment often involved recruiting the company rather than the workers.

> ❛The contractor would suddenly bring in all these membership forms filled in, in a bundle and then deduct the subs. This isn't the usual situation where an individual worker decides

to join the union or a shop steward approaches them and recruits them. This is their employer saying you have to be in the union. I saw this happening because I had to do some of the processing, having previously worked in the membership department. I met some people who were hard-as-nails East End crooks. There was one of them that came into the union office who could have been a 1930s gangster in his pinstripe suit.⁹

This way of doing things very often results in workers being signed up to the union without their knowledge. Relying on large contractors to supply bulk membership means they often end up holding considerable influence over union finances. It is easy to conceive how playing off different unions against each other or withholding subscriptions could result in officials acting in a way amenable to the employer. Images from old gangster movies spring to mind once again.

The practice of friendly contractors providing certain union officials with paper membership, often without the knowledge of the workers themselves, was so well known, that it has been repeatedly acknowledged by senior officials of the construction unions. In 1991, Dominic Hehir, blacklisted painter and former UCATT regional secretary, was asked by *Dispatches* why any employer would pay block membership fees to the union without supplying the names and addresses of the supposed members.

> Dominic Hehir: 'He feels that it would obviously suit him and there is a possibility that some employers may think that UCATT is a union that suits them and they want to see it keep afloat, so they would send a cheque off to General Office.'
>
> Dispatches: 'That's buying industrial peace.'
>
> Dominic Hehir: 'That's the way they would see it.'

This was acknowledged as late as September 2012 when Unite's Gail Cartmail gave evidence to the Select Committee:

> Sometimes employers change tactics. We have a prominent site in London, with Crossrail, and there is evidence of a contractor company suddenly having a conversion on the road

to Damascus and paying the trade-union contributions for its workforce. I raise this because it is another way of sidelining genuine trade-union involvement and sending the message that "we will pay your contributions but we don't expect you to play a role".[9]

At the 1996 UCATT conference, executive council member Tony Farrell said:

> The executive council and the general secretary are not prepared to accept the practice that exists in some regions where subcontractors would give recruits to full-time officials and then cease paying for a similar amount of employees. That is not recruitment, that is a mafia tactic.[29]

Unfortunately, despite the best intentions of Farrell, this tactic appears to have actually been part of the training given to some union officials. Steve Hedley, current RMT assistant general secretary, worked temporarily for UCATT in the 1990s and recalls:

> I was employed by UCATT as a development officer supposedly for one year. On my second week I was given training by UCATT official Jerry Swain. This training consisted of going to the office of a subcontractor called O'Keefe and negotiating a number of membership forms that the subcontractor would fill in and give to the union. At no time were any workers talked to or even approached. I was told I had to get members in this fashion. I told Swain to "fuck off". In subsequent weeks and months I recruited members properly by going site to site and talking to workers in the canteen, probably recruiting around 10 a week. Other officials brought back bundles of forms from subcontractors.

Jerry Swain disputes the incident but has declined to comment on the record in response to this allegation.

The exceptionally cosy relationships between certain union officials and building employers resulted in the very industrial-relations managers responsible for blacklisting union members being invited to attend union conferences. During the day, the main contacts would take notes in the conference hall on speeches made by delegates or leaflets distributed. The details would later appear on blacklist files.

> *At 1998 June Biennial Conference gave short talk:- 'Now is the time to get the wages up'*
>
> *SOURCE: 3280 (main contact A.L.)*

3280 = John Mowlem – now Carillion (JM) Ltd; AL = Alf Lucas

During the evening the blacklisters attended the official receptions and were free with their money in the bar. Stephen Quant was a regular at both UCATT and Amicus conferences, with his late-night antics in the bar described by one observer as 'holding court' with union officials amongst his entourage. When interviewed for this book, Quant admitted attending conferences and claimed never to have had any problems other than from 'the loonies'. Paul Corby, however, remembers naming Quant in a conference speech after the industrial-relations manager had spent the previous evening arguing that no workers should be directly employed.

Dudley Barrett was clear about his reason for attending union conferences:

> ❛I got invited by so many different unions, I had to be careful in case they got jealous. I decided whether I wanted to cultivate them or not. I would have a meal with them, some people I thought "they're not worth very much to me". George Henderson, awkward bastard from the T&G, would take no gifts.❜[30]

Alan Audley of Vinci was a guest at the UCATT conference in Scarborough as late as 2012, three years after his company's involvement in blacklisting was known.

Mary Kerr says that, of all the main contacts, Dudley Barrett and Alan Audley were the ones who especially supplied information that originated from union sources.[31]

Following the discovery of the blacklist, there were renewed calls for industrial-relations officers to be banned from union conferences. In 2013 the UCATT executive council announced that, from 2014, industrial-relations managers would no longer be invited to conference.

Steve Acheson v George Guy

In addition to the blacklist files, other documents relating to blacklisting written by Ian Kerr have come to light. During the preparation for their High Court claim, Sean Curran and Liam Dunne from Guney Clark and Ryan solicitors visited the home of Ian Kerr on two separate occasions. They took witness statements and were also supplied with a number of documents that the ICO had failed to seize during their raid in 2009. Among the documents was a page of notes in Ian Kerr's own handwriting from 6 March 2009, the day the blacklisting story broke in the media. The note records telephone conversations that Ian Kerr had with a number of the main contacts throughout the day and comments on the various press reports.

On Saturday 23 February 2013, the Blacklist Support Group held a meeting in Jack Jones House, in Liverpool. The meeting was chaired by Roy Bentham, with Steve Acheson and Liam Dunne as the main speakers. During his speech, Acheson was continuously barracked by senior members of UCATT, who accused him of making allegations about union collusion without any real evidence and asked him to name names. In response, Steve held up the handwritten note by Kerr and said: 'If you want me to name names, I will: the name that appears on this note is George Guy.' Acheson then read out this section from the Ian Kerr note:

> *AA met Geo Guy UCATT NW Reg Sect + 2 others – who thought a storm in a tea cup*
>
> *G Guy: would you employ St Acheson? 'I bloody wouldn't' (St Acheson IT claimant)*
>
> *We've known for years – just a question of when it would happen.*
>
> *AA Unions will have a problem now as they will get on site & cause problems*

AA = Alan Audley, head of industrial relations at Vinci & Vice Chair of The Consulting Association

As might be expected, following this revelation the discussion was quite heated between those who called for UCATT to launch an immediate investigation and the others in attendance who defended George Guy. An ongoing dispute in the northwest region of UCATT descended into a virtual civil war with claim and counter claim on both sides. Three leftwing blacklisted workers, Tony Sweeney, John Flanagan and Roy Bentham, were subsequently expelled. UCATT threatened to pursue a claim against Acheson for slander, although it never materialized.

George Guy vigorously denied the allegations and issued the following statement:

> ❝I have never discussed Mr Acheson with Mr Audley or anyone else. I have a statement from Mr Audley confirming this... I have never made any comments about Mr Acheson at a regional council meeting and the minutes will show that. I have never discussed the employability of any construction worker, if they were a member or not, with any employer. I have never knowingly ever given any information to anyone which could be used to blacklist anyone.❞[32]

Union internal inquiries

Both Unite and UCATT have carried out internal investigations into possible collusion by union officials, although these took place using only fragmentary documentation before either union had been given access to the full unredacted TCA database as part of the High Court litigation. Some people refused to be interviewed for the internal union investigations and some witnesses only gave evidence under tight preconditions which may have brought their reliability into question.[33] No past or present officials of either union were named or disciplined following the internal investigations, which at the time found there was either no case to answer or insufficient evidence to take any further action.

However, Gail Cartmail, herself from the print sector and therefore with first-hand knowledge of the EETPU, later told the Blacklist Support Group AGM in November 2011 that union collusion may have taken place in the past, 'it shouldn't have happened' and offered the blacklisted workers present an apology.

While this may not have satisfied every blacklisted worker present, the public admission and the wholehearted support she gave to Frank Morris on Crossrail has brought Cartmail a considerable degree of respect from the notoriously hard-to-please construction section of Unite.

Cartmail later told the authors:

> ❦ If there have been failings of union officials in the past, then all can see how Unite has recognized those failings and responded to the magnificent campaign led by the Blacklist Support Group.❦[34]

Meanwhile, in an interview with the authors, then UCATT general secretary Steve Murphy promised a 'warts and all' inquiry, which is the stated policy of the union, though only once it had seen all the files. Asked if he would be surprised if the records showed evidence of union officials supplying names for the blacklist Murphy said: 'Yes I would. Yes, I think any of us would.'[35] Murphy went on sick leave from UCATT in 2014 and never returned to his job.

It is transnational building companies that set up and funded the blacklist, and that victimized construction workers. It was an anti-union blacklist. The Consulting Association scandal provides a once-in-a-generation opportunity to change the industrial relations in the building industry. But that involves changing the way the trade unions have operated as well as the employers. The authors repeat that they make no accusations of illegality or deliberate collusion with blacklisting against any union official. However, the evidence suggests that at the very least, a culture developed among a cohort of union officials and industrial-relations managers that has led to a flow of information to the blacklist files, even if that was inadvertent.

The virtual conveyor belt of union officials immediately taking up posts as senior industrial-relations managers or consultants with construction firms after leaving office adds to the impression of a cosy club. Paul Corby, Jim Simms and Frank Westerman are all working as industrial-relations managers or consultants.

Two of the most explosive industrial disputes in London during 2015 were at Crossrail over the sacking of Dan Collins and at

Morgan Stanley's headquarters at Canary Wharf, where Graeme Boxall was dismissed by Phoenix Electrical just 30 minutes after being elected as shop steward. Rank-and-file activists travelled from as far afield as Teeside to support the victimized Unite member. The company's response was to serve them with a High Court injunction which the demonstrators promptly ignored. Boxall was reinstated by lunchtime. Ex-Amicus official Frank Westerman was the industrial-relations consultant for the companies on both disputes.[36]

Brian Boyd, AEEU official at Pfizers, left Unite in 2011 and only weeks later was representing employers in talks with his former employer at ACAS during the BESNA dispute. Jim Thomas, ex-Unite officer, is currently industrial-relations manager for Laing O'Rourke and involved in disputes with the construction unions over lack of access to the Francis Crick site in Euston, the Cheesegrater in the City of London and Alder Hey Hospital in Liverpool.

On leaving employment as national president of UCATT, John Flavin, blacklisted himself in the 1980s, started acting on behalf of employers, even representing firms in employment tribunals against the union. He is now working on industrial relations for blacklisting firm Laing O'Rourke and was involved in the Hinkley Point negotiations as well as at the Olympic site. A party to celebrate his 40 years in the industry was held in Mayfair, and included high-profile guests from many of the big contractors and global property developers, as well as UCATT officials, including Jerry Swain.[37]

Let the clean-up begin

To imagine that all union officials caught up in the blacklisting scandal suddenly changed the way they operated the day after the Consulting Association database was discovered would be extremely naïve. In 2013, four years after the blacklist had been discovered, two academics from the University of Westminster published research into industrial relations on the London 2012 construction site. As part of the study, six union officials were interviewed. All are quoted anonymously but one official was entirely happy to go on record referring to blacklisting on the

Olympics as 'one of the myths of the site'.[38] It would appear that some officials, at least, still prefer the assurances of the major contractors over the 'anecdotal evidence' of blacklisted workers.

The sooner the trade unions accept that there have been failings in the past, the sooner the clean-up process can begin.

1 Interview with the authors. 2 Ian Kerr evidence to Scottish Affairs Select Committee, 27 Nov 2012. 3 Interview with the authors. 4 Interview with the authors. 5 John McAllion MP (for Dundee East) Hansard, 26 Oct 1999. 6 Interview with the authors. 7 Witness statement seen by the authors. 8 Interview with the authors. 9 *Construction News*, 11 Apr 2002, nin.tl/CNonEscasale 10 'Exposed: Crisis tears at the heart of a great trade union', *Daily Mirror*, 22 Oct 1993. 11 Interview with the authors. 12 'Construction union UCATT and new construction union of EETPU face battle for members', *Construction News*, 23 Aug 1991. 13 Email to the authors, 13 Jun 2014. 14 Reported in North West Cowboy #1 and reproduced on Labournet website 19 Jan 2005. 15 Blacklisting Report to Unite EC, 19 Sep 2011. 16 Interview with the authors. 17 Alan Wainwright's evidence to the Scottish Affairs Select Committee, 6 Nov 2012, EV128. 18 Email to the authors, 5 Jun 2014. 19 Interview with the authors. 20 Interview with the authors. 21 Witness statement seen by the authors. 22 Key documents disclosed pursuant to July Disclosure Order (High Court). 23 Letter from OH Parsons solicitors to Phil Chamberlain, 13 Jun 2014. 24 Email from Spencer Wood, OH Parsons solicitors, to Dave Smith, 4 Apr 2014. 25 Witness statement used in internal UCATT disciplinary hearing. 26 Interview with the authors. 27 Witness statement seen by the authors. 28 UCATT Conference Report 2000, p 129. 29 UCATT Conference Report 1996, p 273. 30 Interview with the authors. 31 Witness statement seen by the authors. 32 Email from Spencer Wood, OH Parsons solicitors, to Dave Smith 4 Apr 2014. 33 Blacklisting Report to Unite EC, 19 Sep 2011 34 Email to the authors, 8 Apr 2014. 35 Interview with the authors. 36 nin. tl/electricianreinstated 37 nin.tl/Kerrylegend 38 Janet Druker and Geoffrey White, 'Employment relations on major construction projects: the London 2012 Olympic construction site', in *Industrial Relations Journal* 44:5–6, 2013, pp 566-583.

9
Under constant watch

Q: Would industrial-relations managers actually meet people from Special Branch?'

A: Well, Special Branch wouldn't be doing their job if they didn't... Sometimes we would go six months without meeting them. Sometimes you would go three to four weeks when you saw them quite frequently.'

Dudley Barrett, head of industrial relations at Costain Group (1982-95)[1]

T he Buckingham Arms pub in central London has the distinction of having been in CAMRA's Good Pub Guide seven years on the trot. It also has the advantage of being just round the corner from New Scotland Yard. As such it was an ideal place for a Special Branch police officer to have a lunchtime pint with a contact without drawing too much attention.

The Buckingham Arms in London,
scene of meetings with the security services

Jack Winder had been schooled to be discreet. He was a senior official with the Economic League, which had spent decades acting as the interface between corporations and the security services monitoring subversives. As Winder told MPs, at these meetings there were certain rules that needed to be followed.

❝ I inherited Metropolitan Police contacts from my predecessor. He stressed to me, "The one thing to remember is that these people can do you a lot of harm, so don't ask them anything that will embarrass them." You never ask them a question about information on individuals or anything like that, because of their contacts. The door was open to those people; we had to put a foot in the door. They could do us a great deal of harm if we got on the wrong side of them and they simply said, "They're dodgy; don't touch them".❞[2]

Winder was being a little coy in his evidence. Former Economic League boss Michael Noar has suggested a much more active relationship. 'Obviously we help them [Special Branch] where we can. If we come across things that we think will be of particular interest to them we send it to them. Now obviously, again in the course of discussions, there is an exchange of information just in the ordinary course of talking.'[3]

These links with corporations and the targeting of union activists were confirmed by Special Branch officers speaking in the BBC's 'True Spies' series of reports. They made clear that the monitoring of trade unions was a key part of their work. One said:

❝ It was very, very important that trade unions were monitored and I as a Special Branch officer did it as efficiently as I could. ❞

At Ford's Halewood factory the company submitted to the Branch the names of the latest job applicants.

❝ We were expected to check these lists against our known subversives and if any were seen on the list, strike a line through it, go and see our contact and say "so and so is a member of the CP [Communist Party]".

You call it blacklisting and that's what it is. If you have a small group of subversives that can bring a factory to a stop then I think the ends justify the means. In any sort of war there are always going to be casualties.[4]

Metropolitan Police Special Branch officer Ken Day, who served from 1969 to 1998, spent time cultivating top union sources. 'People at the very top,' he said.[5] Winder said that the League had good relations with certain trade-union leaders who felt they had problems with the far left. Among them was Kate Losinska, who was president of the Civil and Public Services Association in the 1970s. Losinska was a hero on the Tory right for being, as the *Telegraph* described her in its obituary, 'a scourge of leftwing extremism in the trade unions'. She also chaired the Trade Union Committee for European and Transatlantic Understanding, funded by the US Congress and NATO.[6]

And if they couldn't draw upon ideological soulmates the secret state could put its own people in place. Seumas Milne's book *The Enemy Within*[7] exposes perhaps the most infamous union spy in UK history: Roger Windsor, chief executive of the National Union of Miners (NUM) during the 1984-5 miners' strike. According to an MI5 officer quoted by Milne, Windsor was an *agent provocateur*, deliberately sent in to work for the miners in order 'to fuck up the NUM'. Windsor was, of course, not the only union official providing information to the security services during the miners' strike. As the ex-MI5 officer Cathy Massiter explained: 'Whenever a major dispute came up it would immediately become a major area for investigation.'[8]

The construction industry had its own links with the secret state to ensure that an eye was kept on activists. Former UCATT president John Flavin, now an industrial-relations consultant for Laing O'Rourke, says:

> I was made aware that companies that had industrial-relations [IR] managers met regularly to discuss industrial and trade-union activities. I was also made aware that they had regular meetings with a Special Branch officer at a public house in Hammersmith. One of the IR managers said that he attended one of those meetings and the Special Branch people had revolvers and that he never went back.[9]

That these meetings took place has been confirmed by a number of the industrial-relations professionals that the authors interviewed for this book. It was easy to see how such relationships between the police and the building firms might have come about when you consider the evidence of Ken Mullier, personnel manager for TCA subscriber Mowlem. He told a *World in Action* documentary:

> ❝Most of the major construction companies have their own employees who are ex-policemen and they're employed specifically for their expertise, if you like, at being able to contact old friends who are still serving in the police force to give them the information they need.❞[10]

One such identified by the authors is former detective superintendent Brian Morris who, according to his LinkedIn profile, was employed in 'specialist squads' within the Metropolitan Police. Upon leaving the force, he became group security manager for blacklisting firm Laing O'Rourke. He is now programme security adviser to Crossrail.

The police and blacklisting

Given this history, it was not surprising that campaigners wanted further investigation into the role, if any, of the police and security services in the blacklisting operation. And it was ex-police officer David Clancy who first suggested there was something in this suspicion. At Dave Smith's Employment Tribunal against Carillion, his barrister David Renton specifically asked Clancy about the police and the ICO officer replied: 'There is some information that could only have come from the police or the security services.' There was an audible gasp and a cheer in the public gallery when he said it.

When giving evidence to MPs, Clancy expanded on this. 'There were entries such as a person being removed from the country and coming back into the United Kingdom,' he said.

> ❝This was at a particular time when perhaps people from the Republic of Ireland were being monitored. This was what would appear to have been an Irish national and individuals being given security clearance working on MoD construction

sites. There was information in relation to the registered keeper details of vehicles. Where would that come from? In one particular case there was what was referred to as "a special" within the database attached to one individual's records. That seems to be an in-depth analysis of an individual's home circumstances and what his neighbours thought about him. In my opinion, that would have been part of, in effect, an intelligence record in relation to an individual.[11]

Among all the files released so far, not one relates to any person convicted or even suspected of any kind of terrorist activity.

It took a stroke of luck and some careful digging to develop a much fuller picture. Dave Smith was granted a third-party disclosure order against the ICO that obliged them to disclose all the files that related to him or to the companies in his Employment Tribunal. It was only because the ICO had a lack of staff that they suggested his solicitor, Declan Owens, could look at the files to identify the relevant ones. As Owens was doing this work *pro bono*, he didn't go up but suggested that Smith went instead. When Smith read the files of Dan Gilman, Frank Smith and Lisa Teuscher, he realized that they contained information that only the police could know. It was pure fluke that it was Smith who looked at the files, because anyone else would not have realized the significance.

Two files which raised particular suspicions are held on Frank Smith and his girlfriend Lisa Teuscher. Frank, a bricklayer by trade, was a long-time political activist who had been involved in a number of actions on building sites across London calling for better wages and conditions. It was the late 1990s and London was experiencing a building boom but the stocky Liverpudlian had started to find work hard to get. He said:

I was in poverty – the only jobs I could get were working on little crap jobs. As a bricklayer, you always wanted to get in with a subbie [subcontractor] or a big job that had continuity, that had a decent run of work. You never start a long job in November to January. So you were always aiming for a job that you could get the turkey out of. For me it just became harder and harder to get onto any job where there was any decent run of work – I could only get little tiny jobs. On one occasion, money was quite bad, Lisa couldn't understand it and she took a day driving me around different sites looking for a start. It'd be try that one, that's a big job – I'd go in one after another – nothing. After seeing this and seeing my name on the blacklist, I think my name must have been getting checked out.[12]

Frank Smith's name certainly was being checked out – and not just by the construction companies. Smith's story was to be one of the threads which led the cover-up of security-service involvement to unravel.

When Ian Kerr appeared before the Scottish Affairs Select Committee in November 2012, he used it as an opportunity to make clear he had no links with the police. 'I had no links with any police department whatsoever or any security department whatsoever, and I was never a private investigator, for the sake of this part of the discussion,' he said.

Any information that came in came via the named contacts. The main part of the contacts' jobs was to keep a very good liaison with their opposite numbers in the unions, which was accepted procedure. There is nothing unusual whatsoever about that. In the process of running a site efficiently, they would have made all sorts of odd contacts.[13]

And he agreed that those contacts would have included the police 'even if it was only to do with a theft off-site, an attempted break-in or a grievance matter to keep the site open where there was an unofficial protest.'

MP Pamela Nash then asked about a line in one of the files of an Irish national saying: 'An individual has been given security clearance to work on MoD [Ministry of Defence] construction sites.' She wanted to know if Kerr had a role in the security clearance of Irish nationals working on MoD contracts. There was a very long silence in the room, only broken when Kerr finally asked if that could be answered in private and the chair agreed that it could be. However, it was never followed up and a fortnight later Kerr was dead. Subsequently, his widow Mary said: 'Ian did tell me that he didn't think it was in anyone's best interest to bring up the question of the Irish. I don't know why. I'm afraid that's a secret Ian took with him.'[14]

Kerr's statement to MPs denying any links with the police contrasted with a posthumously published interview with *The Times* just two months later. In it, he recalled a meeting organized by The Consulting Association in 2008 when eight construction industry directors were addressed by a 'key officer' from the National Extremism Tactical Co-ordination Unit (NETCU). According to the *Daily Telegraph*, this then Huntingdon-based police organization had been set up to 'take over MI5's covert role watching groups such as the Campaign for Nuclear Disarmament, trade-union activists and leftwing journalists'.[15] Kerr told *The Times*: 'They were seeking a channel to inform construction companies [of the information] they were collecting [and] they were wanting to be able to feed it out to the companies.'

The Times reported that, in return, the NETCU officer asked the companies to pass on their own information about potential troublemakers and Kerr said that a 'two-way information exchange' opened up. Kerr also disclosed that codes on the files were used to indicate those who were of interest to Special Branch and that 'Irish ex-Army, bad egg' was one example of this.[16] Both terms appear on Consulting Association documents relating to Steve Acheson. It turned out that the Information Commissioner had seized evidence of this 2008 meeting in which the senior police officer from the counter-extremism unit had given a Powerpoint presentation to the secret blacklisting body. The ICO allowed MPs on the Select Committee to view a note taken but has refused subsequent Freedom of Information requests on the grounds of breaching the Data Protection Act. David Smith, the deputy commissioner, said:

> I think it is a bit of an overstatement to call it minutes of a meeting. My recollection is that it is notes of a presentation that the crime unit gave. It is not as though they were having a meeting to agree a course of action.[17]

The ICO says that the document was made available to the Scottish Affairs Select Committee to 'inform their work' but wasn't intended for wider publication. Meanwhile the Metropolitan Police responded to Freedom of Information requests by saying it holds no information about any meetings between NETCU and The Consulting Association, nor in fact any documentation whatsoever from NETCU, which has now been subsumed into the Metropolitan Police. One of the senior managers attending the meeting was John Edwards from Carillion, some two years after the company had supposedly broken all ties with TCA. His presence at Woodstock meetings was confirmed by Mary Kerr in a High Court witness statement and separately to the authors as the person who had been involved in arrangements for a NETCU speaker.

In fact, the ICO's deputy commissioner says that he was not surprised to find evidence of collusion between the police and blacklisting:

> Given that this was about people who had supposedly caused trouble to the construction industry and therefore there are a range of ways you cause trouble, right from the entirely legitimate raising health and safety to criminal damage. There is a link with crime and so it is not surprising there was some connection with the police. I can see a police officer, if they had known the database had existed, going along to Kerr and saying "we have got this person for causing criminal damage on a building site, you might want to put them on your list".[18]

However, on the entire Consulting Association database of 3,213 names, there are no more than 20 files that relate to theft or similar, less than one per cent of the total. The remaining 99 per cent appear there due to trade union and political activism. State co-operation with the blacklisting operation was unlikely to be part of an investigation into criminals stealing copper.

Security service infiltration

The involvement of the security services was the most closely guarded secret of the blacklisting scandal. However, information was seeping out from different sources and careful digging. The most explosive evidence came to light when a whistleblower decided to reveal a hitherto unknown and shocking spying operation.

The Colin Roach Centre in Stoke Newington, London, opened

in 1993 and housed several community organizations including the Hackney Trade Union Resource Centre. It was named after a young black man shot dead in Stoke Newington police station in 1983 – a killing ruled to be suicide but regarded with suspicion by many residents. One of the organizations involved in the centre was the Hackney Community Defence Association, which had proved tenacious in its mission to expose corruption among Stoke Newington police officers. It was also home to trade-union campaigns.

A year after the Centre opened, a man calling himself Mark Cassidy appeared. He said that he was a builder who had lost his father to a drunk driver and come down to London looking for work – but it was just a story. Cassidy's real name was Mark Jenner and he was an undercover spy for the Special Demonstration Squad (SDS). As *Guardian* journalists Paul Lewis and Rob Evans revealed: 'Cassidy delved into radical politics. He had a particularly dubious mission: keeping an eye on campaigners exposing police wrong-doing.'[19] As such he gravitated towards the Colin Roach Centre. Mark Metcalf was a co-ordinator at the Centre at the time and is now a journalist. He said:

> From my campaigning experience it was unusual for someone to simply walk in – most people start their involvement after meeting someone or attending an event. He claimed to have seen TV coverage of a demonstration by the families of people killed at the hands of the police, and radical lawyer Gareth Pierce speaking afterwards, and wanted to get involved. He had come down from his home town of Birkenhead to continue working as a builder and didn't know many people locally.[20]

The Centre was also home to the Brian Higgins Defence Campaign, set up after a UCATT official sued union member Brian Higgins for libel. Jenner chaired some of the Defence Campaign meetings. It may be coincidence but a page in Higgins' blacklist file dated October 1996 is titled 'Known Associates of Brian Higgins – (see their separate cards)'. The ICO has redacted the entire page. In addition there are a large number of articles on his file from the magazine that the Colin Roach Centre printed dating from around the same time that Jenner was chairing these meetings.

The SDS was an elite undercover unit set up by the Special Branch in the wake of protests against the Vietnam War to infiltrate subversive groups. The feeling was that the huge demonstrations had exposed an intelligence gap. The SDS would bridge this gap. The officers would adopt fake identities and live for years among target groups, gaining the trust of those they were spying on. That trust extended to forming relationships and even fathering children with the very people on whom they were tasked to find intelligence.

Though now one of the more notorious spying outfits, the SDS was part of a long policing tradition. Plainclothes police officers infiltrating political organizations and spying on meetings is hardly something new. Co-operation between the state and business in gathering information about people they considered posed a risk to the status quo also has a long history. The first camera purchased by the Metropolitan Police was used to photograph the suffragettes. Despite the end of the Cold War, Special Branch had seen an eightfold increase in officers and those engaged in domestic intelligence gathering and anti-subversion work increased fivefold. As one intelligence expert wrote at the time:

> The Special Branch is supposed to be as accountable as ordinary police forces to local police authorities but this is clearly a fiction. No Chief Constable or Home Secretary would countenance enquiries into Special Branch activities. The Special Branch remains outside of democratic control and is one more element of the secret state which escapes an effective form of oversight.[21]

The expansion of who might be considered a subversive and therefore a legitimate target continued to increase. The catch-all phrase was 'domestic extremism', which had no legal basis or agreed definition, and, as Evans and Lewis point out:

> could be applied to anyone police wanted to keep an eye on. In the most general terms it was taken to refer to political activity involving "criminal acts of direct action in furtherance of a single-issue campaign", but would not be restricted to criminal conduct. Domestic extremists, police decided, were

those who wanted to "prevent something happening or to change legislation or domestic policy", often doing so "outside normal democratic process".[22]

The groups at the Colin Roach Centre, which was as much a trade-union resource centre as anything else, clearly met this definition and so it was little wonder the SDS would try to insert someone into this nexus of dissent. Jenner's cover story of working as a joiner proved ideal not just for making connections with other builders but also in that he could justify his peripatetic lifestyle. During his time there, he ferried construction union activists to demonstrations and attended picket lines over unpaid wages and victimization.

Jenner also spied on anti-racist campaigners and the efforts by anti-fascist activists to confront the British National Party and the paramilitary fascist group Combat 18. In November 1999, Jenner appeared on the ITV news following an anti-BNP protest In Dover. The news coverage shows him at the front of a crowd of anti-fascists, wearing a black hat and robo-cop style padded gloves aggressively taunting the fascists as fireworks were fired at them. That very same month, information about some of his fellow anti-fascist campaigners appears to have made its way on to the blacklist files held by The Consulting Association. Three separate trade unionists who were in contact with Jenner had details on how they were 'observed' or 'apprehended' while protesting against fascists laying a wreath at the Cenotaph in commemoration of Britain's war dead on Remembrance Sunday in 1999.

Among those observed at the Cenotaph were Frank Smith, Dan Gilman and Steve Hedley. All of them have Consulting Association files, though Gilman, who is a teacher, has no connection with the construction industry whatsoever. His sole record in the file is his attendance at an anti-fascist event. Hedley is now senior assistant general secretary of the RMT rail union. His blacklist file covers around 15 years and is filled with details on what he said at union conferences, his involvement in health-and-safety activities, industrial disputes he took part in and his political views. The RMT had its own TCA file, although it was never seized. In addition to Hedley, another RMT assistant general secretary, Mick Lynch, had a blacklist record, leading to concerns in the union about the extent to which it had been targeted.

Hedley's file also has details on his participation in the 1999 Cenotaph anti-fascist demonstration. Hedley said:

> ❝There was absolutely no way a building-site manager would have known that I was on that demonstration. It was nothing to do with work. It was not covered in the papers whatsoever.❞[23]

Hedley points the finger at Jenner, to whom he was introduced at the Colin Roach Centre, as the possible spark for Special Branch interest. Hedley recalls:

> ❝There was something strange about the guy from the start because he looked like a crusty, long haired, and he'd gone to the Kurdish community centre. I just couldn't see the connection why somebody like that would be trying to get involved with the Kurds.❞

Hedley would bump into Jenner a couple of times a month in the late 1990s whenever anti-fascist activities were going on. Jenner for a while became a key activist for Anti-Fascist Action in north London. He was also on several construction dispute picket lines, including Canary Wharf, Southwark, one close to the Old Bailey and another in Waterloo over unpaid wages by subcontractor Dahl-Jensen. Several hundred union members turned up to picket the site and Jenner was there and at other disputes which bubbled up across the capital in the building-boom years. Jenner was also present when Hedley went to Ireland as part of a trade-union delegation to observe the peace process, a trip organized by the Colin Roach Centre. The undercover police officer even stayed at Hedley's mum's house.

TCA blacklist files record a piece of information that activists say was only known to a handful of people involved in anti-fascist activity during the 1990s. The three trade unionists were part of a loose grouping of activists, known colloquially as the 'Away Team', who protected labour movement and anti-racist demonstrations from physical attacks by far-right activists. Only around 50 people in the entire country would have known what the 'Away Team' referred to, as it was a private joke relating to football rather than a term ever recorded in the press. Information about their membership of the Away Team was gathered by SDS officer Peter Francis, who served for years undercover. The activists believe this information that ended up on their TCA files could only have originated from undercover police officers.

The third member of the Away Team who came into contact with the police at the anti-BNP (British National Party) event in November 1999 was Frank Smith. He said:

> ❝I was stopped, searched and spoken to. I wasn't arrested, so there would be nothing in my arrest file. Definitely no press reports about it.
>
> Now what has that got to do with me being a builder? How would a building company know anything about that? It could only come from the police.❞[24]

Yet the Cenotaph incident is recorded in his Consulting Association file. Also in his blacklist file is a line saying:

> **'Under constant watch (officially) and seen as politically dangerous.'**

Frank Smith's blacklist file starts in 1992 and records his involvement with the Vascroft dispute and the Joint Sites Committee. Special Branch also opened a file on him and the officer who opened that file was Peter Francis. The officer recalls:

> ❝The file was created some time around 1995. I knew Frank was involved in Militant but it was primarily his role within the Away Team that I was interested in. So I opened what we call an RF – a registry file.
>
> Then, every time I saw him on a demo or I had a drink with him, that would go on the file. "Seen as politically dangerous" is the assessment I would have had of him. In order for me to create a file on him I need to say something like that because he was regarded as being a subversive.❞[25]

Francis, who subsequently blew the whistle on SDS activities, including spying on the family of murdered black teenager Stephen

Lawrence, was not tasked to monitor Smith because of his union activities but because of his involvement in the Away Team. Yet Smith's blacklist file also describes him as a 'leading light' in the Away Team. Quite how a manager on a building site would know this is difficult to explain.

There was more to Smith's blacklist file than just his union and political activities, though – and it extended to his girlfriend at the time, Lisa Teuscher. One part of his file talks about Teuscher, an American citizen, being involved in 'several marriages of convenience'. This was untrue. It turned out that she also had her own blacklisting file and the only thing on it is that she is the 'girlfriend of Frank Smith'. And, by coincidence, Francis had also opened the

Peter Francis in 1993 – undercover police officer turned whistleblower.

Special Branch file on Teuscher. At one stage Francis recalls being asked, via his superior, to supply information to the Home Office on her marital status. Teuscher was not involved in the construction industry but was actively involved in anti-racist campaigning. Francis told the authors that a file was opened on her because she was identified as an important member of the leftwing group Militant and, in particular, Youth Against Racism in Europe (YRE). Following the Special Branch intervention, Teuscher was refused leave to remain in the UK and the Home Office tried to deport her. When she appealed the decision, the British government seized her passport for seven years, meaning that the young American could not visit her family. Teuscher has now returned to the US but remembers how her treatment by the British state affected her:

> ❝Traumatic because they held my passport for seven years. I loved my family. It was so hard not seeing them for so many years. They tried to deport me; I got a lawyer and fought it. I tried to do everything legally but the British government seized my passport. I couldn't go anywhere. It was very stressful. They accused me of stuff that basically is untrue.❞[26]

Teuscher is particularly upset that her political campaigning was undoubtedly the reason for her battle against deportation.

> ❝ I am outraged. I came to London and was proud to be a member of the YRE. Happy to be spending time usefully fighting racism, especially when we drove the BNP [British National Party] off of Brick Lane. I find it disturbing that throughout my genuine interest to improve society, there was an unknown force in the British government tracking me.❞[27]

The authors informed Teuscher that she was on the Consulting Association blacklist and she has now received a copy of her file from the ICO:

> ❝ I was shocked when I first read my file, it made me feel physically sick. It's absurd. I don't see any reason why my name should be linked with the building industry. I had no professional involvement whatsoever. The only reason I am on the list is because of Frank. And that is not a legitimate reason for the police following me or anybody else making notes on me.❞

Teuscher eventually won her appeal against deportation but after seven years of constant struggle says that she was worn down and she eventually returned to the US when her passport was returned to her, saying 'they won in the end'.

It seems implausible that these very specific, virtually unknown pieces of private information about Smith and Teuscher could have appeared on their blacklist files without first having originated from a state source.

A whole other life

One person taken in completely by the undercover spy was Alison (not her real name), who was in a relationship with Jenner for five years. Alison said that she had no idea that he had a whole other life as a police officer – let alone his own family with three children. They lived together and both worked at Glastonbury one year for the Workers' Beer Company, raising money on behalf of the Colin Roach Centre. Jenner would keep reams of newspaper clippings. His cover as a joiner extended to having a bag of tools and a fake job with Manor Works in Clapham. Jenner even fitted Alison a kitchen – though she noted at the time that he had trouble using the router. When Jenner left suddenly, he took many of his files and all his pictures with him. Only a few snippets remain, including a 1996 diary that indicates he attended UCATT union meetings in February, attended pay talks in May and a union conference in Sheffield in June that year. Other handwritten notes refer to TGWU, EPIU and UCATT members. UCATT records show that, under the name Mark Cassidy, he was a member of the union from 1996 until 1998.[28] His taxpayer-funded SDS bank account was used to pay the union subscriptions and allowed him to infiltrate the Hackney branch of UCATT. Jenner was active in supporting the JJ Fast Foods strike in Tottenham Hale and another note records that he visited a meeting of the RMT Midland District on 12 July 1995.

Alison told the authors she remembers numerous conversations with the SDS spy about the building industry and union campaigns, which she described as a 'key part of his work' and 'a big part of what he did during this period'. She remembers how he even used to ask her mother to type up the handwritten notes that he had taken when returning from union meetings. Some other union activists have described him as a disruptive influence. Whether his role was to spy on union activists or if he was acting as an *agent provocateur*, Jenner's considerable involvement with trade unions in northeast London over many years is beyond doubt.

It would not be unusual for SDS officers to be on picket lines because their targets would often join industrial disputes. Peter Francis recalls picketing outside the Mount Pleasant sorting office in central London because he was interested in a member of Militant who was part of that action.

Another Militant supporter who was not a building worker but an elected politician also has a blacklist file. Former Member of the Scottish Parliament Tommy Sheridan came to prominence when he was elected to Glasgow City Council from his prison cell after he had been jailed for stopping a Poll Tax warrant sale. Two years later, in 1994, his file was opened and regularly updated until TCA was shut in 2009. It has details on his anti-roads protests, social housing, speaking on picket lines outside building sites and the various elected posts he held. Sheridan says most of the early entries in his file are not press cuttings but information often from private political meetings that appears to have been passed to someone while he was carrying out his role as a Glasgow city councillor and later an MSP. Commenting on his appearance on the blacklist, Sheridan said:

> Blacklisting and spying by multinational companies against shop stewards subverts trade unionism. Blacklisting and spying with police collusion on elected representatives of the people subverts democracy.[29]

A number of other prominent Scottish socialist politicians also have TCA blacklist files, including former MSP Colin Fox and former editor of the *Scottish Socialist Voice* newspaper, Alan McCombes. Both were only told of their inclusion on the blacklist when contacted by the authors. Special Branch were also spying on other elected politicians linked with Militant, including the former Coventry Labour MP Dave Nellist.[30]

SDS officers could be tasked to monitor industrial militants. For instance, a major effort went into the policing of the Wapping dispute because of the violence associated with it.[31] According to an analysis of files by the Special Branch Files Projects and released by the Met Police: 'Special Branch subjected the dispute to intense surveillance, producing written daily briefs on all aspects of the pickets, demonstrations, negotiations, and union meetings. They kept files on trade union leaders and had informants. They recorded details of organizations and individuals involved with the protests, and noted the contents of banners, posters and chants.'[32]

When funding for the unit switched from the Home Office to the Metropolitan Police, its million-pound-a-year budget needed to be justified. That meant making its product available to others and one of those was Special Branch's industrial desk. From its glory years in the 1970s, the industrial section within the Met had shrunk to just two detective sergeants and two detective constables by the mid-1990s. Francis, who had a desk next to them before he joined the SDS, said:

> They were purely there for liaison purposes with industry and with unions. They used to swagger around saying how many

lunches they had had. The pub lunches are the cheap end. They would be meeting in hotels.[33]

The role played by the industrial section within Special Branch and the almost identical F2 branch of MI5, once headed by Stella Rimington, particularly during the 1984-5 miners' strike, is well documented.[34] The entire purpose of both was to spy on trade unions and for this information to be shared with major employers when deemed necessary. In relation to political policing, Special Branch officers often acted as the foot soldiers for MI5, with Intelligence gathered by undercover police feeding directly into the security service.

While the SDS was a secret even within Special Branch, its registry files would have been available to other desks. The source of intelligence would have been sanitized, as the jargon puts it, to ensure it was protected. The phrasing of Frank Smith's blacklisting file suggests a conversation between an industry contact and someone with access to the Special Branch file and that conversation being related to Ian Kerr by the company source. In the case of Frank Smith, the entries are referenced to 3228, which is code for Costain.

The industrial-relations manager for Costain from 1982 until 1995 was Dudley Barrett. Now retired and living in Wiltshire, Barrett told the authors he attended quarterly meetings of the Economic League's Services Group and then The Consulting Association. Barrett also revealed he had meetings with Special Branch officers:

> Whenever I thought it was necessary or they thought it was necessary. Sometimes we would go six months without meeting them. Sometimes you would go three to four weeks when you saw them quite frequently. A few of them became personal friends to be quite honest and vice versa. I can say I was much closer than most people were to them.[35]

Barrett claims that 'they never ever gave us names incidentally. Never: absolutely rigid that was.' Although, when pressed, he conceded: 'Occasionally it would happen, if you had strong suspicions and they hadn't got onto the Services Group thing but they [Special Branch] would only deal with people that they were very, very sure and sound with.' Although Barrett admits having particularly close relationships with Special Branch, he claims to have known four or five other senior industrial-relations managers and HR directors who attended similar meetings with the secret political police unit.

According to Barrett, Special Branch had a section that dealt with:

> ❝construction and a lot that dealt with offshore, whereas others were just interested in the Communist Party. The Communist Party was literally trying to overrun this country in 1948-50, names of them were flying about no end: Communist Party members.❞[36]

Special Branch's interest in monitoring leftwing groups continues. Paul Filby, a joiner from Liverpool involved in anti-fascist activities, told the authors about being approached by two plainclothes Merseyside Police officers in 2013. They were interested in any information Filby had about the activities of anarchist groups on demonstrations. In return, the officers said, they would be able to pay Filby's 'expenses' if he was attending events. The construction worker declined the offer.

The activities of campaign groups were also of interest to another spin-off from the Economic League. Caprim was run by Jack Winder, the League's former director of research, and Stan Hardy, its director of operations. Winder joined the League back in 1963 after a stint in the army. Hardy, on the other hand, had worked for and run several companies, again after an army career, and didn't join the League until 1988. He subsequently went to work for the Institute of Directors. Caprim was set up in May 1993 and employed Geoff Hume and Jack Bramwell from the League. Bramwell's expertise was in security. Among Caprim's directors was former League chair and sugar baron Sir Henry Saxon Tate. In a smooth performance before MPs in February 2013, Winder's nonchalant explanation for Caprim's birth was simply to give himself and Hardy a job. He continued:

> ❝We thought we had something to offer, which was to continue

the part of the League's work that I had been involved in – that is to say, warning companies about threats to their well-being from all sorts of organizations. As time went on, of course, it became much less about actual parties like the *Socialist Worker* and so on, and much more about single-issue campaigns.❾[37]

According to Winder, Caprim didn't offer a vetting service because it was the bad publicity attached to that aspect which had helped bring down the League. It didn't make business sense to repeat a failed venture. Instead Caprim focused on organizations such as *Ethical Consumer* magazine, the Campaign Against Arms Trade (CAAT) and Reclaim the Streets. CAAT was also infiltrated by private investigators while Reclaim the Streets was targeted by the SDS. Winder identified three specific sectors to which Caprim provided intelligence: the defence industry, pharmaceuticals and agrochemicals. He named GlaxoSmithKline (GSK), Novartis, Rhone-Poulenc, Zeneca, Monsanto, Rio Tinto, JP Morgan and Morgan Stanley as being among Caprim's clients. Subsequently GSK told MPs that, while it had taken some information from Caprim, it had been so poor that they had terminated the relationship. For those that retained them, Caprim monitored the output of campaigners and attended their meetings. It coincidentally folded in 2009, just a few weeks after the raid on TCA, supposedly because it lost clients and Winder was looking to retire. It had, though, been barely functional for several years before that, as its directors simply lacked the energy and its competitors, including an expanding police interest, enjoyed better resources and equipment. Competitors included risk-management firms such as Control Risks and Kroll.

One former Morgan Stanley banker who blew the whistle on malpractice at the bank came across Control Risks. Chidi Obihara said companies such as these, well staffed with former police and military personnel, 'are known across the industry for keeping records on individual bankers'. Obihara, who found himself unable to get a job after going public, added:

❝ On their websites... they say they carry out bespoke searches on individuals. At a recent industry conference, I asked one officer of Control Risks who told me she was unaware of any laws stopping them from maintaining an "informal" list of individuals.[38]

Unite union members involved in a British Airways dispute in 2014 have also complained about being put under surveillance by the Asset Protection group, which is similarly staffed by ex-police officers.[39] Meanwhile Unite reportedly agreed a million-pound out-of-court settlement with the airline in 2015 over claims that its in-house security department accessed the personal communications of staff – a claim the company denied.[40]

While giving evidence to the Select Committee, Kerr told MPs that, in addition to the files on construction workers, there were around 200 files on environmental activists that the ICO never seized because they did not open the filing cabinet. Kerr subsequently burnt all the files not seized. Nonetheless, an idea as to why these environmental and animal-rights activists might have been targeted can be gleaned from interviews with those named, as well as by looking at the battles the construction industry fought from the mid-1990s onwards.

In 1996, proposals to cut a bypass for Newbury through a sensitive environmental site brought campaigners out in force. Police were confronted by a determined and resourceful effort, including the digging and occupying of tunnels and trees in an effort to frustrate the building process. Sir Charles Pollard, the then Chief Constable of Thames Valley Police, made clear in a subsequent interview that Newbury was a line in the sand as far as he was concerned. 'The ones who were planning and tried to carry out seriously illegal acts are very subversive, in a sense of subversive to democracy,' he said.[41]

Special Branch paid informants for details on the occupation while Thames Valley Police took the unusual step of recruiting from the private sector a spy who was inserted into the camp. This person was eventually credited with allowing a key tunnel to be taken by police and helped cause the protest to unravel.

The Consulting Association set up a special group to consider the wider issue. It was called the Woodstock Group – because of the location of its meetings in The Bear pub in the well-to-do Oxfordshire village of the same name.

Kerr told MPs:

> ❝The targets [for the activists] were the M11, Twyford Down, the Manchester second runway and the Bath eastern bypass. It was those sorts of contracts, which were hit very badly. The M11 had a very large oak tree that stood in the way for ages, which became a postal address and had letters addressed to it.❞[42]

At Woodstock Group meetings, examples came up of people who had gained employment in construction companies or occupied offices. The industry wanted information on who these people were. In his private notes obtained by the authors, Kerr records:

> ❝The outcome of these meetings of the cos [companies] involved in the construction of M11, Twyford Down, Bath Eastern Bypass, Manchester 2nd Runway etc was that the protest movement's tactics were known about from first-hand reporting back via cos' [companies] main security contacts and because of the tenacity of these people, cos [companies] took notice and responded responsibly by becoming sensitive to environmental issues.❞

The intersection of the state, police and the private sector was never clearer than in the response to these road-building schemes. At Newbury, in addition to Thames Valley Police employing an off-the-shelf spook and Special Branch buying informants, security contractors Group 4 used the services of Threat Response International (TRI) to gather intelligence. This company also succeeded in inserting a spy into Campaign Against Arms Trade on behalf of BAe. In the case of Newbury, TRI information also went to the police.[43]

The comedian and activist Mark Thomas was one of those on the receiving end of TRI's efforts to destabilize the anti-arms trade group. He considered Martin Hogbin, who worked for the campaign while passing information to TRI, a friend and it took several years before he realized that he was a paid infiltrator.

The board of TRI is made up of Evelyn Le Chene (who has an intelligence background), Bob Hodges, a former major-general in the British Army, and Barrie Gane, former deputy head of MI6.[44]

Thomas' 2014 show *Cuckooed*, about his experience of being a victim of BAe corporate spying, has won multiple awards, including the Amnesty International Freedom of Expression Award.

Thomas also ended up on Kerr's green list and believes this was because of his role in a campaign against the Ilisu Dam in Turkey. This project, backed by the government's Export Credit Guarantee Department, involved Balfour Beatty. The project would have destroyed a key cultural site and caused thousands of people to be relocated. An alliance of human rights activists, trade unionists, archaeologists, Friends of the Earth, students and the general public came together to get the government and the construction firms to think again.

Thomas said:

> We took over Balfour Beatty's AGM completely, the first one. They shut it down early, lost a load of votes, had to recast a load of votes. We cost them about a quarter of a million, just at the AGM. That was interesting. Second one they were well prepared for us. We lost the vote but the company didn't win it. The abstentions were enormous. They were bigger than those who voted for the company. Which in financial terms is quite a thing.[45]

The Ilisu Dam campaign was officially supported by the London region of UCATT, which passed a symbolic green ban against the proposed scheme and is mentioned on Dave Smith's blacklist file. Balfour Beatty withdrew from the project.

Although a TCA ring binder was the only clue to its environmental files, Unite and the GMB have cross-referenced the names with their membership lists to identify potential victims. One is Ellenor Hutson. Today she works for an SNP MP in Glasgow but during the mid-1990s she was a road protester at the Newbury Bypass, the A30 link road in Devon and the Manchester Second Runway. It didn't occur to Hutson that she might be on an industry blacklist until a letter dropped through her letterbox from Unite. She said:

> It was just random luck that I was a member of Unite at the time. I put on Facebook that I had got this letter. I got talking to people about this and I realized I had opposed a lot of the

projects the big firms were running. Two other people popped up and said they have called the ICO and they were on it and they were as shocked as I was. I set up a Facebook page and found dozens of people all from the 1990s on this blacklist.[46]

These activists had been involved in all the major protests from the mid-1990s up until 2009. Another on the list is Merrick Cork, whose investigative skills successfully uncovered police spy Mark Kennedy. He said:

❝Like many environmentalists, my "greenlist" file comes from details taken by police when I was arrested trying to save woodland that was being felled for Manchester Airport's second runway in 1997. The only credible explanation is that police gave the information about us, illegally, to The Consulting Association. This is not police officers upholding the law, it's police officers breaking the law to uphold something they clearly consider more important, the profits of construction companies.The Information Commissioners Office only seized a list of people who had greenlist files, rather than opening the drawer and taking the files themselves. Thanks to that incompetence, we'll never have a full picture of what info was held on us.❞[47]

Another on the list is John Stewart, who chairs the pressure group Heathrow Association for the Control of Aircraft Noise. Described by his Conservative MP Zac Goldsmith as a superbly effective but civilized campaigner, Stewart was told by the GMB that he was blacklisted. Stewart fears this may explain why, when he landed in America in 2011 for a speaking tour, he was escorted off the plane by armed guards and sent back to the UK. He said:

❝The list seems to have been around for some years. It's worrying that somebody like me, without convictions, can find myself on a blacklist like this.❞[48]

The files for the prominent Scottish leftwing political activists Tommy Sheridan, Colin Fox and Alan McCombes are all referenced as 'green' on the Consulting Association index system. This suggests that the greenlist was not solely for environmental activists but also for wider 'security' concerns, again raising the spectre of possible police collusion.

Hutson says the fact that her date of birth and home town are next to her name suggests the police as the original source. Hutson was arrested between 7 and 10 times, without press coverage, and each time was asked for her date of birth and her home town, which was Colchester. She would not have given that detail to private security guards or detective agencies looking to gather information for injunctions. One person with a now-destroyed file is listed as Grace Quantocks (the Quantocks is a range of hills in Somerset). However, Hutson points out that it was standard practice for activists to adopt the name of a landmark as a surname and give that to the police. For instance Dongas, named after ancient tracks on Twyford Down, was a name adopted by campaigners against a road-building scheme in that area.

The virtue of anonymity

Being targeted by those in authority has always been a hazard for those trying to improve the living standards of working people, so the need to keep workers' organizations secret was well known. In 1834, the Tolpuddle Martyrs were sent to Australia for swearing a secret oath while forming a trade union in the Dorset countryside. But the martyrs were just one example of vindictiveness by the authorities against agricultural labourers at the time. Eighteen people were hanged during a prolonged bitter battle over rural unemployment and poverty wages. With no legal means of raising their grievances, the fictitious character called Captain Swing was blamed whenever large crowds took retribution against landowners' threshing machines.

Some 20 years earlier, a slowdown in the industrial revolution had seen workers use the name of Ned Ludd when they fought back against the destitution facing mill workers made unemployed by new looms. As Luddite leaders faced execution, the need to hide one's true identity was a matter of life or death.

Workers in the building industry facing extremely hostile management have also resorted to using false names to avoid detection. At the simplest level this amounted to deliberately mis-spelling a name during a site induction or using a middle name when making an application. The leading lights in the Joint Sites Committee used the aliases Sean Prophet, Joe Stewart, Jack Mundey and Jerry Kelly when writing articles or talking to employers. All four alter-egos have their own blacklist files. Joe Stewart's file records:

> **1992 Mar:**
> **Described as Treasurer of the JSC and Newham UCATT Branch**
> **Long time reporter of various disputes in militant**
> **Note: could be pseudonym**

Sean Prophet's file is 11 pages long and even includes a photograph of the fictional person, as well as an article written about 300 bags of asbestos dumped by a company in a school playground and numerous press cuttings. It contains entries such as:

> **1997 March 26th: Along with** ▬▬▬ **visited 3230's**
> **Tottenham Court Road Building job to distribute current edition**
> **of 'Builders Crack', paper of Joint Sites Committee at breakfast**
> **in canteen. Gave their names verbally when asked by the site**
> **manager. Hence possibility that surnames are spelt differently**
> **to that assumed above. Alternatively – names may be false.**

Another activist that appears on the blacklist is the Australian union leader Jack Mundey. The legendary leader of the Australian Builders' Labourers' Federation (BLF) in the 1970s instigated the Green Bans strategy. BLF mass meetings voted to impose 'Green Bans' on particular projects that would destroy the environment if they were approached by local campaigners. Imposing a green ban meant that BLF members refused to demolish green space as part of the project. During the construction of Sydney Opera House, the Royal Botanical Gardens, which included ancient trees of spiritual significance to the aboriginal community, was intended to be demolished to make way for a car park. The BLF imposed a green ban and, as a consequence, the Gardens still remain today. The Rocks community in Sydney, meanwhile, was the site of the first European settlement and the oldest buildings in the entire country, which were to be demolished to make way for tower blocks. The BLF imposed a green ban that saw mass blockades by builders' labourers rallying thousands of Sydney residents and environmental activists. After a bitter battle, including arrests of BLF leaders, The Rocks was saved and is now a major cultural attraction in Australia; it has recently been granted World Heritage Site status.

In the late 1990s, London building workers used their antipodean hero's name as a pseudonym and leaflets were published by building workers in the name of *'Friends of Jack Mundey'*. The reference was clearly lost on company main contacts, undercover police officers and Ian Kerr processing the intelligence. So Jack Mundey was added to the blacklist: something he will no doubt be proud of.

During the 2012 sparks dispute over BESNA, the two most interviewed rank-and-file electricians, quoted extensively in the press throughout, went by the names Alan Keys and Eddie Current. But a more sinister usage of pseudonyms has been uncovered. During interviews for this book, blacklisted electrician Steuart Merchant revealed his dark secret, 'I gave a false name when I joined the single, widowed and divorced club in Dundee.'

Meanwhile, Hutson believes that it may well have been her first action as a 16-year-old which earned her a file. She took part in a demonstration in London in support of striking transport workers, ended up occupying London Transport offices and was arrested. Unknown to her, one of those involved was Jim Sutton, known to colleagues as Grumpy Jim. Sutton was actually an undercover police officer, real name Jim Boyling, who had targeted Reclaim The Streets. She said:

> ❛I found him quite unapproachable because he was associated with Reclaim The Streets and they had a whole cache. They did actions that were organized very secretly. Later on we found the reason he was grumpy was because he was almost having a breakdown because of the pressure he was under. Later on it was so obvious that he was having problems and was conflicted.❜

Boyling was arrested along with Hutson and others. He sat in on privileged legal meetings and went all the way to court without telling anyone that he was actually a member of the Special Demonstration Squad. In the end all but one of them were acquitted. 'I don't think he was on that action to mess it up or even to spy on me,' said Hutson. 'His primary reason was in order to show willing and demonstrate he was willing to get arrested.'

Also on Kerr's green list is a 'Gibby Zodal' which mirrors the mis-spelt name of a journalist quoted in an article in the *Sunday Times* about radical newsletter SchNEWS. Gibby Zobel was the co-founder of SchNEWS in Brighton in 1994. The weekly alternative paper arose out of the squatting of a disused courthouse in Brighton and the attempt to turn it into a community centre. It covered animal rights, protests against arms companies, anti-fascist action and the burgeoning anti-capitalist movement that coalesced around anti-roads protests, Reclaim The Streets and other direct-action movements – all familiar areas of TCA and police interest. Zobel subsequently went on to become the news editor for *The Big Issue* and is now a freelance journalist based in Brazil.

On 18 June 1999 ('J18') a huge demonstration called Stop the City of London took place. Thousands of people took to the Square Mile with a mixture of humour and defiance. As Hutson said:

> J18 was the point where all of the environmental activists started to become anti-capitalist. There had been a current of anti-capitalism before then but it hadn't really been in the ascendancy. That was the point where it became more common than not to identify as an anti-capitalist.[49]

It was a major target for the police spies to discover who was going and what their plans were.

Interestingly, several blacklist files mention sightings of their subject at the event. It seems unlikely, to say the least, that some site manager happened to be passing through, saw a construction worker they knew, and thought to pass the details on to The Consulting Association. The elusive Sean Prophet's file records: 'Involved with J18 "Stop the City of London" events on 18 June 1999.' Dave Smith's file says:

> *Re: J18 (Stop the City of London) At Finsbury Square site, then*
> *to Bank of England demo returning to site with 4 Eco warriors*
> *– attempted entry, but unsuccessful. Leaflet distributed (see*
> *JSC file for copy)*
>
> *Concern is over the developing links between JSC, D Smith*
> *and environmental activists. Leaflet from JSC states: 'Unity*
> *between Building Workers & Eco-Campaigners.*
> *Reported that building unions, UCATT specifically want*
> *D Smith/Schal issue sorted out. UCATT worried that*
> *issue is attracting attention of other pressure groups (ie:*
> *environmentalist) not interested in construction.*

Quite who is expressing concern is not made clear, but the inference is that the number of groups making common cause that might otherwise have acted independently was prompting observation and, presumably, infiltration. There is one possible source for the entry on Smith's file. Police spy Jim Boyling, whom we met earlier, had secured a key organizing role on the day through his work with Reclaim The Streets. One of his tasks was to reconnoitre the area and a witness remembers Smith's picket line at Finsbury Square being mentioned. The witness is almost certain that Boyling visited that part of the demonstration on the day.

Sexual and emotional abuse by undercover officers

Another female activist who found herself the target of undercover police monitoring and on the Consulting Association blacklist is Helen Steel. In the 1990s, the gardener and former London Greenpeace activist was sued for libel by the McDonald's Corporation for a pamphlet the group had distributed outside fast-food restaurants exposing the company's record on environmental issues, nutrition, animal and workers' rights. Steel and fellow activist Dave Morris decided to defend themselves in court and McLibel went on to become one of the longest and most famous court cases in UK legal history and a public-relations disaster for the fast-food giant. During the trial it emerged that McDonald's had paid for up to seven private investigators to infiltrate London Greenpeace meetings and that Metropolitan Police officers, including Special Branch, had passed private and in some cases false information about the McLibel Two and other activists, including their home addresses, to McDonald's and to one of the private investigators.

The Met agreed to pay £10,000 to the McLibel 2, plus their legal costs, and most significantly 'to bring this settlement to the attention of the three Area Commanders of the Metropolitan Police Force and ask them to remind their officers of their responsibility not to disclose information on the Police National Computer to a third party.'[50]

Under the consent order finalized, detective sergeant Valentine also stated he 'regretted any distress of the claimants caused by the disclosure of their details' to a private investigator hired by McDonald's. Sid Nicholson, McDonald's head of security and a former Met chief superintendent, had stated from the witness box that McDonald's security department were 'all ex-policemen' and if he ever wanted to know information about protesters he would go to his contacts in the police.[51]

Years later, Steel was to find out that one of the police officers spying on her was her long-term boyfriend John Barker. The SDS officer, whose real name was John Dines, had been tasked to infiltrate environmental activists and used his relationship with Steel to ingratiate himself. Dines' cover as a kitchen fitter allowed him to be away for several days apparently working. Steel also recalls Dines writing her letters about being involved in union action – including on the Channel Tunnel. 'It's possible that he was down there spying,' she said.[52]

In 2013, Steel found out that she is one of the green activists on the Consulting Association database. So is her McLibel co-defendant Dave Morris. Steel is convinced that if intelligence gathered by undercover police was routinely given to McDonald's in the 1990s, that the police were also providing similar information to major construction companies at the same time.

It has also now emerged that another undercover SDS officer, Bob Lambert, was one of the co-authors of the original London Greenpeace pamphlet that caused the entire McLibel court case in the first place. Despite being married and having children of his own, Lambert fathered another child with Jacqui, an activist he was spying on. He abandoned the mother and son when his deployment ended following the conviction of two animal-rights activists involved in planting incendiary devices in 1987. Lambert's deployment was considered one of the high points of the SDS. He was promoted to detective inspector and put in charge of the entire unit, mentoring the next generation of undercover officers.

In November 2014, Jacqui was awarded £425,000 in an out-of-court settlement by the Metropolitan Police for the emotional trauma she had suffered. In a series of media interviews, she claimed her experiences felt like being 'raped by the state'.[53]

In 2012 Green MP Caroline Lucas used parliamentary privilege to name Bob Lambert as the person who planted an Animal Liberation Front bomb which burned down the Debenhams department store in Harrow. Lambert denies the allegation. The two ALF activists who were imprisoned for that crime are currently appealing their convictions. By December 2015 the courts had overturned 57 convictions due to the *agent provocateur* role of undercover police officers and it was estimated that another 83 people could have their sentences quashed.[54]

On leaving the police, Lambert was awarded an MBE and took up a post as lecturer at St Andrews and London Metropolitan Universities, where he purported to be a liberal-minded expert in counter-terrorism and tackling Islamophobia. After a long-running campaign Lambert resigned from both posts at the end of 2015. In a statement he said: 'Henceforward I will pursue my academic interests in responses to terrorism and political violence as an independent researcher. I will also continue to co-operate with the investigations and inquiry into undercover policing.'[55] However, stalwart anti-racist campaigner Suresh Grover from the Newham Monitoring Project, who helped co-ordinate the Stephen Lawrence family campaign over many years, has said Lambert 'has absolutely no credibility whatsoever with the Muslim community'.[56] Grover has also stated:

> I now know that a number of other campaigns that I co-ordinated, such as the Michael Menson, the Ricky Reel and the Blair Peach campaigns, were spied upon. These campaigns that I have been involved in had absolutely no intentions other

than peaceful ones. But from Blair Peach to Stephen Lawrence, from Michael Menson to Nicky Jacobs, from the New Cross Massacre to the Campaign Against the Police Bill, from the Cherry Groce campaign to Broadwater Farm, every single one of these campaigns has been subject to surveillance.'[57]

During the McLibel trial another undercover police officer who used the cover name Matt Rayner was also involved in environmental and animal rights activism in the London area. Rayner was part of London Animal Action, which was based in Housman's bookshop, a location also used by London Greenpeace and the McLibel Support Campaign at the same time. He regularly drove activists long distances, including to Aintree racecourse in 1993 when 15 animal-rights protesters forced the cancellation of the Grand National when they ran in front of the horses at the start of the race. This was described as 'probably the single most successful feat of direct action ever carried out in the name of animal rights', with an estimated cost to the racing industry of £75 million. The undercover officer was a key logistical link in sabotaging the most famous horse race in the world, broadcast live on BBC TV. All of the 15 activists were released without charge.[58]

'Domestic extremism'

The police subversion-monitoring unit NETCU, which gave the presentation to The Consulting Association in 2008, is now no more and the SDS has also been wound up. Instead, responsibility for monitoring extremism was handed over to the National Domestic Extremism and Disorder Intelligence Unit (NDEDIU) in September 2011. That organization also absorbed the National Public Order Intelligence Unit and the National Domestic Extremism Team as it rationalized competing agencies. Sitting under the Metropolitan Police, rather than the more unaccountable National Police Chiefs Council (as the Association of Chief Police Officers was renamed), NDEDIU describes itself as supporting: 'all police forces in helping reduce the criminal threat from domestic extremism across the UK. It works to promote a single and co-ordinated police response by providing tactical advice to the police service alongside information and guidance to industry and government.'[59]

The NDEDIU goes on to say that it provides 'intelligence on domestic extremism and strategic public-order issues in the UK. Police will always engage to facilitate peaceful protest, prevent disorder and minimize disruption to local communities. Where individuals cross over into criminality and violence, the police will act swiftly and decisively to uphold the law.'[60]

In June 2013 it was revealed that the NDEDIU was monitoring some 9,000 people considered domestic subversives.[61] Baroness Jenny Jones, Green Party member of the House of Lords and London Assembly member, is one of those on the domestic extremist database.[62] A whistleblower subsequently alleged that the Metropolitan Police had deliberately shredded documents about the peer so that she couldn't find out the extent of her surveillance.[63] All monitoring of domestic extremism is now under the auspices of the Metropolitan Police Counter Terrorism Command SO15 unit with police spies now deployed by the Special Project Teams of SO15. So state spying on trade unionists and peaceful leftwing activists is now categorized as counter-terrorism.

The increasingly draconian ways in which legal protests were viewed by the state and private sector affected those on the blacklist. In December 2008 Steve Acheson, with the support of Warrington Trades Council, started a picket outside the Fiddlers Ferry power station in Cheshire after he was dismissed from the site. Owners Scottish & Southern Energy (SSE) tried to bring an injunction against Acheson under the Prevention of Terrorism Act. The firm claimed that Acheson's protest presented a potential threat to the national grid and national security. In October 2009 Acheson won an appeal at the High Court in London with the judge describing SSE's argument as 'fanciful bordering on paranoia'.[64]

As construction workers took part in various days of action to highlight concerns over terms and conditions as well as blacklisting, they also drew the attention of the police. The City of London police issues a weekly 'Terrorism/extremism update for the City of London business community'. The first section has a round-up of terrorist activity around the globe from bombings in Iraq to the execution of prisoners in Colombia. Underneath are the domestic issues. On 28 October 2011 this included a construction industry day of action. On 2 December it warned of an electricians' strike targeting Balfour Beatty. Underneath it reminds people to remain alert and gives the anti-terror hotline number.[65]

When it comes to the police investigating themselves there appears to be a pattern of behaviour aimed at frustrating any attempts to discover what the state is doing. In October 2011, Operation Herne was formed by the Metropolitan Police to look into allegations raised by the *Guardian* about the questionable practices of the Special Demonstration Squad.[66]

In November 2012, Imran Khan and Partners solicitors made a complaint to the Metropolitan Police on behalf of the Blacklist Support Group about collusion between the police and The Consulting Association. Initially the Met refused even to record the complaint, arguing that 'the complaints process is not the correct vehicle to forward [your] concerns or allegations' but, after an appeal, it was eventually passed to the Independent Police Complaints Commission. In an astonishing admission as part of correspondence with solicitors, the IPCC said: 'It was likely that all Special Branches were involved in providing information about potential employees.'[67] This was then immediately contradicted by Operation Herne, which said there was no such evidence. However, the IPCC stood by its claim, which it said came about after discussions with the Met. The ability of the Met to police itself clearly wasn't working, so in February 2013 the Chief Constable of Derbyshire, Mick Creedon, took over the inquiry.[68] It didn't get much better.

When Operation Herne published its report in March 2014 on the allegations raised by SDS whistleblower Peter Francis, it quoted an unnamed Special Branch officer as saying 'the information [in TCA files] was purely one way', from the blacklisters to the police, and that it was driven by a sense of 'civic duty'.[69] The suggestion that the information flow was one way is described by ex-SDS officer Peter Francis as ridiculous. 'I've never heard of a back-scratching scenario where you get one thing and you don't give anything back,' he told the authors.

The report adds:

> There is no dispute that individuals named by Peter Francis appear on the "blacklist". However, Peter Francis claims to

have been deployed between 1993 and 1997. The Consulting Association record is dated from 1999, two (2) years after Peter Francis' claimed deployment ceased. There is no available evidence to suggest that SDS exchanged any information with either the Economic League or The Consulting Association.[70]

Francis dismisses this conclusion as 'total rubbish', pointing out that just because the TCA files date from 1999 only shows that was when the information was added – the Special Branch files had been opened for at least three years prior to that.

As part of its investigation Operation Herne looked at 20 sample blacklist files sent to it by the ICO which the data watchdog suggested could imply police collusion. The details on which files were sent have not been released but the authors have established that Dan Gilman, Frank Smith, Lisa Teuscher and Steve Hedley were not among them. Francis said:

I would like somebody independent of the police to forensically examine all the blacklisting files, to be cross-referenced with Special Branch records to look at the areas of collusion and where they may or may not be.[71]

The Blacklist Support Group declined to co-operate with Herne, believing it ineffective. Nonetheless Sarah McSherry, solicitor from Imran Khan and Partners, said:

While correspondence from the police in relation to this complaint continually raises concerns about the quality of their investigation, it is interesting to note that they confirm that they have identified a potential "flow of information between Special Branch and the construction industry".[72]

In October 2014, over five-and-a-half years after the ICO raid and the repeated denials by Operation Herne of any involvement by the police with The Consulting Association, John McDonnell MP named detective chief inspector Gordon Mills, head of police liaison at NETCU, as the senior officer who had given the Powerpoint presentation to the blacklisting organization.[73]

In a letter to then Home Secretary Theresa May, McDonnell identifies the companies in attendance as Vinci, AMEC, Skanska,

Costain, Sir Robert McAlpine, Emcor and SIAS Building Services and writes:

> Given this record of attendance at this meeting, it is shocking that, in their evidence to the Scottish Select Committee's inquiry into blacklisting, directors of Skanska and Sir Robert McAlpine denied any involvement of the police. Despite numerous requests under the Freedom of Information Act for documents relating to NETCU's activities, the response has been that no documents relating to the meeting of DCI Mills with The Consulting Association exist. It appears odd that no report of such an important meeting was written and that no evidence of the meeting is now held by the Metropolitan Police.

A year later Mills broke cover to tell his side of the story. The former police officer said his life had been blighted, leaving him fearful for the safety of his family. This was after the GMB union turned up outside a Cambridge police station (where he no longer actually worked) with a man dressed in a pantomime crocodile suit. Mills opened his heart to the London *Evening Standard* saying: 'All I have ever tried to do is fulfil my duties as a police officer and protect the public'. While admitting his attendance and the presentation, the intelligence officer said it was a 'misunderstanding' and that he did not realize that it was a meeting of The Consulting Association. 'I only became aware of this organization as a result of a newspaper article in 2014. I did not know Ian Kerr at the time or have any subsequent dealings with him. It was not a meeting about the activities of trade unionists or anything to do with so-called blacklisting.'

For the avoidance of all doubt, the Woodstock meeting DCI Mills attended was a Consulting Association meeting. The senior managers were all invoiced by The Consulting Association for their attendance. Ian Kerr organized and was present at the meeting in the Bear Hotel. At best, Mills' version of events implies that as a senior intelligence officer from the UK's key domestic extremism unit, he attended events held in pubs without even checking which organization he was meeting. If a top 'terror cop' was so easily duped by TCA, it hardly bodes well for the rest of his intelligence gathering or assessment skills. But of course a meeting of white middle-class businessmen in a Cotswold hotel did not fit the typical profiling for serious criminality, so therefore the experienced high-ranking officer would have no reason to suspect.

Mills' account of events is in slight contrast to the witness statement signed by Ian Kerr in preparation for the High Court trial in which he claims that NETCU 'wanted an output for the information they had gathered about animal-rights and environmental activists on site where the construction companies were working. I gave them the email addresses of the contacts in the construction industry and they would feed them information.'

Mary Kerr's witness statement for the High Court trial also mentions the meeting when Gordon Mills spoke and recalls that it was to cover 'the role of activists and how they intend to infiltrate commercial organizations and cause trouble – which was clearly a concern for a number of the members working on sensitive environmental projects'. This was essentially the *raison d'être* for the very existence of TCA itself and specifically for the creation of the 'green list'.

Three pages of handwritten notes by Ian Kerr from the meeting record the phone number for the NETCU office and Gordon Mills' mobile number, as well as that the police body was set up under ACPO to cover domestic extremism. The note minutes sections of the PowerPoint presentation and the discussion that took place, including: 'National Extremism Tactical Coordination Unit, set up originally for animal rights issues but expanding…' 'Extreme leftwing' activists are described as 'emerging threats'… There is a paragraph that deals with gathering of information about extremists which signals that 'temporary workers come into the company and take information at key times eg: Jan / Aug hols / Christmas – companies need to have strong vetting procedures in place'.

The sole purpose of NETCU was to gather intelligence for the police domestic extremism database and to provide information to business. Many of those on the domestic extremism database are environmental, animal rights and leftwing union activists, often without any criminal record. TCA was an organization that kept a database of union and environmental activists in the building industry with the aim of keeping these individuals off major construction projects. The dovetailing between state and corporate spying could not be more obvious. NETCU was looking for an outlet to disseminate information; TCA was looking for that information to use in its unlawful blacklisting operation. According to Mary Kerr, at its close TCA held information on 813 animal-rights and environmental activists, which in relation to the size of the potential cohort seems an extraordinarily large number. There appears little doubt that the 'two-way exchange of information' described by Ian Kerr in his interview with *The Times* did take place and that some names and information on the greenlist held by TCA were supplied by NETCU, either directly to TCA or via the subscribing construction companies. So far, despite numerous FOI requests and the required disclosure of information for the Pitchford inquiry, no documents from the NETCU period have been disclosed by the police. The Woodstock TCA meeting was no doubt one of many that NETCU held with businesses across the UK.

As an aside, Mary Kerr recalls that Gordon Mills was invited to speak by John Edwards, the head of security for Carillion. This was in 2008, when Carillion claimed to have severed all ties with TCA. An invoice addressed to John Edwards at the Carillion Wolverhampton head office for attending TCA meetings in 2008 was publicly disclosed as part of litigation.

Mills' story appeared as the front-page headline in the *Evening Standard*, a newspaper that in the seven years since the blacklisting story broke has barely covered the scandal. It was widely viewed as an attempt by the rightwing anti-union paper to sling mud at John McDonnell now that he had been made Shadow Chancellor of the Exchequer and using his letter to Theresa May as the basis for a defamation claim. Following the newspaper article, Mills sent letters via his lawyers, Slater and Gordon, who represent the Police Federation, threatening to sue McDonnell, the *Guardian*, *Morning Star*, the GMB union and two small websites, Union Solidarity International and Northern Voices. None of those who received threatening letters apologized for linking DCI Mills with the blacklisting meeting or paid him any money. All legal actions subsequently ran out of time. Ben Chacko, editor of the *Morning Star*, commented:

❝I gather Mills thought the *Morning Star* was a soft target and would panic the moment we received legal threats. He was wrong. Wrong because we were confident about our claim, but also because we had no intention of letting anybody derail the campaign to get full disclosure on what the blacklisters had been up to. We were proud to stand firm in the knowledge that we were not just fighting for ourselves but for thousands of blacklisted workers. And that solidarity was also expressed by the labour movement with Unite assisting us with our case.❞

Articles by the authors of this book are among those that Gordon Mills complained about. We stand by every word we have written. Mills did not respond to a request by the authors to provide a comment for this book.

Meanwhile Mills' former boss, superintendent Steve Pearl, who ran NETCU, is now a non-executive director at Agenda Security Services, which provides employment-vetting services. His former boss is ex-assistant chief constable Anton Setchell, who was the senior officer in charge of the police's domestic extremism machinery between 2004 and 2010. A few months after the ICO raid he was interviewed by the *Guardian* and said:

❝Just because you have no criminal record does not mean that you are not of interest to the police. Everyone who has got a criminal record did not have one once.❞[74]

He is currently head of global security at Laing O'Rourke – one of the construction companies which belonged to The Consulting Association. He did not respond to requests for an interview.

Blacklisted workers are not only concerned about the gathering of intelligence by the police; more importantly, they fear that information on the Special Branch registry database is routinely shared with external organizations, with negative consequences for those spied upon. Passages in a 2010 report written by former associates of Bob Lambert highlight that just such a policy of sharing police intelligence with third parties already exists, especially in academia.

❝Some senior university and college staff are security cleared and have access to local Special Branch briefings, and security managers who are former police officers can often obtain information or informal briefings because they have pre-existing trusted relationships. But this is not necessarily true for those from other backgrounds. The Office of the National Coordinator Special Branches (NCSB) has urged police forces and counter-terrorism units to be more proactive in declassifying local threat assessments, and we saw evidence of this happening in some areas, but progress must be monitored. ACPO is also conducting a review into how local counter-terrorism threat assessments are compiled and shared, which provides an opportunity to shape a new approach.[975]

The 'Institute of Community Cohesion' report focuses on the perceived threat of Muslim extremism. However, given that state spying on trade unions is now located within SO15 Counter-Terrorism Command, it does not take a great leap of the imagination to think that a similar sharing of information already exists between those charged to keep tabs on domestic extremists and other third parties such as industry.

Given the neoliberal agenda of mass privatization of the public sector, many campaigners argue that an investigation is needed to find out whether activities previously carried out by state security services have now been outsourced to private companies.

The idea that the work of MI5 or Special Branch could be privatized, potentially putting national security at risk, may seem far-fetched to many. But the widespread use of military contractors in Iraq and Afghanistan sharing logistical support provided by the armed forces seems to blur any strict distinction between the public and private sector. Most of these modern-day mercenary companies have been set up by retired senior military personnel and no doubt their intimate knowledge of operations and existing contacts within the armed forces have assisted in winning lucrative contracts.

In these circumstances, it is not so difficult to imagine that the security services might also have outsourced some of their spying operations to private companies. In the UK, finding any information about contracts in these areas is hugely difficult. But in the US, a report published by the Office of the Director of National Intelligence in 2008 estimated that private contractors make up 29 per cent of the 'intelligence community workforce',[76] with Edward Snowden being its most famous former member.

There are a number of ex-senior police officers and security-service personnel who oversaw state spying on British citizens living in the UK who now run or work for private intelligence companies that provide 'vetting' services. We have already mentioned Steve Pearl and Anton Setchell. But they are not the only ones. Rod Leeming, the head of Special Branch's Animal Rights National Index, which spied on animal-rights activists, founded the security firm Global Open advising transnational pharmaceutical giants. His company played a role in Paul Mercer's infiltration of the Campaign Against Arms Trade, and later employed Mark Kennedy after he stopped working for NPOIU.[77]

MI5 and Special Branch, which in 2006 merged with Anti-Terrorist Branch to become Counter Terrorism Command or SO15,[78] already operate in an opaque environment. However, these private companies are exempt even from laws governing the police and the security services. If they are carrying out contracts on behalf of the British state, this raises serious questions about political oversight and transparency.

The Blacklist Support Group, alongside the abused women activists, the Stephen Lawrence family, anti-racist, socialist groups and environmental campaigners had all taken a conscious decision to boycott the work of Operation Herne. Virtually all of their legal teams were part of the Haldane Society of Socialist Lawyers and, despite all running autonomous campaigns, an umbrella organization was set up called the Campaign Opposing Police Surveillance (COPS). Then, in 2014, came the announcement of a judge-led public inquiry into undercover policing. The activities of corporate spies might be well hidden – was this the opportunity to tease out the truth of state-sponsored infiltration?

1 Interview with the authors, 6 Dec 2014. 2 Scottish Affairs Committee, Blacklisting in Employment: oral and written evidence, The Stationery Office Limited, London, Apr 2013, p 205. 3 Mark Hollingsworth and Richard Norton-Taylor, *Blacklist: the inside story of political vetting*, The Hogarth Press, London, 1988, p 158. 4 BBC2 TV True Spies series, Oct-Nov 2002. 5 Ibid. 6 *Telegraph*, 15 Jan 2014, **nin.tl/Losinskaobit**

– accessed 12 Mar 2014. 7 Seumas Milne, The Enemy Within: The Secret War Against the Miners, Pan, London, 1994. 8 Ibid, p 383. 9 Witness statement submitted to the Committee. 10 World in Action report, 'Boys on the Blacklist', broadcast 16 Feb 1987. 11 Scottish Affairs Committee, op cit, p 110. 12 Interview with the authors. 13 Scottish Affairs Committee, op cit, p 155. 14 Email to the authors, 14 Jan 2014. 15 'Did police cutbacks allow extremists to hijack student demonstrations?' Telegraph, 14 Nov 2010, nin.tl/policecutbacks 16 'Police were brief on industry extremists and bad eggs', Times, 23 Jan 2013, nin.tl/extremistbadeggs – accessed 9 Feb 2013. 17 Interview with the authors. 18 Interview with the authors. 19 Rob Evans and Paul Lewis, Undercover: The true story of Britain's secret police, Faber and Faber, London, 2013, p 182. 20 From Mark Metcalf's blog post 'I Spy Mark Cassidy', nin.tl/ispyfightingtalk 21 Stephen Dorril, The Silent Conspiracy: Inside the intelligence services in the 1990s, Heinemann, London, 1993, p 170. 22 Evans and Lewis, op cit, p 202. 23 Interview with the authors. 24 Interview with Phil Chamberlain. 25 Interview with the authors. 26 The British National Party is a far right political group which stands candidates at the ballot box but it is also active on the streets and has a number of members with convictions for violence. For a period in the 1980s and 1990s it was the premier such political force, though infighting has now reduced its influence. Brick Lane is a multi-racial area of London which has long been home to migrants. 27 Interview with the authors. 28 ucatt.org.uk/ucatt-exposes-infiltration-police 29 Interview with the authors. 30 BBC2 TV, True Spies documentary, broadcast 3 Nov 2002, nin.tl/bbctruespies 31 Interview with Phil Chamberlain. 32 Wapping Strike Story, Special Branch Files Project, specialbranchfiles.uk/wapping-strike-story See also Solomon Hughes Special Branch 'political police' spied on Wapping leaders, Morning Star, 24 Apr 2015, nin.tl/Wappingleaders 33 Solomon Hughes Plain Dealer blog, 8 Apr 2014, nin.tl/spyingonwappingstrike 34 Milne, op cit, and BBC2 TV, op cit. 35 Interview with the authors. 36 Interview with the authors. 37 Scottish Affairs Committee, op cit, p 192. 38 Written evidence to Scottish Affairs Select Committee, Mar 2013, nin.tl/chidiobihara 39 Guardian, 5 Sep 2010, nin.tl/BAsurveillance 40 Independent, 27 Feb 2015, nin.tl/BAspyingscandal 41 'Taylor hired spy stopped Newbury Protest', BBC news, 6 Nov 2002, nin.tl/hiredspy – accessed 10 February 2014. 42 Scottish Affairs Committee, op cit, p 149. 43 Eveline Lubbers, Secret Manoeuvres in the Dark, Pluto, London, 2013, p 159. 44 Ibid. 45 Interview with the authors. 46 Interview with the authors. 47 Interview with the authors. 48 Interview with the authors. 49 Interview with the authors. 50 BBC News, 5 July 2000, news.bbc.co.uk/1/hi/uk/820786. stm 51 McLibel Support Campaign press release, 5 Jul 2000. 52 Interview with the authors. 53 Guardian, 23 Oct 2014, nin.tl/Metpayout 54 Guardian, 17 Dec 2015, nin.tl/policespydisclosure 55 Guardian, 23 Dec 2015, nin.tl/academicexspy 56 Speech at Campaign Opposing Police Surveillance meeting at London Metropolitan University, 12 Nov 2014. 57 Speech to parliamentary meeting, 23 Jun 2014, nin.tl/1xblmOf 58 nin.tl/GrandNationalsabotage 59 ACPO, nin.tl/aboutNDEDIU 60 Ibid. 61 'National police unit monitors 9,000', Guardian, 26 Jun 2013, nin.tl/9000extremists – accessed 16 Jun 2014. 62 BBC news, 16 Jun 2014, nin.tl/Jonesondatabase 63 Guardian, 8 Jan 2016, nin.tl/improperdestruction 64 youtube.com/watch?v=8e9gtdLdDKo 65 City of London Police, nin.tl/OccupyFOI 66 nin.tl/OperationHerne 67 Letter from IPCC, 19 Jun 2013. 68 Guardian, 11 Feb 2013, nin.tl/Mayinvestigation 69 Operation Herne: report 2 – allegations of Peter Francis, p 6. 70 Ibid. 71 Interview with Phil Chamberlain. 72 Email to authors. 73 According to the Observer, Mills has since lectured at Anglia Ruskin and his LinkedIn profile describes him as 'senior officer in national extremism unit dealing with UK domestic extremism'. *Observer*, 8 Nov 2014, nin.tl/BLpolicecoverup 74 *Guardian*, 25 Oct 2009, nin.tl/rebrandingprotest – accessed 16 Jun 2014. 75 Rachel Briggs and Harris Beider, 'Promoting Community Cohesion and preventing violent extremism in higher and further education', Institute of Community Cohesion, 2010. 76 Dana Priest, *Top Secret America*. Little, Brown and Company, 2011, p 320. 77 http://undercoverresearch. net/2015/03/22/488/ 78 nin.tl/CTCommand

10
#spycops

Members of the House of Parliament have legal protection when speaking in the chamber. Parliament has always considered itself a place where free speech should not be abridged, otherwise democracy is weakened. It was ironic then that a whistleblower aiming to highlight a secret and undemocratic practice should feel unsafe even in the Palace of Westminster. Peter Francis had hoped to attend the launch of *Blacklisted* in March 2015 and to reveal more about the activities of the undercover police unit of which he had been a member. However, because he feared prosecution under the Official Secrets Act, he had to make do with a written statement that was distributed to the packed Westminster committee room and read out by John McDonnell. In it, Francis stated:

> This remarkable, well-researched and must-read book clearly shows how police spying on political activists has destroyed lives and that I, most unfortunately and regrettably, played a part in this.
>
> The forthcoming Home Secretary's public inquiry into undercover policing must include a forensic, independent (in other words, non-police) examination into all the blacklisting files compiled by The Consulting Association and then cross-reference them with corresponding Special Branch individual activists' records to look at the areas of collusion. There will be multiple duplicates. Of that I have no doubt at all.
>
> I would also like to take this opportunity to unreservedly apologize to all the union members I personally spied upon and reported back on whilst deployed undercover in the SDS.
>
> Including those not only engaged in working in the construction industry but also those in the National Union of Students (NUS), National Union of Teachers (NUT),

Communication Workers Union (CWU), UNISON and the Fire Brigades Union (FBU).[91]

Matt Wrack, General Secretary of the FBU, was sitting in the audience as the statement was read out.

The Peter Francis story was taken up by the media, with union general secretaries queuing up to join the call for a full public inquiry. Dave Prentis from UNISON commented: 'The revelation that union members were spied on by undercover police officers simply because they belonged to a union is shocking. Being in a union is not a crime and this dirty secret is just the latest in a long list of attacks on unions and their members.'

While CWU general secretary Billy Hayes at the time said: 'Once again the secret state is revealed. It seems trade-union activists are still the enemy within. More transparency on such matters would perhaps have avoided some of many miscarriages of justice, including Hillsborough and the Jimmy Savile cases. We need a full public inquiry to address the blacklisting scandal.'[2]

In addition to the Herne Report, Theresa May had also commissioned a separate investigation by Mark Ellison QC (who in 2012 successfully prosecuted Gary Dobson and David Norris for the murder of teenager Stephen Lawrence) to look into the allegations made by Peter Francis about police corruption. The review included allegations about undercover police spying on the Stephen Lawrence family and was published at the beginning of March 2015. Less than a week later, on 12 March 2015, the very same day as the book launch for *Blacklisted* in Parliament, May announced that Lord Justice Pitchford would head a public inquiry, with the terms of reference to be published in the summer.

The then Conservative Home Secretary told Parliament that the Ellison report had unearthed 'serious historical failings' in undercover policing practices.

May added:

> I was profoundly shocked by Mark Ellison's findings and committed to establishing a public inquiry to thoroughly investigate undercover policing and the operation of the SDS. In the interest of learning the lessons of past failures, I have decided to establish the inquiry now while ensuring existing

work is not affected. Undercover policing is an essential tactic in the fight against crime but to improve the public's confidence in undercover work we must ensure there is no repeat of these failings in the future.[93]

Months of intense lobbying and legal submissions took place with lawyers representing those spied upon arguing for the widest possible remit to enable all those touched by the scandal to be covered by the Inquiry. The print and broadcast media covered the story and public meetings were held around the country. The Centre for Crime and Justice Studies brought together many of those at the heart of the issue for a conference on Police Corruption, Spying and Racism in Conway Hall in London.[4]

In July 2015, the Home Secretary finally announced the terms of reference for the Inquiry.[5] It would look at undercover operations since 1968 but only for English and Welsh police forces. The Inquiry would consider how they were authorized and the oversight as well as the impact on those involved. The issue about how evidence from undercover officers should be used in trials would also be examined. The terms said: 'The Inquiry's investigation will include, but not be limited to, whether and to what purpose, extent and effect undercover police operations have targeted political and social justice campaigners. The Inquiry's investigation will include, but not be limited to, the undercover operations of the Special Demonstration Squad and the National Public Order Intelligence Unit. It includes operations conducted through online media.' Some commentators considered the Inquiry to be an exercise in kicking the scandal into the long grass rather than truly interrogating the practices of the police. The announcement that the Inquiry was expected to be completed by the summer of 2019 suggested that the long-grass theory had some merit.

One obvious omission from Theresa May's original terms of reference was any specific mention of trade unions. The Blacklist Support Group statement echoed the thoughts of many activists:

> Many in the trade-union movement may be sceptical about whether the Pitchford Inquiry, or indeed any investigation by the British establishment, will expose the full extent of state spying on unions. Spying on trade unionists is not an aberration but

standard operating procedure, outside of democratic oversight and out of control. The effects on those targeted were often life-changing. It is a human-rights abuse that cannot be tolerated – and which Pitchford cannot ignore. Campaigners will be arguing forcibly that other instances such as the Miners' Strike, Shrewsbury, Grunwick, Wapping and blacklisting should all be investigated. There is *prima facie* evidence in all these cases of undercover police involvement. The internal police inquiries so far have been a sham. Pitchford may not get the full story of state surveillance on trade unions but an opportunity like this only comes along once in a generation. After decades of campaigning, we cannot tolerate a whitewash.[9]

The first major ruling that Lord Justice Pitchford needed to make was who would be granted 'core participant' status. 'Core participant' is a designation that affords individuals or organizations additional rights within a public inquiry. It is granted to those at the centre of the issues to be investigated. An inquiry into a train crash, for example, would grant core-participant status to the families of the victims as well as to the train companies. Evidence disclosed to the inquiry is seen prior to its general publication and core participants are allowed to make submissions to the inquiry through their lawyers. Moreover, the lawyers' fees are paid for by the British state. Without such a provision, the legal expense connected to a public inquiry would make participation impossible for all but the wealthiest individuals or large institutions. If issues around police spying on union activists were to feature in the Pitchford Inquiry, it was essential that unions and blacklisted workers were granted core-participant status.

However, it is the Chair of the Inquiry who decides whether to grant core-participant status based upon whether 'the person has played, or may have played, a direct and significant role in relation to the matters to which the Inquiry relates, or whether the person has a significant interest in an important aspect of the matters to which the Inquiry relates. The Chairman will also consider whether the person may be subject to significant or explicit criticism during the proceedings of the Inquiry, or in the report when it is written.'[6]

A very public lobbying campaign now kicked in to ensure that when Pitchford made his final decision about which areas to investigate, the union dimension was not left out, and specifically that unions were granted core-participant status: another round of newspaper articles, alongside public meetings in universities, and party conferences addressed by spied-on activists and union general secretaries. The FBU organized a packed-out fringe meeting at the TUC Congress in Brighton where Shamik Dutta of Bhatt Murphy solicitors told delegates that he was submitting multiple applications for core-participant status.

> ❝The families, organizations and individuals I represent share the following two characteristics: firstly, state agents were directly implicated in the killing or misconduct that was the subject matter of their campaigns. Secondly, undercover state agents gathered, or are reasonably believed to have gathered, intelligence on their campaigns through covert means. Their cases give rise to a particular abuse of power concern. At worst, undercover officers were deployed to infiltrate and undermine campaigns that were organized in order to expose police misconduct.❞

In September 2015, for the first time in its 147-year history, the Trade Union Congress unanimously passed a motion on undercover police spying on trade unions. The first edition of this book and the work of the Blacklist Support Group were applauded and there was a demand that the BSG and the TUC should be granted core-participant status. It repeated the demand for a full public inquiry into blacklisting and support for those members who had been spied upon. It was moved by UCATT and seconded by the FBU. During the debate, Anita Halpin from the NUJ told delegates about a battle to expose spying upon journalists, after some of its members had obtained their police surveillance files. 'They discovered that records had been made not only of phone numbers, past addresses but also appearance, sexual orientation, names of ex-partners and, in one case, a family member's medical history was on file,' she said. The parallel with some of the personal detail on TCA files was clear.

GMB delegate John McDonnell (not the MP of the same name) spoke in support of Composite Motion 16, saying:

❝These actions involved intrusive surveillance, undercover police officers invading activists' homes and families, even beginning relationships and having children with them. Scumbags, every one of them! During the Cammell Laird's dispute in 1984, 37 GMB members, and my family was one of them, on Merseyside ended up in jail after exercising their legitimate right to protest for their right to work. The files dealing with the circumstances surrounding their prosecution and unjust imprisonment mysteriously vanished. No trace anywhere!❞

As with the Shrewsbury dispute, where official documents have been hidden from view, the Cammell Laird affair has been smothered in official secrecy. The shipyard workers occupied vessels, including a Royal Navy frigate, in a dispute over compulsory redundancies. They were sentenced in their absence for contempt of court while carrying out the occupation, though no court documents have ever been produced. The action was at the height of the miners' strike and there was considerable police and military activity on the dock. The men were warned that unless the occupation ended there would be loss of life. The strikers came out and were immediately taken to a maximum-security prison and kept in isolation for a month before being released. None ever worked in the shipbuilding industry again.[7] Since then, efforts to find official documents have failed. One of the strikers, Eddie Marnell, has taken his case to the European Court with the backing of the GMB, which has called it a clear miscarriage of justice.[8]

Alongside the public lobbying, legal submissions were sent in on behalf of those spied upon. A 31-page application was made for core-participant status on behalf of the BSG and 11 individual blacklisted workers using *Blacklisted* as a basis for the claim. It identifies a key issue relating to police spying on trade-union activists:

❝There is an imperative to investigate the apparent complete absence of contribution made by police in passing information to TCA in the prevention and detection of crime, given that not a single arrest or charge arose out of the material contained in the blacklist files. It follows, therefore, that there is a further pressing imperative to examine the motivation for the actions of the police if what it did was not for the purpose of the prevention or detection of crime.[9]

This is a direct rebuttal of the police assertion set out by Chief Constable Mick Creedon, responsible for the internal police investigation (Operation Herne) which reached the diametrically opposite conclusions to Ellison, arguing that: 'Undercover policing is a vital police tactic that has saved lives, protected victims and brought dangerous criminals to justice.'[10]

Some campaigners have even questioned whether Creedon is a fit person to be carrying out the internal police investigation given his role at Derbyshire Police, where he was the senior officer responsible for undercover operations. Donal O'Driscoll from the Undercover Research Group commented: 'Piecing together the timeline of his career showed us that Creedon has been overseeing operations of undercover officers targeting protest groups at various points in time.'[11]

On 10 February 2016, Pitchford announced his decision on core-participant status. Spying on trade unions is now a stand-alone category, with the BSG, FBU, UCATT and NUM all granted core-participant status in the Inquiry along with the following named individuals: Frank Smith, Lisa Teuscher, Dan Gilman, Steve Hedley, Brian Higgins, John Jones, Steve Acheson and Dave Smith. The supposed 'conspiracy theorists' were now being funded by the British state to expose the real-life conspiracy, with John Hendy QC acting as counsel for all those in the union strand.

The NUM's inclusion as a core participant is clearly linked to the widespread use of undercover police to infiltrate the union and its support networks during the year-long miners' strike of 1984-5. Granting the FBU such status relates not just to the admissions made by Peter Francis but also to Special Branch files indicating that the former FBU General Secretary Ken Cameron was spied upon at the *News of the World* dispute at Wapping – as well as to suspicions that the FBU were illegally targeted during their 2002-3 pay strike.[12]

FBU General Secretary Matt Wrack commented:

❝Any intrusion, even as someone who is around the movement and knows what goes on… it comes as a shock to experience it. People will find the degree of [the blacklisting operation] and the degree of state involvement staggering. Anyone directly involved has the right to know what spying was done, who carried it out and what reports were compiled. All special units targeting people engaging in legitimate political and industrial activity should be scrapped and their archives made accessible.❞[13]

One of the doubtless unintended consequences of the Pitchford Inquiry is the bringing together of activists from across the radical spectrum who in normal circumstances would never meet each other. Through informal contacts and formal meetings, the shared experience of being spied upon has built links between a diverse range of campaigns.

Lois Austin lived a few miles away from the British National Party bookshop in Welling and as a young woman was co-chair of Youth Against Racism in Europe, helping to organize protests against the BNP in the immediate aftermath of the Stephen Lawrence murder. The current chair of the Campaign Opposing Police Surveillance, she said:

❝We were campaigning against a bunch of horrible racist fascists who had a headquarters in Southeast London. The police, instead of spending their resources trying to combat racist attacks and racist murders in that part of London, were spying on a grieving family and spying on anti-racist activists. It is inexcusable. We want recommendations to make sure that this never happens again. What we are campaigning for is the end of political policing in this country.❞[14]

Suresh Grover from The Monitoring Group explained how many in the Black and Asian community have been treated:

❝We've been part of and we have initiated many Black and Asian justice campaigns, families who have lost their loved ones where the police have been negligent in their investigations or deaths in custody where the police are directly involved in the murder or the death of someone. We know that a number of families and community groups have been spied on by the police unlawfully.9

Stafford Scott, from the community advice organization Tottenham Rights, has been under police surveillance since his involvement in the Broadwater Farm Defence Campaign, which successfully fought against the miscarriage of justice that saw Winston Silcott, Engin Raghip and Mark Braithwaite sent to prison in 1987 for the murder of PC Keith Blakelock. The convictions of the Tottenham Three were overturned in 1991 and two detectives were tried for perverting the course of justice but later acquitted. Stafford Scott expresses the anger of many:

6We knew then that we were being spied on and they were making attempts to infiltrate us. In the case of Winston Silcott, he has been proved to have been fitted up for Blakelock's murder. So it is incredible that not only would they frame someone for a crime that he didn't commit but they would then go on to spy on the families who were running campaigns while they were in prison. Like was said 30 years ago, we want to give the police a metaphorical "bloody good hiding". So that they will learn and they will understand that their job is to maintain the law, not to undermine it with this type of behaviour.9 15

Paul Gravett from London Greenpeace commented:

6London Greenpeace was spied upon by the SDS and one of them was Bob Lambert – I knew him very well. He was one of the writers of the "What's wrong with McDonalds?" leaflet that LGP produced. Five people got sued for libel and I was one of those people. None of us had actually written the leaflet but by the time we got the writ, he was long gone.9

Kate Wilson, an environmental activist who lived with undercover police officer Mark Kennedy, said:

6I am one of an ever-increasing number of women who discovered that I had been abused by an undercover police officer who was sent into my life, into my home, into my parents' home and into my bed by the Metropolitan Police. I think there are many more women that will discover that this has also happened to them.⁶¹⁶

The undercover officers given that status include Peter Francis, Mark Kennedy plus 16 officers only identified by the letter N and a number. Most of these have already been uncovered by activists, with their names appearing in the media, and are assumed to include: Bob Lambert, Jim Boyling, John Dines, Mark Jenner, Mike Chitty and the officers using the aliases Marco Jacobs, Lynn Watson, RC, Matt Rayner, Rod Richardson, Jason Bishop and Simon Wellings. N81 is the code number for the officer who spied on the Stephen Lawrence campaign.

Some sections of Pitchford's first ruling on core-participant status are breathtaking even for those already aware of the scandal. Paragraph 74, for example, deals with Category J (justice campaigns):

⁶Celia Stubbs (Blair Peach), Lee Lawrence (Cherry Groce), Myrna Simpson (Joy Gardner), Bernard Renwick (Roger Sylvester), Patricia Armani Da Silva (Jean Charles De Menezes), MSS and MWS (Michael Menson), Sukhdev, Balwant and Tish Reel (Ricky Reel) all represent family campaigns for justice in respect of the deaths of those close to them. In several cases death occurred at the hands of the police or while the deceased was detained in police custody. In some cases no-one was held accountable, while in others there were unsuccessful prosecutions. All have been informed by Operation Herne that their campaigns were the subject of intelligence gathering. The extent to which the intelligence was gathered by undercover police activity is at present unclear. Winston Silcott was convicted of the murder of Police Constable Blakelock but on 25 November 1991, after a campaign for his release, his conviction was overturned on appeal. He has received copies of 16 heavily redacted intelligence reports relating to the campaign. Mrs Sharon Grant is the widow of Bernie Grant MP. Mr Grant supported campaigns for justice raised by his constituents. Peter Francis has claimed that Mr Grant was a target of undercover policing.⁶¹⁷

There have been well in excess of 4,500 deaths in prison or police custody since 1990. Between 2002 and 2012, there were 380 deaths either in police custody or through police shootings, with a disproportionately high number of deaths of people from a Black or ethnic-minority background. Only a handful have resulted in criminal action against the police and not a single officer has ever been found guilty of homicide.[18] All of the individuals and campaigns named above were granted core-participant status but the application by the charity Inquest, which provides legal support to families of those killed in police custody, was declined.

The Pitchford ruling on the justice campaigns is in contrast to the public statement made by Chief Constable Mick Creedon, in charge of the police's own internal investigation Operation Herne, which in 2014 said:

> No evidence, either witness or documentary, was found that any SDS undercover officer was ever targeted into the Stephen Lawrence campaign or into his friend, Duwayne Brooks. There was likewise no evidence that any SDS undercover officer was ever targeted into any black justice campaign. There was no evidence that SDS undercover officers were ever tasked to obtain intelligence specifically on a black justice campaign or the Stephen Lawrence campaign. And lastly there was no evidence that any SDS undercover officer was directed to smear the Lawrence family, or Duwayne Brooks.[19]

Creedon explained away the numerous entries relating to grieving family members and justice campaigns in Special Branch intelligence reports by using the euphemistic and now infamous term 'collateral intrusion'.

One instance of 'collateral intrusion' was against the family of Ricky Reel, a young Asian student at Brunel University who went missing after a racist attack in October 1997. His family campaigned for the police to look for him and his attackers, only to be told not to worry. His body was found in the River Thames in Kingston a week later. Ricky's mother, Sukhdev Reel, led a tireless campaign for justice alongside her constituency MP, John McDonnell, and the anti-racist activist Suresh Grover. McDonnell remembers:

❝Throughout the campaign our one overarching desire was to get more resources to effectively search for those people who may well have produced Ricky's death. All through that time we were saying "we need a better investigation, more resources". Last year we met with the Herne Inquiry and were told that the police did have police officers involved in the campaign but they were undercover and we were under surveillance. But don't worry, you were simply collateral intrusion.❞[20]

The core participants are divided between those on the side of the establishment – the police and the Home Office – and those who for many years have fought for justice only to be spied on by undercover police for activities that are perfectly lawful in a democratic society.

But as Jules Carey, the solicitor from Bindmans representing Jaqui, one of the women who had a relationship with an undercover officer, pointed out:

❝All this damage and all this harm that has come to light since 2011 relates to the activities of only 12 police officers. What we know for a fact is that there were at least 102 undercover officers in the SDS and we don't know how many were operating in NPOIU.❞[21]

The police have already indicated that there were 460 campaigns that were infiltrated by the secret political policing units,[22] while the number subject to incidental surveillance would be greater still. To release them all would amount to a people's history of the UK from 1968 to the present day. What activists and researchers have discovered so far is just the tip of an epic anti-democratic iceberg.

A number of organizations are conspicuous by their absence. The TUC and the NUJ were both refused core-participant status, for example, despite NUJ members appearing on the domestic extremism database and trade unions being identified as targeted by undercover police, for which the TUC had agreed to act as a clearing house. The Hillsborough families' campaigns were also refused core-participant status. In August 2016, actor Ricky Tomlinson was refused this status by Pitchford. This is despite the fact that in the BBC series 'True Spies' in 2002 a former member of Special Branch says he saw a file which had been opened on the former union member because of his activities. Pitchford ruled that Tomlinson was unable to demonstrate that the information in the file came from an undercover officer. The judge said: 'Special Branch files may be created from a variety of sources, including the uniformed police, detectives, informers, police records and public knowledge.' He also ruled: 'However, sufficient information has been received by the Inquiry to require further investigation. Mr Tomlinson's application will be kept under review.' Tomlinson, who called for a full inquiry to force the release of documents, said: 'Why not give us the benefit of the doubt? Why is [it] always in the establishment's favour?'[23]

Police Spies Out of Lives

One of the most appalling aspects of the undercover police scandal is the abuse suffered by the women activists whose emotions, human rights and even fecundity were viewed as disposable by-products of covert operations by those in charge of undercover deployments. For many years, these women activists, who were deceived into long-term sexual relationships with police spies, fought a lonely battle against the Metropolitan Police in the courts. And at every turn the police denied everything until the activists themselves uncovered another piece of information.

The women might have hit a brickwall in the High Court but their heroic efforts exposed the scandal in the media. At Liberty's Human Rights Awards 2014 the Police Spies Out of Lives women were nominated for human-rights campaign of the year and their solicitor, Harriet Wistrich of Birnberg Peirce, received the award as human rights lawyer of the year.

On 20 November 2015, after many years of legal wrangling, the Metropolitan Police finally agreed to publish a full apology that was given personally to seven women involved in the litigation. Assistant Commissioner Martin Hewitt read out the statement live in which he addressed concerns that such practices were still ongoing. Hewitt said:

> I acknowledge that these relationships were a violation of the women's human rights, an abuse of police power and caused

significant trauma. I unreservedly apologize on behalf of the Metropolitan Police Service. One of the concerns which the women strongly expressed was that they wished to ensure that such relationships would not happen in future. They referred to the risks that children could be conceived through and into such relationships and I understand that.

These matters are already the subject of several investigations, including a criminal and misconduct enquiry called Operation Herne; undercover policing is also now subject to a judge-led public inquiry which commenced on 28 July 2015. Even before those bodies report, I can state that sexual relationships between undercover police officers and members of the public should not happen. The forming of a sexual relationship by an undercover officer would never be authorized in advance nor indeed used as a tactic of a deployment. If an officer did have a sexual relationship despite this (for example if it was a matter of life or death) then he would be required to report this in order that the circumstances could be investigated for potential criminality and/or misconduct. I can say as a very senior officer of the Metropolitan Police Service that I and the Metropolitan Police are committed to ensuring that this policy is followed by every officer who is deployed in an undercover role.[24]

The supposed contrition shown by the Met regarding the treatment of the Police Spies Out of Lives women activists is in stark contrast to the explicit direction given to SDS undercover officers during their training. The total lack of morality at the heart of this state-sectioned surveillance was demonstrated when, after repeated failed freedom-of-information requests, the official 'tradecraft' manual provided to Special Demonstration Squad new recruits was finally published. SDS officers were taught how to steal the identities of dead babies with Frederick Forsyth's *Day of the Jackal* explicitly referenced. The spies were expressly encouraged to have sexual relationships with women activists as a way of gaining trust within the campaigns they were targeting. The vast majority of the 60-page training manual is redacted, but among the few paragraphs that are readable, the official document suggests that

SDS officers should 'try to have fleeting, disastrous relationships with group members' while on deployment.[25]

Kate Wilson, one of the women in the case, responded to the Met, saying:

> In the apology the police say that these relationships were a gross violation and may well have reflected an attitude towards women that should have no place in the culture of the Metropolitan Police. You can feel them desperately trying to stretch the language in order to avoid using the word sexism. Any woman inside or outside the police force who has come into contact with those attitudes towards women knows that what we are talking about here is institutional sexism.[26]

At the end of June 2016, the College of Policing, the professional standards body for the police service, published a consultation document giving guidance for undercover officers.[27] The guidance forbids officers to 'form an intimate sexual relationship with those they are employed to infiltrate and target or may encounter during their deployment'. It adds: 'This conduct will never be authorized, nor must it ever be used as a tactic of a deployment.' Taking drugs is also off limits. However, as Emily Apple has pointed out, the guidance does have holes.

> It is great that the report says it is never acceptable for a UCO [undercover officer] to form an intimate sexual relationship... but it is immediately followed by a massive caveat: "UCO engages in unauthorized sexual activity for whatever reason (for example, they perceive an immediate threat to themselves and/or others if they do not do so) this activity will be restricted to the minimum conduct necessary to mitigate the threat." Pretty much the same get-out clause is given in relation to drug taking. And this is the problem. How an officer perceives an "immediate threat". It is far more likely that this excuse will be used as a "well, it would have been obvious I was a cop if I didn't have sex with someone". This attitude was reflected in comments from a former undercover officer. "Everybody knew it was a very promiscuous lifestyle. You cannot not be promiscuous in those groups. Otherwise you'll stand out

straight away.' This isn't true – but it shows how both an undercover officer and their superiors could and probably will twist that "immediate threat" to suit their purposes.'[28]

Lawyer Jules Carey said: 'It is disappointing that the guidance fails to spell out that in a democracy the first consideration should be whether it is necessary to use an undercover officer at all, or whether the intelligence could be obtained through some other means. The guidance should also make it clear that the degree of intrusion should be proportionate to the seriousness of the crime being investigated.'[29]

The document also says that for an undercover deployment to be effective it may be necessary for personnel to participate in criminal activity about which they have been tasked to report. It warns all undercover unit staff should be aware of the dangers posed through 'exposure in true identity' on social media.

The case of Carlo Neri

During the research for this book, the authors organized a number of meetings with blacklisted workers and activists spied on by undercover police units. One of those meetings was held at the

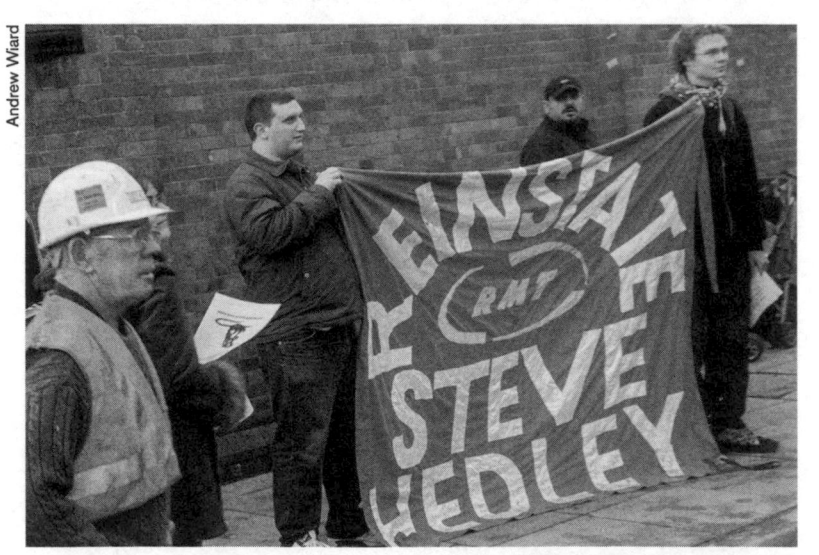

Undercover police officer 'Carlo Neri' (in baseball cap behind banner) on an RMT picket line in 2005.

offices of the *Guardian* in the summer of 2014 and in attendance was journalist Rob Evans, co-author of the book *Undercover* that exposed the undercover police scandal. Also present were blacklisted workers Dan Gilman, Frank Smith and Steve Hedley, alongside anti-fascist activists Joe Batty, Dennis Rudd and Paul Heron (now an award-winning human rights lawyer). The meeting was primarily to share information about how the undercover police spied on activists, including a number of standard practices used. During the discussion, all of the activists flagged up suspicions about a particular individual. This initial meeting started off a chain of events that would make the suspicions into something concrete, especially when the formidable research skills of Donal O'Driscoll from Undercover Research Group (URG) were deployed. O'Driscoll is himself a core participant in the Pitchford Inquiry. He explained his organization's role:

> ❛We at the URG are there to work alongside them, involved and supporting at the same time. We are only all too aware of how painful a process this can be for people as they slowly come to terms that an old friend with whom they shared so much of their lives was not who they said they were. We are here to alleviate fear and destructive uncertainty. If we can prove that a friend, lover or colleague is not an undercover or corporate spy then that is equally important to us.❜[30]

Once the URG had produced a definitive report,[31] in January 2016 they provided the information to the *Guardian*[32] and the BBC2 *Newsnight* programme. The media organizations simultaneously outed the undercover police officer who used the cover name Carlo Neri.[33] He had infiltrated the Socialist Party and a number of anti-fascist campaigns between 2001 and 2006. He remains a serving police officer. The officer's surname is particularly distinctive and publication would have the potential to invade the privacy of others who are not involved with undercover policing in any way. For that reason the real name of the undercover police officer who used the alias Carlo Neri has not been published. Neri is undoubtedly one of the 'N' numbers granted core-participant status in the Pitchford Inquiry. Lois Austin, Socialist Party member and former chair of YRE, said: 'Far from being secretive, we publicly advertised our events. The police could have read our leaflets and newspapers, or attended our public meetings, to find out what was going on.'[34]

During his deployment, Neri followed a similar pattern to many of the previously exposed police spies. He claimed a troubled childhood in Italy, including a dislike for his father due to supposed abuse of his sister at a young age, which accounted for why none of his relatives were close. He pretended to be employed as a locksmith for the Franchi company in Hackney and a member of the GMB union. The job explained why he could not be found at a specific place of work every day. His training, combined with some judicious spreading of paranoia, meant that, during his deployment, Neri changed the locks for a number of the activists he was sent to spy on. This included the Walthamstow home of Dan Gilman, who noted wryly: 'The police need a warrant to enter someone's house but in my case, Special Branch have already got the front door key.'[35]

This police spy had a British passport in the name Carlo Neri but no credit cards. He always paid for bills in cash, of which he always seemed to have a ready supply, especially for expensive restaurants. He had a car and was willing to drive his supposed comrades long distances, including on trips to Cornwall.

Neri took a keen interest in the Socialist Party's international links. He went to Florence for the European Social Forum in 2002, travelling on his own a few days early supposedly to meet up with his previous Italian comrades, who subsequently did not make an appearance. He also took great interest at international meetings in befriending members from other European countries.

During the period of his deployment, Neri had long-term sexual relationships with three separate women activists: Andrea, Lindsay and Beth (all of which are pseudonyms). Andrea had a two-year relationship with Neri after meeting him at an anti-war protest in September 2002. After a six-week whirlwind romance, they had moved in together and, on New Year's Eve that same year, he proposed. Andrea recalls: 'We had friends round, he cooked lots of food for them and he asked me to marry him. It was quite quick, quite intense, but it felt right and I said yes. And we started to make plans to get married. It felt utterly real, completely real.'[36] The undercover officer was already married with a child at the time.

Andrea and Neri visited Cornwall and Italy together, even joining Andrea's family on their summer holiday in Whitby. They travelled from London to Scotland to watch the punk band Stiff Little Fingers in concert with one of Neri's new acquaintances, Sean Cregan. In hindsight it appears to have been a way for the police officer to befriend this prominent anti-fascist activist. Cregan, a motorcycle courier, was also spied on by Mark Jenner during campaigning against the BNP and came into contact with Mark Kennedy a number of times while planning Anti Fascist Action (now known as Antifa) mobilizations against the Red, White and Blue festivals.

Neri discussed having children with Andrea but, following a familiar exit strategy, he became increasingly volatile and, feigning suicidal tendencies, left her in the summer of 2004. Andrea describes the way she was deliberately deceived by Carlo and his handlers as 'abusive, cold-hearted, psychological torture'. She is now suing the Met and has been granted core-participant status in the Pitchford Inquiry.

Margot was a guest at the New Year's Eve party where Carlo proposed to Andrea. She commented:

> We were a bunch of people working in the caring professions trying to make the world a better place. For that we were targeted for intimate personal betrayal by the state. Neri was but one officer in an industrial-scale policing operation that makes political dissent in the UK seem a very dangerous thing indeed. Especially if you're female.[37]

After splitting up with Andrea, Neri stayed in Paul Heron's flat for nine months until October 2005, although Heron remembers that he 'barely stayed a dozen nights', adding: 'If I had known the Met Police were paying all his bills, I would have put his rent up.'[38]

In the same period, Neri also told the prominent RMT union activist Steve Hedley about being made homeless and that he was looking for a place to stay. Hedley allowed him to use the spare room in his house in East Ham, which he did for eight weeks, although again his stay was sporadic. In October 2004, Neri turned up at an industrial dispute after Hedley was sacked by the signalling firm Westinghouse at the Channel Tunnel Rail Link (CTRL). The industrial action meant that Hedley was re-employed on CTRL but, as Hedley recalls: 'When that bit of work came to an end, they made sure it came to an end. I was totally blacklisted, I didn't get any work for about a year.'[39]

The undercover officer attended various anti-fascist protests, including one in Bradford in 2001 and the BNP Red White & Blue camp at Hanningfield Reservoir in Essex in 2004, often driving carloads of activists to the events. Neri appears to have targeted a looser network of socialist and anarchist anti-fascist activists in north and east London. Many of the same individuals had been under observation by SDS officers Peter Francis and Mark Jenner since the early 1990s. Frank Smith was one of those targeted and questions the purpose of the entire police strategy.

> ⁶We were targeted by three separate undercover police officers for over a decade. If we were such a threat, why were none of us arrested at the time? This has nothing to do with preventing crime but everything to do with keeping political activists under surveillance. This is political policing.⁹[40]

Neri bragged about unspecified links with the Red Brigades in Italy and a particular element of his deployment raises cause for concern. On one occasion, activists claim that the police officer suggested that they should petrol bomb a charity shop in north London that he claimed was run by the fascist Roberto Fiore. The leader of the extreme rightwing Forza Nuova party, Fiore fled to London after the 1980 Bologna railway station bombing in which 85 people were killed. Despite being arrested by Scotland Yard, he repeatedly evaded extradition by the Italian authorities. In his absence, he was cleared of planting the bomb but convicted of a subversive association and jailed for nine years. The jail term eventually 'timed out' under Italy's statute of limitation laws.[41] Fiore settled in London and formed close personal and political links with former BNP leader Nick Griffin, an association that exists to this day. Dan Gilman reflects on the suggestion by the police spy:

> ⁶Carlo tried to persuade me and Joe Batty to fire-bomb a charity shop on Elgin Avenue which he said was a front for the fascist Bologna bomber. This was at his flat at the same New Year's

Eve party where he asked Andrea to marry him. Then a couple of months later he mentioned it again at an anti-war demo. Carlo was really keen. Looking back, I think he was trying to set us up, like the ALF got done by their undercover.[42]

Appendix F of the SDS manual which has to be signed by new undercover officers, states that 'a police officer must not act as an *agent provocateur*', going on to explain that he must not incite anyone to 'commit an offence, nor an offence of a more serious character, which that person would not otherwise have committed'.[43] It is difficult to view the actions of Neri as anything other than a conscious attempt to entrap activists into acts of terrorism. This is the very same accusation made against Bob Lambert by a number of animal-rights activists referred to by Gilman above.

Gilman has been granted core-participant status by Pitchford but Joe Batty, one of those targeted by Carlo because of his campaigning against the BNP, has been turned down. Joe reflects on his interactions with the undercover police officer:

❝It's not the legitimate, or otherwise, targeting of leftwing activists as if they are a type of terrorist that concerns me. It's the endless weekends spent chewing the cud about life, the universe and everything, in the nude at Ironmonger Row Steam Baths, with Carlo that gets me. I fail to see of what possible benefit this was to police work apart from racking vast amounts of overtime at taxpayers' expense. Yeah, I was duped, violated even, but to be honest I am still grasping for a reason why. Anti-racism and fighting fascism is not a crime, it is a civic duty.[44]

Green MP Caroline Lucas, who previously used parliamentary privilege to name Bob Lambert in relation to the the firebombing of Debenhams, told the authors:

❝It's deeply worrying to learn that more than one undercover police officer stands accused of inciting the use of explosives, especially as we have to assume that none have been held to account for their actions and whatever actions they might have taken were sanctioned by their superiors.[45]

Holyrood

Scotland had always been a major battleground in the blacklisting campaign. An exceptionally high number of Scottish workers have files and blacklisting via the NRB system in the offshore sector is notorious. According to testimony heard by the Scottish Affairs select committee, the Glasgow-based company Balfour Beatty was reportedly one of the harshest users of the blacklist and even continued to victimize union activists long after TCA was closed down. The first ever march against the blacklist was in Dundee and a number of former MSPs appear on the TCA database.

It is little wonder then that the Scottish Parliament has debated the issue on a number of occasions. But it was not until November 2015 that a meeting was held inside the Holyrood building to discuss the links with undercover police. Neil Findlay MSP convened a meeting attended by dozens of parliamentarians, including Elaine Smith, Deputy Speaker of the Parliament.

Blacklisted environmental activist Ellenor Hutson, now a rights worker in the constituency office of the SNP MP Alison Thewliss, explained that, during protests against the G8 summit at Gleneagles in 2005, she had worked alongside the undercover police officer Mark Kennedy. The serving officer was one of the central organizers of the anti-globalization protests which took place at the same time as Bono was asking world leaders to 'Make Poverty History'. Kennedy had infiltrated the Dissent network, the main group organizing the protests, and was the transport co-ordinator for the 'Horizone', a camp of several thousand anti-G8 activists near the summit itself. The undercover officer's key logistical role during the summit protests involved hiring flatbed lorries for transporting heavy materials and minibuses for people, all apparently paid for by the British taxpayer.

However, the original remit for Pitchford is restricted to 'undercover police operations conducted by English and Welsh police forces in England and Wales'.[46] The activities of the police officers playing leading roles in the protests at Gleneagles and who may have spied on trade unions in Scotland would be excluded from the investigation. Findlay, Hutson and Smith all called for a full public inquiry into the role of undercover police operating in Scotland, whether by the Scottish government or by Lord Pitchford extending the geographical scope of his inquiry or else setting up a separate inquiry.

Scottish journalists took up the issue and a wave of articles appeared in the papers featuring revelations about both blacklisting and police spying on activists and interviews with Ellenor Hutson, Francie Graham, Steuart Merchant and Brian Higgins. One of the activists pushing the agenda with the Scottish media was Jason Fitzpatrick, former vice mayor of the city of Arcata in California, now living in Berlin. For a number of years Fitzpatrick was a key spin doctor for a variety of anti-globalization campaigns, including the protests which took place around G8 in Scotland. His skills ensured that, whereas the English mainstream media virtually ignored the issue except for occasional big splashes, new spycops stories appeared in the Scottish press on an almost daily basis.

The story gained added traction when it was discovered that Police Scotland's new chief constable, Phil Gormley, had previously been in charge of Special Branch at the Metropolitan Police. Gormley became the Met Special Branch Commander in January 2006 and as such was in overall control of the operations of the SDS. Later that year, all of the UK political policing units, including SDS, NPOIU and NETCU were amalgamated into the Counter Terrorism Command (SO15). A statement from Police Scotland states that at this point Mr Gormley's job title 'would have' changed to Commander SO15.[47]

In April 2016, it was discovered that former MSP Rosie Kane appeared on the Consulting Association database, becoming the third member of the Scottish parliament to have been targeted by the blacklisting organization. The ex-Scottish Socialist Party MSP was elected to Holyrood in 2003 and appears on TCA's greenlist, meaning, like many others, that her actual file was not seized by the ICO and was later destroyed by Ian Kerr.

When Dr Nick McKerrell, a law lecturer and regular media commentator about policing issues in Scotland, also found that TCA kept a file on him, undercover policing became an even bigger issue in the elections for the Scottish Parliament. Scottish Justice Secretary Michael Matheson even made a personal phone call to the then Home Secretary Theresa May asking for the expansion of the Pitchford remit, but to no avail.[48] But within minutes of MSPs returning to Holyrood after the May 2016 elections, Neil Findlay presented a parliamentary motion entitled 'Scotland, Pitchford and Undercover Policing', arguing that 'should this request be refused, the Scottish Government should set up its own inquiry so that all UK citizens, who have been affected by what it considers this scandal can have the opportunity to get to the truth.'[49] The motion has gained the signatures of Labour, Green, Conservative and Liberal MSPs. A similar Early Day Motion has been submitted in the Westminster parliament by the Lib Dem MP Alistair Carmichael.[50] The issue was raised again by Findlay in a debate in the Scottish Parliament on 30 June 2016 where he told MSPs that, as it stands, none of the huge number of questions about undercover operations in Scotland will be investigated unless Pitchford widens its remit: 'We cannot have a situation in which the only people in mainland UK not to have access to the Inquiry and to potential justice for them and their families are Scots.' His call for a Scottish inquiry if Pitchford fails to widen its remit has been resisted so far by the SNP.

In Northern Ireland, former Justice Minister David Ford confirmed that, following legal pressure from Jason Fitzpatrick, he had written to Theresa May to ask her to consider cases in which the undercover operative travelled to the region. Fitzpatrick had travelled with Mark Kennedy and other activists to Northern Ireland in 2005 to attend various anti-globalization events including one at the City Church in south Belfast. Fitzpatrick told the *Irish News*: 'These undercover officers operated in many places, not only England and Wales, and it's absolutely essential anybody who was targeted by these undercover officers have a right to receive justice in whatever places these injustices have occurred.'[51]

In June 2016, the German government also wrote to Theresa May formally calling for the Pitchford Inquiry to be extended to cover the covert operations of British undercover police in Germany.

In July 2016, in one of her very last acts as Home Secretary before becoming Prime Minister, May decided not to allow Pitchford to be extended to Scotland. The decision was disclosed in a letter, sent by the new policing minister Brandon Lewis to Neil Findlay MSP, which claims that covering Scotland would 'require further consultation and delay the progress of the Inquiry'. It adds: 'in the interests of learning lessons from past failures and improving public confidence, it is important that the Inquiry can proceed swiftly'.[52] Findlay responded that 'victims of unethical and illegal undercover policing' would have access to 'truth and potential justice' if they lived in England and Wales but not those in Scotland.[53] The Campaign Opposing Police Surveillance, meanwhile, described the 'geographical blinkers' as a 'snub to Scotland'.[54] Legal action is now being considered.

Neither Confirm Nor Deny

One of the biggest legal arguments so far in Pitchford is over the issue of how public the public inquiry should actually be. The police claim that in order to protect officers and their families at the centre of the Inquiry from harm, they should be granted total anonymity and their evidence heard in secret. Non-disclosure of documentary evidence and refusal to inform those who have been spied on that their human rights may have been breached is also justified, they say, in order to protect vital secrets about the process of undercover policing. The policy of Neither Confirm Nor Deny (NCND) has been elevated to the level of a divine commandment. The fight over NCND is central to how the public inquiry will operate and a battle has raged between the police and activists both inside the Royal Courts of Justice and in public campaigning leading up to the Inquiry.

Back in 2012 the authors requested under the Freedom of Information Act any files on the Blacklist Support Group held by the Metropolitan Police, Scottish Police and a selection of other forces. After consulting with what was then the Association of Chief Police Officers, every force decided that it would 'neither confirm nor deny' it held such information. This is the exact same response given by the police to the Hillsborough campaigners and the women like Alison and Helen Steel who had long-term relationships with proven undercover police officers sent to spy on them, some of whom also appear on The Consulting Association's blacklist. The Blacklist Support Group believes that it is currently a target of ongoing undercover police surveillance. A request by Dave Smith under the Data Protection Act for information held on him by the police was refused because it might jeopardize ongoing criminal investigations and on the basis of national security.

Before Pitchford published his ruling on NCND, a seminal conference took place at London South Bank University which brought together non-state core participants and their legal teams to discuss the evolution and practice of political policing in the UK.[55] Piers Doggart and Stephen Brown, official solicitors from Pitchford's legal team, were present throughout to hear the voices of those spied upon and to present an Inquiry update.

The message sent out by Doreen Lawrence must have been uncomfortable for those in authority to hear. Lawrence accused the Commissioner of the Metropolitan Police, Sir Bernard Hogan-Howe, of making a hollow promise when he previously stated that he was committed to transparency and that he hoped it would 'go some way to start rebuilding the trust she has lost in us'. Responding to the submission by the Met's lawyers that the hearings should take place in secret to protect the identities of officers, Baroness Lawrence expressed her fury:

> In my view the Commissioner should be ashamed of himself. Our son was the victim of an unprovoked racist attack. We were a grieving family. We had done nothing wrong. In my view, because of what the undercover police officers did, they don't deserve this special treatment. I didn't do anything to be spied upon. They chose to spy upon me. And they have been caught out. They now have to deal with the consequences of what they did.[56]

In March 2016, Pitchford held a two-day hearing to discuss restriction orders for which the police had applied. So many people turned up that an overflow court with huge widescreen TVs was needed for those who could not fit into the public gallery. Jonathan Hall QC laid out the police reasoning behind their call for restriction orders in line with NCND. His opening remarks expressed 'how committed the Metropolitan Police Service is, from the Commissioner down, to ensuring that you get at the truth'; however, he continued, 'it would be unfair and therefore unlawful to approach disclosure on the basis that there is a presumption of openness'.[57]

Referring to some of the core participants, he indicated that 'they were not made up of a bunch of eccentric, if well-meaning, hippy idealists' but were in fact often 'violent extremists', adding, without an ounce of irony, 'there are those who may not be entirely frank with the Inquiry about what their activities were'. The undercover police officers had supposedly all been offered lifelong anonymity as part of their deployment but were now apparently living in constant fear and would suffer 'heartbreak' if exposed, possibly forcing their children to move schools.[58]

Certainly there were regular protests and public meetings at London Metropolitan and St Andrews universities, where Bob Lambert was employed as a lecturer until the end of 2015. These were aimed at highlighting the links the ex-head of SDS has with the McLibel case, the Debenhams arson attack and sexual relations with female activists. Protesters said that all of this constituted a safeguarding issue for young adults in those institutions, a claim denied by his employers. In April 2016, the Met announced that it was reinvestigating the Debenham bombing following a review of undercover operations.[59] Lambert has always vehemently denied any involvement in the bombing.

To date, not a single officer named in the media or publicly outing themselves in the press has been threatened, let alone assaulted. Tackling this point, Jonathan Hall QC put forward an improbable line of argument that there is a 'difference between something that is in the public domain and something that is officially confirmed' and 'it may be that the lack of official confirmation is all that is holding individuals back from taking aggressive action. It may be that they are still in doubt, but that official confirmation would provide them with the justification in their eyes for taking some action against an officer.'

Hall was stridently unapologetic about the work of undercover officers in the Special Demonstration Squad, arguing that some mistakes in the past should not overshadow 'the work the police did to uphold the democratic values of this country by avoiding influence by industrial or extremist means'.[60]

The deliberate usage of the term of 'industrial' flags up that the state considers trade unions a legitimate target of undercover policing. Used alongside the term 'extremist', the statement gives a clear indication as to the stance the police intend to adopt throughout Pitchford. Mirroring Victorian morality, the police are attempting to differentiate between the 'deserving' and 'undeserving'. The police will fall over themselves to apologize to Doreen and Neville Lawrence, Duwayne Brooks and Michael Mansfield for the way they were treated. The same with the women activists who were deceived into sexual relationships to provide cover for police spies. However, the general principle of spying on leftwing political or trade-union activists who may on occasion participate in civil disobedience will be presented as totally legitimate. To justify their defence of vested interests, it will be necessary to paint activists as troublemakers, violent extremists and agitators.

Echoing his counterpart from the Met, Andrew O'Connor QC, representing the National Crime Agency, added the now-familiar refrain that 'hearing evidence about those matters publicly will undermine the prevention and detection of crime today' and that 'the Neither Confirm Nor Deny policy is, in principle, an important tool for maintaining and sustaining policing operations, in particular undercover operations'.

Sukhdev Reel attended the High Court hearing and afterwards described her feelings:

> ❝I am not a lawyer but just a mother who has spent the past 17 years trying to find out who murdered my son and why. Sitting at the Inquiry, I became quite distressed because there was a lot of talk by the Met about the police's rights to privacy. But nothing about the core participants who were spied upon. Our rights to privacy were completely ignored. I wonder if transparency will be core to the Inquiry or will it be another case of police abuse and corruption being hidden behind closed doors.❞[61]

But despite the repeated assertions of police lawyers, NCND in relation to undercover policing is far from being a long-established principle that could never be deviated from. In normal criminal trials (often concerning individuals who truly are violent) it is common for undercover officers to give evidence in open court, but when political policing units are involved, the police now demand total secrecy. But even this is a new development.

On 19 December 2010, the *Sunday Times* newspaper published an article about Mark Kennedy's deployment in the environmental movement, including his participation in the protest at Ratcliffe-on-Soar power station, where a number of protesters were convicted. Their convictions were later overturned as a miscarriage of justice. The newspaper reported that the activist known as Mark Stone was in fact an undercover police officer called Mark Kennedy who had been spying on activists for over seven years. The article stated that: 'Last week two police forces confirmed Stone's status to the *Sunday Times*. "The individual is a Met officer," said Nottinghamshire Police. "He is an undercover officer." said the Metropolitan Police, "so we can't say more".[62]

In January 2011, revelations appeared in the media about the undercover officer Jim Boyling, who, while spying on the anti-capitalist group Reclaim the Streets between 1995 and 2000, had married 'Rosa' and fathered two children. The relationship became so abusive that she eventually fled to a women's refuge. 'Rosa' told the authors:

> ❝I had a "welfare" visit from Bob Lambert and his superiors. It was not a welfare visit really, but it took me years to understand what it was. It was a security risk assessment. That was a confirmed by a whistleblower, they call it a "containment exercise".❞[63]

The *Guardian* reported at the time: 'In a statement the Metropolitan Police said a serving specialist operations detective constable has been restricted from duty as part of an investigation following allegations reported in a national newspaper.'[64]

Helen Steel recalls being contacted by 'Rosa', who has now been granted core-participant status in Pitchford:

> ❝There was not just the confirmation in the media. I was with her when she was interviewed in March 2011 by the Department of Professional Standards, who were investigating the conduct of Jim Boyling. Her account was absolutely harrowing and, at the end of it, the police officers apologized on behalf of the Metropolitan Police. At no point in that interview did they mention Neither Confirm Nor Deny. On the contrary, they

confirmed that Jim was a serving police officer. They also named Jim Boyling and referred to him as a serving officer in correspondence sent relating to that interview and potential disciplinary issues arising from it from February 2011 until June 2012.'[65]

In relation to the Spies Out of Lives women who took cases against the Met, numerous exchanges of correspondence between lawyers took place in which the true role of the undercover officers was openly admitted. In one letter dated 10 February 2012, the police lawyers state: 'If it assists, I can confirm Mark Kennedy was a Metropolitan Police officer and did not serve with any other force. He left the Metropolitan Police Service on 18 March 2010.'[66] But in November 2012 the Met changed its position, arguing Neither Confirm Nor Deny in relation to their application to strike out claims on the basis that NCND meant that they could not defend themselves properly in court. A policy has been effectively invented by the police in order to protect themselves from public scrutiny that through repetition has been elevated to the status of principle in the interests of national security. The women activists have received a public apology and financial compensation from the Met for the trauma they suffered but, to this day, the police will neither confirm nor deny whether the individuals concerned are undercover police officers or not. This is Kafkaesque.

In March 2015 in the High Court case of Welsh anarchists targeted by undercover officer Marco Jacobs, the police agreed that they will not contest that Jacobs was an undercover officer, nor require the claimants to prove he was. If the claimants win their case then the Met, the South Wales force and ACPO will be liable for any damages. This is an admission of guilt and an abandonment of NCND in all but name.

But when it came to the opening of the Pitchford Inquiry, the police stuck religiously to the NCND mantra. Phillipa Kaufman QC represents over 15 solicitors and around 200 core participants in the Inquiry who were spied upon by the Special Demonstration Squad and the National Public Order Intelligence Unit because of their political beliefs or because they were seeking to hold the police to account for racist policing. In her open remarks to Pitchford she made it clear the feelings of many of those who had suffered at the hands of the police in regards to NCND.

> **❝**If this proceeds on the basis of a presumption of secrecy, this is the end for many of the non-state core participants. That is not said as a matter of threat, it is simply a statement of fact because they are not prepared, some of them, to prise themselves open, to re-open wounds, wounds caused by police abuse, wounds perpetrated under a veil of secrecy, in circumstances where the police are again availing themselves of that veil of secrecy, that veil of secrecy being one that has kept them in the dark until now. In those circumstances they simply cannot and will not be prepared to move forward and involve themselves in this Inquiry... There was an issue of dignity that goes with a situation in which they are forced to give evidence in open before everybody, where the self-same evidence will be given by the police in total secrecy. There's a major issue of dignity that arises in that situation. So, for them, this is a make-or-break situation.**❞**

Kaufman argued that the police should not be allowed to adopt NCND in relation to the small number of police officers who have already been exposed by activists. Not only that, but the police should be obliged to publish the cover names of all the undercover police officers and provide a list of all 460 campaigns that they infiltrated. Kaufman argued that a 'key public interest that this Inquiry has to serve and achieve, one which the Secretary of State herself identified, is justice for the victims. If they don't know they are victims and if they don't know what has been done to them, they can't possibly have justice.'

Dan Squires QC, representing politicians given core-participant status, including Diane Abbott, Ken Livingstone, Dave Nellist and Dame Joan Ruddock, has argued the need for transparency because the Inquiry would be investigating 'matters of fundamental public importance as well as... the constitutional and democratic issues relating to the targeting of Members of Parliament'.

At the NCND hearing was Peter Francis, the former undercover cop turned whistleblower, represented by Ben Emerson QC. The court was told on behalf of Francis that 'as an undercover officer himself, he was never given a lifelong assurance of confidentiality, nor briefed on the existence or meaning of the policy of Neither Confirm Nor Deny'. There was a deathly silence from the police lawyers at this stage. Emerson argued that failure to reveal the cover names of officers would shield from public scrutiny the very thing the Inquiry was set up to investigate.

After two long days in court, during which the public gallery had been at times infuriated, at other times bored, with occasional bursts of excitement, the courtroom was about to witness high drama. Helen Steel stood up, becoming the only core participant to represent herself, and demolished NCND.

Helen Steel

John Dines confronted by Helen Steel at Sydney airport 24 years after his deployment.

The weekend before the hearing, Steel had appeared on TV news around the world after she had flown to Australia and confronted her ex-partner, the undercover police officer John Dines, at Sydney's Kingsford Smith airport. Dines is now a director at the Australian police training college. He 'apologized unreservedly' to her and the incident was caught on a hidden camera by the *Guardian*.[67] Her story was beamed into homes across the globe and she was present in the New South Wales parliament as the issue was raised by Australian Greens MP, David Shoebridge.[68]

In a speech brim-full of restrained emotion, Steel gave chapter and verse not only of the abuse suffered by the women activists but of the disrespect shown them by the continued policy of NCND, which only compounded their suffering.

Discussing the Commissioner of the Metropolitan Police, Bernard Hogan-Howe, Steel told the court:

> You would think that this is someone who would stick to NCND if it truly was a policy adopted by the Metropolitan Police. But, no, at a public meeting of the Metropolitan Police Authority on 27 October 2011, he confirmed that Jim Sutton

was under investigation as a serving officer. Is it really credible that, if there was a NCND policy in place, the Commissioner himself would not know about it and not adhere to it? I would submit that NCND was suddenly adopted in June 2012, when the Metropolitan Police Service wanted a wall to hide behind after they realized that they could no longer write these relationships off as a result of rogue officers and that, in fact, there was clear evidence of multiple abusive relationships that could only have arisen through systemic failings and institutional sexism.

The blacklisted environmental activist then went on to describe the making of the BBC TV documentary series 'True Spies', broadcast in 2002, which was about the work of the Special Demonstration Squad. Steel told Justice Pitchford:

> As I am sure you have heard, the programme was made with the support and assistance of the Metropolitan Police Service. While no individual officer's identity is disclosed, undercover officers speak extensively to the camera about their work. They talk about the groups they infiltrated and the methods used. There are significant details of the undercover operations actually carried out. I submit that they were perfectly happy to reveal their methods and the groups that they were spying on when it suited them for public-relations purposes and that the reason they want to bring in Neither Confirm Nor Deny is actually just to cover up serious human rights abuses. It is being used as a shield for the police from any form of accountability and to avoid any proper scrutiny of their actions to cover up illegal and immoral activities of political undercover police officers and prevent them coming to light.

Like a scene from a Hollywood blockbuster, seething with repressed anger Steel went on:

> There was a lot of talk yesterday about the police rights to privacy, but there was nothing at all from the police about the rights of core participants who were spied on. It took me 24 years to get acknowledgment of wrongdoing from the Metropolitan Police and from John Barker, my former partner.

Other core participants should not have to wait that long, It is insulting in the extreme that, despite the apology, the police are still seeking to neither confirm nor deny John Dines. It is also farcical in light of my meeting with him last week and his apology to me. But it was not just insulting to me. It is insulting for everybody who has had their privacy invaded to be told that they can't know the truth about the wrongdoing that was done against them because the privacy of those who carried out that abuse has to be protected.*

By this point the public gallery and social media were cheering Helen on as she ended by demanding all the cover names be released.

Without the names of undercover officers who targeted each group, it is impossible to start to assess the whole impact of their surveillance or the extent of the abuses committed. Without full disclosure, we won't get to the full truth and we can't ensure that preventative measures are put in place to stop these abuses happening again. These were very, very serious human rights abuses committed by this unit. We want to stop them happening again. That is our purpose in taking part in this Inquiry and that is the real public interest that requires that there must be openness and transparency. Thank you.

As she sat down, the court erupted in cheering and a standing ovation. It was a piece of political theatre that no-one who witnessed it will ever forget.

The ability of NCND to frustrate efforts to gain insights was evident again when Lord Justice Pitchford made his ruling on the issue. He effectively said that there will be no blanket application of NCND but individual police officers will be able to apply for it in each case. It pushes debate on the issue further down the road which, if nothing else, means an even longer inquiry.[69]

Spying on trade unions

To date, all of the evidence about police surveillance of unions and union activists has been uncovered by activists and investigative journalists. Not one document has been voluntarily disclosed to Pitchford or to the trade unions by the police. Instead, freedom-of-information requests have been refused time and again. The official police position is that unions were not the specific target of undercover police spies, nor does any evidence exist that points towards that conclusion. At best, unions were victims of collateral intrusion similar to the Lawrence and Reel family. But the more the police trot out that line, the more activists seem to uncover evidence to the contrary.

In the spring of 2016, Brian Higgins called in a plumber to fix a burst pipe in the loft of his Northampton home. The 75-year-old grandfather and former national secretary of the rank-and-file Building Worker Group (BWG), asked if there were any old papers left up there. Lo and behold, more evidence emerged of undercover police spying on union activists. The documents gathering dust give an insight into how deeply the police embedded themselves in even grassroots union campaigns. On 21 March 1997, the undercover police officer Mark Jenner wrote a letter under his cover name of Mark Cassidy to a number of different organizations regarding the 'Building Workers Safety Campaign', which he described as a 'rank-and-file organization run by building workers', asking for support in getting 'information on deaths on building sites' in order to visit 'the site within one week after the event and ask workers to stop work'. The police-authored letter continued: 'We believe that only by hitting production can we hope to stop the killings on building sites.' This was in 1997, when the fatality rates in construction were averaging around three deaths a week.

The identical letter was sent to a number of trade-union bodies, including Haringey UNISON, Hammersmith UNISON, TGWU North London Textile branch and civil servants in the CPSA union (forerunner to PCS). The police spy also sent the letter to the charity Inquest, which provides free legal advice to people bereaved by a death in police custody. Why a charity dealing with deaths in custody would be an obvious source of information about deaths on building sites is difficult to fathom but it again raises questions of public interest as to what the undercover police officer was trying to achieve.

One response from Mick Holder on behalf of the London Hazards

Centre identifies HSE inspectors, the Coroners' Office and the local police as sources of information on site deaths. The letter goes on to highlight that the authorities 'can be very tight-lipped when it comes to giving out information', no doubt bringing a smile to Jenner's face when he read it.

Brian Higgins commented:

> The police would be infinitely better employed investigating, prosecuting and jailing the corporate criminals responsible for the killing and maiming of many building workers, rather than spying on those of us who dedicate our industrial lives to trying to put a stop to this wanton carnage and the terrible grief which accompanies it. Intelligence gathered by these police spies has found its way onto an illegal blacklist in the construction industry. They say justice never sleeps: time it woke up over this!

Mark Jenner's former partner 'Alison' told the *Morning Star* that the letter was almost certainly typed by her mother who regularly prepared correspondence for the undercover cop in his trade-unionist guise.

> I don't remember this particular letter, but I do know that he convened meetings for the Building Workers Group. It's just another in the litany of the shameful abuses of power. I think he's doing two things. One thing he's doing is trying to build relationships and build trust, so with all the places these letters were sent, there was an opportunity to say at a future time: "You remember me, I wrote to you, I'm Mark Cassidy." The other thing he's doing is shutting down the ability to protest, so the people he sent it to would not know anything about deaths on building sites, and therefore they're not going to get any responses and not be able to take any action. All I can say about this is that nothing surprises me any more.[70]

Solicitor Shamik Dutta, who represents the Colin Roach Centre (which has been denied core-participant status) at Pitchford, commented:

> We have all known for some time that Mark Jenner was

an undercover police officer and that he formed a deceitful relationship with "Alison" and spied on members of the Colin Roach Centre (CRC) and Hackney Community Defence Association (HCDA) while those organizations supported the victims of police misconduct and fought to expose serious police criminality. This recently discovered letter now provides evidence that Jenner also tried to ingratiate himself with Inquest, an organization that has, for over 30 years, been commended for supporting the families of those who have died at the hands of, amongst others, the police and prison service. Just as with CRC and HCDA, it is difficult to comprehend any reasonable justification for an undercover police officer being deployed to form a relationship with, and gather intelligence on, Inquest. My clients deserve to know who deployed Mark Jenner, why they did so and what steps he might have taken in an attempt to undermine their vital work.[71]

Trade Union Bill

Concerns about the British state gathering intelligence on trade unionists are not confined to the Pitchford inquiry, on Monday 12th October 2015, the BSG sat alongside the human-rights NGOs Amnesty International and Liberty to give evidence to MPs at the committee stage of the Trade Union Bill. The invite had been wangled by Chris Stephens MP, who, until being elected to Westminster for the SNP in May 2015, had been the branch treasurer for Glasgow Unison. Dave Smith told MPs:

> My concern about the Bill is all geared around this concept of picket supervisors having to have their names provided to the police, because if the names have got to be provided to the police, it is inevitable that the police will collate these names and they will appear on some kind of database. I am very, very sceptical about the state keeping a list of picket supervisors. This could clearly be turned into a state-sponsored blacklist.[72]

Sara Ogilvie, policy officer from Liberty, reminded MPs that trade-union rights are a fundamental part of the human rights framework, with Article 11 of the European Convention on

Human Rights enshrining the freedom of association and assembly. She found the proposed compulsion for unions to appoint a picket supervisor, in order to exercise their human rights, 'extremely concerning', adding 'the thought that we would require a person in 2015 to wear an armband and carry a letter of authorization at the behest of the state in order to exercise their rights does not seem right'.[73]

On 4 May 2016, the Trade Union Act 2016 received royal assent and became British law. The armband, letter of authorization and list of names were all included.

The effect of the new legislation is that any strike can now be declared unlawful if the trade union does not provide the police with the name, address and mobile phone number of the local shop steward likely to be co-ordinating the strike action. For major disputes covering multiple locations over a number of days, such as a Tube strike, this would mean the rail unions providing hundreds of names of union activists to the police. Failure fully to comply with the requirements will see employers rushing to the High Court in search of an injunction against the unions.

In addition to costly litigation, the Trade Union Act makes a potential state-sponsored blacklist a very real prospect. Smith highlighted the fears of many in the union movement when he asked MPs, 'once the police information about trade-union activists is written on a database or a computer somewhere, give me any possible way that you could exclude Special Branch from finding the information?'[74]

The Conservative government is currently pushing the Investigatory Powers Bill through Parliament. This 'snoopers' charter' will make it easier for the police and security services to spy on private emails, internet usage and phone conversations, including being granted warrants for phone tapping and covert surveillance. On 6 June 2015, Shadow Home Secretary Andy Burnham told the House of Commons: 'I have received confirmation from the security services that, in the past – under governments of both colours, it has to be said – trade unions have indeed been monitored.' Referring to the evidence gathered by the authors and the Blacklist Support Group, the Liverpool MP went on to say: 'People have a right to know what information was passed by whom in the police service, who sanctioned the passing of that information to such organizations and the policy under which passing that information was justified.' He called for a public inquiry into blacklisting and Orgreave, saying: 'There is clear evidence that such monitoring was used for unjustified political and commercial reasons, breaching privacy and basic human rights. The blacklisting of construction workers was used to vet people and deny them work. We need to understand how covertly gained police information came into the hands of the shady organization compiling the blacklist. This is yet another scandal from our country's past that the public have a right to know about.'[75]

Burnham submitted a successful amendment to the Bill that will ensure union activity is not enough of a reason in itself to grant a warrant to look at private data, even forcing the Conservative Home Office Minister John Hayes to admit it was 'neither proportional nor lawful' to investigate legitimate trade-union activity.[76] Many believe, however, that the wording will allow GCHQ to drive a coach and horses through the declared aim of the amendment.

How we got here

The only reason the issue of undercover policing broke into the public domain, forcing the establishment of the Pitchford Inquiry, was because of the relentless campaign by activists and investigative journalists.

Helen Steel makes the point forcibly:

> We are not here because the police unearthed evidence of bad practice within these political policing units and were so concerned that they brought it to the attention of the Home Secretary. We are here because of the bravery of Peter Francis coming forward to blow the whistle on the deeply alarming, abusive and undemocratic practice of the Special Demonstration Squad and we are here because of the detective work of women who were deceived into relationships with undercover police officers and who, despite the wall of secrecy around these secretive political policing units, managed to reveal the true identities of our former partners and expose these and other abusive practices to the wider world.[77]

Phillippa Kaufman QC agreed that, except for the whistleblowing by Peter Francis, none of the failings were uncovered because of self-disclosure by the police, 'but all the other abuses came out as a result of the efforts of the individual victims of those abuses to uncover them. On the contrary, when it comes to miscarriages of justice, those miscarriages themselves arose precisely because the police failed to discharge their legal obligations to disclose their involvement in the circumstances leading to the prosecutions.'[78]

Guardian journalist Rob Evans, co-author of *Undercover*, the definitive book on the police spying scandal, commented:

> What we are seeing is the people who were spied upon are turning the tables on the spies and beginning to dig out the information about what has happened to them, putting together all the pieces of the jigsaw. I think that is a very powerful form of accountability and it is something that is very uncomfortable for the police.[79]

At the first Pitchford hearing the Undercover Research Group (URG) was asked directly 'was its purpose to out undercover policemen?' URG responded with a post on its website, stating: 'To be clear, we do not have a list of unconfirmed undercovers through which we are steadily working in preparation to systematic exposure. What we have is a bunch of fears and concerns from individuals and groups, who we think have valid questions... All undercovers to date, with the exception of whistleblower Peter Francis, have only been exposed by activists doing the work of investigation. This is people doing the difficult work of investigating a close friend, not an abstract bit of detective work.'[80]

In relation to police collusion with blacklisting of trade unionists, the final paragraph of the Imran Khan &Partners submission to Pitchford says: 'But for BSG and the revelations that the group uncovered, very little of the information that is now known about the relationship between undercover policing and blacklisting would be in the public realm. It is, accordingly, BSG, through the individuals that form the group, is able to claim a significant interest, in that they are in a truly unrivalled position to provide information in this particular aspect of matters to which the Inquiry relates.'[81]

This point was reiterated by Andy Burnham in the House of Commons: 'We would not know about the practice were it not for the outstanding work of the Blacklist Support Group... who have exposed how much of the information held on individuals appeared to emanate from police sources.'[82]

In July 2016, Unite general secretary Len McCluskey was interviewed by Decca Aitkenhead in the *Guardian* during the battle over Jeremy Corbyn's leadership of the Labour Party. The union leader mentioned that it would be naïve to think the security services would not at least be interested in the dispute.

McCluskey said: 'Do people believe for one second that the security forces are not involved in dark practices? I have been around long enough... the type of stuff that we ultimately find out about, about who was involved in who, the 30-year rule. We found out just a couple of years ago that the chair of my union then, the Transport and General Workers Union, was an MI5 informant at the time that there was a strike taking place that I personally as a worker was involved in. [In] 1972, I was on strike for six weeks. And 30 years later it comes out that the chair of my union at that time was an MI5 informant.'

Then, in a section which predictably led to headlines that MI5 were destabilizing Corbyn, the *Guardian* wrote: 'Asked again if he believed that classified documents would eventually reveal the involvement of security forces in Corbyn's leadership difficulties, McCluskey said: "Well I tell you what, anybody who thinks that that isn't happening doesn't live in the same world that I live in... Do you think that there's not all kinds of rightwingers who are not secretly able to disguise themselves and stir up trouble? I find it amazing if people think that isn't happening."'[83]

McCluskey clarified the comments a few days later, citing blacklisting, Shrewsbury, Hillsborough, Orgreave and the abused women activists, saying: 'My comments to Ms Aitkenhead were a wry observation, not a direct allegation, as subsequent headlines claimed, when power and authority face challenge, as many will consider Jeremy Corbyn's leadership does to the prevailing political and economic orthodoxy, they do not sit idle.'[84]

The response on the Left to McCluskey's observations showed clearly that, for some, the security services remain no more than a disinterested observer. Former Labour MP Jacqui Smith tweeted in response: 'A downright insult to the dedicated staff of MI5 who are actually working day & night to protect us from terrorism.' Smith was Home Secretary from June 2007 to June 2009, coinciding with the operation of the construction blacklist and subsequent discovery, despite frequent denials, and when we know that undercover police officers were infiltrating unions and protest groups that have led to dozens of convictions overturned and hundreds of thousands of pounds paid out in compensation.

Amid all the allegations and counter-allegations over undercover police spying on activists, Courtenay Griffiths QC, who has appeared in some of the most high-profile trials of the past few decades, injected a degree of reality into the debate. Pulling the rug from under both the conservative and liberal outlook in one concise statement, he recently commented:

> ❝ I can understand the sense of outrage which has greeted recent disclosures about police surveillance but I can't understand the sense of surprise. Those disclosures merely serve to confirm, beyond challenge, that the surveillance of dissent is an institutional pillar of our political order: it is a mode of governance.❞ [85]

The Pitchford Inquiry is due to report in 2019.

1 Statement by Peter Francis read by John McDonnell MP at launch of *Blacklisted*, 12 Mar 2015. 2 *Morning Star* 14 Mar 2015. nin.tl/infiltrations 3 Undercover policing: Inquiry established by Theresa May bbc.co.uk/news/uk-31852220 4 Conference film, nin.tl/policespying 5 Home Office website 16 Jul 2015, nin.tl/HomeSecretaryterms 6 nin.tl/UCPIfaqs 7 GMB news, nin.tl/GMBCammell 8 *Liverpool Echo*, nin.tl/Cammellworker 9 Submissions for core-participant status on behalf of the Blacklist Support Group. 10 bbc.co.uk/news/uk-31852220 11 Billy Briggs, *The Ferret*, 30 May 2016, nin.tl/chiefunfit 12 'Special Branch "political police" spied on Wapping leaders', *Morning Star*, 24 Apr 2015. 13 *Morning Star*, 16 May 2015, nin.tl/policeagents 14 Reel News video, nin.tl/reelnewsUC 15 Ibid. 16 vimeo.com/164225448 17 Core-participant ruling 1 – 26 Oct 2015. 18 Deaths in Custody statistics inquest.org.uk/issues/home 19 Operation Herne press conference, 24 Jul 2014. 20 Speech to conference, nin.tl/TMGvideo 21 Reel News video, nin.tl/reelnewsUC ins 22 Operation Herne press conference, Thursday 24 Jul 2014. 23 *Guardian*, 2 Aug 2016, nin.tl/Tomlinsonfamily 24 Met Police news, nin.tl/Metnews 25 Special Demonstration Squad Tradecraft Manual, published Jun 2015, nin.tl/SDSmanual 26 vimeo.com/164225448 27 app.college.police.uk/wp-content/uploads/2016/06/UCAPP_consultation-draft.pdf 28 *The Canary*, 1 Jul 2016, nin.tl/CanaryUC 29 *Guardian*, 29 Jun 2016,

nin.tl/sexdrugsofflimits 30 undercoverresearch.net/1082-2 31 nin.tl/
Nerialias 32 *Guardian*, 18 Jan 2016, nin.tl/Neritorture 33 Ibid. 34 Socialist Party,
socialistparty.org.uk/articles/22049 35 Interview with the authors. 36 *Guardian*,
18 Jan 2016, nin.tl/Neritorture 37 Interview with the authors. 38 Interview with the
authors. 39 Interview with the authors. 40 Interview with the authors. 41 *Guardian*,
18 Sep 2000, nin.tl/catholiclink 42 Interview with the authors. 43 Special Demonstration
Squad Tradecraft Manual, published Jun 2015, nin.tl/SDSmanual 44 Interview
with the authors. 45 Interview with the authors. 46 Undercover policing: Inquiry
established by Theresa May bbc.co.uk/news/uk-31852220 House of Commons,
Home Secretary statement, 16 Jul 2015. 47 Paul Hutcheon, *Sunday Herald*, 13 Apr
2016. 48 *Daily Record*, nin.tl/SNPprobe 49 Scottish Parliament Motion Number:
S5M-00003. 50 BBC News, nin.tl/inquirycall 51 nin.tl/FordandMay 52 Letter
from Brandon Lewis MP to Neil Findlay MSP, 25 Jul 2016. 53 Rob Evans, 'Theresa
May accused...', *Guardian*, 4 Aug 2016 54 Scotland Excluded from Pitchford Inquiry
– Campaign Opposing Police Surveillance website. 55 Speech to conference,
nin.tl/TMGvideo 56 *Guardian*, 17 Apr 2016, nin.tl/DoreenLawrence 57 https://www.
ucpi.org.uk/wp-content/uploads/2016/03/160322-transcript-of-hearing-on-22-
March-2016.pdf 58 nin.tl/hearingtranscript 59 BBC news, 20 Apr 2016, bbc.co.uk/
news/uk-36095317 60 nin.tl/hearingtranscript 61 nin.tl/sabotagespying 62 Tim
Rayment and Jonathan Leake, '7 year snitch', *Sunday Times*, 19 Dec 2010. 63 Interview
with the authors. 64 Jo Adetunji, 'Police spy who married activist suspended from
duty', *Guardian*, 21 Jan 2011. 65 nin.tl/hearingtranscript23rd 66 Campaign
Opposing Police Surveillance, nin.tl/HelenSteel 67 *Guardian* news video, 9 Mar
2016, nin.tl/Steelvideo 68 nin.tl/spyapology 69 Undercover Policing Inquiry,
nin.tl/underpi 70 *Morning Star*, nin.tl/newlowforpolice 71 Interview with the
authors. 72 Hansard, nin.tl/Hansard131015 73 Ibid. 74 Ibid. 75 *Mirror*, 6 Jun 2016,
nin.tl/workersvictory 76 Ibid. 77 Helen Steel speech to Pitchford inquiry, 23 Mar
2016. 78 nin.tl/hearingtranscript23rd 79 nin.tl/sabotagespying 80 Undercover
Research Group undercoverresearch.net/1082-2/ 81 Submissions for core-
participant status on behalf of the Blacklist Support Group. 82 Speech on Investigatory
Powers Bill, 6 June 2016, nin.tl/Hansard060616 83 *Guardian*, 22 Jul 2016, nin.tl/
McCluskeyinterview 84 *Guardian*, 25 Jul 2016, nin.tl/McCluskeyupdate 85 nin.tl/
sabotagespying

11
Vindication

'I want to make an apology, an apology for the way that you have been betrayed by the state, by the courts, by the Information Commissioner's Office, by the political parties – all of them – by the police and by the media. All of the institutions of our state have utterly failed you and I am utterly ashamed to be part of a state that has allowed this to happen. You have been the victims of the worst conspiracy of silence and inaction that I have ever known in my parliamentary life.'[1]

The speech by MP and former minister Michael Meacher to blacklisted workers in March 2013 sets out clearly that the failure to bring justice is borne by every section of the state. The more campaigners uncovered, the worse the conspiracy appeared and still no-one had properly apologized. Court cases revealed mountains of evidence, a TV documentary exposed ongoing blacklisting, a parliamentary investigation condemned the guilty parties: and still no-one offered any redress. The truth was beginning to be exposed – but painfully slowly. So slowly that some blacklisted workers who played a key role in the campaign have passed away without seeing justice.

Own Up! Clean Up! Pay Up!

Eight months after Michael Meacher's speech to blacklisted workers at the BSG AGM, the TUC organized the first ever national day of action against blacklisting under the slogan 'Own Up! Clean Up! Pay Up!' Protests were held around the country and blacklisted workers hailed it as a marvellous success. They were at the front of union-organized events at the Scottish Parliament and the Welsh Assembly building. UCATT protested outside every Sir Robert McAlpine office in the country, while the GMB targeted the

Carillion head office in Wolverhampton. In Leeds, two blacklisted pensioners, Sandy McPherson and Pete Shaw, were hospitalized when they were thrown to the floor by a building security manager described as being built like a 'rugby league prop'.[2] Pete Shaw has been undergoing treatment since the incident that caused damage to his eye and shoulder plus contributed to the worsening of his pre-existing angina. A private prosecution backed by Unite the Union is under way.

In the City of London, Leadenhall Street was closed for an hour during the morning rush hour as a BSG and Unite protest spilled into the road outside the Cheesegrater development being built by Laing O'Rourke opposite Lloyds of London. Green Party leader Natalie Bennett joined blacklisted workers as they blockaded the Francis Crick Institute, also being built by Laing O'Rourke. Just a few days earlier a young builder, Richard Laco, had been killed on the site, which refuses to allow trade-union officials access. TV cameras filmed union general secretaries and Scabby the Rat at College Green opposite the House of Commons with the BSG banner blocking the road as it led an impromptu march on parliament singing the Bob Marley lyrics 'Get up! Stand up! Stand up for your rights! Don't give up the fight!'

The trade unions might have been generating publicity and demanding that the companies 'Own Up!' But to admit one's sins requires a degree of honesty, self-criticism and contrition: attributes the firms seemed to lack. Former MP Nick Raynsford said that the industry was 'in denial' over its role in the affair. The introduction to the Scottish Affairs Select Committee first interim report on blacklisting describes the evidence given by directors of transnational companies thus: 'We are far from certain that all of our witnesses have told us "the truth, the whole truth and nothing but the truth", despite many of them being under oath.'[3]

This damning assessment of the firms' response was one shared by campaigners.

The TUC also called for the companies to 'Clean Up!' This is of course very difficult, if you don't think you've done anything wrong in the first place. Internal investigations were the opportunity to self-cleanse but at best these discovered that staff may need training or a new clause should be added to a company policy. In response to questions from MPs Stephen McPartland and Kevin Hopkins, Costain, NG Bailey and Morgan Sindall said that new but undefined procedures have been introduced. Skanska gave them a detailed explanation of training on data protection for staff, highlighting that: 'Ethical dilemmas are discussed at management meetings to keep the code of conduct and ethical behaviour high on the agenda within the company.'[4] This was despite The Consulting Association being a permanent agenda item at regular internal Skanska industrial and employment relations meetings chaired by TCA chair Stephen Quant during his time as HR director at the company.[5]

An outside observer may think involvement in blacklisting brought the company into disrepute. Yet, as Will Hurst revealed in *Building* magazine, of the 39 alleged TCA contacts named by Kerr and known to be working, '78 per cent remain in senior HR roles within construction while 61 per cent are still working in HR at the same firms they were when, it is alleged, they interacted with TCA'.[6]

Dianne Hughes, for instance, is now HR director for the Big Lottery Fund. She had previously been a senior HR professional at Carillion and its then mechanical and electrical subsidiary Crown House, and a main contact for Ian Kerr. Others have moved up the corporate ladder. Paul Raby, named by Kerr, now sits on Balfour Beatty's executive board. Sheila Knight, former personnel director for Drake & Scull on the Jubilee Line and assistant director of ACAS, now runs two consultancies called Anderson Knight Associates and Synatus. Her consultancy practice includes acting as a visiting lecturer, and teaching employment law and human resource management to MA students at the University of Reading. Gayle Burton, Costain's main contact who was named in the Scottish Parliament as a source of information between TCA and Special Branch, holds a senior role at the Jockey Club.

The Chartered Institute of Personnel and Development (CIPD) carried out an investigation in secret, which to this date has still not been published, and not a single HR professional suffered any public sanction by the organization. In November 2014, Mike Emmott, CIPD employee relations expert, was a keynote speaker at the Manchester Industrial Relations Society 50th anniversary conference and told 200 of the UK's leading academics that blacklisting was 'a big fuss about very little' and that he found 'union moral outrage over blacklisting rather distasteful'.[7] The employers' federations have never even discussed the matter at their meetings. Only a handful of members of staff were even disciplined as a result and fewer still actually ceased employment with the blacklisting firms.

At the TUC day of action on blacklisting in November 2013, Frances O'Grady, TUC general secretary, called on the firms to 'pay up', telling a packed rally inside parliament: 'It's a disgrace that none of the companies involved have faced any criminal sanctions. It's an abomination that many continue to use blacklists. And it's an outrage that not a single penny has been paid to the victims.' Blacklisted workers were about to take the call for compensation into their own hands.

The High Court

It was clear that, regardless of the public outrage and political pressure, the blacklisting firms would never own up, clean up or pay up unless they were forced to. Fortunately, from the moment the ICO announced the discovery of the blacklist back in 2009, there had been a team of people preparing to exert the required pressure. The battleground for the final scenes in this campaign was to be the High Court in The Strand but, like many other parts of this story, it required a little bit of luck to get started.

One of those blacklisted following his work on the Jubilee Line was an electrician called Bobby Hawkes, whose amiable Irish son-in-law is a former rock guitarist turned barrister called JC Townsend. Hawkes remembers what happened when he received his letter from the ICO in the spring of 2009. 'When I got my file I showed it to JC and told him "I want to do these bastards". He said, "OK, I'll see what we can do".'[8]

And so it began.

Townsend is engaged by a small solicitors' firm in north London called Guney, Clark and Ryan (GCR) and works regularly at the High Court. GCR doesn't usually take high-publicity human rights cases. It is a small law firm specializing in criminal and family law, with an office next to a Turkish restaurant. Townsend persuaded

GCR to take up the blacklisting cases on a no-win no-fee basis. This was in the summer of 2009 when the unions were just starting to engage with Employment Tribunals.

Sean Curran, a partner at GCR, said:

> ❝This is the type of case that all lawyers dream of working on – a case where ordinary people have been trampled on by those in positions of power and privilege and one where the justice system appears to provide the means to redress the balance.❞

The GCR case to the High Court is based around the legal notion of an unlawful conspiracy, the very thing for which the Shrewsbury pickets were sent to prison. Conspiracy comes into play when a group of people (or companies) participate in a joint venture to carry out an illegal act. By actively participating in the preparation and execution of the legal breach, all of the conspirators become equally responsible, regardless of whether they personally carry out the unlawful act.

The groundbreaking GCR case first conceived by JC Townsend argues that The Consulting Association was an unlawful conspiracy. Ian Kerr's prosecution for breaches of the Data Protection Act and the successful tribunal cases won by Unite demonstrate the illegality. The covert nature of the Association's blacklist, the invoices and blacklist files demonstrate the conspiracy. The argument for a joint venture is strengthened by the Association's constitution which describes the body as an 'unincorporated trade association' owned and controlled by the member companies. If the court agreed with the 'unlawful means conspiracy' argument, it would mean that every one of the companies that subscribed to TCA would be equally liable for the actions of all the other companies.

Initially only a handful of blacklisted workers contacted GCR. Among the first were two electricians: John Spillane and Jim Lafferty. Spillane was blacklisted because of his union activity on various sites in London, while safety rep Lafferty, from County Roscommon in Ireland, had been a union activist on major sites including the NatWest Tower, Broadgate and the Royal Opera House. He was an active member of the JSC and a regular contributor to *Builders Crack*. Lafferty and Spillane had held meetings with GCR and spoke about the High Court claim at the BSG founding meeting back in 2009, persuading those present to put their trust in the Irish law firm. Lafferty was to play the lead role of liaison between the blacklisted workers and GCR until his untimely death in December 2010. His 12-page blacklist file recorded his contribution fighting for working people but he is another of the blacklisted workers who never saw justice.

One difference between the Tribunal system and the High Court is in legal costs. At a Tribunal, so long as there is a case to answer, even if the claimant loses, they do not have to pay the other side's costs. Only in exceptional circumstances, where the Tribunal considers a case to be a completely 'vexatious' mudslinging exercise or if the judge at a pre-hearing stage states the claim has no reasonable prospect of success, will there be costs awarded against an unsuccessful claimant. Without such a rule, the disparity of resources between a worker and their employer would allow companies to hire very expensive lawyers and simply scare the workers into dropping their claims.

In the High Court it is different. Whichever side loses pays the other side's legal costs. Without funding, the High Court claim was going nowhere. The only option is a no-win no-fee agreement funded by an insurance policy to cover the costs should the case lose. This is not the kind of insurance you can get by ringing a call centre for a quote and a free Meerkat toy. Many insurance brokers offer such policies to cover minor legal claims but a High Court case for unlawful conspiracy relating to blacklisting was unheard of. To convince the money people, a QC needs to write a legal opinion about the prospect of success. Within weeks, GCR had managed to convince one of the superstars of the British legal system, Hugh Tomlinson, of Matrix Chambers, to act as lead counsel. Tomlinson literally wrote the book on human rights law and is QC of choice for celebrities in need of a super injunction. He is a founder member of Hacked Off and was the silk that represented victims of the *News of the World* phone-hacking scandal that led to the Leveson inquiry. Tomlinson not only agreed to represent the blacklisted workers, but he also agreed to do it on a no-win no-fee basis. This was a real coup and soon Tomlinson and Townsend had produced a written legal opinion on the likely success of the High Court claim.

The crunch moment came in March 2012 when the claim was lodged at the High Court and there was still no insurance scheme in place. Inevitably the claimants were worried but Sean Curran had invested his law firm's time and money on the High Court case when no-one else was even talking about such actions and was now asking people to trust him. After a nerve-wracking few weeks, the Lloyds insurance syndicate QBE agreed to provide insurance cover for the High Court case. There was a huge sigh of relief from everyone involved in the legal action.

In the preparation for the High Court claim, Curran and Liam Dunne visited the home of Ian and Mary Kerr. Liam Dunne recalls:

❝ It was hard to reconcile the fact that these warm and welcoming people were involved in a practice that we knew had affected so many decent hard-working men in such an egregious manner. It seems they were disengaged from the reality of the damage their actions had caused to people's lives. They became tools to be used by the companies in their campaign to eliminate any dissenting voices.❞[10]

After GCR agreed not to make him party to any proceedings, Ian Kerr handed over a number of documents that had not been seized during the ICO raid and the lawyers assisted in drawing up a draft witness statement. This witness statement had not been put in the public domain before publication of this book.

After meeting with Kerr on a number of occasions it became clear to GCR that Sir Robert McAlpine Limited was the key company in the entire blacklisting conspiracy. It was Sir Robert McAlpine Limited that paid for The Consulting Association to be set up and bought the historic blacklist files from the Economic League. Key decisions about Kerr's employment were taken by Cullum McAlpine, as Ian Kerr's witness statement makes clear:

❝ I was always an employee of Consulting Association, as shown by my correspondence with Cullum McAlpine about my salary and a copy of my original employment contract... As part of my employment package I also got life assurance and a car allowance. I have a memo to Cullum McAlpine dated 8 March 1994 on which he has written a handwritten reply querying the expense of the life insurance... as part of my employment package with TCA I was given a Black Mercedes C class which came from the Sir Robert McAlpine fleet.[9][11]

Cullum McAlpine had been the founding chair of the Association, while David Cochrane, head of human resources at Sir Robert McAlpine Limited, was chair at its demise and was responsible for paying the fines and legal costs incurred by Ian Kerr. Invoices also show that Sir Robert McAlpine Ltd spent around £28,000 in the final year of TCA's operation, requesting in excess of 10,000 name checks.

On 20 March 2013, GCR served notice at the High Court against just one defendant, in the case of *Steve Acheson and others v Sir Robert McAlpine Limited*. If the conspiracy claim were successful, it would mean that McAlpine would be held responsible for the actions of all of the companies involved, even though none of them were in court. From the claimants' point of view it did not matter if one or all of the companies were in the dock – the evidence would be aired and, if successful, any award would be the same.

Sir Robert McAlpine Limited filed its defence in July 2013. The company admitted that it was a member of The Consulting Association but denied that there was a conspiracy intended to cause injury to the claimants. The defence then named 34 other companies that, if the ruling went against McAlpine, would be equally liable for any damages. The 34 companies were all subsidiaries of the eight construction giants: AMEC, Balfour Beatty, BAM, Carillion, Costain, Laing O'Rourke, Kier, Skanska and Vinci (including Taylor Woodrow).[12] Within weeks, the eight companies all found themselves as co-defendants in the High Court and, due to the name of their joint solicitors, quickly became known as the MacFarlanes defendants.

But the GCR claim was not to be the only one brought to the High Court. In mid-2012, the GMB held a meeting in Swindon Hospital among a group of low-paid ancillary workers. The workforce, mainly from Goa in India, were complaining about the attitude of their supervisors. When the workers joined the union and complained about alleged racist bullying, a number of them found themselves disciplined by the employer. GMB organized public meetings as well as a huge march through the middle of Swindon in support of the Goan workers, and took 21 days of official strike action involving over 130 members – around 3,000 strike days in total, amounting to more than one per cent of all days lost to industrial action in 2012.[13] In a massive industrial victory, every manager and supervisor accused of racist bullying was removed from the contract and the union later won some Employment Tribunals for indirect race discrimination and union victimization. All of the GMB strikers were employed by Carillion, which built and runs Swindon Hospital under the Private Finance Initiative. The lead negotiator for the company during the dispute was Liz Keates, who was named in documents disclosed at the Dave Smith tribunal as a TCA main contact. The files show that Carillion actually blacklisted workers during the construction of Swindon Hospital.[14]

In June 2012, GMB published a report on blacklisting by Carillion as part of the Swindon Hospital dispute. A year later, GMB national secretary Justin Bowden announced to 500 delegates at the union's annual conference that a High Court claim had been started against Carillion for conspiracy and, crucially, also for defamation. GMB member Dirk McPherson, a welder from Redhill in Kent, was blacklisted after complaining about the lack of safety equipment at the Pfizer site.

> If me and five other workers have started on a job where there is, say, 18 months' work ahead of you, all of a sudden after two weeks I am no longer required but the other welders are still there. Or, conversely, you phone up for a job on the Wednesday, they say "can you start Monday?" then all of a sudden on the Friday you get a phone call saying the job's been cancelled. When you apply for jobs with welders that are perhaps not as good as you and they are earning money and you are sitting indoors skint, it is not a great deal of fun.

The GMB research discovered ever more of their members who were blacklisted, including national officer Martin Smith, who is political director for the union fundraising organization, the Workers Beer Company.

Class action

Finally, on 29 November 2013, more than four-and-a-half years after the ICO raid, blacklisted workers made it to the Royal Courts of Justice. There were not enough seats for all the lawyers and nearly 50 blacklisted workers crammed into Court 65, with some forced to sit in the aisles of the raised public gallery. As Unite and UCATT had both joined the claim the week before, there were 30 lawyers in wigs and robes with a plethora of QCs in court to hear Hugh Tomlinson describe The Consulting Association as 'a blacklist for trade-union and political activities' and accuse the firms of being involved in 'a conspiracy to injure'.

Up until this point, every blacklisting case had involved individual workers seeking redress for specific incidences of dismissal or victimization. But the superstars of the legal profession – Hugh Tomlinson QC (Guney Clark & Ryan solicitors), John Hendy QC (Unite), Guy Vassall-Adams (GMB) and Matthew Nicklin (UCATT) – asked the Court to agree a Group Litigation Order (GLO), equivalent to a US class action. This was to allow all of the cases for the blacklisted workers to be heard together against all of the blacklisting companies. On 10 July 2014, Senior Master Leslie granted the GLO: effectively putting the entire construction industry on trial for blacklisting.

Leading BSG activist Stephen Kennedy – a blacklisted electrician from Johnstone, Renfrewshire – was in court to see the proceedings and summed up his thoughts:

> ❝ After five years of pursuing the beast, we have witnessed the first harpoon landed. I wish more of our number could have lived to see this seed of justice. But blacklisting is a malady not yet cured or beaten.❞[15]

The battle lines were drawn and plain to see. The companies' strategy was to deny everything and at all costs try to avoid their directors being cross-examined in the witness box. Meanwhile the blacklisted workers' lawyers tried to wring everything they could from the defendants. The months that followed were a combination of behind-the-scenes legal negotiations and brief bi-monthly appearances in court. The MacFarlanes defendants used every legal loophole possible to prevent or delay the exposure of the dirty

Hugh Tomlinson QC (in middle with scarf) with Guney Clark & Ryan legal team and Blacklist Support Group outside the High Court

secret the construction industry had tried to keep hidden for the previous half a century.

Admissions of guilt

When the blacklist was first discovered, the firms had robustly denied any wrongdoing. A variety of justifications had been put forward by the companies to excuse their role in blacklisting. Harvey Francis of Skanska claimed that the company used The Consulting Association to improve safety on site. Others claimed that the purpose of blacklisting was to combat theft or vandalism. On the entire blacklist database there are no more than 30 files that relate to theft or fraud: less than one per cent of the files. The overwhelming reason why people were added to the blacklist and denied work was because of their trade-union activities or leftwing political outlook. It is not against the law to be a member of a trade union or to hold political views that are left of centre.

Balfour Beatty even attempted to defend its use of The Consulting Association. Chief operating officer Andrew McNaughton expressed regret, emphasized that it never sought to suppress lawful union activity and enjoyed relations with unions. However:

❛The reason for our involvement with the TCA was to seek to mitigate and prevent any disruption caused on our construction sites throughout the UK by unofficial and unjustified industrial action. Unfortunately, this type of unofficial industrial action was prevalent for decades and was a symptom of an extremely difficult and turbulent industrial-relations climate which, in turn, had an adverse effect not only on our company but on our industry, our customers and the country as a whole.❜[16]

Witness statements drawn up for use in the High Court continued to justify the blacklisting operation. Trevor Watcham, former TCA chair from Balfour Beatty, was in his youth a member of the NUM, organizing flying pickets of power stations during the 1970s. He was prepared in 2016 to claim:

❛Into the 1990s there was a very small cabal of individuals with a disproportionate influence looking to come onto construction sites with the deliberate and sole intention of causing disruption... There were a small number of political individuals – almost always leftwing – very much intent on disrupting projects with a view to seeking increases in pay (mostly bonuses or a reduction in hours) outside the working-rule agreements or in an attempt to get the project abandoned. My understanding was that such individuals adhered to the Trotskyite theory to cause as much disruption as possible to create another national strike. They believed they could bring down the government and replace it with a popular revolution under workers' control.❜[17]

Dudley Barrett, the main TCA contact from Costain, was prepared to tell the High Court about:

❛concerns within the construction industry, which I shared at the time, that a number of politically motivated individuals saw construction projects (and other commercial activities) as appropriate means for placing pressure upon employers... one objective of such individuals (especially from the extreme far left) was to cause such widespread disruption that it would enable workers' councils to bring about a change of government... it was therefore imperative that the construction companies had some way of ensuring that anyone who was thought to pose a risk of causing disruption, was not given the opportunity to do so.[9][18]

These are the actual words, approved by their lawyers, of the people who ran the building industry's blacklist.

After two years of procedural wrangling and behind-the-scenes negotiations, everything was still geared towards a 9 May 2016 scheduled start date for the trial. October 2015 was supposed to be just another hearing among many. This time only a handful of blacklisted workers even bothered attending because prior expectation was that the entire day would be taken up with a technical dispute over expert witnesses and timetabling. And then, out of the blue: BANG. In an almost throwaway remark by Nourse QC, acting on behalf of the MacFarlanes defendants, there was a breakthrough when the firms admitted that The Consulting Association 'infringed workers' rights to confidentiality, privacy, reputation and latterly data protection'. The companies offered an unreserved apology for their involvement in TCA, for any adverse employment consequences and for the distress and anxiety caused to workers and their families.[19]

This was an admission of liability for the unlawful use of the private details of unions' members and that union members had also been defamed. Accepting defamation was a tactical move by the firms to deflect the spotlight away from unlawful conspiracy. What is very noticeable was the deliberate avoidance of the word 'blacklisting' in any of the employers' statements. However, admitting liability for defamation and misuse of personal data also meant that in order to assess any awards for damages the companies still had to answer to how and why they had defamed people. They could no longer hide behind any non-disclosure rules. The firms had admitted their guilt; the only real question now was what a victory for blacklisted workers would actually look like.

Pay Up

The British legal system administers the law, not justice. A guilty verdict in a civil trial at the High Court will not see anyone sent to prison. The outcome is financial: it is all about the money. It was surely a coincidence then that, back in 2013, only days after the High Court granted the Group Litigation Order, Balfour Beatty, Carillion, Costain, Kier, Laing O'Rourke, Sir Robert McAlpine, Skanska and Vinci launched their own compensation scheme. It was also coincidental that the eight companies were the same eight MacFarlanes defendants in the blacklisting trial. The Construction Workers Compensation Scheme (TCWCS) was decided upon as a suitably innocuous name for the scheme which again avoided mentioning the term blacklisting. The firms employed John Taylor, the recently retired former chief executive of ACAS, as a figurehead. Their compensation scheme was devised by Richard Slaven, a partner at Pinsent Mason solicitors (which had previously specialized in representing bankers and the finance sector).

If they thought that their scheme would be greeted with applause, they were sorely mistaken. Dave Smith, Steve Kelly and Roy Bentham of the BSG met with representatives of the Construction Workers Compensation Scheme at the offices of Pinsent Mason in the City of London. The meeting finished abruptly once the initial draft proposals for the scheme revealed that the vast majority of those on the blacklist were likely to be offered a one-off payment of £1,000 without an apology but with the proviso that all legal claims were dropped. The BSG delegation walked out and issued a statement saying:

> These are not proposals designed for genuine negotiations. It is a piss-take masquerading as a publicity stunt. We were not prepared to continue with the charade. They can shove their grand right up their profit margin.[20]

Then GMB general secretary, Paul Kenny, declared contemptuously:

> A few pounds would not buy off the bloodstains of the victims. Throwing a few quid on the table is not the answer here. We need that public inquiry and justice.

The Select Committee meanwhile produced a second interim report which argued that the firms should fully compensate the workers they blacklisted and that the level of compensation should be set not by the companies themselves but jointly with the trade unions.[21] Lawyers for the claimant groups presented Pinsent Mason with a detailed 10-page letter which highlighted serious inadequacies and presented a series of proposals that they considered were needed to make the scheme acceptable and therefore allow for a jointly supported scheme in line with the Select Committee recommendations. These included some kind of positive-action scheme to allow blacklisted workers back into employment, with compensation levels to be set at a level to compensate for human rights violations. Ian Davidson and the Select Committee were in constant contact with the scheme in order to encourage a collaborative approach.

Instead, when the scheme was launched, on 4 July 2014, it was on a unilateral basis, without the support of any of the trade unions, of the BSG or of the lawyers working on their behalf. But it would have been difficult to guess that from the public-relations blitz that announced the arrival of the scheme, which saw it trumpeted on the BBC flagship morning news programmes. The spin put on the launch and a letter sent to every single MP in parliament gave the impression that the unions jointly supported the scheme. So much so, that a group of leftwing MPs putting down an Early Day Motion in the House of Commons welcomed the development and pointed out that 'the scheme has been agreed between trades unions and employers'.[22]

Only a few days later, the Select Committee called Nick Pollard, chief executive of Balfour Beatty, Andrew Ridley-Barker, managing director of Vinci Construction, and Callum Tuckett, finance and commercial director at Laing O'Rourke, plus Richard Slaven from Pinsent Mason and Richard Jukes from the PR company Grayling to explain why the firms had completely ignored the recommendations of the MPs' interim report.

Conservative MP Simon Reevell condemned the letter sent by the industry's hired spin doctor Richard Jukes, which he said was 'intended to mislead every Member of Parliament' by claiming falsely that unions and representatives of blacklisted workers supported the scheme. Labour MP Jim McGovern told the industry bosses bluntly that they had 'misled this committee and misled

Parliament', while Ian Davidson accused the scheme of being 'purely damage limitation' rather than a genuine desire to show 'repentance'.

The levels of compensation being offered by the scheme were also forensically taken apart by MPs and Richard Slaven, partner at law firm Pinsent Mason, was forced to admit that he could not quote a single authority to justify the pitifully low figures being offered by blacklisting firms that MPs identified as having a combined annual turnover of £34 billion.

Despite grovelling apologies to MPs and promises to go back and make amendments to the scheme, no changes were made, though there were slightly elevated levels of financial award. The scheme involved a Fast Track option offering between £4,000 and £20,000 based purely on the information written on the files (which were considered to be a true record of events). The £4,000 offer was 20 per cent less than the £5,000 minimum compensation provided under the 2010 Blacklisting Regulations, which were so roundly criticized for being inadequate. Alternatively, a Full Review option requiring a written submission detailing loss of earnings, offered a maximum award of £100,000. A retired judge was to make the final decision on the level of compensation without any hearing.

The employers' scheme sent letters or emails to blacklisted workers informing them of the package being offered. The response of Jack Fawbert, blacklisted joiner, was typical.

> £4,000 from you criminals for decades of human-rights abuses that forced many decent people including myself out of the industry, leading to me suffering years of deprivation to build another career in education, seeing my kids on free school meals and the family nearly splitting up. And for what? For simply representing my fellow workers on a building site as a UCATT shop steward and legally appointed safety rep. This PR stunt makes no admission of guilt or gives me an apology for what you did to me and my family.[23]

Contemporary blacklisting

The most glaring omission from the firms' compensation scheme was any offer of jobs. Pound notes and crocodile tears mean nothing until blacklisted workers can again provide for their families and stand alongside their fellow trade unionists on major construction projects. But the transnationals now rigidly stick to their denial that any blacklisting has occurred after 2009 and trot out their much-repeated mantra that there was no evidence to back up the claims that the unlawful practice is still ongoing. Therefore they claim that they do not need to pay any compensation post-2009 or make any provision to eliminate contemporary blacklisting.

But even with the most cursory inspection of projects run by the very same companies who have admitted their guilt in the High Court, it would appear that blacklisting remains rampant. MPs on the Select Committee investigation concluded that blacklisting was in operation on the Olympics and Crossrail projects. And a new younger generation of rank-and-file construction activists in London have found themselves repeatedly dismissed, even though they are supposedly self-employed and working through employment agencies. At the Fawley Oil Refinery near Southampton, unions have protested after prominent union activists were denied work on the projects, while in Teesside, well-known activist Tony Seaman, who sits on the Unite national industrial sector committee, has won out-of-court settlements over current blacklisting.

On Merseyside, BSG held a series of meetings with Liverpool City Council and clients of major projects in the city. But despite assurances that, if CVs were supplied, blacklisted union members would be engaged, nothing concrete has materialized. Both Alder Hey and Royal Liverpool hospitals have seen a series of major protests against blacklisting of workers by Laing O'Rourke[24] and Carillion[25] respectively. Carillion are also redeveloping the Anfield stadium and Roy Bentham held meetings with Liverpool Football Club about the ongoing blacklisting but the hollow promises again failed to result in employment for prominent union activists. In response, BSG organized a protest during the televised Premier League match against Manchester United that attracted support from the Hillsborough Justice Campaign, the Orgreave Truth & Justice campaign and jailed Shrewsbury picket Arthur Murray.[26]

Blacklisted electrician Brian Horne told the authors about his experiences trying to find work in 2016:

❛Blacklisting is still going on; I have got personal experience of it. I phoned up for a job and was told that there wasn't one. But I knew there was, so I got a couple of mates to ring up the same people. A couple of minutes later they called me and said they've got the start on Monday!❜27

The fact that blacklisting is still ongoing is virtually universally accepted by all trade unionists in the UK construction sector. Gail Cartmail of Unite commented:

❛Blacklisting hasn't gone away, it is a contemporary issue. The major contractors are reliant mostly on agencies as labour suppliers and we know that those agencies are vetting our members.❜

Alan Wainwright, the man who blew the whistle originally and as a result ended up with his own blacklist file, is currently preparing Employment Tribunal claims against 35 companies. The former Haden Young labour manager turned whistleblower said: 'These new claims arise because the companies involved continue to victimize me. I should not have to go through all this again.'28 Nor, of course, should anyone else.

The NRB ('Not Required Back') system is an open blacklist in the North Sea, while there is strong anecdotal evidence that similar practices operate in other sectors such as retail, the railways, airlines and banking. Organizations such as Compassion in Care, Whistleblowers UK and Public Concern at Work have repeatedly highlighted the plight of experienced and highly qualified NHS whistleblowers who have found it immensely difficult to find employment in the Health Service after exposing patient-safety scandals.

In February 2015, Sir Robert Francis published his Freedom To Speak Up review, which looked at how to create an honest reporting culture in the NHS. In his findings Francis wrote:

❛The message from staff who have suffered as a result of raising concerns has been loud and clear. I heard shocking accounts of the way some people have been treated when they have been brave enough to speak up. I witnessed at first hand their distress and the strain on them and, in some cases, their families. I heard about the pressures it can place on other members of a team, on managers, and in some cases the person about whom a concern is raised. Though rare, I was told of suicidal thoughts and even suicide attempts.❜[29]

Even those at the centre of the blacklisting operations do not think that blacklisting has stopped. Stan Hardy, former director general of the Economic League, told MPs:

❛The Consulting Association lasted for the best part of 20 years as a stand-alone but way-below-the-parapet operation. It was not recorded and was not registered as a company; it was operating as what I think is described as an un-incorporated association. The League was a limited company, up front, easily identified and publicly known about; The Consulting Association was way below the parapet. Does that not beg the question that there may be more than one somewhere?❜[30]

Yet despite all the indications of the practice being widespread across British industry, the regulators and the police seem unable or disinclined to carry out any inquiry. Some would like to present The Consulting Association as an aberration, exclusively restricted to a few bad apples in the UK construction industry. But blacklisting is a global phenomenon that has been going on for centuries. Wherever working people organize against big business, targeting of activists in an attempt to behead the movement is to be found. Stan Hardy told MPs:

❛Blacklisting has operated since the Pyramids were being built... I do not think there is an HR professional in the world who does not have a filing cabinet with a drawer in it that is marked "do not re-employ".❜[31]

Bertolt Brecht, Paul Robeson, Pete Seeger, Harry Belafonte and Dalton Trumbo are all superstars of the arts world whose careers suffered for their campaigning. McCarthyism during the 1950s resulted in harassment by the state and blacklisting by employers for those with 'un-American' attitudes, which often meant little more than being a left-of-centre trade unionist. The Hollywood blacklist gained global notoriety but thousands of local union activists in schools, engineering and car plants suffered too.[32] In the US today, evidence has emerged of police using covert spies to infiltrate the Black Lives Matter protests and campaigns against fracking.[33]

In 2011, Mexican migrant workers were reportedly added to a Canadian government blacklist after they joined a union.[34] In 2012 it was alleged that Swedish furniture company IKEA had used a security company to pay for access to police intelligence files in France in order to spy on customers and staff.[35]

In 2014, companies in Jakarta producing World Cup footballs for Adidas sacked and circulated a blacklist of 300 workers who supported union demands for better wages.[36] In New Orleans, in the US, campaigners with the National Guest Workers Alliance and the Workers Center for Radical Justice have filed federal complaints against employers for blacklisting mainly Hispanic guest workers who joined a trade union.[37] Denmark's DR1 TV exposed blacklisting by the Atlanco Rimec employment agency, with offices in the UK and Ireland supplying staff to the construction industry and the NHS.[38] The UK head office of the labour supplier was occupied by the BSG in 2014.

At the same time as the blacklist scandal was unfolding in the UK, Australia saw high-profile criminal trials brought against Construction, Forestry, Mining and Energy Union (CFMEU) organizers Michael Greenfield and Andrew Sutherland[39] and rank-and-file activists Ark Tribe[40] and Bob Carnegie[41] because of union meetings on building sites. All charges were subsequently dropped or defeated in court.

A police taskforce called 'Hercules' was specifically established to investigate and bring criminal charges for matters identified by the Royal Commission into trade unions under the former Justice of the Australian High Court Dyson Heydon. CFMEU organizer and former Rugby League international Johnny Lomax was charged with blackmail following a complaint by a contractor that negotiations leading to an agreement with the union amounted to coercion, as he felt that not signing would have meant his company was less likely to win contracts on unionized projects.

In October 2015, the charge was dropped after prosecutors

offered no evidence.[42] But in December 2015 police raided the offices of the CFMEU in Victoria, seizing computers and documents as evidence against John Setka and Shaun Reardon (the union's state secretary and deputy) in a new blackmail charge. Dave Noonan, CFMEU national construction secretary, criticized the police, saying the arrests were 'designed to create maximum political damage to the union with little regard for their families. The arrests were conducted in front of both families and reek of overkill.'[43] The criminalization of union officials for applying perfectly normal pressure during negotiations would virtually make collective bargaining illegal, as well as signalling open season for the police to target unions. The fall-out would affect not just construction but the entire Australian trade-union movement. Given the globalized nature of industrial relations, the attacks on the CFMEU could have worldwide significance.

The list goes on and on. The Consulting Association may have been an extreme example but, far from being a rarity, victimization and blacklisting of workers prepared to stand up for their rights is used daily in the war between labour and capital.

Rather than passively waiting for their lawyers or those in authority to save the day, BSG repeatedly used direct action to expose the blacklisting scandal. Occupations took place at the offices of Sir Robert McAlpine and Laing O'Rourke.

Throughout all the protests, occupations and walkouts over a seven-year campaign not a single worker had been arrested. That was until February 2015, when BSG blockaded all four lanes of traffic outside the Park Lane Hilton while the Construction News Awards were taking place inside. Dave Smith was arrested almost immediately he walked into the road. Eighteen months later, despite a 'right to protest' defence ably supplied *pro bono* by JC Townsend and Liam Dunne, and with police witnesses admitting that they were given intelligence about the protesters before the event took place, Smith was found guilty of unlawful obstruction of the highway. As Smith observes: 'Now the only two people to have gone in the dock related to blacklisting are me and Ian Kerr.'

Just days before the High Court trial was scheduled to start, the ultra-modern headquarters of Skanska were targeted, with blacklisted workers unfurling banners and chanting 'gizza job' until removed by the police. As whole sections of the HQ were evacuated by security, blacklisted bricklayer Paul Crimmins told the employees via a mobile PA: 'People from Skanska should hang their heads in shame, hopefully they are gonna get done in court, not just with an apology but hopefully we'll see some of these bastards in prison.'[44]

Part 36

There is a mechanism within the legal rules for British civil cases called a 'Part 36 offer'. This was introduced by Lord Woolf, Master of the Rolls and Lord Chief Justice under John Major and Tony Blair. The purported intention is to save all the litigants and the legal system time, money and stress. As the only outcome in a civil trial is a financial award, the Part 36 offer allows a defendant to make an offer to the claimant, effectively to buy themselves out of a trial. Any offer is always 'without prejudice', which means they are subject to a legal restriction and are not allowed to be discussed publicly. So in the courtroom the lawyers are still arguing their corners but behind the scenes there are offers and counter offers taking place that no-one is allowed to talk about. Litigation, as with major industrial disputes, is all about who blinks first. At Christmas 2015, the McFarlanes defendants sent Part 36 offers to every claimant in the High Court case.

Part 36 offers come with a whole bunch of legal implications. The defendants (in this case the blacklisting firms) make different individual offers that individual claimants are invited to accept or reject. This is where it gets technical. If someone rejects the offer and the case ends up going to court, even if you win the case, if a claimant is awarded less by the judge than they were offered, then the claimant is liable to pay the other side's legal costs.

So if someone rejects £30,000 but then at full trial is awarded £25,000, they will still have to pay the firm's legal costs – even though they have won! The legal costs in the blacklisting litigation are extortionate and no-one could afford to pay them on their own. It is the threat of having to pay the other side's legal costs that make this so vital. Blacklisted workers could end up winning their claims in court but being forced to pay out more to the other side in legal costs than they get awarded by the judge.

In theory, no-one is forced to accept a Part 36 offer. Anyone has the right to carry on and have their day in court. In practice, it becomes all about whether the lawyers think that the Part 36 offer is close to what you would be likely to win in court. If it is more than you are likely to win in court, then the lawyers are duty bound to advise you to accept the offer. If you ignore the lawyer's advice, then you are on your own – and you will be representing yourself in the High Court against the most expensive QCs in the profession.

If someone is a multi-millionaire, they can go to court regardless because they will be able to afford the legal costs either way. If you are a retired ex-construction worker who has been blacklisted and therefore is on a limited pension, the options are more limited. Part 36 offers sound very reasonable in principle but the effect is to neuter any attempt to force rich people into the dock. It was designed to protect litigants from themselves but it was also giving control to those with the deepest pockets to ensure they could buy their way out of appearing in court.

Christmas 2015 proved a pivotal moment in the case. The pressure from companies for claimants to accept the Part 36 settlements had increased and there was a fear that the action could collapse. It caused anger and frustration among the blacklisted workers. With more than 700 claimants, there was always going to be a divergence of opinions and approaches. Some were happy to have got some money back after years of suffering, while others would give it all up to see the companies in the dock. As blacklisted offshore worker Lee Fowler explained, 'This has never been about the money for me.'[45]

The difficulty was that the decision was not really in the hands of the individual claimant because all the cases were funded

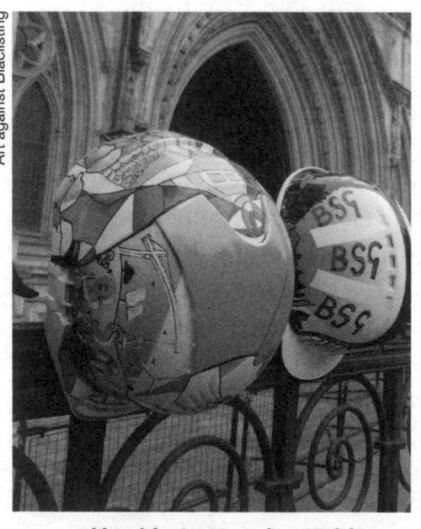

Art against Blacklisting

Hard hat artwork outside the High Court

by someone else. They were funded either by the trade-union funds or, in the case of the GCR claimants, by a no-win no-fee insurance policy. To reject the Part 36 offer would mean they were taking a huge gamble on winning in the dock and the insurance rules precluded such a gamble.

Art Against Blacklisting response to the Part 36 offers.

When they make a Hollywood feature film about blacklisting, this will be the part where old friends and comrades who have stood shoulder to shoulder through many years of battle start to fall out and question one another. For some, the financial offers were life changing, for others this was like having a gun put to their head, virtually forcing them to withdraw almost within touching distance of the trial.

Lawyers were giving people advice to accept the Part 36 offers. This was especially difficult for the claimants represented by Guney, Clark and Ryan (GCR), whose offers were noticeably lower than the union-backed cases. This was almost certainly because the firms knew that QBE, GCR's insurance company, would not be prepared to take any sort of risk. Grown men, big hard men who are used to a hard day's work, were in tears. It looked like all the cases would collapse and the blacklisting trial would go out with a whimper rather than a bang. There were sleepless nights all round and hour after hour of verbal abuse for those lawyers who had to make the phone calls.

At this point, good old-fashioned union solidarity kicked in. By an absolute fluke of timing, the deadline for when these decisions on whether to accept the offers needed to be made was the very same week that the Unite national industrial sector committee (NISC) for construction was due to meet in its Holborn offices. The chair of the committee is blacklisted electrician Billy Spiers and several blacklisted workers are also members. Gail Cartmail and Howard Beckett both attended the meeting and the NISC voted unanimously for Unite to offer financial support to the

GCR claimants. Frank Morris and Dave Smith then met privately with Unite general secretary Len McCluskey. That evening, BSG held simultaneous mass consultation meetings with blacklisted workers in London, Glasgow, Liverpool and Bristol joined together via teleconference. It was an explosion of working-class anger in the raw. It took a lot of bottle when Liam Dunne from GCR attended the London meeting to explain the legal situation in a simmering atmosphere of repressed violence. The next day, Unite agreed to underwrite GCR for any costs over and above what its insurance firm would cover. It is hard to put a number on this, but if everything had gone wrong that could be have been as much as £6 million. That was a big ask and Unite stepped in. They were the only game in town with the resources and the logistical muscle to pull it off. It was solidarity but it also allowed Unite's more militant negotiating stance to come to the fore.

Disclosure of documents

The blacklisting companies hoped to quash the entire group litigation around Christmas 2015 and keep a lid on their dirty secrets; but they failed. And, whether they liked it or not, the tide had started to turn. The firms had been forced to admit their guilt but their lawyers still fought tooth and nail to keep the sordid conspiracy secret. Every attempt to force the firms to divulge evidence or disclose documents to the court was resisted but, after years of bravado, the firms were now clearly on the back foot.

A major ongoing legal argument throughout the group litigation was over the disclosure of evidence. Any trial requires both the defendants and the claimants to exchange documentation that might be used in evidence. Holding back potential evidence is seen as a serious issue. But that did not stop the firms arguing that they should not have to disclose evidence from over such a long period, claiming that searching for archived emails and historic electronic documents would require the need for the specialist computer company, Epiq. Their costs alone were 'conservatively' estimated at £27 million.[46]

Lord Justice Supperstone was having none of it and in July 2015 ordered the companies to search for any relevant documents. After six months of searching, on 26 January 2016, the defendant companies disclosed five small boxes of documentation that they said was their full disclosure of their 50-year involvement in the Economic League and The Consulting Association. The claimants' lawyers were fuming and claimed that the companies, by refusing to carry out in-depth searches of old computer files, had failed to comply with the court order. In legalistic language they accused the firms of deliberately attempting to cover up the secret conspiracy. The firms claimed that forensically searching through old archived computer databases and emails was so costly that it was grossly unfair on them. There was always going to be an argument.

Dinah Rose is a QC with swagger. Rather than the public schoolboy in-jokes and tedium that permeates much high-level litigation in the British courts, when the petite figure of Rose stands up to speak, people listen. And in January 2016, she delivered a master class in how to destroy a corporate defence. Hand on hip, standing sideways on to the public gallery for more dramatic effect, with an absolute air of disdain, she gave the blacklisted workers what they had waited a long time to hear. Rose presented the court with a 'greatest hits' of the misconduct found in the documents that the firms had so far been forced to disclose.

Rose said the evidence showed the firms had 'deliberately both refrained from creating evidence to conceal their activities and destroyed evidence to conceal their activities'. She added: 'The claimants will, in support of their claims in this action, rely on a plea of spoliation. The defendants were responsible for the deliberate destruction, non-provision and concealment of evidence. We can show that the defendants have destroyed documents systematically from the date of the ICO raid onwards in an effort to conceal their guilt.'

Rose also said that companies kept internal lists as well as using the TCA list, not least for the simple expediency that: 'once you have made an enquiry of the Services Group or of The Consulting Association about a Mr X on one occasion and been told that he is a troublemaker, you don't need to make that enquiry again. You can build up your own internal list of undesirables.'

Despite the defendants' lawyers denying the use of internal databases, their own witnesses time and again admitted to compiling such lists. Dudley Barrett from Costain admitted compiling handwritten postcards on several hundred individuals, including their name, address, national insurance numbers and a summary of relevant information including 'alleged political activism'. These were stored in two A4-sized plastic boxes with alphabetical dividers, which were maintained by his then secretary, Gayle Burton.[47]

A letter from Michael Aird sent to Trevor Watcham, dated 10 July 2000 and found on the Balfour Beatty Engineering Services shared drive, read:

> ❝I have enclosed a listing of operatives who we would not re-employ following the recent dispute at our Pfizers project in Kent. Not all of these individuals are troublemakers, some are but most are either poor workers or "sheep" who will follow any cause!❞[48]

Further disclosure found an email from Elaine Gallagher to Gerry Harvey tucked away on Harvey's laptop and dated 16 March 2009. The email includes attached lists of workers recorded as 'Not Required' or Code 11 'do not employ' and an internal data base kept by Balfour Beatty. This was from March 2009, after the ICO raid on the TCA. Included on the internal blacklist were a number of workers with TCA blacklist files, including the Manchester electrician Sean Keaveney.[49]

Harvey now admits: 'In addition to the Consulting Association database, Balfour Kilpatrick had its own HR database which had been in operation since well before I joined.' While claiming that this was to record individuals with poor time-keeping or inadequate qualifications, the HR director went on to name Andrew Alison, Michael Shortall, Colin Trousdale, Danny Regan, Steve Acheson, Graham Bowker, Tony Jones, Sean Keaveney, Robert McKechan and Howard Nolan as workers who appear on the internal database as unsuitable for employment. They are also all blacklisted by TCA for their union activities. There was even a code (Co11) on the internal spreadsheet that recorded feedback from The Consulting Association after a decision had been taken not to employ a worker. Harvey does reassure the court that 'regardless of the Consulting Association checking service neither

I nor my staff would have employed Acheson, Bowker or Jones given their very high profile'.[50] It seems that so long as you didn't use a secret list to deny them work because of their union activity, everything was fine.

Balfour Beatty came in for more criticism over the destruction of documents, when Rose pointed out to the court that the defendants admitted having destroyed all data on the desktop and laptop of Elaine Gallagher, one of the main contacts for The Consulting Association, when she left the employment of BB Engineering Services in April 2013. This was despite three separate instructions to retain potentially relevant documents issued in March 2009, March 2013 and April 2013.

But the main vitriol was saved for Sir Robert McAlpine Limited. Despite a court order, Rose said that only a 'tiny number of documents had been returned from people that we know were key players in the operation of The Consulting Association, and most particularly Sir Robert McAlpine'. Rose pointed the court to a handwritten note made by Ian Kerr on 2 March 2009, immediately after the ICO raid, which records a meeting between Kerr and David Cochrane from McAlpine's.

> At the conclusion of the meeting, Mr Cochrane instructed Mr Kerr to telephone all the member companies of The Consulting Association and to instruct them to destroy data and to stop processing data. Mr Cochrane instructed Mr Kerr: "Ring everyone. Cease trading, close down, we don't exist any more, destroy data, stop processing.

Rose said McAlpine's paid redundancy to Ian and Mary Kerr plus the legal costs and fine after he was prosecuted by the ICO was subsequently channelled secretly through his daughters. Every effort was made to keep Cullum McAlpine's name out of the investigation. Mary Kerr records that Cochrane was less than happy when he discovered that her husband had provided information to GCR. During one phone conversation Cochrane is said to have asked of Kerr: 'How can you call yourself a Christian?'[51]

Despite being the father figure of the entire TCA operation for over 16 years, barely a single letter or email to or from Cullum McAlpine was disclosed. This was because, according to evidence supplied by the company: 'Hard-copy correspondence sent to Cullum McAlpine was destroyed at the time of an office move that commenced in 2011. Hard-copy correspondence sent or received from The Consulting Association by Mr McAlpine was retained in a file by his personal assistant, Pat Crosdale. In 2011, due to an office move, Ms Crosdale disposed of the file.'

Rose witheringly compared the conduct of McAlpine's with its fellow defendants when it came to document disclosure. 'Sir Robert McAlpine, the company at the heart of this entire operation, has disclosed only 252 documents pursuant to the July disclosure order. We see how that contrasts with other companies: Balfour Beatty 2,500; Skanska over 1,000; Laing O'Rourke over 7,000 documents. Less than 2.5 per cent of the disclosure has come from Sir Robert McAlpine. We say that in itself gives rise to real questions about the disclosure exercise.'

Another reason given for the lack of material such as emails is that Cullum McAlpine does not have a laptop!

Cullum McAlpine literally owns the company. He was not just a potential witness in the trial, he was a named defendant. As the trial date approached, witness statements were beginning to be exchanged. When McAlpine gave evidence to the Select Committee he did so sitting next to his lawyer and refusing to answer a number of questions put to him by MPs. For this, and many other reasons, lawyers were looking forward to getting the prime mover behind the blacklist into the dock. The resistance to that was made clear in April 2016, when Sir Robert McAlpine Limited filed its legal defence. It was a month before the case was formally due to start and director Cullum McAlpine signalled that he would not take the stand.

Unite's legal director Howard Beckett was scathing:

> You judge the character of a person if they are prepared to stand up and defend their actions in open court – you don't skulk in the legal twilight protected by a platoon of expensive City lawyers. How can a company run by a man who hides from his victims and the justice system ever hope to convince ministers that they have learnt from the sins of the past and deserve to be involved in public procurement contracts?[52]

Like a matador impaling a wounded bull, Dinah Rose told the packed courtroom in January 2016:

> Cullum McAlpine is a very senior, very important man. It is very important that he should not be seen to have got away with what was clearly a protracted period of unlawful activity which it is plain that Mr Cochrane was seeking to cover up.

The entire purpose of the January 2016 hearing was for the judge to determine whether the pitiful amount of disclosure was adequate or if the court would force them to carry out the costly forensic checks through back-up emails and archived documents. Rose made the position of the blacklisted workers in the case crystal clear:

> It is no doubt true that, where there is a conspiracy, the conspirators are careful not to leave written records of their conspiracy. However, it is also well known that people say things in emails which they would not dream of putting into a letter or a minute or a formal note... The tendency of conspirators is to conceal rather than reveal. Proper disclosure is all the more important in a conspiracy claim.

The defendants contested the damning allegations but Lord Justice Supperstone was just as shocked by the antics of the construction companies as the blacklisted workers sitting in the public gallery. The judge ordered the firms to go back and search for all relevant documentation and emails – whatever it might cost them. He also ordered the firms to pay the claimants' hearing costs, estimated at £100,000. This was just the kind of thing the firms had hoped to avoid by trying to settle the claims at Christmas. It was a good day in court and Dinah Rose had won herself a new fan club.

Vindication

The High Court trial was due to start on Monday 9 May 2016. But with more newly disclosed documents naming and shaming the guilty being released all the time, the behind-the-scenes negotiations over compensation and other clauses within an overall settlement that had been on the backburner for months, suddenly reached boiling point at the end of April.

Mark Ellis, industrial correspondent for the *Mirror*, first broke the story on 29 April that the firms had agreed to pay out millions in compensation, with some workers receiving as much as £200,000.[53] Frantic last-minute negotiations took place, with the start date of the trial having to be delayed as Part 36 offers continued to increase even into May. Talks resulted in a further £4 million for 97 Unite claimants in the final few days alone, bringing the union's total compensation to £10.5 million plus improved non-financial provisions around retraining. Thompson's lead solicitor Richard Arthur commented: 'Whilst no amount of money can bring justice for a life wrecked by blacklisting, this is a landmark victory for the victims and their families.'[54] A large number of workers who, under the original compensation scheme proposals, would only have received £1,000 were paid around 25 times that amount.

UCATT confirmed it had won £8.9 million on behalf of its members. 'This is the largest ever compensation payment won by this union on behalf of our members,' said acting general secretary Brian Rye.[55] GMB secured £5.4 million for its members. Newly elected GMB general secretary Tim Roache said the companies involved had thought that they were above the law: 'Finally they have been held to account in public and at great cost to them financially and reputationally. Government and employers' organizations must never forget this sordid episode.'[56]

Guney Clark & Ryan solicitors, who initiated the entire High Court litigation, won £6.6 million for 78 construction workers. When the settlement was announced, Sean Curran, partner at GCR, was named as 'Lawyer of the week' by the *Sunday Times*.[57]

The multi-million-pound compensation settlement was shared between 771 workers. Pay-outs to individuals ranged from £25,000 to £200,000. Several hundred others accepted money from the companies' compensation scheme.

In addition to the compensation payouts, the firms also had to pay their own and the combined legal costs of four sets of lawyers for the GCR, Unite, GMB and UCATT claimants. The firms have kept very quiet regarding the total costs but estimates in the press place the figure somewhere between a conservative £75 million[58] and a whopping £250 million.[59] Given the fact that, as *Private Eye* pointed out, on some occasions there were '30 wigs in the courtroom' and MacFarlane's claimed that the disclosure order to search for archive computer records alone would cost around £27 million it is likely that the figure is somewhere between the two.

Lucky breaks

Information Commissioner's Office investigator David Clancy talked about 'the stars being aligned' when he led the raid on The Consulting Association – and there is a series of lucky breaks in this story. For instance, the fact that someone at the ICO happened to read the article in the *Guardian* about blacklisting and thought it worth dropping on David Clancy's desk. That when Clancy visited blacklisted Steve Acheson he had that very morning received notification of another job offer turned down. That, when the ICO raided Haden Young, for some reason no-one tipped off Ian Kerr even though they had months to do so. That Kerr returned from holiday and put his files back in the office just three days before the raid. That a staff shortage gave Dave Smith access to the files – and that he then recognized a name that pointed towards police involvement. That the deadline for the Part 36 offers was the same week as Unite's national construction committee met. All these show how often it was a close-run thing whether the scandal would be revealed.

As Mark Thomas, one of those on the blacklist, said: 'The tragedy of this is we were lucky to get this. The tragedy is we have grabbed a snippet of this.'[60] On numerous occasions the government asked corporations if they were behaving themselves, companies said they were, and that was enough to end any prospect of legislation. Even when legislation did make it on to the books it was not enacted. At every stage the benefit of the doubt was given to the companies and the evidence from thousands of blacklisted workers was marginalized. If ever there were a sign that regulations were systematically failing, it is in the case of blacklisting, because it took numerous lucky breaks to get this far. And if, in the future, such cases recur, what chance is there that they will be uncovered?

What does justice look like?

It is Wednesday 11 May 2016 outside the High Court in the Strand,

Shadow Chancellor John McDonnell talking
outside the High Court after the victory.

London, and Shadow Chancellor John McDonnell MP has joined blacklisted workers on the pavement. They were about to go in and hear the formal end to their case. This should be the scene where blacklisted workers spray large bottles of champagne over their supporters while the paparazzi jostle for the best photos. But it didn't quite feel like that.

At 9:30am McDonnell reminds the crowd how he chaired the first-ever meeting of the Blacklist Support Group back in 2009, with fewer than 10 people present – but now we have won a famous victory. McDonnell tells the hundreds of supporters and the world's media and his thousands of Twitter followers that 'compensation is one thing, justice is another'.

Everybody files into the court, which can barely contain the crowd. The hearing gets under way at 10am but, to the consternation of the firms' lawyers and the judge, there is one more attempt to get the firms in the dock. Roy Bentham, a blacklisted carpenter from Liverpool, stands up unrepresented except for the assistance of Helen Steel sitting beside him and makes an application not to be bound by the settlement agreement but to be able to continue to the full trial by representing himself. Bentham knows full well that, even if he is successful, this could mean losing his home and being bankrupted. But he tells the court how, as a Hillsborough survivor, he had waited 27 years for justice with many false hopes in courtrooms over the decades. He explains that he wants to continue to ensure that those responsible for the blacklist are called to account. 'A bit of compensation here and there is not justice.' There is a spontaneous round of applause and cheering from the packed public gallery.

To stony silence Lord Justice Supperstone rules against Bentham and denies him the right to appeal. Responding, Bentham says: 'I look at the episode in this courtroom as a failure of the British justice system.' Gesturing at other blacklisted workers in court, he continues: 'It has been a privilege to stand beside them and this battle will go on. This will be judged in time because this hasn't been justice today.'[61]

In that moment, Bentham epitomizes both the bittersweet feelings of the day and the camaraderie of the entire campaign. One of the pieces of art produced by Art Against Blacklisting is a sculptured hardhat with the words 'justice for blacklisted workers' on it alongside an engraving of dandelion heads. The explanation for this from the BSG Artists in Residence was: 'The construction companies thought they had buried us, but little did they know they had planted seeds.'

It is now 11am and time for the construction firms to make a grovelling apology 'for the distress and anxiety caused to workers and their families'. The six-page agreed statement (see appendix) reads like a history of blacklisting in construction from the 1960s, covering the covert operations of the Services Group within the notorious Economic League until the discovery of the Consulting Association blacklist in 2009. Senior company directors, including Cullum McAlpine, are named in the statement, which ends with an apology from the firms.

Lawyers read out the statement, which says in part: 'Since at least the early 1970s and on the Claimants' case the late 1960s a large number of Britain's leading construction firms were involved in secretly collecting, storing and distributing amongst themselves information about workers who had, or who were applying for, work in the construction industry. The simple purpose of this operation was to create a database of information to vet particular workers in the construction industry. Long-held suspicions that this was taking place were finally confirmed in 2009 when, following the execution of a search warrant, the Information Commissioner (the "ICO") seized various documents, including a list of 3,300 names with additional identifying details and extant record cards for 1,800 individual workers on the list. The Claimants have always characterized this list of names and index cards as a blacklist. As the Defendants are here now publicly to accept, their secret vetting operation should never have happened. It caused harm to the employment opportunities of many workers. The secret nature of the operation meant that those on the database had no way of establishing whether they were included in it, or any chance to challenge the information that was kept and available for dissemination.'

While welcoming the agreed statement for putting on public record the shameful activities that have tarnished the reputation of an entire industry, blacklisted workers remain extremely sceptical about how genuine the apology really is. Even now, the firms cannot bring themselves to use the toxic word 'blacklisting', despite the British Parliament passing the Blacklist Regulations 2010 in order to outlaw the disgraceful practice as a direct response to the Consulting Association scandal.

Howard Beckett insists:

> Unite do not accept that this apology was the end of the matter, we do not accept that the apology was genuine. Anybody who was genuine about wanting to apologize would call it for what it is: a blacklist. And call the people responsible for creating the blacklist to task and dismiss them. It is exactly what the statutory definition is of a blacklist. What is missing is accountability. So Unite calls for a public inquiry and says that those companies who are guilty of this behaviour should not be allowed to involve themselves in public procurement on taxpayers' contracts.[62]

It has taken some 30 minutes and the statement is still being read. As Caldecott QC reaches the very end and is summing up his apology on behalf of the firms, the High Court is suddenly interrupted as 40 workers wearing their iconic BLACKLISTED T-shirts stand up in unison chanting 'No Justice – No Peace'. After several minutes where the judge has lost control of the court, there is an impromptu speech by Dave Smith, who tells Lord Justice Supperstone and the assembled aristocracy of the UK legal profession: 'Under no circumstances do we consider this to be a sincere apology.' Eventually the chants subside. It is now noon and the firms' lawyers have finally managed to conclude the statement. The judge rules that the High Court blacklisting group litigation is concluded. Blacklisted workers, lawyers and supporters go to the pub. And now the champagne corks finally do get popped.

Justin Bowden, GMB National Officer and someone who has been close to the saga for many years, said:

> In the Royal Courts of Justice today, with their heads bowed before Lord Justice Supperstone, Carillion, Sir Robert McAlpine and the biggest construction companies in the land apologized for the part they played in the secret blacklisting of 3,213 building workers and environmental activists. They will hang their heads in shame for the lives they destroyed with their arrogance and contempt. Government and employers' organizations must never forget this sordid episode.[63]

Blacklisted electrician Dick Grey was more cynical about the way the legal system has responded to the blacklisting scandal: 'They are very rich, these people, and if they can just buy their way out of this, that is not justice, is it?'[64]

The Blacklist Support Group press release concurred, adding: 'The statement put on public record the shameful activities that have tarnished the reputation of an entire industry but the only thing the firms are sorry for is getting caught. This is not the end of the matter – this is unfinished business until we get a public inquiry.'

The blacklisting High Court victory was a front-page story in the mainstream media and was covered on the TV and radio news. Within days, Chris Stephens MP, the SNP lead on trade unions, had put down an Early Day Motion in the Westminster parliament welcoming the apology and admission of wrongdoing while calling for 'the government to conduct a full public inquiry into the scandal of blacklisting'.[65] At Holyrood, Neil Findlay MSP submitted a similar Early Day Motion calling for 'the Scottish government, councils, public bodies and the UK government to end the issuing of contracts to the companies responsible until they have proven that they have self-cleansed.'[66]

Since the High Court victory Jeremy Corbyn has made a number of speeches about the need for workers' rights to be a central theme of any future Labour government.

Long before the ICO raid, workers battled against blacklisting, most of the time in small unpublicized skirmishes. Since 2009, the fight has come out of the shadows into the political arena. Blacklisted workers themselves have driven the campaign forward, pulling in support from their trade unions, investigative journalists, lawyers, politicians, artists and musicians along the way. In the political, legal and industrial sphere, the fight for justice is still ongoing and many issues remain unresolved. But what has already been uncovered means that blacklisting is no longer just an industrial-relations issue: it is a human rights conspiracy involving big business, the police and the security services.

For the past half a century union activists in the construction industry have been victimized with impunity. Seven years ago, the firms denied everything and refused to offer anyone even a penny in compensation. Four years ago they were offering the princely sum of £1,000 to most blacklisted workers. In 2016, the blacklisting wretches were forced into a grovelling apology, their dirty laundry has been aired in public and they have been forced to pay out a multi-million-pound settlement, with the potential to cost billions in lost public-sector contracts. Just as importantly, blacklisting has become part of mainstream political dialogue.

Make no mistake, the High Court is a famous victory not just for blacklisted construction workers but for the entire trade-union movement. The lesson is clear: that, even in a period of concerted neoliberal attacks on the organized working class around the world, when the labour movement unites and fully mobilizes against a common enemy, the most powerful vested interests can be defeated. Ex-crane driver and BSG activist Mickey Guyll reflected: 'Not bad for a few aging building workers with a Facebook page.'[66]

The whole anti-blacklisting campaign stands as a beacon of how working people can fight back and win. The abiding memory of the victorious day in the High Court will be the chants of blacklisted workers: 'No Justice! No Peace!'

1 Michael Meacher speech to BSG Conference, March 2013. 2 *Socialist Worker*, 20 November 2013, nin.tl/BLdayofaction 3 Blacklisting in Employment, interim report from the Scottish Affairs Select Committee, p 5, nin.tl/SelCommreport 4 The MPs wrote to all the companies they could find who had subscribed to the Association asking what they were doing to put things right. All the responses can be seen here: nin.tl/corpresponses 5 Witness statement prepared for the High Court seen by the authors. 6 'Blacklisting: Human impact', *Building*, 31 May 2013, nin.tl/BLhumanimpact , accessed 17 June 2014. 7 *Hazards* blacklist blog, 25 November 2014, nin.tl/CIPDblunder 8 Email to the authors. 9 Interview with the authors. 10 Interview with the authors. 11 Ian Kerr's witness statement, prepared for the High Court. 12 Sir Robert McAlpine Ltd, part 20 schedule, 22 July 2013. 13 Labour Disputes – Annual article 2012, Office of National Statistics. 14 nin.tl/GMBswindonwin 15 Interview with the authors. 16 Evidence to the Scottish Affairs Select Committee. 17 Witness statement prepared for the High Court seen by the authors. 18 Witness statement prepared for the High Court seen by the authors. 19 Unions hail blacklisting breakthrough, bbc.co.uk/news/business-34481921 20 *Independent*, 17 November 2013, nin.tl/BLcomp100k 21 SASC, 'Blacklisting in Employment: addressing the crimes of the past, moving towards best practice', 12 March 2014. 22 Early Day Motion 220 Compensation for Blacklisted Workers 7 July 2014. 23 Labour Representation Committee, 8 July 2014, nin.tl/BSGLRCnews 24 *Liverpool Echo*, nin.tl/alderheydemo 25 *Liverpool Echo*, nin.tl/LiverpoolHospital 26 Reel News video, nin.tl/Liverpool3film 27 Interview with the authors. 28 *Guardian*, 21 Apr 2016, nin.tl/whistleblowervictim 29 Freedom To Speak Up, National Archives, Feb 2015, nin.tl/freetospeakup 30 SASC, 'Blacklisting in Employment: oral and written evidence', Apr 2013, p 218. 31 Ibid. 32 Albert Fried, *McCarthysim: The Great American Red Scare*, Oxford University Press, 1997. 33 *Daily Kos*, nin.tl/BLMinfiltrated 34 Littlegate Publishing, 31 March 2013, nin.tl/BLMexicans 35 France 24, 20 Nov 2013, nin.tl/BLIKEA accessed 2 Apr 2014. 36 *Jakarta Post.* 12 Jun 2014. 37 National Guest Worker Alliance, 6 Jun 2014, guestworkeralliance.org 38 DRDK Nyheder, 'Blacklisted for union dealings', 12 May 2014, nin.tl/BLDenmark 39 *Guardian*, 23 Feb 2016, nin.tl/intimidationchargedropped 40 *The Australian*, 24 November 2010, nin.tl/Ausarktribe 41 *The Australian*, 11 February 2013, nin.tl/Carnegiecontempt 42 *Canberra Times*, 1 Oct 2015, nin.tl/Lomaxchargesdropped 43 ABC News, 6 Dec 2015, nin.tl/CFMEUblackmailcharge 44 Reel News video, nin.tl/Skanskaoccupation 45 Interview with the authors. 46 Disclosure report of the MacFarlanes defendants, 3 Dec 2014. 47 Witness statement prepared for the High Court. 48 'Key documents disclosed pursuant to July Disclosure Order' exhibit in the High Court trial. 49 Ibid. 50 Witness statement prepared for the High Court. 51 Witness statement prepared for the High Court. 52 Unite website, 12 Apr 2016, nin.tl/blacklistmastermind 53 *Mirror*, 29 Apr 2016, nin.tl/compensationwin 54 Thompsons Solicitors, nin.tl/tsvictory 55 *Morning Star*, 10 May 2016, nin.tl/blacklistedVictory 56 'Construction companies that blacklisted workers pay £75m', *Financial Times*, 9 May 2016. 57 *Times*, 19 May 2016, nin.tl/SeanCurran 58 *Financial Times*, 9 May 2016, nin.tl/payoutdetail 59 *Morning Star*, 10 May 2016, nin.tl/blacklistedVictory 60 Interview with the authors. 61 *Guardian*, 11 May 2016, nin.tl/firmsapology 62 Unite video, nin.tl/Unitevideo 63 GMB statement, 11 May 2016, nin.tl/GMBstatement 64 Reel News video, nin.tl/trialbeginsfilm 65 parliament.uk/edm/2016-17/47 66 nin.tl/ScottishEDM 66 Interview with the authors.

Appendix I

Full list of names of managers involved in blacklisting as disclosed during litigation and appears on GMB website[1]

Michael Aird (MA) – Balfour Kilpatrick – Glasgow

Kathy Almansoor (KA) – Kier Group – Sandy, Bedfordshire

Dave Aspinall (DA) – Carillion / Crown House – Wolverhampton

Alan Audley (AA) – Vinci – Watford

John Ball (JB) – Carillion / Crown House – Wolverhampton

Ron Barron (RB) – CB & I – Tonbridge, Kent

Valerie Bennison (VB) – Whessoe – Darlington

Ernie Boswell (EB) – Kier Group – Sandy, Bedfordshire

Richard Bull (RB) – HBG Construction (BAM) – Colindale, London

Gayle Burton (GB) – Costain – Maidenhead, Berkshire

Iain Coates (IC) – Emcor – Kew Bridge, Twickenham

David Cochrane (DC) – Sir Robert McAlpine – Hemel Hempstead, Hertfordshire

Ann Cownie (AC) – Balfour Beatty Civil Engineering – Edinburgh

Tony Crowther – AMEC – Knutsford, Cheshire

John Dangerfield (JD) – Balfour Beatty Scottish & Southern – Basingstoke, Hampshire

Lynn Day (LD) – Cleveland Bridge UK – Darlington

John Dickinson (JD) – Skanska – Rickmansworth, Hertfordshire

Frank Duggan (FD) – Carillion / Crown House – Wolverhampton

John Edwards (JE) – Carillion / Crown House – Wolverhampton

Elaine Gallagher (EG) – Balfour Kilpatrick – Glasgow

Kevin Gorman (KG) – Carillion / Crown House – Solihull

Gerry Harvey (GH) – Balfour Kilpatrick – Glasgow

Roy Hay (RH) – Tarmac – Solihull

David Hillman – Sir Robert McAlpine – Birmingham

Keith Horner (KH) – Ballast Wiltshire

Dianne Hughes (DH) – Tarmac / Crown House – Solihull

Geoff Hughes (GH) – Costain – Maidenhead, Berkshire

Greg Ingleton (GI) – Emcor – Kew Bridge, Twickenham

Prue Jackson (PJ) – Haden Young – Watford

Vince James (VJ) – Balfour Beatty Scottish & Southern – Basingstoke, Hampshire

David Jenkins – Costain – Maidenhead, Berkshire

Armar Johnston (AJ) – Balfour Kilpatrick – Livingstone

Liz Keates (LK) – Carillion / Crown House – Wolverhampton

Sheila Knight (SK) – Emcor – Kew Bridge, Twickenham
Ian Leake (IL) – Taylor Woodrow – Watford
Tim Llewellyn (TL) – Walter Llewellyn & Sons Ltd – Eastbourne, East Sussex
Alf Lucas (AL) – Mowlem
Bridget May (BM) – Nuttall – Camberley, Surrey
Cullum McAlpine – Sir Robert McAlpine – Hemel Hempstead, Hertfordshire
Paul McCreath (PM) – HBG Construction (BAM) – Colindale, London
Steve McGuire (SM) – Morgan Est plc – Warrington
Sean Mobbs – Costain – Maidenhead, Berkshire
John Morrison (JM) – Morrison Construction – Edinburgh
Arnold Nestler (AN) – AMEC – Knutsford, Cheshire
Lisa O'Mahoney (LOM) – Laing O'Rourke – Dartford, Kent
Danny O'Sullivan (DOS) – Kier Group – Sandy, Bedfordshire
Sandy Palmer (SP) – Carillion / Crown House – Wolverhampton
Harry Pooley (HP) – Rosser & Russell – Watford
Derek Price – Morgan Ashurst – Stratford upon Avon
Stephen Quant (SQ) – Skanska – Rickmansworth, Hertfordshire
Paul Raby (PR) – Balfour Kilpatrick – Glasgow
Murray Reid (MR) – NG Bailey – Ilkley, West Yorkshire
Roger Robinson (RR) – Carillion / Crown House – Wolverhampton
Sylvia Smith (SS) – Laing O'Rourke – Dartford, Kent
Trevor Spice (TS) – Costain – Maidenhead, Berkshire
Lisa Stevenson (LS) – Shepherd Engineering Services – York
John Stoddart (JS) – SIAS Building Services – Keighley
Alan Swift – Crown House Technologies – Manchester
Pat Swift (PS) – BAM Nuttall – Guildford
Symon Taylor – Costain – Maidenhead, Berkshire
Alan Thorniley (AT) – Vinci – Watford
Brian Tock (BT) – Carillion / Crown House – Solihull
Alex Vaughan – Costain – Maidenhead, Berkshire
Ken Ward (KW) – Costain – Maidenhead, Berkshire
Trevor Watcham (TW) – Balfour Beatty Major Projects – Redhill, Surrey
Steve Wigmore – Crown House Technologies – Solihull
Allison Wilkins – Skanska – Rickmansworth, Hertfordshire
Carolyn Williams (CW) – Haden Young – Watford

1 gmb.org.uk/newsroom/crocodile-tears-blacklist-tour-leeds

Appendix II

The companies that subscribed to The Consulting Association were:

Amec Building Ltd, Amec Construction Ltd, Amec Facilities Ltd, Amec Industrial Division, Amec Process & Energy Ltd, Amey Construction, B Sunley & Sons, Balfour Beatty, Balfour Kilpatrick, Ballast (Wiltshire) PLC, BAM Construction (HBG Construction), BAM Nuttall (Edmund Nuttall Ltd), C B & I, Cleveland Bridge UK Ltd, Costain UK Ltd, Crown House Technologies, Carillion, Tarmac Construction, Diamond M & E Services, Dudley Bower & Co Ltd, Emcor (Drake & Scull), Emcor Rail, G Wimpey Ltd, Haden Young, Kier Ltd, John Mowlem Ltd, Laing O'Rourke (Laing Ltd), Lovell Construction (UK) Ltd, Miller Construction Limited, Morgan Ashurst, Morgan Est, Morrison Construction Group, NG Bailey, Shepherd Engineering Services, SIAS Building Services, Sir Robert McAlpine, Skanska, Kvaerner, Trafalgar House Plc, SPIE (Matthew Hall), Taylor Woodrow Construction Ltd, Turriff Construction Ltd, Tysons Contractors, Walter Llewellyn & Sons Ltd, Whessoe Oil & Gas Willmott Dixon, Vinci PLC (Norwest Holst Group).

Taken from Information Commissioner's Office press release, 6 March 2009.

Appendix III

Acronyms

AEEU: Amalgamated Engineering and Electrical Union (merger between EETPU and AEU) subsequently became part of Amicus, now merged into UNITE

Amicus: predecessor union of UNITE

AUBTW: Amalgamated Union of Building Trade Workers (forerunner of UCATT)

BLF – Builders Labourers' Federation (1960-70s Australian union)

BSG: Blacklist Support Group

CFMEU: Construction, Forestry, Mining and Energy Union (Australia)

CIPD: Chartered Institute of Personnel and Development

COPS – Campaign Opposing Police Surveillance

EETPU: Electrical, Electronic, Telecommunications and Plumbing Union – subsequently became part of UNITE

ETU: Electrical Trades Union (Australia)

GMB: General and Municipal Boilermakers Union – general union representing mainly blue-collar workers in public and private sector

HSE: Health and Safety Executive – government watchdog for enforcing health and safety legislation

ICO: Information Commissioner's Office – independent watchdog for enforcing data legislation

IER: Institute of Employment Rights

JIB: Joint Industry Board (electrical contracting national agreement)

NETCU – National Extremism Tactical Coordination Unit

NPOIU – National Public Order Intelligence Unit

OILC: Offshore Industry Liaison Committee

RMT: Rail, Maritime and Transport union

SASC: Scottish Affairs Select Committee

TCA: The Consulting Association

TGWU: Transport and General Workers Union

UCATT: Union of Construction, Allied Trades & Technicians

UGR – Undercover Research Group

UNISON: Largest public-sector union

Unite: Largest union in the UK – formed by the merger of TGWU and Amicus

Appendix 4

Composite Motion 16 – passed unanimously at the TUC Congress 2015

Blacklisting and undercover surveillance of trade unionists

Congress notes that in March 2015 it was revealed that Mark Jenner, a police officer serving in the Special Demonstration Squad (SDS), had infiltrated construction union UCATT and spied on its members.

Congress further notes that former police officer Peter Francis, acting as a whistleblower, has admitted that during his time in the SDS he spied on trade unionists in the construction industry and activists in the NUT, CWU, FBU and the National Union of Students.

Congress is aware that information on the files of workers blacklisted by The Consulting Association could only have been provided by the police or the security services.

Congress applauds the tremendous work done by unions and the Blacklist Support Group in campaigning against the blacklisting of workers for trade-union activity.

Congress is alarmed that attempts to find out further information on the involvement of police officers in infiltrating unions, activist organizations, environmental and anti-racist campaigns, including the Stephen Lawrence campaign, have been blocked by the Metropolitan Police on grounds of security.

Congress believes that trade unionists who were spied on by the police have an absolute right to know why they were targeted in this manner.

Congress notes the Home Secretary's announcement on 12 March 2015 of the Pitchford Inquiry into the operation of undercover police bodies.

Congress further notes the blacklisting meeting at Westminster on 12 March 2015, which heard the statement from a former undercover police officer disclosing that he spied on members of the FBU, UNISON, CWU, NUT and NUS.

Congress notes the significant evidence contained in a number of published books and media articles of police monitoring of, and interference in, the trade union movement during industrial disputes, union-backed anti-racist and environmental campaigns, as well as routine trade-union activity.

Conference demands that these issues are fully addressed by the Pitchford Inquiry and that relevant information is sought by the inquiry without threat (e.g. of prosecution) to those agreeing to provide evidence.

Congress believes that a trade union body such as the TUC, as well as the Blacklist Support Group, should be given 'core participant' status in the Pitchford Inquiry.

Congress resolves to campaign for the democratic rights of trade unionists and against secret state interference in the labour movement. This will substantially further the interests of trade union members and elected representatives to engage in their legitimate trade-union activities.

Congress further resolves to support the NUJ campaign against surveillance of journalists and calls for further legislative changes, including an independent judicial process; automatic mandatory prior notification and mechanisms to challenge and appeal in cases where the authorities, including the police, are attempting to access journalists' communications, materials and sources.

Congress calls on the General Council to:

i   campaign for a full independent public inquiry into blacklisting in order for these and other matters relating to how the lives of workers were ruined are fully revealed

ii   ensure that the inquiry being led by Lord Justice Pitchford into undercover policing and the SDS fully investigates the links between the police and blacklisting

iii   provide support and assistance to all unions whose members were subjected to secret police infiltration and surveillance.

Congress further calls on the European Parliament to ensure both the EU Data Protection Regulation and the EU Health and Safety Strategy 2014-2020 explicitly ban blacklisting of workers for their trade-union and health-and-safety activities.

Mover: Union of Construction, Allied Trades and Technicians
Seconder: Fire Brigades Union
Supporters: GMB; National Union of Journalists

Appendix 5

Agreed joint statement and public apology read out in High Court on 11 May 2016

Counsel for the Claimants

1 In these claims, I act for the Claimants identified in the First Schedule attached to this statement. Those Claimants were at all material times members of one or other of two trade unions: UCATT or GMB (or their predecessors) or were clients of the law firm Guney, Clark & Ryan.

2 Since at least the early 1970s and in the Claimants' case the late 1960s a large number of Britain's leading construction firms were involved in secretly collecting, storing and distributing amongst themselves information about workers who had, or who were applying for, work in the construction industry. The simple purpose of this operation was to create a database of information to vet particular workers in the construction industry. Long-held suspicions that this was taking place were finally confirmed in 2009 when, following the execution of a search warrant, the Information Commissioner (the 'ICO') seized various documents including a list of 3,300 names with additional identifying details and extant record cards for 1,800 individual workers on the list. The Claimants have always characterized this list of names and index cards as a blacklist. As the Defendants are here now publicly to accept, their secret vetting operation should never have happened. It caused harm to the employment opportunities of many workers. The secret nature of the operation meant that those on the database had no way of establishing whether they were included in it, or any chance to challenge the information that was kept and available for dissemination.

3 A large number of claims have been brought against the companies in this group litigation. Individual construction workers have brought claims for breach of confidence, misuse of private information, defamation, conspiracy and breach of the Data Protection Act 1998.

4 My learned friend, Andrew Caldecott QC, appears for the construction companies who are respectively Defendants to these various claims, and to apologize on behalf of them publicly for any harm caused. In most cases the Claimants have accepted Part 36 offers. In three cases they have additionally accepted offers of amends made under the Defamation Act 1996. Insofar as other Macfarlanes Defendants are not joined in these actions, they associate themselves with the general apology made today on behalf of those who are.

The Vetting Operation

5 Between the early 1970s and 2009, a group of major construction industry companies were involved in setting up, funding, operating and/or subscribing to and using a secret scheme for vetting those working or seeking work in the construction industry.

6 Initially this was done by the Services Group and then, from 1993, by an organization called The Consulting Association.

The Economic League and the Services Group
7   he Economic League (the 'League') was originally founded in 1919 and kept national and regional databases of alleged leftwing activists and campaigners, including trade unionists. The Services Group was a group of construction industry companies which was formed within the League following the national strike in the early 1970s.
8   The Services Group created and operated a database on certain individual construction workers (the 'Services Group Database'). Included within the Services Group Database was information provided, from time to time, by individual members of the Services Group. Information from the Database was then disseminated to individual member companies in response to inquiries about individual workers. Often, the provision of information led to a worker being refused employment.
9   Information held in the Services Group Database varied widely but commonly included such details as workers' names, dates of birth, addresses and changes of address, national insurance numbers, trade, employers' names, alleged employment history and, in a number of cases, suspected political affiliations or sympathies or perceived militancy, trade-union affiliation or activities such as complaints about health-and-safety conditions or breaches of employment rights. Individuals' entries sometimes contained express recommendations against employment. A few cards referred to private matters relating to health or personal relationships. Some record cards included press clippings about workers or newspaper articles by them, although there is an issue as to whether such material was passed on. What is described as the 'Vetting Information' varied from Claimant to Claimant.
10   Ian Kerr joined the Economic League in 1969 and had a significant role in preparing and maintaining the Services Group Database. He collated and disseminated information that Services Group member companies had supplied. There are issues in the outstanding actions as to the precise legal status of the League and Mr Kerr's legal relationship with the League and the construction companies at the material times.
11   Names of potential employees were sent by Services Group member companies to Mr Kerr for checking. This process often led to the failure of an application for employment or to the dismissal of an individual if they were already employed when the relevant name coincided with a record card.
12   Measures were taken to ensure that the existence and operation of the Services Group and its Database did not become publicly known. For example at each company subscribing to the Services Group a designated 'main contact' was generally the only person to whom information would be passed. It was a secret operation conducted without the knowledge or consent of the individuals who were the subject of these records. In consequence they could neither identify the information held about them nor challenge inaccuracies in any entries.

The formation of The Consulting Association
13   he Services Group's existence was not publicly known until around 1989 when it was referred to in a series of newspaper articles and parliamentary debates and in a report of the House of Commons Employment Committee in

February 1991. In consequence the Economic League as a whole, including the Services Group, was wound up in 1993. At least some of the records from the Services Group were used to form the basis of the card index system of The Consulting Association, which was set up by some of the former members of the Services Group.

14 The Consulting Association commenced operations in April 1993. It was an unincorporated association. McAlpines provided £10,000 towards the start-up costs of the new organization. Mr Kerr acted as The Consulting Association's salaried Chief Officer from 1993 until it was disbanded in February 2009.

15 The membership of The Consulting Association consisted of the construction companies that subscribed to its services. The membership altered from time to time over the course of The Consulting Association's existence. The members determined which other companies in the industry could join The Consulting Association.

16 The member companies periodically elected a chairman, who retained the office for a two- or three-year term. The chairmen over the course of The Consulting Association's existence were, giving approximate years only in some cases, as follows:

1993-1996	Cullum McAlpine	(McAlpines)
1996-1999	Tony Jennings	(John Laing Construction Limited)
2000-2001	Danny O'Sullivan	(Kier Limited)
2002-2003	Stephen Quant	(Skanska UK)
2004-2005	Trevor Watcham	(Balfour Beatty plc)
2006-2009	David Cochrane	(McAlpines)

17 The subscribing companies paid an annual subscription for membership of the association on a quarterly basis and, in addition, a fee to check each name.

The Consulting Association Database
18 The Consulting Association Database included a colour-coded list of 3,300 names in alphabetical order (the 'Monodex List'), commonly with additional information to identify those individuals. Record cards for approximately 1,800 individuals were seized by the ICO in February 2009.

19 Information held in The Consulting Association Database varied widely but commonly included such details as workers' names, dates of birth, addresses and changes of address, national insurance numbers, trade, employers' names, alleged employment history and, in a number of cases, suspected political affiliations or sympathies or perceived militancy, trade-union affiliation or activities such as complaints about health-and-safety conditions or breaches of employment rights. Individuals' entries sometimes contained express recommendations against employment. A few cards referred to private matters including health or personal relationships. Some record cards included press clippings about workers or newspaper articles by them, although there is an issue as to whether such material was passed on. What is described as the 'Vetting Information' varied from Claimant to Claimant.

20 Typically, at the end of each entry on a record card the source of the information would be stated, in the form of a numeric code. Each subscribing company was assigned its own code number. In some cases the initials of the individual from a subscribing company who had communicated the information

to The Consulting Association was also included. On other occasions this individual would be identified by the phrase 'Main Contact'. This was a designated individual or a small number of designated individuals, usually senior employees in the human resources department, from whom information was received and to whom it was passed.

21 When lists of names were received from an inquiring member company they would be checked against the Monodex List. If a record card existed in relation to a name on a list from an inquiring company, the information contained on the card would then be passed to the inquiring company and the faxed lists were destroyed.

22 The record cards sometimes included recommendations about whether to employ the individual in adverse terms. Record cards often recorded the failure of an application for employment. This is why the Claimants have referred to it as a 'blacklist'.

23 The Consulting Association also operated in secret. The relevant workers had no way of knowing that they were included and no way of challenging what was recorded about them. The Claimants were very distressed to find they were included in these secret Databases on the basis of which some were refused employment.

The ICO raid in February 2009

24 The Consulting Association's activities were brought to an end after the ICO executed a search warrant at The Consulting Association's premises on 23 February 2009.

25 After the raid in February 2009 Mr Kerr was prosecuted by the ICO for failing to register as a data controller under the Data Protection Act 1998. He pleaded guilty and his fine and costs were paid by McAlpines. None of the companies who were members of The Consulting Association was prosecuted.

Admissions

26 Although they had originally denied liability in these proceedings, on 6 October 2015, the Macfarlanes Defendants made wide-ranging admissions about their involvement and roles in the Services Group and in The Consulting Association. The Defendants represented by Macfarlanes LLP are listed in the attached Second Schedule, but they include in alphabetical order: Balfour Beatty companies, Carillion, Costain, Kier Limited, Laing companies, Sir Robert McAlpine Limited, Skanska UK, Vinci, Taylor Woodrow, and various individual defendants, including Cullum McAlpine, Danny O'Sullivan, David Cochrane, and Stephen Quant.

27 The Macfarlanes Defendants admitted generally that the communication of information included in record cards in the Services Group Database bore the defamatory message that the worker concerned might pose a risk of unjustified disruption on any site on which he was employed at the time when the entry was made and for a reasonable time thereafter apart from any additional specific allegation(s) recorded. The company providing the information accepted responsibility as the publisher. It was also accepted that aspects of the information held in the Services Group Database were confidential and should not have been used and that the information sometimes included private and personal details. Like admissions were made in relation to

The Consulting Association and, in addition, admissions were made regarding data protection. It was accepted that these activities had consequences for certain workers in terms of lost work opportunities or refusals of work and that they had an impact on some workers' personal lives.

28 Together with their admissions, the Macfarlanes Defendants offered their unreserved apologies for their involvement in the secret systems, for the adverse employment consequences caused to workers and for the distress and anxiety caused to such workers and their families. The Claimants accept those apologies as sincere. The Macfarlanes Defendants also made monetary offers from December 2015 to March 2016, which the Claimants have accepted as reasonable and proportionate compensation for the harm suffered. The parties now hope that this matter can be treated as a closed chapter.

Counsel for the Defendants

29 My Lord, on behalf of the Defendants, I accept everything my learned friend has said. The Defendants are here today to offer, through me, their sincere and unreserved apologies to the Claimants for any damage caused. The Defendants apologize as providers of any information and for the loss of employment suffered as a result of communication of information during the operation of The Consulting Association. They also apologize for the anxiety and hurt to feelings caused as a result.

30 The Macfarlanes Defendants as a whole agree and endorse that apology. They openly accept and acknowledge that the essential failing of the Consulting Association system was its secrecy and the nature and content of the information it held. They apologize generally for the fact that information was communicated and kept in secret and was not subject to any or any effective verification process.

31 The Macfarlanes Defendants have agreed to pay to the Claimants appropriate sums by way of damages and their costs. In addition, suitable undertakings have been agreed between the parties.

Counsel for the Claimants

32 On behalf of the Claimants whom I represent today, they are pleased that their claims have been resolved.

Index

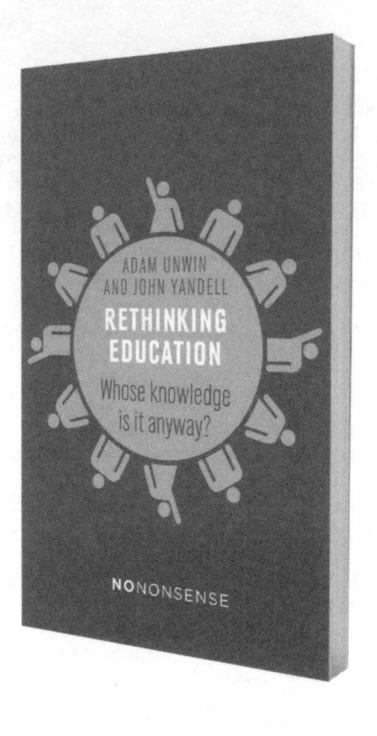

ADAM UNWIN
AND JOHN YANDELL

RETHINKING
EDUCATION

Whose knowledge
is it anyway?

NONONSENSE

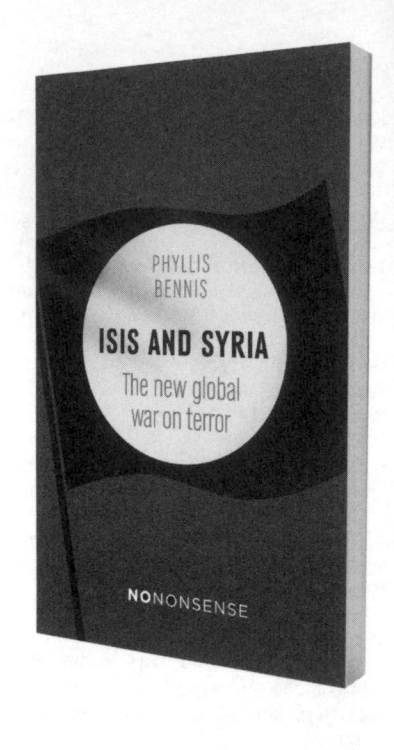

PHYLLIS
BENNIS

ISIS AND SYRIA

The new global
war on terror

NONONSENSE

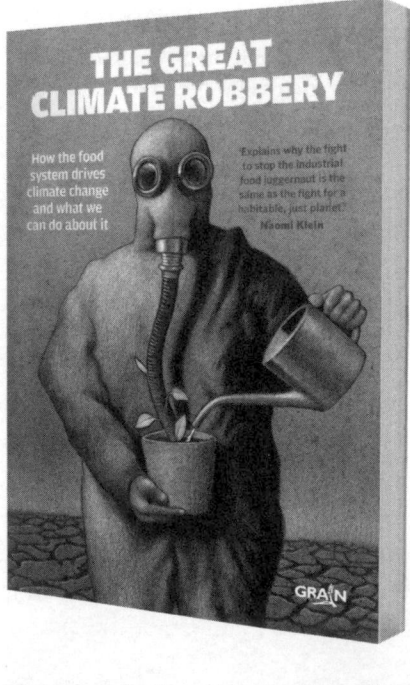

THE GREAT
CLIMATE ROBBERY

How the food
system drives
climate change
and what we
can do about it

'Explains why the fight
to stop the industrial
food juggernaut is the
same as the fight for a
habitable, just planet.'
Naomi Klein

GRAIN

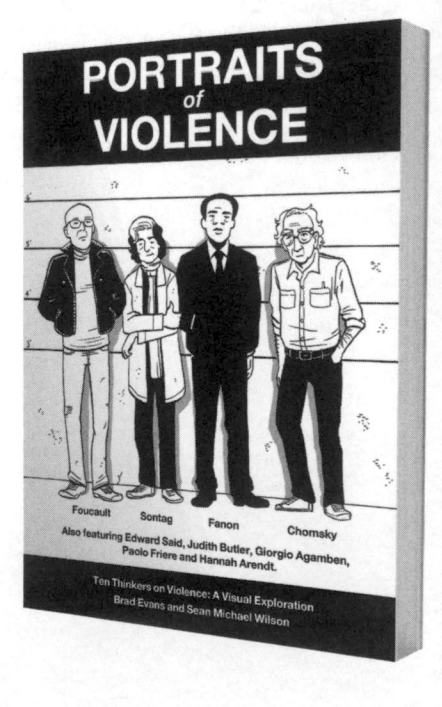

PORTRAITS of
VIOLENCE

Foucault   Sontag   Fanon   Chomsky
Also featuring Edward Said, Judith Butler, Giorgio Agamben,
Paolo Friere and Hannah Arendt.

Ten Thinkers on Violence: A Visual Exploration
Brad Evans and Sean Michael Wilson

More books from New Internationalist

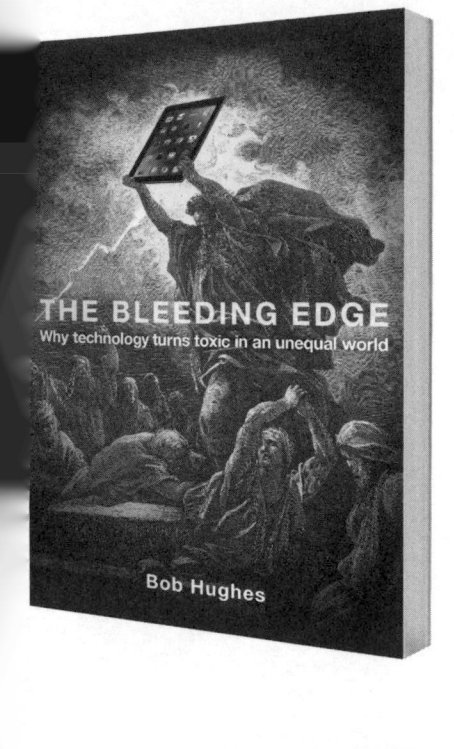

THE BLEEDING EDGE
Why technology turns toxic in an unequal world

Bob Hughes

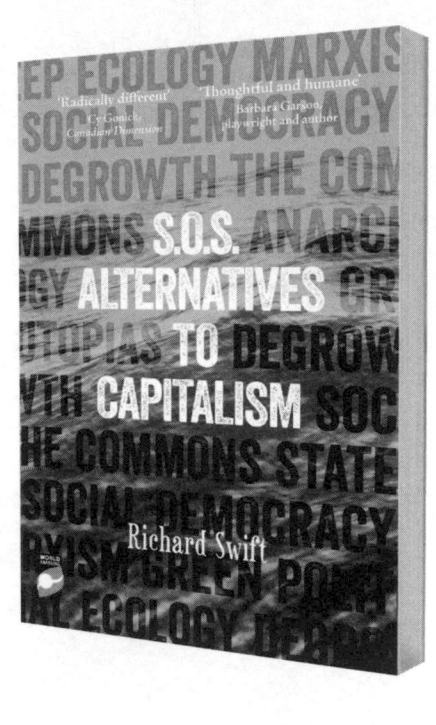

'Radically different' *Cy Gonick, Canadian Dimension*

'Thoughtful and humane' *Barbara Garson, playwright and author*

**S.O.S.
ALTERNATIVES
TO DEGROWTH
CAPITALISM**

Richard Swift

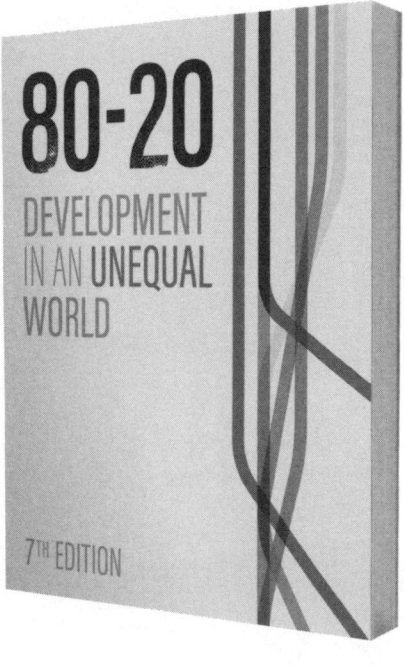

80-20
DEVELOPMENT IN AN **UNEQUAL** WORLD

7TH EDITION

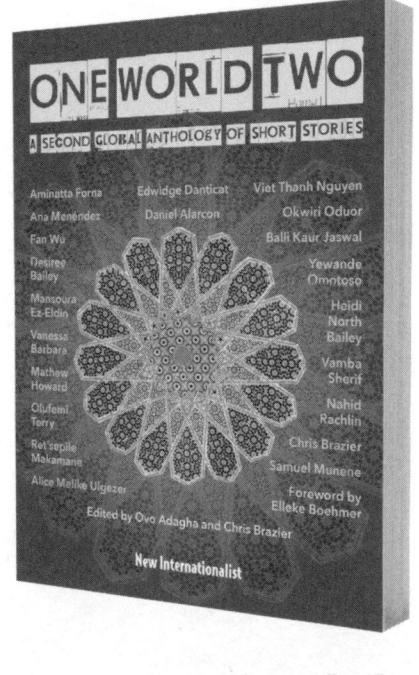

ONE WORLD TWO
A SECOND GLOBAL ANTHOLOGY OF SHORT STORIES

Aminatta Forna	Edwidge Danticat	Viet Thanh Nguyen
Ana Menéndez	Daniel Alarcon	Okwiri Oduor
Fan Wu		Balli Kaur Jaswal
Desiree Bailey		Yewande Omotoso
Mansoura Ez-Eldin		Heidi North Bailey
Vanessa Barbara		Vamba Sherif
Mathew Howard		Nahid Rachlin
Olufemi Terry		Chris Brazier
Ret'sepile Makamane		Samuel Munene
Alice Melike Ulgezer		Foreword by Elleke Boehmer

Edited by Ovo Adagha and Chris Brazier

New Internationalist